Communes and Workers' Control in Venezuela

Historical Materialism Book Series

The Historical Materialism Book Series is a major publishing initiative of the radical left. The capitalist crisis of the twenty-first century has been met by a resurgence of interest in critical Marxist theory. At the same time, the publishing institutions committed to Marxism have contracted markedly since the high point of the 1970s. The Historical Materialism Book Series is dedicated to addressing this situation by making available important works of Marxist theory. The aim of the series is to publish important theoretical contributions as the basis for vigorous intellectual debate and exchange on the left.

The peer-reviewed series publishes original monographs, translated texts, and reprints of classics across the bounds of academic disciplinary agendas and across the divisions of the left. The series is particularly concerned to encourage the internationalization of Marxist debate and aims to translate significant studies from beyond the English-speaking world.

For a full list of titles in the Historical Materialism Book Series available in paperback from Haymarket Books, visit:
https://www.haymarketbooks.org/series_collections/1-historical-materialism

Communes and Workers' Control in Venezuela

Building 21st Century Socialism from Below

Dario Azzellini

Translated from the Spanish by Ned Sublette

Haymarket Books
Chicago, IL

First published in 2016 by Brill Academic Publishers, The Netherlands
© 2017 Koninklijke Brill NV, Leiden, The Netherlands

Published in paperback in 2017 by
Haymarket Books
P.O. Box 180165
Chicago, IL 60618
773-583-7884
www.haymarketbooks.org

ISBN: 978-1-60846-829-4

Distributed to the trade in the US through Consortium Book Sales and Distribution (www.cbsd.com) and internationally through Ingram Publisher Services International (www.ingramcontent.com).

This book was published with the generous support of Lannan Foundation and Wallace Action Fund.

Special discounts are available for bulk purchases by organizations and institutions. Please call 773-583-7884 or email info@haymarketbooks.org for more information.

Cover design by Jamie Kerry of Belle Étoile Studios and Ragina Johnson.

Printed in the United States.

Entered into digital printing May 2019.

Library of Congress Cataloging-in-Publication data is available.

Contents

Acknowledgements IX
Abbreviations X

1 **Introduction** 1
   1 Venezuela's Specific Path 4
   2 The Dilemma of the State 6
   3 Two-Track Construction 9
   4 Local Self-Government, Communal Councils (CCs), and Communes 11
   5 Cooperatives, Co-Management, Self-Management, and Workers' Control 12
   6 The Revolution without Chávez 15

2 **Class, Constituent Power, and Popular Power** 18
   1 Updating the Concept of Class 18
      1.1 *Theoretical Notes on Class and Multitude* 20
      1.2 *Class Composition and Breadth in Venezuela* 25
   2 Socio-Territorial Segregation and Class Formation 31
   3 From Taking Power to Process: Constituent Power and Popular Power 33
      3.1 *Crisis as a Motor of History: Constituent Power vs. Constituted Power* 35
      3.2 *The Popular Constituent Process* 41
      3.3 *The Simultaneity of Foci: Resistance, Insurrection and Constituent Power* 48
      3.4 *Popular Power: The Knowledge of Resistance* 49

3 **Movements and Alternative Construction in Venezuela** 52
   1 Social Movements or Popular Movements? 57
   2 The Historical Current for Change and the Ruptures of the Continuum 62
   3 The New Framework of Action 66
   4 Popular Actors and Autonomous Construction 70
      4.1 *The Bolívar and Zamora Revolutionary Current* 71
      4.2 *The Settlers' Movement* 73
      4.3 *National Network of Communards* 76

4 The Communal Councils: Local Self-Administration and Social
   Transformation 81
   1   The Origins of the CCs and Their Antecedents in Local
       Participation 84
       1.1 *Participatory Budgeting* 85
       1.2 *The Failed CLPP Initiative* 86
       1.3 *Metropolitan Council for Planning Public Policies (CMPPP)* 89
       1.4 *The Municipal Constituent* 90
       1.5 *The Local Work Cabinets in Caracas* 92
   2   The Communal Councils 93
       2.1 *The Genesis of the CCs* 96
       2.2 *Makeup and Structure* 98
       2.3 *Rigid Law and Flexible Praxis* 100
       2.4 *Financing and Financial Administration* 102
       2.5 *Projects* 105
       2.6 *Decentralisation or Centralisation* 107
       2.7 *Development, Situation, and Contradictions* 108
       2.8 *Relationship between CCs and Institutions* 112
       2.9 *CCs and Popular Movements* 117
       2.10 *Relations between CCs and Communities* 119
       2.11 *The Appropriation of CCs by Communities and the Question of the
             State* 122
   3   The CCs as a Means of Participation in the Barrios of Caracas 124
       3.1 *The 'Emiliano Hernández' Communal Council, Magallanes de
             Catia, Caracas* 126
       3.2 *The CC as a Body of Self-Administration* 128
       3.3 *Participation as a Process of Development and of Social
             Recognition* 133
       3.4 *New Social Relations and Community Transformation* 137
       3.5 *Participation as a Process of Democratisation and of Building
             Collectivity* 138
       3.6 *The CC 'Unidos por el Chapulún', Parroquia Nuestra Sra. del
             Rosario, Baruta* 145
       3.7 *CCs in Caracas: Conclusions* 148
       3.8 *Participation* 149
       3.9 *Relationship between Communities and Institutions* 152

CONTENTS VII

5 New Collective Business Paradigms   157
   1   Cooperatives   162
       1.1   Roots of Cooperativism in Venezuela   163
       1.2   Governmental Policies of Support for Cooperatives   164
       1.3   Limitations of State Support for Cooperatives   165
       1.4   Internal Organisation of Cooperatives   167
       1.5   The Problematisation of Cooperativism   169
   2   New Entrepreneurial Models   172
       2.1   Private Enterprise and Co-Management   172
       2.2   Co-Management in State Businesses   173
       2.3   Social Production Companies   176

6 Workers' Control, Workers' Councils, and Class Struggle   178
   1   Recuperated Companies and Nationalisation   181
   2   Workers' Control and Workers' Councils   188
       2.1   The Movement for Workers' Control   191
       2.2   The Socialist Workers' Councils   195
       2.3   The CVG and the 2009–19 Socialist Guayana Plan   199
   3   Workers' Control: The Example of Inveval   202
       3.1   From the Struggle for Pay to the Struggle for the Factory   203
       3.2   The Workers Abandon the Cooperative and Form a Council   205
   4   Alcasa: Class Struggle for Productive Transformation Against Bureaucracy and Corruption   208
       4.1   Revolutionary Co-Management   209
       4.2   The Victory of Bureaucracy and Corruption   212
       4.3   Workers' Control Returns   214
       4.4   The Organisational Structure of the New Alcasa   216
       4.5   Worker Inventiveness Workshops   220
       4.6   The Alcasa Initiatives and the Institutional Embargo   221
       4.7   The Attack on Workers' Control and the Negation of the Socialist Guayana Plan   223
   5   New struggles for Workers' Control   227
   6   Approaching the Issue of New Worker Subjectivities in the Context of Participation and Class Struggle   232
       6.1   Horizontality in the Factory and Change Throughout Society   237
       6.2   The New Collective Self   241

7 Communes, Production, and the Communal State   243
  1   Communes   244
      1.1   *Origin and Form*   244
      1.2   *Communes and Constituted Power*   248
  2   Companies of Communal Social Property and the Construction of a Communal Economy   252
  3   Communal State: State or Non-State?   258

8 Local and Worker Self-Management, Two-Track Construction, and Class Struggle: A Preliminary Assessment   263
  1   The Bolivarian Process and Class Struggle   267
  2   Communal Councils, Communes, and Communal State   268
  3   Property Models, the Administration of the Means of Production, and Class Struggle   271
  4   Nationalisation, Workers' Control, and the Socialist Workers' Councils   274
  5   The Relation of Constituent and Constituted Power to Class Struggle   279

Interviews   281
References   286
Index   301

Acknowledgements

I want to thank first and foremost all the people in Venezuela active in various groups and organisations at the base, the communal councils and communes, the alternative media and various collectives, as well as those who fight and take over production sites and those who support them in different ways. I thank also a long list of researchers and organisations who have inspired radical thinking about self-administration, communes, workers' struggles and social transformation, and who are supporting and conducting research on these subjects. Special thanks goes to all who have contributed to this book through letting me be part of their struggles, giving me interviews, making contacts and contributing important information. The list is not complete. If I inadvertently forgot anyone, I beg your pardon. Many thanks to: Andrés Antillano, Jaqeline Ávila, Luz Carrera, Eduardo Daza, Roland Denis, Rafael Enciso, Frente Campesino Ezequiel Zamora, Atenea Jímenez, Karina Lanz, Melisa Maytín, Red Nacional de Comuneros y Comuneras, Adriana Rivas, Ligia Duerto, Alcides Rivero, Marina Sitrin, and the Johannes Kepler University Linz for partly funding the editing. Special thanks also to Ned Sublette, the translator, for his excellent work.

This book is dedicated to my partner, comrade, friend and wife Marina Sitrin and to our wonderful son Camilo Turi Azzellini Sitrin.

Abbreviations

ANC	Constituent National Assembly
CLPP	Local Public Planning Councils
CC	Communal Council(s)
Copei	Independent Electoral Political Organisation Committee (social-Christian party)
CRBZ	Bolívar and Zamora Revolutionary Current
CTU	Urban Land Committees
CVG	Venezuelan Corporation of Guyana
EPS	Social Production Company, Social Property Company, or Socialist Production Company
FALN	Armed Forces of National Liberation
FNCEZ	Ezequiel Zamora Peasant National Front
FNCSB	Simón Bolívar National Communal Front
FONDEMI	Fund for Microfinance Development
Fundacomunal	Foundation for the Development and Promotion of Communal Power
Freteco	Revolutionary Front of Workers of Co-Managed and Occupied Companies
LCR	Cause R
MAS	Movement toward Socialism
MBR-200	Bolivarian Revolutionary Movement-200
Milco	Ministry of Light Industry and Commerce
Minep	Ministry of Popular Economy
Minpades	Ministry for Participation and Social Development
M21	Movement 21
MDP	Settler's Movement
MTA	Water Technical Boards
MVR	Venezuelan Republic Movement
PCV	Communist Party of Venezuela
PDVAL	Venezuelan Production and Distribution of Foodstuffs
PDVSA	Venezuelan Petroleum S.A.
Podemos	For Social Democracy
PPC	Popular Constituent Process
PRV	Party of the Venezuelan Revolution
PSUV	United Socialist Party of Venezuela
Safonacc	National Autonomous Fund for Communal Councils Service
Sinatecc	National System of Technical Support for Communal Councils

Sintralcasa	Workers' Union of Alcasa
Sunacoop	National Superintendency of Cooperatives
UBE	Electoral Battle Entities
UBV	Bolivarian University of Venezuela
UCV	Central University of Venezuela
UNT	National Workers' Union

CHAPTER 1

Introduction

> The idea is to conceive of politics as a gamble rather than as something known in advance, external, objectified. A politics that requires of us the uninterrupted construction of temporary syntheses and of new social relations that anticipate the coming socialist society. The elaboration of a strategy that does not renounce the possibility of re-signifying the state, so that at least the state does not overly contribute to the 'hostile ecosystem' of capitalism, but instead develops policies that strengthen social movements without subsuming them into the state machinery. A politics that synthesizes the dynamics of sovereignty and autonomy, in perpetual tension-contradiction with the state because its ultimate goal must be the classless society.[1]

...

> We have a political project to construct a power that does not exist today, a power that is in the hands of the *pueblo*. The people have to make their own articulated, organised government – not as a repository of resources, but as something that can and must govern itself, something that must make plans and put them into execution. That generates a proposal for what socialism today must be.[2]

∴

Ever since Hugo Chávez began his first term as president of Venezuela in 1999, the Venezuelan process he championed has stimulated interest and controversy everywhere. Traditional left currents, and some anti-systemic approaches as well, see in the Venezuelan process a liberal-capitalist project in disguise, based on populism and reformism, without any emancipatory potential for transformation. Others praise its great advances in social justice, but without

---

1 Nicanoff 2007, p. 11.
2 Atenea Jiménez, National Network of Communards 2012.

carrying out a deeper analysis of social and economic relations or, especially, examining the internal contradictions of the transformation process in action.

Most such commentary betrays a lack of understanding of what is happening in Venezuela, a country whose reality has little or nothing to do with how it is portrayed in the international propaganda campaign against it. In spite of Venezuela's enormous social advances – plainly evident, and demonstrable by research and statistics of organisations both national and international – its media image is one of a country in which poverty and misery have expanded because of changes in policy made 'overnight' by Chávez, which supposedly have brought the country to the brink of an economic, political, and social collapse, even as Venezuela's democracy is purportedly being dismantled and replaced by an authoritarian, repressive regime.

The emphasis placed on the figure of Chávez by many scholars and by media, and even by those in favour of the process, has diverted attention away from the extensive social transformation processes going on in Venezuela, within which the massive protagonism of the previously excluded majority is emerging. As a consequence, after the death of Chávez, many journalists and commentators asked whether the transformation process in Venezuela would continue, and not a few announced the rapid decay of Bolivarianism.

Outside Venezuela, almost nothing is known about the process through which local self-government structures with direct, non-representative democracy have been created by means of communal councils and communes.[3] Nor is there awareness of Venezuelan workers' struggles over different initiatives from above and below to democratise the possession and administration of the means of production.[4]

With the assumption of the Presidency by the ex-lieutenant colonel of the Armed Forces in early 1999, a profound social transformation process was implemented in Venezuela that has obliged the left to rethink traditional concepts, along with some non-traditional ones. How that process started – very differently from other historical social transformation processes – appears to contradict the previous theories and ideas of the left. It was not led or influenced by a workers' organisation, a party, or a partisan alliance; before it, there was not even an important newspaper or other communication medium on the left. It did not follow a firm ideology, but rather grew out of a broad spectrum of groups and organisations, with different trajectories and reference points, different social and structural policies, and different historical backgrounds.

---

3 See Azzellini 2010; Azzellini 2013; Azzellini and Ressler 2010.
4 See Azzellini 2011; 2012; 2014; Azzellini and Ressler 2006.

In their totality these groups are identified as the *movimiento bolivariano*, or 'Bolivarianism',[5] which represents more a complex of values and concrete practices than a fully elaborated ideology.

The left has been divided since the 1980s over the issue of the taking of the state, and over the collateral issue of whether the state should be the central agent for change. But in Venezuela, state-centric and anti-systemic perspectives converged following two general visions (with all imaginable shades of difference) that we could roughly characterise as 'from above' or 'from below'.[6]

The Venezuelan process includes participation by sectors generally considered incompatible: traditional-style organisations and parties on the one hand, and new, autonomous groups and organisations on the other. This 'two-track' process has become characteristic in several contexts of Latin American social transformation, but its greatest development has occurred in Venezuela, where it has manifested in concrete policies.[7] Despite all the conflicts within the process, there have been no sharp points of rupture between the Venezuelan government and popular movements, as there have been, for example, in Ecuador and Bolivia.

Since 2006, the Venezuelan transformation process has explicitly followed the line of the 'council-socialist' tradition, and as of 2007, possibilities for wide participation and for 'council structures' increased. These council structures, existing in different sectors of society, are understood as the basis of the desired Venezuelan socialism: they must cooperate and coordinate at a higher level, so that they can ultimately replace the bourgeois state with a communal one. The basis of this transformation process, and the most advanced initiatives, are communal councils (CC) and communes. As part of the process, there has been a series of different initiatives and measures to stimulate the democratisation of the relations of property, work, and production.[8] Some of these measures are directed at reducing, and hopefully overcoming, the boundaries that separate the economic, the political, and the social, rejecting the vision of society and politics as distinct spheres, separated one from the other, that is foundational to capitalism and the bourgeois state. Capital reproduces this vision constantly, while the state regulates its divisions: not coincidentally, this concept appears for the first time in Niccolò Machiavelli's (1467–1527) *The Prince*, a guide for the power elite of the new republican cities in the early days of capitalism.

---

5   In honour of Simón Bolívar, hero of South American independence.
6   See Ellner 2006.
7   Zibechi 2006, p. 226.
8   See Azzellini and Ressler 2006; Azzellini 2007a; 2011; 2013; 2014.

The question of overcoming these divisions is of fundamental importance from an emancipatory perspective, although it has not been dealt with in the majority of the transformation processes of the twentieth century. Because of that, this book is not intended narrowly for specialists in Latin America or Venezuela. A critical analysis of the transformation process in Venezuela and of the relations between the state and the movements is important for everyone on the left in search of democratic and socialist alternatives to the capitalist system.

In Venezuelan political practice – which does not deny theory or its importance – the big challenge is to reinvent, constantly, relations and social mechanisms, institutions, and strategies for the transition to 'socialism', observing and learning from past experience, but without a predetermined line of inquiry or goal. In Venezuela, that kind of inquiry is basic to the transformation process, as reflected in the oft-quoted words of the philosopher and educator Simón Rodríguez, teacher of Simón Bolívar and central reference for Bolivarianism, who said at the beginning of the nineteenth century: 'Where will we look for models? Spanish America is original. Its institutions and its government have to be original, along with the means for founding them. Either we invent or we fail'.[9]

1   Venezuela's Specific Path

The Venezuelan economic crisis of the early 1980s triggered a crisis of the entire political system, in which the *caracazo* (the popular uprising against neoliberal structural adjustment measures) of 1989 and the two leftist, military-led, civic-military uprisings of 1992 were foundational events for the Bolivarian movement. With traditional power in crisis, the popular movements took ever more autonomist positions: their specific demands for solutions to concrete problems gradually became demands for self-determination, self-management, and constituent power.[10]

A growing social polarisation and the decay of the existing representative body favoured the December 1998 election of Chávez, who had previously headed the first civic-military uprising, as President of the Republic, in a campaign supported by political parties, organisations, and private entities on the

---

9   In Spanish: '*O inventamos o erramos*.' Cited by Contreras 1999, p. 112.
10 Constituent power refers to the legitimate collective force that humans possess to think of something new, to model it, and to produce it without having to derive it from, or submit to, what already exists.

left. After the election, Chávez launched a constituent process; the National Constituent Assembly was elected, and, with great popular participation, a new Constitution was written, which was ratified in a December 1999 referendum. This Constitution postulates a 'participatory and protagonistic democracy' based on a broad conception of participation that, besides redefining political participation, encompasses social, economic, and cultural rights, with collective rights for specific groups. Chávez was re-elected President in December 2000, in accordance with the new Constitution. In 2003, the creation of structures parallel to the government began, with a strong participation 'from below', above all in the social programmes called missions. After that, the government ran up against obstacles at all levels in trying to reorient public policies, especially in the area of social policy.[11]

From the beginning, participation was framed in a democratic discourse, which postulated a 'third way' beyond capitalism and socialism. This path led toward the left, and in January 2005 at the Social Forum in Porto Alegre, Brazil, Chávez designated 'socialism' as the only alternative in the context of a necessary overcoming of capitalism. This radicalisation happened after the extremely successful popular mobilisations against the *coup d'état* of April 2002, and against the 'business lockout' of 2002–3.[12]

From 2007 onward, participation in the official politics of the Government was increasingly located in the context of 'popular power' (*poder popular*), revolutionary democracy, and a socialism in development (called '21st-century socialism', to differentiate it from earlier state socialisms).

Venezuela's search in recent years has been shared at the global level by various socio-political actors: the participatory budget of Porto Alegre (Brazil); the autonomy posed by the Zapatista movement in Chiapas (Mexico); the popular movements of Argentina; the landless movement (MST) in Brazil; or the popular and indigenous movements of Ecuador and Bolivia. These and other movements share a rejection of the mechanisms of representative democracy, meaning that the zealous use of liberal-democratic criteria to measure how well Venezuela implements those mechanisms makes no sense. It has been precisely the failure of the liberal-democratic model to satisfy the material necessities of the population or to permit popular political participation that has produced in Venezuela a rejection of the logic of representation and the demand for a direct democracy, expressed in the Constitution as 'participatory and protagonistic democracy'. This is especially significant in the context of

---

11   Lander 2007, p. 71.
12   See Lander 2009.

the popular movements that surged from 2011 on in the US, as well as in various European countries and on the African continent. Besides rejecting the logic of representation and proposing models of direct democracy, these movements have many practices in common with movements that surged in Latin America during the 1990s.[13]

The transformation process in Venezuela is the expression of a new, heterogeneous left that draws power from its diversity, and does not seek homogenisation. Officially, it seeks to redefine the state from below and proposes a renewed concept of popular power. This process is complex and contradictory, entailing both cooperation and conflict, and is characterised by a two-track construction: from below (constituent power) and from above (constituted power).

2   The Dilemma of the State

Until the mid-80s, the dominant political concepts in Latin America were those of 'national liberation'. These generally contemplated a highly institutionalised party that would conduct state affairs with the support of a large central workers' union and other mass organisations (of peasants, for example, or of women) structurally tied to the government and/or party, acting as its 'long arm'. (According to the traditional division between the social and the political, the latter remains the exclusive domain of the state and the party). Along with a 'national bourgeoisie', to which was attributed an interest in internal development, the state would undertake interventions directed at the economy and society in order to stimulate development and national transformation, orienting it toward sovereignty, and against the countries to the North, especially the US. The state would adopt anti-imperialist positions and seek alliances with other states of the 'third world'.

There is no complex analysis of the bourgeois state in the writings of Marx. His occasional statements over the years clearly develop a position that discards the simple taking of the state. In a new preface to the 1872 German edition of the *Communist Manifesto,* Marx and Engels stated that the 1848 manifesto had become antiquated with regard to some of its points; a careful analysis of the Paris Commune, they declared, had demonstrated that 'the working class cannot simply lay hold of the ready-made state machinery and wield it for its own purposes.'[14]

---

13   See Sitrin and Azzellini 2014.
14   Marx 1986, p. 533.

Lenin's *The State and Revolution* introduced into the Communist movement, and into many revolutionary movements influenced by Marxism-Leninism, the idea that revolutionaries' central task was the taking of the state in order to subsequently direct the masses in building a socialist economy:

> The proletariat needs state power, the centralised organisation of force, the organisation of violence, both for the purpose of crushing the resistance of the exploiters and for the purpose of guiding the great mass of the population – the peasantry, the petty-bourgeoisie, the semi-proletarians – in the work of organising Socialist economy.[15]

Antonio Gramsci observed that modern societies, which function in a more complex way than feudal Russia did, are based not only on repression, but also on creating an active consensus among the governed. This is done in civil society, which also forms part of the 'integral state'. In this way, Gramsci analyses incisively the working of modern states; still, in his counter-strategy, the end is the party, which through gaining hegemony would direct the different sectors of civil society in a long war of positions for the taking of the state, in order to transform it afterward into the 'ethical state' of a 'regulated society'.[16]

The general idea among communists was that by advancing through socialism toward communism, the state would simply die. In countries of 'actually existing socialism', however, the state did nothing that would cause itself to die or disappear, but, on the contrary, assumed the form of a repressive state in order to survive, a contradiction that provoked a more intense analysis in the 1960s and 70s. Neo-Marxist approaches analyse the state as a 'bourgeois state' – as a structural part of capitalism, not something external. This implies that the state is not a neutral instrument in the transformation process, and that its possession does not necessarily signify a social transformation toward overcoming capitalist relations, since it is a product of those same relations.

Louis Althusser differentiates between the state's 'ideological apparatus' and its 'repressive apparatus', drawing a distinction between the 'apparatus' and 'power' of the state while questioning the division between 'state' and 'private'. In his analysis, even though state power can be occupied by different political forces, the state apparatus persists as such; for that reason it must be destroyed.[17] Similarly, Nicos Poulantzas differentiates between state apparatus

---

15   Lenin 1932, p. 28.
16   Gramsci 1999, p. 526.
17   See Althusser 1971.

and state power: 'A change in state power is never enough to transform the materiality of the state apparatus'.[18]

A process of emancipatory transformation cannot be carried out through state apparatus. The state is not the simple instrument of those who appropriate its power; it is much more than the power of the state or its institutions. Advocates of 'seizing state power' consider that the state, in spite of all its complexity, is the central, regulating, and directing influence capable of guiding a transformation. Adversaries of the idea, on the other hand, reject participation in or cooperation with the state, since they consider the state to be structurally opposed to revolutionary transformation, corrupting and co-opting all the forces related to it. In this latter line of thought, only popular movements are entrusted with the capacity for transformation. Between these two polarised positions there are many shades of difference.

With the strengthening of globalisation processes and the failure of national liberation concepts, the idea has gained force among intellectuals and political organisations that it is impossible for 'third world' countries to act independently in a globalised world. Along with this has come the denial of the possibilities of radical change and the 'social-democratisation' of many ex-revolutionaries who have maintained their state-centrism.

In the 1980s, when various Latin American intellectuals and social researchers turned their attention to independent movements and the segments of the population mobilised 'from below', this perspective was accompanied by the interpretation that these movements could be active only within the sphere of the social. The possibility of a profound social transformation, characteristic of the worker movement, was thus denied to the 'new' movements. In turn, these movements – still anti-systemic – mostly reject traditional models of organisation and the idea of a path to emancipation via the state. The problem is that the state permits the building of parallel structures only when they do not aspire to self-management or autonomy, and not when they dispute the state's competence. If self-organisation is considered actually or potentially challenging to state power, historical experience demonstrates that it will be submitted to massive state repression and destroyed.

---

18   In his analysis, the state is neither a neutral instrument nor an actor, but rather a social relationship and therefore a battlefield: 'The (capitalist) state should not be regarded as an intrinsic entity: like "capital", it is rather a relationship of forces; or more precisely, it is the material condensation of such a relationship among classes and class fractions, such as this is expressed within the state in a necessarily specific form'. Poulantzas 2000, pp. 128–29.

3 Two-Track Construction

The election of leftist and progressive governments (with all their differences, and though some were leftist and progressive only in popular expectation) in Latin America from 1998 onward has obliged the Latin American left – state-centric or not, and especially the movements – to redefine their relationship to the state and its institutions:[19] '[B]road sectors of our societies seem to be understanding that the best possible scenario consists in the continuity of progressive administrations, who must always be pressured not to limit themselves to administering the inherited situation'.[20] In parallel, it can be observed in Latin America, principally in Venezuela, that a left is taking shape that, as Ernst Bloch put it, understands politics as a challenge to praxis. The process of constituting a new emancipatory left in many parts of Latin America is attended by the demands and experiences of praxis, creating 'a combination of historical experiences, practices of struggle, theorisation about these practices, and knowledge, illuminating a "new-new left"'.[21]

Venezuela's two-track transformation process contradicts much existing theory in terms of the role it creates for state interaction with the movements.[22] On the other hand, it also contradicts the positions of the state-centric left because its normative orientation assigns a central role to popular movements and self-organisation.

We are speaking of a new way, unheard of in previous struggles and strategies for social transformation, that combines concepts 'from above' and 'from below' to pursue an anti-imperialist politics of national sovereignty. In this process, the state and its institutions are strengthened, and follow a strategy of active regulation of economic process in a mixed (capitalist) economy. On the other hand, according to the declared normative orientation, movements must assume the central role in the process of change and must have autonomy. The dominant role of the popular movements was evidenced by the mobilisations convened from below, which were decisive in overthrowing the 2002 coup and in resisting the 2002/3 lockout and oil strike and the 2004 revocatory referendum against Chávez. Different popular organisations within the transformation process have repeatedly assumed positions contrary to the government's positions and policies, although they support the government generally. Among these are the National Workers Union (UNT), founded in 2004, the

---

19 See Denis 2001; 2005; Mazzeo 2007; Rauber 2003; 2006; Wainwright 2003.
20 Zibechi 2006, p. 227.
21 Nicanoff 2007, p. 12.
22 See Hardt and Negri 2000; 2004; Holloway 2005.

National Peasant Front Ezequiel Zamora (FNCEZ), and the Urban Land Committees (CTU).

This process from below is reinforced by self-management structures and, with the decentralisation of state decision-making, by taking an active part in building a new state and society in which the division between political and civil society can be reduced or even erased. In the Bolivarian process, there is an understanding that the state and its structures are situated in an antagonistic relation to emancipation, to liberation, and to the aspiration to construct a socialist social system.

Two-track construction moves social antagonism into the state. It creates new institutions directed at supporting the popular base and the movements in their construction of structures intended to supplant the state and its institutions, despite resistance to such construction both institutionally and structurally within the state. This tension is reinforced by the centrality of petroleum to the Venezuelan economy, which foments state-centrism, centralisation of power, and vertical structures.[23] This distortion of the economy also engenders another Venezuelan peculiarity: the rentier economy[24] displaced class struggle in such a way that it takes place within the state. In other words, the class struggle in Venezuela centres on access to the resources to be administered, on the assumption that the state is the dispenser of social wealth.

In contrast to common notions of social transformation, the Venezuelan process is attempting to invent a new way by means of which a re-signification of state and society can be effected, opening up the possibility of overcoming capitalist relations as the result of the interrelation between above and below. The great challenge is to keep this process open-ended and develop a *modus operandi* from above that will support, accompany, and reinforce from-below strategies without co-opting or limiting them, making it possible to actively build the new without being absorbed from above or losing the initiative when confronted with the state or its institutions. It becomes an issue, then, of a relationship between *constituent power* and *constituted power*, in which constituent power continues to be the driving creative force. Even so, questions remain as to how it might be possible that the state with its institutions could overcome itself acting in interrelation with the movements.

According to the normative orientation of the process, constituent power must be the force that creates the new, while constituted power guarantees the

---

23 See Coronil 1997; Lander 2009.
24 Rentier economy: an economy that, instead of being productive, lives principally from the rent of resources or of capital.

space and the material conditions with which to do so. In practice, however, the asymmetry of power favours the logic of constituted power, with the consequence that constituted power tends to dominate, regulate, and restrain the creative capacity of constituent power. The deeper the transformation process becomes, the more the points of conflict multiply between constituent power and constituted power: on the one hand, the grassroots and agents of the process of change; on the other, the institutions and part of the Bolivarian process itself, which has brought into existence a new bureaucratic and economic bourgeoisie.

As changes become more profound, the old state's resistance increases. At the same time, struggles for further change increase, and become directed more and more against institutional obstacles. With the passage of time, then, class struggle has penetrated the institutions and the state, which are also a battlefield, although conditioned by their systemic limits.

4   Local Self-Government, Communal Councils (CCs), and Communes

Since 1999, many different mechanisms for citizen participation have been tried, mostly local or regional in scope; but these were interconnected with the representative institutional structure, and failed for that reason. A similar fate befell the first initiative of local participation at the national level, the Local Councils of Public Planning (CLPP). The search for a framework for participatory and protagonistic democracy has led to popular power and socialism, both of which are connected to the tradition of the commune and not to that of the state. The idea of local self-administration also connects with the historical experiences of indigenous people and Afro-Venezuelans, as well as with Latin American Marxist thinkers such as the Peruvian José Carlos Mariátegui.

With the beginning of the presidential term in 2006, the possibilities for participation and for council structures were broadened, reinforced, and renovated. These different 'councilist structures' have become fundamental to Venezuelan socialism in development. At their base are the communal councils, commonly referred to as 'CC' – a non-representative democratic form with higher levels of development that include communes and communal cities. Communes are formed by various CC and grow from below. Although, as in the case of the communal councils, the role of the state has been of great importance, with more than 40,000 communal councils and 1,169 communes formed by June 2015, they represent the most important field of participation and the principal instrument for building popular power, and they are assigned a central role in the supposed overcoming of the bourgeois state.

The communal councils emerged from below, as a revolutionary form, in a *sui generis* expression of class struggle (similar to that of the Soviets in the Russian Revolution). Then Chávez renewed the CCs, propagated them, and gave them an important push beginning in January 2006. This meant that, on the one hand, there was an enormous diffusion and strengthening of the CCs, but, on the other hand, it interfered in their organic growth. Today, some are autonomous forms, plural and locally organised for self-management, while others form part of the long arm of the institutions.

In this context, it is necessary to analyse how far the self-organisation mechanisms of the base, accompanied and promoted by the state, might go in developing the autonomy with which they can transform the state – a potential that would be lost if they were reproducing state structures and mechanisms.

5 Cooperatives, Co-Management, Self-Management, and Workers' Control

Although Chávez assumed the presidency in 1999, it was not until he overcame the 2002 coup and the 2002/3 'oil lockout' that he initiated a new economic policy with a more alternative orientation, increasing the promotion of cooperatives and introducing models of co-management. The systematic implementation of means of support for building a new productive sector of collective or social property began only in 2004 with the creation of the Ministry of Popular Economy.

The Venezuelan government officially declared a socialist orientation in 2005. It had previously begun nationalisations in the petroleum sector and the first expropriations of large agricultural estates, or *latifundios*; now it began to expropriate and nationalise industries, firms of strategic importance, and unproductive enterprises, strengthening the expansion of the productive sector of state or collective property. Although the first worker takeovers of firms were during the oil lockout, in the government's first years it treated the takeovers as a legal conflict and left its resolution to the courts. Only in 2005 did it begin – though still not in a systematic manner – to treat the occupation and reactivation of firms by their workers as a political question.

In 2007/8, Chávez assumed what had previously been a minoritarian position in the Bolivarian process, proposing the transformation of the mode of production. This means transforming the means of production, the productive forces, and the social relations of production. The latter faces transformations in three fields: power relations, commercial relations, and overcoming the social division of labour. The transformation of the possession and administration of the means of production is more conflictive than merely increasing participation in any other field, since it strikes directly at the foundations of the rentier model of capitalism and the economic interests of powerful sectors within and without the transformation process, who are against change in the relations of production.

However, workers' experiences over the last decade have promoted a radicalisation in the best sense of the word (which comes from the Latin and refers to going to the root, *radix*, of things). As the great expectations tied to the state fade, it becomes ever clearer that the materiality of the state apparatus is not transformed by a change in state power.[25]

The workers' movement has assumed a growing protagonistic role in the Venezuelan transformation process. Previously, the sector of industrial workers had been one of the weakest social structures in the Bolivarian process in terms of its capacity for building socialism. But in recent years, the struggles for worker participation on the job have become stronger, and the demand for workers' control is gaining force. What Marx postulated in his analysis of the Paris Commune is also valid in the case of Venezuela: the council structure is 'the political form at last discovered under which to work out the economical emancipation of labour'.[26]

After Chávez's first call to form the Socialist Workers' Councils (CST) in 2007, pressure from below led some institutions as of 2010 to permit or even promote the formation of CST, although there was still no law to that effect. While there is still an effort within the majority of institutions to impede the formation of CST, in some others and in some state companies, institutions have tried to take the lead in forming CST, distorting their meaning and reducing them to a representative body of workers dealing with labour-related demands within the governmental bureaucracy. This has made the CST a new zone of conflict, and in several cases has transformed the CST and the struggle for their creation into new struggles for workers' control.

There is not even a pretence at present of centring the transformation process on industrial workers in a country where 44 percent of the economically active population works in the informal sector. (When Chávez assumed the presidency it was 54 percent). Besides the low level of industrialisation in Venezuela, the classic factory councils have been made impractical in many situations by a combination of post-Fordist changes in production and labour; the disappearance of large factories that brought together great numbers of

---

25   Poulantzas 2000, p. 131.
26   Marx 1986, p. 334.

workers, homogenising their conditions of work and life; the fragmentation of the processes of production; and the widespread practice of externalising and subcontracting parts of the production process.

The struggle for workers' control must be seen as an element in the building of what in Venezuela is discussed as the communal state. It is, however, an especially important field to analyse for various reasons. It is there that the most direct (or least mediated) conflict takes place between capital and labour – a struggle between two antagonistic models that cannot coexist. More than any other, this conflict penetrates the rank and file of the Bolivarian process, challenging those who do not truly seek to transform the social relations of production.

The agents of transformation can only be the workers and the communities. As has been demonstrated in all the twentieth-century variants of 'actually existing socialism', state ownership of the means of production did not accomplish the hoped-for abolition of exploitation, nor did state ownership of the means of production change either the mode of production or the mode of exploitation. Private control was simply replaced by a frequently more inefficient state control, with a new privileged bureaucratic elite who appropriated a good part of any surpluses produced. Only workers and communities, collectively assuming control of the means of production, can construct a new social economy leading to overcoming capitalist relations.

There is no automatic mechanism to achieve this. As Marx said, existence determines consciousness; capitalism does not generate a consciousness of solidarity and collectivity, which is necessary for the transformation. Elio Sayago, ex-worker-president of the aluminium plant Alcasa, correctly says:

> If you don't make an exercise of involving yourself, it's wrong to think you can generate a different consciousness. The essence and the strength of capitalism is that the structure under which we all function obliges the worker to compete with his co-worker to bring food home to the family, because there's a job a little higher up the ladder that can permit him to take home a little more salary.[27]

In order to progress in the creation of a new social economy in the service of humanity, overcoming capitalist logic, it is necessary to involve the workers actively and participatively in building other relations of work and of production. There is a growing pressure from below in the workplace, that seeks to aug-

---

27   See Sayago 2011.

ment workers' protagonistic participation on the job, and – increasingly – to assume workers' control, seeing in it the only guarantee of a transformation of the social relations of production and of Venezuela's economic model, and of putting production at the service of the *pueblo*.[28]

6 The Revolution without Chávez

Hugo Chávez's death from cancer on 5 March 2013 sparked fears over the future course of the transformation process, since Chávez was the movements' most important interlocutor and ally in government. Since his death, the opposition and strong economic powers have engaged in political and economic destabilisation, seeing his death as an opportunity to topple the government and reverse the transformation process. Many observers have drawn parallels to the economic sabotage against the socialist government of president Salvador Allende in Chile before the military coup of September 1973.

Former Foreign Minister Nicolás Maduro won the presidential election of April 2013 with a margin of two percent over his right-wing opponent Henrique Capriles – half a million fewer votes than Chávez received a few months earlier. Although the elections were once again confirmed as free, fair, and democratic by hundreds of international observers, the opposition refused to recognise Maduro's victory, promoting violent demonstrations that left nine government supporters dead. Nevertheless, Maduro's victory has proven that the Bolivarian Revolution is a solid transformation project and not a one-man show based on populism.

Maduro committed publicly to Chávez's programme and declared several times that creating communes is central to Venezuela's own path towards socialism. During his electoral campaign he promised not to negotiate with the bourgeoisie and to put popular power at the centre of his policies. Among other changes Maduro made, he appointed a new Minister of Communes, Reinaldo Iturriza, removing his widely criticised predecessor. The new minister changed the approach of the Ministry of Communes, recognising the limitations of the Ministry and the primacy of the constituent power organised in communes. His work has been welcomed by the communards. Movements, rank-and-file *chavistas*, and other leftist leaders advocate for further radicalisation of the process and a decisive turn in revolutionary politics – a *golpe de timón* (taking

---

28 [Translator's note: In the Venezuelan context, I have chosen to leave the Spanish *pueblo* untranslated, with its sense of community and place intact, rather than translate it as 'people'].

of the rudder), as Chávez titled one of his last written political interventions. Initiatives for a better coordination of movement forces are proliferating, as are concrete struggles in communities and workplaces.

Some critics from the left, and also polemicists from the right, argue that there is no socialism in Venezuela, attempting thus to disqualify the entire process. However, in Venezuela there is no pretence that socialism has arrived, which is the implication behind these criticisms (even if it is not framed so explicitly). Beyond all the governmental rhetoric of putting the seal of socialism on everything, Venezuela is only trying to construct the fundamentals for the development of a future socialist society. If the criticism is that Venezuela is not a socialist country, and that it cannot construct a socialist system if it does not develop internal production, and continues living by collecting internationally produced surplus value, the response can only be affirmative. But neither will a different development model lead to socialism.

The programme for the Chávez government in the period 2013–19, assumed by the president-elect of 14 April 2013, Nicolás Maduro, declares: 'Do not be deceived: the socioeconomic formation that still prevails in Venezuela is of a capitalist, rentier character. Socialism has barely begun to implant its own dynamic among us'.[29] The main problem in the dialectical framework of capitalist-dependent-petrostate accumulation is that the rentier model is reinforced when the GNP grows, since the 'fruit of dependence can only be more dependence, and its liquidation necessarily supposes the suppression of the relations of production that it entails'.[30]

To advance in the building of socialism in Venezuela according to the declarations in the government programme for 2013–19, it will be necessary to continue strengthening the communal councils, communes, and communal cities, and 'the development of social ownership of the basic strategic means of production is crucial',[31] and 'to develop bodies of coordination between the communal councils and workers' councils, on the one hand, and the direct social property companies on the other'.[32]

'The history of all hitherto existing society is the history of class struggle', wrote Karl Marx and Friedrich Engels in the *Communist Manifesto*.[33] Raniero Panzieri, one of the founders of Italian workerism (*operaismo*), arguing for the necessity of co-research as a way to intervene in factories and as means of

---

29   Chávez 2012, p. 2.
30   See Marini 1991.
31   Chávez 2012, p. 7.
32   Chávez 2012, p. 22.
33   Marx and Engels 2007, p. 9.

analysis, emphasised the necessity of 'refusing to extract, from the analysis of capital, the analysis of the working class'.[34] In contrast to historian Marc Bloch, who saw history as the science 'of men in time'[35] and wrote that 'the object of history is, by nature, man. Let us say rather, men',[36] traditional Marxism locates capital at the centre of its analysis.

The present work, which shares the perspective of critical Marxist and workerist currents, locates human beings and their struggles at the centre both of history and of social transformation processes, and concentrates on the question of class struggle. In the analysis of the Bolivarian process, class struggle is central, since class struggle tends toward a struggle for a different social system rather than a struggle within the capitalist framework. Only in this way can the emancipatory potential of the Bolivarian process be analysed.

As Antonio Gramsci indicated, under the economic and political domination of the bourgeois class, the real development of the revolutionary process takes place invisibly within the organisations and institutions of the bourgeois representative system, hidden away within the 'darkness of the factory and in the obscurity of the consciousness of the uncountable multitudes that capitalism subjects to its laws'.[37]

In this way the central question in analysing the Venezuelan social transformation process cannot be whether Venezuela has already built a socialist society, which is obviously not the case, nor can it be whether the state is putting the correct socialist policies into practice. The central question has to be how social relations and popular experiences have developed since 1998.

That is what this book seeks to do. It studies and discusses various popular movements; the communal councils and their forerunners in community organisation; different types of alternative forms of entrepreneurial organisation, like cooperatives or co-management; companies recuperated by their workers and the initiatives and struggles for workers' control; and the forming of the communes as self-government at a higher level. Out of the different experiences and initiatives, a profile emerges from below of what Chávez called 'the communal state', which has become the political and social project of the popular movements in Venezuela. This analysis and discussion necessarily include the politics of constituted power and of government institutions, and of the relationship between the movements, the organised *pueblo*, and the state and its institutions.

---

34   Panzieri 1965, p. 109.
35   Panzieri 1965, p. 23.
36   Panzieri 1965, p. 21.
37   Giachetti 1972, pp. 157–8.

CHAPTER 2

Class, Constituent Power, and Popular Power

In order to analyse and understand the Bolivarian process, it is necessary to clarify some conditions and specific concepts that have marked its development. It is not possible to decode Venezuelan reality with a traditional class analysis; a concept of class adequate for analysing the composition and range of classes in Venezuela must be developed, necessarily factoring in the roles of socio-territorial segregation and of community in the creation of class and the development of class struggle.

What follows is an analysis of the process of two-track construction and of the centrality of constituent power. Within the Bolivarian process, the main agent of change is understood to be constituent power – the legitimate, sovereign, collective, creative capacity of human beings that is expressed through movements in the organised social base. Therefore we look at the theoretical concept of constituent and constituted power and the genesis and development of the concept in Venezuela. This chapter closes with an analysis of the concept of popular power as it is being handled in Venezuela (and other Latin American countries) at present, which represents an important base for the building of a new society, and which is fundamentally different from previous historic concepts about popular power or dual power.

1   Updating the Concept of Class

> In a capitalist society all issues bear on class, even if they are not all about class and even if a great many problems we face are across class boundaries.[1]

> ∙∙∙

> If there is no struggle there is no progress. Those who profess to favor freedom and yet deprecate agitation are men who want crops without plowing up the ground; they want rain without thunder and lightning.

---

[1] See Panitch 2003.

They want the ocean without the awful roar of its many waters ... Power concedes nothing without a demand.²

∴

Why continue using the category of 'class'? Does it not belong to an analysis of industrial societies centred on the industrial worker? Obviously now that the relations of production have changed, the traditional reading that equated industrial workers with the working class, assigning them the protagonistic role in central change because of their location within the productive process, is behind the times (if it was ever applicable). However, that does not mean that the contradiction between capital and labour, which gives rise to the formation of classes, has disappeared. Instead, redefining the concept and the composition of class requires that we deal in specifics.

The category of class continues to be important. Unlike categories based on identities, class is based on doing. Since doing is more questionable and more subject to decision than identity, it interrogates its subjects more, and better indicates their capacity for changing the world. Moreover, 'class' expresses the struggle of what John Holloway calls 'doing against labour'.³ The category of class also indicates the unity of the rich diversity of struggles without hierarchising them. The existence of class struggle, then, indicates to us that the character of the struggle tends in the direction of a struggle for different systems, since it is based in the antagonism between capital and labour. This antagonism finds expression in the fact that the classes do not struggle within the framework of a system, but instead tend toward a struggle for new systems.⁴ This aspect of class is basic for analysing the character and perspective of the transformation process in Venezuela.

In the Venezuelan context, the necessity of a new definition of the concept of class is in view, given that the traditional paradigms have never been able to include or identify the agents of change:

> The popular insurgence of February 27, 1989, was not organised, nor directed, nor protagonised, by the revolutionary subject *par excellence*: the

---

2 Frederick Douglass, quoted in Martin 1986, p. 175.
3 Holloway 2004a, p. 15; Holloway defines 'doing against labour' as 'the revolt of one form of activity, which we choose, against another form of activity, which we reject'. See Holloway 2010, p. 85.
4 Bonefeld 2008, p. 128; Dos Santos 2006, p. 30.

proletariat ... [But] if the working class was not the protagonist of those actions, why conclude that there was no political actor? Does not this impossibility of perceiving the imprint of a distinct political subjectivity in the working class constitute a severe reduction in the political sphere?[5]

1.1 Theoretical Notes on Class and Multitude

In the *Communist Manifesto*, the classes are the two 'great hostile camps' into which society is divided: bourgeoisie and proletariat.[6] Marx, however, left no highly developed concept of the various aspects of class, meaning that Marxist interpretations of class are based on commentary found in various parts of Marx's work. Even so, the analysis of class on which *Capital* is built is that of a single class relation: capital and labour.[7]

Following Marx, political economy analyses social relations created by humans, which appear to be relations with and between things; classes, like capital, are not predetermined positions, but are, like capital, a social relation.[8] Marx rejects the idea that classes are constituted by their form of income or by 'market situation', as Max Weber argues from a sociological perspective in the course of differentiating a large number of social classes.[9] Marx did not understand classes as places or groups, the way empiricists, structuralists, or sociologists do, but rather as social relations.[10] According to Marx, only at first glance are classes constituted by conditions of wages, earnings, or ground rent – i.e. the exploitation of the workforce, of capital or of land ownership. A dialectical Marxist approach, which understands class and class struggle as social relations, can also reveal how different individuals are differently affected by the capital-labour contradiction. If class is a social relation, then

---

5   Iturriza 2007, p. 1.
6   The fact that in the third volume of *Capital* Marx speaks of three classes ('The owners merely of labour-power, owners of capital, and land-owners', Marx 1967, p. 885) has prompted some critics to accuse him of contradiction. Dos Santos attributes this criticism to a lack of dialectical comprehension (2006, p. 11, p. 30). But this is not a superimposition of different interpretations of the concept of class; rather, it is a dialectical interpretation in which the concept of class is adapted to the level of abstraction (2006, p. 30). The quote describes a concrete historical revolutionary situation in which the formation of groups is the result of class struggle as a tendency, rather than as absolute reality.
7   Gunn 1987, p. 20.
8   Gunn 1987, p. 16.
9   Weber 1922.
10 Gunn 1987, pp. 17, 19, 20. This difference is important because a sociological interpretation does not help us understand class or class struggle. Nevertheless, a classification of groups or strata may be very useful in analysing society.

the relation between classes does not derive from the countervailing interests of exploited and exploiter (which would presuppose groups that are almost naturalised); instead, the relation between exploited and exploiter creates antagonistic interests. Classes are the expression of such relations; because of this, the concept of class is constituted theoretically within the concept of class struggle.[11] Class therefore is a relation of struggle: '*class struggle* is the fundamental premise of *class*. Better still: class struggle is class itself',[12] the goal of which is to overcome, destroy, and dismantle a system (or to defend it). That the revolutionary conflict should take the form of conflict between groups is the result of class struggle.[13]

As a consequence, class is not an affirmative concept. Class condition is not something to be romanticised, as Communist parties and their worker-organisation appendages have done for a century, nor as some more autonomist or anarchist concepts of recent decades have done. As Marx noted: 'To be a productive worker is therefore not a piece of luck, but a misfortune'.[14] The condition for the liberation of the working class is the abolition or overcoming of classes. The struggle, therefore, takes place on two levels: between the constituted classes, and against class and classification.[15]

In this context, it is necessary to remember that it is not the primacy of economic motives in historical explanation that constitutes the decisive difference between Marxism and bourgeois thought, but the 'point of view of the totality'.[16] Along with this focus on the totality comes the rejection of the split between political and civil society: 'In the Marxist view, the category of "politics" becomes as wide as the forms which class struggle (and class itself) unpredictably takes'.[17]

As a consequence, class is absolutely varied and diverse, irreducible to a specific subject with a certain position in the process of production, and struggle does not have to assume pre-established forms. Class struggle is made up of many struggles, and the collective is not an abstraction, but is the 'ideal form of existence that is produced as an "instant" of negation/overcoming'[18] of the divisions of capital.

---

11   Dos Santos 2006, p. 31.
12   Gunn 1987, p. 16.
13   Gunn 1987, p. 23.
14   Marx 1990, p. 644.
15   Bonefeld 2008, p. 117; Dos Santos 2006, p. 31; Holloway 2004a, p. 13; 2004b, p. 78.
16   Lukács 1971, p. 27.
17   Gunn 2004, pp. 29–30.
18   Tischler 2004, p. 113.

Among the many present efforts to redefine the concept of class at the level of the relations of production of class composition, the most widely disseminated and controversial has been the concept of 'multitude'. Answering criticisms of having abandoned the concept of class, Michael Hardt and Antonio Negri (2004) have insisted that multitude is a renovated concept of class that breaks with the limited vision of the political sphere and attempts to encompass the variety and diversity of class without homogenising it. The multitude is constituted in struggle; it rejects representation and homogenisation by its very nature, and is not limited to a fixed position in the production process.

Both Hardt/Negri (2004) and Virno (2004) base their concept of multitude on the work of Baruch Spinoza, who in the seventeenth century (unlike Thomas Hobbes) saw the multitude as the basis of civil rights, being that in its multeity and its collective action it does not become one people.[19] The multitude is a 'set of singularities', singularity in this case meaning a 'social subject whose difference cannot be reduced to sameness, a difference that remains different'.[20] It is precisely these differences that become socially enriching by means of the multitude's communication and common action. The form of organisation of the multitude is the network, without a centre and with open boundaries.[21]

Hardt and Negri contrast the open condition of the 'multitude' with the notions of 'working class' and the 'people'. While the latter two concepts are based on exclusion, division, and homogenisation, the multitude is based neither on identity or unity (like the people), nor on a certain position in the production process (like the traditional working class). Virno and Hardt and Negri also differentiate between *multitude* and *mass*, and contrast the 'plural singularities' of the multitude to the 'undifferentiated unity' of the people.[22] The mass is composed of social actors who are basically passive, who cannot act independently but need leadership.[23] Within the masses, differences tend to disappear, though they cannot be reduced to a unity. While the multitude has no external limits and is inclusive, the idea of the 'people' is connected in all its historical variants with a 'habitual "inside" and an unknown and hostile "outside"'.[24]

Nevertheless, despite Hardt and Negri's and Virno's critiques of Hobbes, who with his state-centrism was panicked by the idea of the multitude, they end

---

19   Virno 2004, p. 25.
20   Hardt and Negri 2004, p. 99.
21   Hardt and Negri 2004, pp. vii–xv, 54–5; Virno 2004, p. 33.
22   Hardt and Negri 2004, p. 99.
23   Hardt and Negri 2004, p. 106.
24   Virno 2004, p. 33.

up adopting Hobbes's definition of *people*, which sees them as the actors of nation-state building. They oppose the concept of multitude to that of the people, which according to them always converges in the state. So in the definitions offered by Hardt and Negri and Virno, *people* ends up being almost an existentialist concept. In their vision, the people are not formed through historical experiences, struggles, and collective memory, are not diverse in their goals, and are not flexible or capable of transformation; the definition varies between a republican one, based on homogenisation for the construction of the national (as a legacy of the French Revolution), and an existentialist one (as natural executor of the historic task of building the nation, following the definition of the German philosopher Johann Gottlieb Fichte).

This Eurocentric vision completely ignores other historical experiences. In Latin America, *pueblo* (people) may have many totally different interpretations, as per the example of 'indigenous *pueblos*', which, far from implying an intention to build a nation state, carries the contrary interpretation: it is based on a concrete critique of the concept of the national state (as has been seen, for example, in Bolivia, where on the base of the indigenous *pueblos* the new Constitution defines the state as a 'plurinational state').

An even greater conceptual problem arises from what according to the authors is the basis of the post-Fordist multitude: namely, what it has in common. According to Hardt/Negri, 'all forms of labour are today socially productive, they produce in common, and share too a common potential to resist the domination of capital'.[25] Or, in Virno's words: 'The multitude, unlike the people, is not defined by qualities, but by capacities. This way of being corresponds to post-Fordism and to the "general intellect": a point of departure, inevitable but ambivalent'.[26] But if the multitude is the 'mode of being' that corresponds to post-Fordism, then the capacities that define the multitude are derived from the capitalist production regime and not from the struggles that ought to be central. In this case, the 'revolutionary subject' would be once again defined by location in the production process and not through social relations and struggles, and here resides one of the basic contradictions of the concepts of multitude.[27]

The post-Fordist multitude's 'way of being' impels the search for non-representative democratic forms and for the collapse of representation. Since its lack of homogeneity prevents delegating to a sovereign, the multitude, which wants

---

25 Hardt and Negri 2004, pp. 106–7.
26 Virno 2003, p. 19.
27 Tischler 2007, pp. 126–7.

neither to take power nor to construct a new state, inherently tends toward annulling both ideas. This is where Virno sees the most direct connection with the seventeenth-century multitude, which also supposedly wanted not to take power, but to construct 'plural experiences, forms of non-representative democracy, of non-governmental usages and customs'.[28] This reference, however, seems forced, because the present multitude is derived from post-Fordism, and also because the 'non-statal uses and customs' of the seventeenth-century multitude were frequently focused on the defence of rights, privileges, or specific practices without implying an acceptance of plurality.

Hardt and Negri conclude that because of the multitude's condition of being and its form of organisation, it is 'the only social subject capable of realizing democracy, that is, the rule of everyone by everyone'.[29] Nevertheless, there is not even a hint of how this could begin to take shape. Virno, on the other hand, rejects what he calls a postmodern focus for the multitude. For him, the multitude does not mean the end of the working class, but rather that the working class is assuming characteristics of a multitude and not of a people.[30] According to Virno, unity continues to be necessary, but it resides not in the state, as in the case of the people, but rather in 'language, intellect, [and] the communal faculties of the human race'.[31] It is important to underscore that unity cannot be in the state, since the state is a product of capitalist relations, and thus to go beyond capitalism it is necessary to go beyond the state.

Virno does not draw concrete conclusions from his analysis. But unity must converge in a political project that includes all of society, 'a world in which many worlds fit', as the Zapatistas say. For that to happen, there must be a moment of political linkage that the term 'multitude' does not cover. To speak of many worlds should not blind us to the world in which the many worlds fit.

Ranciére and Corcoran criticise Hardt and Negri's mere positive definition of multitude. They accuse it of being a concept that 'manifests a phobia of the negative, of any politics that defines itself "against"'.[32] According to Ranciére and Corcoran, politics always involves the addition of one people to another people, as well as pitting one people against another, and the latter is precisely what Hardt and Negri's concept of multitude rejects.[33]

---

28 Virno 2004, p. 43.
29 Hardt and Negri 2004, p. 100.
30 See Virno 2004.
31 Virno 2004, p. 25.
32 Ranciére and Corcoran 2010, p. 86.
33 Ranciére and Corcoran 2010, p. 85.

In Ranciére's analysis, the people are a political actor. In the fifth of his *Ten Theses on Politics*, he summarises his concept of the people:

> The 'people' that are the actors of democracy – and thus the principal actors of politics – are not the collection of members in a community, or the labouring classes of the population. They are the supplementary part, in relation to any counting of parts of the population that makes it possible to identify 'the part of those who have no-part' [*le compte des incomptés*] with the whole of the community.[34]

This definition gets us closer to the understanding of *pueblo* as class that is found in parts of Latin America and specifically in Venezuela. In the following chapter, the points previously discussed are applied to Venezuelan reality in order to develop a concept of what class is in this specific context, and how class struggle is expressed in the Bolivarian process.[35]

1.2   Class Composition and Breadth in Venezuela

Chávez's constant affirmation of the importance of supporting the poor more than the other sectors of the population shows a clear class orientation, representing a novelty within the history of Venezuelan heads of state.[36] The polarisation of Venezuelan society tends to manifest itself in class struggle, fundamentally as a struggle between the accommodated and the marginalised.[37]

Analysis of mobilisations and struggles in Venezuela provides evidence that 'the marginalised' cannot be reduced to a specific actor. On the contrary, it is precisely from the variety and multiplicity of the struggles that the Bolivarian process derives its revolutionary potential. Between the organisations and movements that participate in and support the transformation process, we find neighbourhood residents organised in communal councils, labourers and informal workers like motorcycle taxi drivers, walking street vendors, peasants, women, migrants, indigenous people, Afro-Venezuelans, ecologists, producers of independent media, LGBT people, and others. Iturriza writes:

---

34 See Rancière 2001.
35 Theoretical Marxist categories are derived from historical reality and as such are not eternally valid universal categories: a society historically formed in a concrete way cannot correspond directly to abstract categories. Marxism does not use abstraction formally, but elaborates concepts abstractly and denies them immediately, demonstrating its limits in doing so (Dos Santos 2006).
36 Ellner 2006, p. 87.
37 Medina 2001, p. 124.

The multiplicity of actors implies the multiplication of fronts for struggle, the diversity of strategies of struggle for radical democratisation of Venezuelan society, and its capacity for mobilisation to defend the revolutionary process when it has been in danger.[38]

The widest focus of class, the multiplicity of actors in the process of change, and the recognition of the variety of struggles: all are at the roots of the Bolivarian movement. Even politico-military organisations like the PRV (Venezuelan Revolutionary Party), or later the MRT, were already diverging in the 1970s and 80s from traditional concepts with their analysis of class, taking as points of reference a wide range of struggles, including those of neighbourhood residents, indigenous peoples, cultural movements, sexual diversity movements, and sex workers. The PRV in the 70s referred to the 'crowd' (*muchedumbre*) to indicate the diversity of the community in struggle.[39]

In creating a space for a redefinition of the collective and a critique of the actually existing, the movements developed a revolutionary utopia envisaging the end of human suffering like that described by Ernst Bloch in *The Principle of Hope*,[40] and updated the question of class and class struggle:

> Class can be conceptualized, then, as a community of struggles, diverse modes of collective resistance. That position goes against the idea of class as a homogenous, synthetic social form. The unity of the monad is not homogeneity but, it could be said, the actually existing [*concreta*] community. The actually existing community, then, is the irruption of *messianic time* in the *continuum* of the abstract community.[41]

The irruption of 'messianic time' in the 'continuum' signifies the advance presence of elements of the aspired-to classless society, which indicate what the future might hold. For Walter Benjamin, *messianic time* is the symbol of a classless society, and therefore it is a collective time, not an individual one. Benjamin speaks of *now-time* (*Jetztzeit*) to describe the moment when the present is interrupted by messianic time.[42] Now-time is the time of the presence of advanced elements and of the densification of the possibilities and dangers of

---

38   Iturriza 2007, p. 6.
39   Twickel 2006, p. 51.
40   See Bloch 1986.
41   Tischler 2007, p. 112.
42   Benjamin 1968, p. 261.

emancipation. This breaks with the bourgeois temporal concept, which postulates a time that is empty, homogeneous, constant, and linear.

In messianic time, emancipation is not transferred to the future or to the great beyond. Everything is possible and imaginable – which also means that there is not necessarily a liberating outcome. Messianic time presents in short form all the history of humanity. It is also found in the living memory of traditions and practices in which the experience and praxis of past generations is reflected. The actually existing community, which can in flashes appear a classless society, is class as a community of diversity and plurality built in the struggle to abolish class. It is the community constituted on the basis of difference rather than synthesis and homogenisation.

Since 1998, the government's official discourse, and more explicitly that of Chávez, has been directed to the 'sovereign *pueblo*', referring to the marginalised majority of the population.[43] Chávez explicitly rejected the term 'mass' (*masa*) and was accustomed to speak of the *pueblo*, and in some cases the *multitud*,[44] precisely in order to make multiplicity visible. The *pueblo* is comprised of the poor, the unemployed, workers, students, retirees, etc. – sectors that, as Chávez emphasised, carried out hundreds of 'microrevolutions' in the 1980s and 90s.[45] Multiple, diverse and contradictory, it is the *pueblo* of the oppressed, the present-day form of Víctor Hugo's *Les Misérables* or of *Los de Abajo* in Mariano Azuela's novel of revolution in Mexico.[46] It does not exist *a priori*, but is constituted in relation to struggle, as a social project. In this conception, the *pueblo* is

> the protagonist of the great transformations of history. At times the *pueblo* disappears, but others emerge when customs are shared and there is intense communication. The multitudes, then, associate with each other in the liberation of 'metaphysical solidarity'.[47]

The counterpart of the *pueblo* is the *oligarchy*. Although some opposition politicians and parties have adapted the term *pueblo* to fit their discourse to the new social context, the middle and upper classes do not see themselves as *pueblo*. They identify as people, good people, decent people (*gente, gente*

---

43 García-Guadilla 2003, p. 247.
44 Chávez 2008, p. 66.
45 Chávez 2007, p. 4.
46 *Les Misérables*, referred to occasionally by Chávez in his discourses, has been printed in three volumes and freely distributed by the Venezuelan state.
47 See Chávez 1993.

bien, gente decente), while viewing the *pueblo* as comprised of poor people and marginals.[48] The middle and upper employees of PDVSA, who lost their jobs as a consequence of the 'petroleum sabotage' (*sabotaje petrolero*) of 2002–3, called themselves *gente del petróleo*.

Chávez reinforced his class-oriented discourse by declaring a socialist orientation in 2005. In November 2008, with reference to Marx, Chávez declared:

> I firmly believe that our battle is an expression of the class struggle. The *pueblo*, the popular classes and the poor against the rich. And the rich against the poor. That's the broad outline, though one needs to know how to appreciate its subtleties and intermediate stages.[49]

What characterises other struggles – that of the Zapatistas in Chiapas, for example – that 'do not promote a policy of homogenisation and centralisation of political action, that is, they do not propose to be a synthesis',[50] can also be applied to the process of change in Venezuela. *Pueblo* is not a homogenising term; it does not deny diversity. Chávez included the diversity of struggles and organisations in his discourse and at the same time he directed his discourse to specific elements of the *pueblo* – to workers, barrios, peasants, women, youth, LGBT, disabled people, etc., and included indigenous people and Afro-Venezuelans, who look back on centuries of oppression and struggle. With his constant positive references to Venezuela's indigenous and African heritage, including himself, he contributed centrally to empowering the population.[51] Chávez did not speak for the poor and the marginalised, but added his voice to theirs. This is why the opposition, with its bourgeois racist and classist culture within a Eurocentric colonial tradition, despised Chávez so heartily, because they saw him as part of the 'rabble'.

Denis also uses the terms *pueblo* and multitude, although he rejects using the two terms in opposition.[52] Andrés Antillano, in contrast, considers the concept of multitude unsuitable to the Venezuelan context and refers to the *pueblo*. In an interview, he further specified that a more apt term for the condition of the Venezuelan *pueblo* would be a positive use of the pejorat-

---

48 Moreno 1999; 2005; Parker 2006, p. 90.
49 YVKE Mundial: Chávez lee nueva lista de ataques a misiones: 'Aquí hay una lucha de clases', available at: http://www.radiomundial.com.ve/yvke/noticia.php?1553 (accessed 30 November 2008).
50 See Tischler 2007.
51 On racism in Venezuelan society and in the opposition, see Herrera Salas 2004.
52 Denis 2005, p. 72.

ive term 'horde', which better captures the antagonism between constituent and constituted power in the face of massive ambivalence. The horde leads itself; it neither has nor wants political leadership, but is chaotic and oriented around a collective intelligence. These characteristics, however, render it more readily influenced and administered by the state, which has an inherent tendency to control social processes.[53] For Barreto, the term *pueblo* is the most apt for the necessary building of political actors in the process of change.

The common use of *pueblo* in Venezuela includes the characteristics of difference, of crowd, and of multitude; it has several characteristics in common with the multitude of Hardt/Negri and Virno. The *pueblo* has no determined position in the production process and is organised in the form of a centre-less web. This *pueblo*-multitude does not seek unity in the state, but in the building of 'a world in which many worlds fit'. Nevertheless, there are important differences. The *pueblo* is constituted in relation to struggle and, unlike Hardt/Negri's multitude, the *pueblo* in Venezuela does 'sign pacts', with the end of better accomplishing its goals and consolidating its gains.

> We as a *pueblo* have given everything. We have gone out to the street every time they have asked us because we believe in it, we know that the hope of all of us, is the hope of the humble people who are with *comandante* Chávez, and for this we struggle and for this we defend the revolution.[54]

By doing so, the *pueblo* neither delegates nor surrenders its sovereignty, but rather tries to create a framework for amplifying its sovereignty. Complying with 'pacts' and the conditions of compliance are constantly redefined in a relation of conflict and cooperation. Transformation is a non-linear process, beset with ruptures.

According to the understanding of the term *pueblo* current among active participants of the transformation process in Venezuela, it is always composed of different parts, which maintain their diversity and come together in a social project. It is a community built on heterogeneity. It is an open category, constituted in struggle, which people can join. It is important to underscore that the *pueblo* is in no way predetermined by social status, nationality, or any other category. It is not composed of 'the poor' or 'the oppressed' as such, but is col-

---

53 See I-AA 2008.
54 Yusmeli Patiño 2006, Commune-in-construction 'Eje de MACA', Petare, Gran Caracas, in Azzellini and Ressler 2006.

lectively constituted in relation to specific struggles and in a struggle for a social project in which all struggles can have a place.[55]

> For socialism, *pueblo* is the formula that articulates subaltern pluralities; the rough outline of struggles, creations, and resistances of those from below; the name of a revolutionary subject self-created in class struggle. Erected against hegemony, its universal signification derives from the particularity of its organised base. Its horizon is a collective creation.[56]

According to Mazzeo, who comes from the Darío Santillán Popular Front organisation of Argentina, *pueblo* is an 'ethico-political and dialectical' category, 'and because of that it is constitutive praxis':[57]

> We say that the 'masses,' the 'multitudes,' transform into *pueblos* [...] when they are constituted in collective organisations, social movements, political liberation movements; that the *pueblo* is the form through which the collective project of the exploited begins to be realized; that it is the will and the utopia of subalterns that conjures some, but not all, contradictions and paradoxes. This notion of *pueblo* does not presuppose division, but refers more to linkage among distinct fragments of the subaltern classes.[58]

Nevertheless, it is necessary to clarify that *pueblo* cannot be constructed as a positive universal category based on its use in Venezuela or other Latin American contexts. That is as unworkable as a categorical opposition between people and multitude. Like any community that goes beyond face-to-face interaction, *pueblo* is an imagined community, for which reason it is an ambivalent category, whose dimensions and characteristics can only be explained in the specific context.[59] Historically, the term *pueblo* has also been used to create interclass alliances and to mobilise in the name of exclusive projects and wars. The danger of erasing class contradictions under a national unity against the 'other', whether internal or external, imaginary or real, is always latent in the concept of *pueblo*.[60]

---

55   Acha 2007, p. 19.
56   Mazzeo and Stratta 2007, p. 10.
57   Mazzeo 2007, p. 41.
58   Mazzeo 2007, pp. 41–2.
59   See Anderson 1988.
60   Acha 2007, p. 21.

2   Socio-Territorial Segregation and Class Formation

Venezuela is the second most urbanised country of Latin America after Uruguay, with 87 percent of its population living in urban areas. About 14.3 million of Venezuela's approximately 27 million inhabitants live in *barrios*, which is to say, in urban zones with precarious infrastructure, which occupy around 650 square miles in total.[61] (In Venezuela, the term *barrio* refers specifically to popular, i.e. not middle- or upper-class neighbourhoods). Most barrios were formed by means of occupying private or public land, since the cities offered no space for the newly arrived, and therefore are not only precarious, but also officially invisible:

> Material negation accompanies symbolic negation: the barrios are not represented in the images of the city, they don't appear on its maps, they're not listed in its land registries, don't show up on its censuses, aren't covered in its news, and are not included in inventories of heritage. The barrios don't exist in the city's rhetoric, except as danger or anomaly.[62]

In the urban zones of Venezuela, the barrio is the most important template of identification and collective organisation. Given its Latin American context, it is unsurprising that it should be the most important and stable support for the transformation process.[63] The barrio's territorial identification should not be confused with nostalgic localism, but, because of territorial segregation, goes hand in hand with the dimension of class. In Venezuela, two totally different realities of life meet in the same geographical and political space – on the one hand, the medium and high strata, which have traditionally been the only ones with political influence; on the other, the lower strata, that of the *pueblo* in the barrios and the rural communities.

The sharing of a collective, precarious daily life in the barrio or the community represents a fundamental identification by the lower strata, which make up the majority of the population. Facing the conditions of life is a dimension marked by struggle, solidarity, and a relational network. It is not a place, nor a given community, but a vivid framework of social relations. Moreno calls it coexistence (*convivencia*), and underscores that it is not necessarily

---

61   See I-AA 2008; Colau 2008, p. 1.
62   Antillano 2005, p. 206.
63   Denis 2005, p. 31; I-AA 2008.

harmonious, but may also be conflictive.⁶⁴ Coexistence, nevertheless, has to be built and constantly maintained. Many of the barrios look back on a long history of struggles, having had to defend themselves for decades against eviction, struggle to obtain services, and develop collective mechanisms of mutual aid.⁶⁵ They are thus the result of urban marginalisation, as is the resistance against segregation, and as such, they are the guardians of alternative values.⁶⁶

In the early 1990s, organisations called Water Committees were formed, along with other organisations that worked to improve the supply of gas, provide health services, organise the collective purchase of residences, and even arm self-defence militias, as well as sponsor sporting organisations and, especially, cultural groups. Fiestas, dance, and music play a very important role in Venezuelan society, and there exist a large number of local cultural groups in the barrio that perform on certain dates. These groups frequently dedicate themselves to strengthening regional musical traditions, which promotes a sense of community permanence and historical self-consciousness. As of this writing, the communal councils represent the mechanism of self-organisation in the more advanced and developed councils, and the most important form of local territorial organisation.

The centrality of territory in the Venezuelan struggles is in contrast with the centrality of the workplace or the metropolis that has been traditionally identified with 'old' and 'new' social movements. The most active agent of change in Venezuela has been and continues to be the residents of the urban barrios and the peasant communities. The building of workers' councils, for example, has been much more difficult. The lack of identification by the greater part of the Venezuelan population with factory-industrial labour is due in part to the rentier economic model. Factory-industrial labour does not correspond to the reality of life for the majority of the people, although there have been important worker struggles, like that of the independent unions in the basic industries of Bolívar state. However, industrial workers were frequently privileged, and official unionism has mostly been corporativist, corrupt and co-opted by the political system.

> Class is found not in the factory but in territory, it's organised around territory. It's a service-sector class, very exposed, that comes and goes in

---

64   Moreno 2005, p. 213.
65   Antillano 2005, p. 200.
66   See I-AA 2008.

the informal economy and is mostly non-unionised. Territorial struggles, barrio struggles, have always had a very strong importance, more than workers' struggles, and quantitatively, this sector is also the large majority.[67]

Nevertheless, there have been important struggles in the industrial sector, and they have been increasing, especially since 2007 (see Chapters 5 and 6). Most of the successful ones have been connected with territory and have had ties to the surrounding communities. Among industrial workers there exists a consciousness of the importance of community relations and a feeling of responsibility toward them:

> We want everyone at the national and international level to know that when the workers recover a company, it is not to grab it for themselves, but to generate more jobs and help the communities.

> We only restarted the plant six months ago, but we have done our social labour, which is the most important task. We have to understand that we cannot recover a business to become capitalists all over again. We have to recover a business to be socialists, to get to the social. Because if not, I don't believe it's worth the trouble for the *pueblos*, for the people of the communities, to join the struggle of workers who will one day abandon them.[68]

3 From Taking Power to Process: Constituent Power and Popular Power

To speak of constituent power is to speak of democracy.[69]

...

All of modern history has been characterized by the indistinguishability of the social and the political in the exercise of constituent power by the subordinated classes. Not a single episode of the rebellion that for

---

67 Antillano 2006b.
68 Rowan Jimenez, worker, Invepal, in Azzellini and Ressler 2006.
69 Negri 1994, p. 17.

some centuries opposed capital and proletariat has emerged unscathed from this common process of social and political that the proletariat has imposed. With a violence adequate to the importance of the stakes. What else is this if not the definitive hegemony of constituent power, of free creative work, that is the extinction of the political as a separate category? Constituent power does not eliminate the political, it makes it live as a category of social interaction where one lives, in the integrity of the social relations among men, in the density of cooperation ... The category of the political, like independence or 'relative autonomy,' is brought up only to block, order, dominate the omnipotence of the living work: the category of the political forms part of constituted power.[70]

∴

Commonly, *constituent power* refers to the legitimate creative force that resides in humans collectively: it comes into effect when the multitude meets the *potentia*, the capacity to emanate, design, mould, create something new, without having to derive it from, or be subject to, that which already exists. The Bolivarian process prioritises constituent power, which is understood not as a temporary situation of delegating power and/or sovereignty – in the creation of a constitution, for example – but rather as the permanent creative force of the *pueblo* that imposes itself on constituted power. The concept, which in Venezuela emerged from the movements of the 80s, rejects the logic of mediation between 'civil' and 'political' society as represented by, for example, the non-governmental organisations. Rather, it is focused on promoting the grassroots' potential and direct capacity to analyse, decide, execute, and evaluate their concerns. Constituent power refers to the councils in general, to popular power, and to the basic concept of the communal state.

Being omnipotent and expansive, constituent power is and has been the justification and the basis of all revolutions, democracies, and republics. It is, then, the great motor of history, the most powerful innovative social force. Even though it is the source of legitimacy, however, constituent power has historically been silenced and robbed of the possibility of acting on its own, so it has barely complied with its function of legitimising the existence of constituted power.

---

70 Negri 1994, pp. 325–6.

The question, then, is what to do in order that constituent power might constantly have the possibility of irrupting to model the present, of impelling and creating something new that does not derive from the old. Revolution, then, is not understood as an act of taking power, but as a wide process of construction of the new, an act of creation and invention.[71] This is also a legacy of the Bolivarian process within the movements of the American continent and beyond.

In the absence of an extensive theorisation of the concept of constituent power by Venezuelan movements, which instead have disseminated it in practice, we turn to Antonio Negri's concept (1994), which is not only broadly applicable to Venezuela, but has also been widely referenced by the Bolivarian movement.

3.1 Crisis as a Motor of History: Constituent Power vs. Constituted Power

In the debates of previous centuries about democracy, constituent power was considered to be the omnipotent, expansive source that produces the constitutional norms of the entire legal order, but which is also subject to that production.[72] Nevertheless, if constituent power is revolution, it is omnipotent.[73] Therefore every constitutional and legal definition of the role of actor of constituent power contradicts its nature, since its rebellious spirit is incompatible with integration into a standardised, hierarchised system.[74] Constituent power represents a constant threat to constituted power. In spite of this, it cannot be neglected or ignored by legal definition, since democratic legitimacy and the legal system's meaning and justification are based on it. It has thus been limited in time and in reach, reduced to legal categories and forced into an administrative structure.[75]

In the philosophy of law, there are three different traditions of argument that all end up neutralising the potent historical motor of constituent power. The traditional posture, which characterises the German school of public law from the mid-nineteenth to the mid-twentieth centuries, considers constituent power as transcendent in the face of constituted power. In this definition, although constituent power could be the antecedent of constituted power, it always remains external. The autonomy of the constituted legal order is abso-

---

71 See Negri 1994.
72 Negri 1994, p. 17.
73 Negri 1994, p. 19.
74 Negri 1994, p. 18.
75 Negri 1994, pp. 18–19.

lute. Following this line of argument, constituent power almost disappears.[76] The second interpretation, assumed by some who are positioned near the workers' movement, like Ferdinand Lassalle and Hermann Heller, sees constituent power as inherent in constituted power. This focus places importance only on constituent power during the act of creation of a new Constitution, after which constituent power is absorbed and subjected to constituted power. The immanence of constituted power is absorbed into the Constitution in 'the form of a natural evolution' of the state, while the originality and creativity of constituent power is negated and annulled.[77] The third focus, that of the great institutional schools of the twentieth century, denies the 'original and liberating quality' of constituent power: neither transcendent nor inherent, constituent power is integrated into constituted power and expands together with it.[78]

Summarising the philosophical-legal interpretation:

> In general constituent power is seen as the power that justifies a system and nothing more. The system does not count constituent power among the sources of immanent law, since it is considered an element outside of law. It has to yield its space to constituted power.[79]

As 'the sign of a radical expression of democratic will', constituent power is in contradiction with constitutionalism, which is always the 'mediation of and within inequality', having as its base an undemocratic paradigm. Constituent power 'is tied to the idea of democracy as absolute power';[80] it is an expansive force that ruptures the existing equilibrium, leaving it to the future to explain the present.[81] Constituent power is formed and reformed in all its parts, constantly.

Two historical through-lines of the action of constituent power can be traced. The first, more common, is the line of constitution of the political order for a new society, faithful to the tradition of the revolutionary principle of the Renaissance. It is visible in the great revolutions, which were a response to the rationalisation of power: the crisis that emerges of the relation between the potential productivity of the society and the legitimisation of the state. Republican, democratic, and socialist constitutions all failed to solve this con-

---

76 Negri 1994, p. 21.
77 Negri 1994, pp. 24–5.
78 Negri 1994, pp. 26–7.
79 Negri 2008, p. 10.
80 Negri 1994, p. 28.
81 Ibid.

tradiction.[82] One must therefore view constituent power as a concept of crisis, with its essence in that negativity: the legal and politico-constitutional definitions of constituent power have limited or neutralised it without ever resolving in constitutions a synthesis of the dualism between constituent power and constituted power.[83]

Negri bases the development of his concept of constituent power in the second through-line of constituent power, in turn grounded in Machiavelli, Spinoza and Marx: the continuity of the constituent passion of the *Multitudo*, as Spinoza calls it. This is found within the first through-line and is the cause of the process of constitutionalisation and its crisis.[84]

Machiavelli sees creative force as the talent of the new man. For him, constituent power is the passion and capacity of the multitude to organise its forces dynamically and to create form. It moves in a state of permanent crisis, which is also its stimulus. Taking Machiavelli's idea as a point of departure, Spinoza defines constituent power as the creative force that unfolds its full potential in order to constitute itself as a socially determined force following its progressive, omnipotent desire. The motor is supplied by the inevitable contradictions and conflicts it encounters along the way.[85]

It is Marx who transforms into a real possibility the idea of democracy as an absolute form of government, which in Machiavelli and Spinoza does not add up to more than a philosophical variation. For Marx, the force of constituent power creates the power of production and along with that the artificial second nature of the world.[86] Constituent power is creation that joins, inseparably, the *potentia* and the multitude. The constituent principle both represents and concludes modernity, since the structure of modern production returns to the actor of production, who is responsible for production and its meanings. The project is no longer to construct the correspondence between the political and the social, but to include the production of the political in the creation of the social.[87]

> All emancipation is a reduction of the human world and relationships to man himself ... Only when the real, individual man re-absorbs in himself the abstract citizen, and as an individual human being has become a

---

82   Negri 1994, p. 369.
83   Negri 1994, p. 30.
84   Negri 1994, p. 370.
85   Negri 1994, pp. 348–9.
86   Negri 1994, p. 372.
87   Negri 1994, p. 373.

species-being in his everyday life, in his particular work, and in his particular situation, only when man has recognised and organised his 'own powers' as social powers, and, consequently, no longer separates social power from himself in the shape of political power, only then will human emancipation have been accomplished.[88]

According to Negri, two obstacles block the open relation between multitude and *potentia*. The first is the vision of unification common to Machiavelli, Spinoza and Marx, which has its roots in Judeo-Christian tradition. Unification contradicts and blocks the multitude, which draws its force from its irreducible diversity.[89] The second limitation derives from the tradition of natural law in modern rationalism. If the creative force of constituent power is viewed as a mere expression of a precondition of natural law and is forced into a pre-established scheme, the connection is cut between multitude and *potentia*.[90]

From the history of constituent power, according to Negri, three conclusions can be drawn. First, as a creative principle, constituent power cannot be neutralised, and the fundamental obstacles reappear every time it turns into constituted power. Second, as long as constituent power remains a possibility, it represents a dimension of time that is open to the future. And third, the contradictions continue in effect, since constituent power does not free itself from the concept of progress and the rationalism of modernity. The eagerness to overcome those limitations

> … carries constituent power from liberalism to democracy and from there to socialism, but it fails every time in the face of the impossibility of setting itself the absolute limit. The state, the constituted power, sovereignty in the traditional sense, always reappears and winds up finishing off the constituent process.[91]

Constituent power is neutralised by means of the separation, inherent in modernity, of the spheres of the social and the political, so that the political potential of constituent power is split off from political power. Instead, constituent power is subjected to the social division of labour and absorbed by the representative system.[92]

---

88   See Marx 1844.
89   Negri 1994, p. 374.
90   Negri 1994, p. 377.
91   Negri 1994, p. 380.
92   Negri 1994, p. 396.

The English and American revolutions of the seventeenth and eighteenth centuries effected the rationalisation of the 'political sphere' and transformed it into a space structured by representation, in which constituted power assumes the central role of mediator. While representation is ideally horizontal, mediation is always vertical. Constituent power loses all its potentiality and exists only formally in the representative institutions and the organs legitimised by them.[93]

The Russian and French revolutions imposed the rational organisation of time.[94] In the dynamic of constituent processes, constituent power is seen as a form of society's productive force, as living work; but constitutionalisation subjects the collective creativity to the instrumental rationality of the capitalist mode of production and to the command of constituted power. In this way the rationalism of modernity is reaffirmed, with its linear time and its tendency to annul the living variety of the world (because of this, we see the Communards of Paris shooting at and smashing clocks in 1871). The terror in which these revolutions were derived was due precisely to the acceleration of time with which constituent power, following the rationalism of modernity, desires the elimination of obstacles.

Constituted power constantly interrupts the historic force of constituent power, putting the latter in a permanent state of crisis. This crisis, however, is not insurmountable by the force of the multitude, but is only an obstacle. The crisis does not even represent a disadvantage; quite the contrary, it is the motor of constituent power. This impossibility of reaching a positive synthesis causes the potential of the multitude to return again and again in search of another way out. Constituent power has no relation with modernity's progressive linear rationality, nor does it, according to Negri, with utopia. Instead, it is crisis and dystopia.

Utopia as a prefigured rough draft has indeed nothing in common with constituent power. However, one must object that constituent power has utopian leanings by means of historical experiences and defeats, values based on cognition and experience, as well as on feelings. All of that finds its expression through myths, popular culture, etc., and these leanings are in turn visible in the eagerness to go beyond the rationality of modernity. This accumulation of leanings, values, and feelings exists in the collective memory of the multitude and has no linear order, but it is constitutive for movements. Negri calls this the ontological background, the historical philosophy of constituent power. To

---

93 Negri 1994, Chapters 3 and 4.
94 Negri 1994, Chapters 6 and 7.

take effect it must exist beforehand, albeit in a hidden, slumbering form. This is collective memory, which does not produce continuity, but which flourishes in certain conjunctures and moments to strengthen constituent power.

According to Negri, the political form of constituent power is dystopia: a democracy that is not determined, not even minimally, by external factors and which, radically, is nourished only by its own potential. Constituent power breaks with the rationalism of modernity, opposing it with its own rationality. Constituent power, then, represents another time and another space, and can open up other spaces and times;[95] it is an ongoing movement beyond modernity. The rationality of constituent power is a creative action from below that is not subject to previous or external rules and develops its own mechanisms of control. It is a process of building that is renegotiated to create a space in which to move while it penetrates all areas: the social and the political, the law and its institutions. Constituent power does not yield or transfer its sovereignty.[96]

Equality is the essential material condition that provides the base from which the multitude can arise as a force. With equality, there can be no privilege of external intervention, which is automatically based on external superiority, and which would constitute a blockage of the relation between multitude and *potentia*. Equality in this context cannot signify an absolute reduction to unity or uniformity, because the creative force of constituent power develops from connection and cooperation between singularities, precisely because they are not reduced to a unity. This is in marked contrast to the command that constituted power represents, which is based on the alienation of the multitude and the expropriation of its creativity and cooperation. The central category of the new rationality is cooperation under conditions of equality.[97]

The political, then, is the 'ontological potential of a multitude of cooperating singularities'.[98] Without constituent power, the political is degraded to an administrative measure and a despotic exercise of power, but by expanding the effectiveness of constituent power, it is reinforced and moderated.[99] The limitation in time and space of constituent power that impels it toward the acceleration of time no longer determines its activity. By broadening the definition of the political and opening it, the political becomes the territory for the change of social relations, to which constituent power can always return to impose itself.

---

95   Negri 1994, p. 396.
96   Negri 1994, p. 402.
97   Negri 1994, p. 403.
98   Negri 1994, pp. 403–4.
99   Negri 1994, p. 405.

What does this mean in practice? How can the omnipotence of constituent power then be liberated for use as a social motor? Negri imagines the form of a 'constituent republic' as a 'Republic that emerges before the state, outside the state. It is the paradox of the constituent Republic: that the process of constitution will never end and the revolution will always remain unfinished'.[100] Revolution, then, is not a process based on unification, but maintains the multitude's productive diversity. It is a constituent power that does not produce external constitutions, but constantly self-constitutes as a collective process.

In practice, this means:

> [T]o see in the institution a reality that has to open constantly, in order to include constituent power in place of excluding it: an institution in continual genesis ... Constituent power can be an element of law, or rather, an institution that has to continually produce new institutions.[101]

Since there exists an asymmetry between constituent and constituted power in favour of the latter, and since the logics of the two powers contradict one another, the path of constituent power is replete with contradictions and limitations that continually appear in the course of colliding with constituted power.

3.2 *The Popular Constituent Process*

> The Bolivarian revolution is nothing without this political invention, without this basic sowing and the harvests that it brings: laws, new spaces of transformation, liberties, places of self-organisation and popular self-government, unfinished struggles that announce new areas of liberation.[102]

∴

> Constituent power cannot freeze, cannot be frozen in place by constituted power ... Some authors speak of the terrible character of constituent power. I believe that constituent power is terrible, but that is how we need it, terrible, complex, rebellious. Constituent power cannot submit

---

100   Negri 1998, p. 80.
101   Negri 2008, p. 10.
102   See Denis 2007.

..., constituent power is and must be – compatriots – permanent potential, transformative capability, a revolutionary injection to reactivate, very occasionally, our Bolivarian process.[103]

∴

The idea of constituent power as an ongoing social transformation process began to spread rapidly among the Venezuelan movements at the end of the 1980s. In the face of the failure of the traditional ideas of organisation and transformation, the defeat of the representative way, and the political invisibility of the non-traditional forces, the direct protagonism of the popular bases without representative mediation was proposed. The concept of revolution changed, since it was no longer about taking power, but about a broad process, extended in time, of construction of the new. The concept of constituent power became more radicalised and became the horizon of revolutionary transformation.[104] With that, the state ceases to be the central referent of change, since the centre of the revolutionary process has become the act of creation and the invention of the new. The similarity of this to Negri's concept was noticed; previously Italian workerism had been viewed with interest by different movements in the base and even by armed groups like the MRT.[105]

The different forms of struggle and resistance that were developed during the 80s, the new political culture in the movements, and the experiences of the *caracazo* and of the civic-military uprisings of 1992 brought about a paradigmatic change in the movements. The slogans changed. 'We don't want to be government, we want to govern'[106] is the main slogan of the Assembly of Barrios, an assembly that articulates a coalition of some 700–800 leaders and movement spokespeople with a strong socio-cultural base in the barrios of Caracas.[107] The force of constituent power appears in the new actors of radical change, in the poor and marginalised: 'where there was no "actor of emancipation", as imposed in idealistic form according to Marxist orthodoxy, now it

103   Chávez 2007, pp. 4–5.
104   Denis 2001, p. 65.
105   Denis 2001, pp. 143–4; I-AA 2009; I-OL 2008.
106   Twickel 2006, p. 93.
107   Denis 2001, p. 22.

will begin to emerge without asking permission of sociologists or revolutionaries'.[108]

During the 1990s, the idea of revolution as a constituent process spread among the popular movements.[109] The concept of constituent power became part of the historical current for change. In parallel with the growth of the movements at the beginning of the 90s, the discourse of constituent power assumed a hegemonic role in the political-ideological debate. From that moment forward, the traditional political organisations, along with many of the high-level military commanders involved in the subversive movements (whether from political conviction or because of the balance of forces within the movements), had to accept the uncontrollable concept of constituent power as part of a dual revolutionary strategy.

> The proposal for the Popular Constituent Process was developed with the perspective of the socio-political construction of the revolutionary process. It was seen as a process of building and affirming constituent power by means of organised social action, and not by constitutionalist representation. And it was developed with reference to the strategic mechanisms that serve to give form and body to the popular insurgency – a point with which everyone agrees in principle – empowering the thesis of 'Three in One', that is, of insurgency understood as strategic interaction among the rebel military forces, those nuclei of guerrillas that are still organised, and the popular militia that is under construction.[110]

Some circles of the MBR-200 and some grassroots barrio organisations formed militias. However, along with the traditional left, many nationalist-oriented military personnel rejected the creation of militias. Among the military, only Chávez and other young officials supported fully the proposition of 'Three in One', so it was never fully applied in its totality. The concept of Popular Constituent Process (PPC) continued extending into society. Chávez read Negri in prison (1992–4) and acknowledged his work as an important influence in the development of the Bolivarian project.[111] He cited Negri frequently, as during his swearing-in as president in January 2007.[112]

---

108   Denis 2001, p. 158.
109   Denis 2001, pp. 40–5.
110   Denis 2001, p. 140.
111   Chávez 2008, p. 47; Harnecker 2002, p. 18.
112   Chávez 2007, pp. 2–4.

The PPC concept has been disseminated by means of hard work at the grassroots. The collective Guacamaya, with which Roland Denis was affiliated, dedicated itself as of 1995 to elaborating methodologies and materials to disseminate the idea of PPC. It developed flyers and training materials, and organised workshops with activists from the base, who come principally from the barrios, from area organisations of education and culture, and from the MBR-200, achieving a common debate with movements who had kept their distance from the MBR-200 because of their scepticism about the military.

The process of collective discussion and production brought diverse forces to postulate an ongoing constituent process, realised by an indelegable constituent power, that served as the path of transformation. This 'permanent revolutionary process, without limits of time or space, without predetermined stages or territories',[113] is collectively led by a protagonism from below. This logic attempts to overcome the logic of institutional representation and the rationalism of the traditional left (partisan/worker), while taking away from the state 'the institutional monopoly over collective transformative action'.[114]

> The 'institution of the state,' not the most revolutionary of states, in such space as it imposes and administers the movements and the rules of collective will, from now forward will not be the only place with the right to establish the horizons of building a new order; quite the contrary, it will tend permanently to be overwhelmed by the irruption of a popular power that unfolds at the base of the society.[115]

Unlike the ideas expressed in the theoretical framework of the PPC, the Constituent Process of 1999 had representative elements. The process that brought forward the new constitution of the present-day Bolivarian Republic of Venezuela was, rather, a hybrid between protagonism and representation. Though the Constituent National Assembly (ANC) was primary and sovereign, not subject to any other body, it was composed of elected representatives. The population participated massively via various collective mechanisms in the process of producing the new constitution, contributing proposals to the ANC; although these proposals were non-binding, their influence was great, but nevertheless it is a question of principles, not of results. Several important mechanisms deriving from the concept of constituent power were reflected in the new

---

113   Denis 2001, p. 145.
114   Ibid.
115   Denis 2001, pp. 145–6.

Constitution. First of all, the basis of the new Venezuelan Republic, 'participatory and protagonistic democracy', tends toward suppressing the separation of the social, political, and economic spheres. Beyond that, the Constitution formulates various explicit rights that function as a base to ultimately develop the putting into practice of participatory and protagonistic democracy, like the introduction of citizen and constituent assemblies that can make binding decisions.[116]

Constituent power as a force of change, nevertheless, had emerged and made its way in broad sectors of society. Prior to the 1998 presidential election, hundreds of Constituent Circles and Constituent Committees of the Base were formed, which discussed both general and specific topics. These circles grew and multiplied following the elections. In Caracas, constituent assemblies were formed in six of the 32 parishes [*parroquias*, administrative subdivisions of Caracas].[117]

The traditional forces, which dominate the representative spaces of the Bolivarian process because of their experience, their inclination, their political apparatus and their practice, struggle against the application of the concept of constituent power to representative mechanisms, since for many of them it signifies a threat to their mechanism of political reproduction. In the Bolivarian electoral alliance Movimiento v. República (MVR), those responsible for building the party rejected the proposal of the revolutionary militant William Izarra and others to bring to fruition the building of the party and the elaboration of its proposed programme by means of local grassroots assemblies.[118]

The idea of a popular constituent process lost force in the following years because of the prominence of the central figure of Chávez, and because of the conflictive internal situation that obliged the movements to defend the process against opposition attacks instead of dedicating themselves to the building of the process. With only a few exceptions, like the Urban Land Committees (CTU), there were not many broadly diffused experiences of protagonistic participation, while the Constitutional mechanisms went practically unexploited. Moreover, the *chavista* government saw constituent power as an annex to representative structures and not as the central decision-making source.[119] Even in those years, however, the self-constitution of the base as constituent power was decisive for the continuation of the process at least twice: during the coup of

---

116   Azzellini 2010, pp. 72–82.
117   Denis 2001, p. 146.
118   Ellner 2008, p. 4.
119   Ibid.

2002, and the petroleum sabotage and business lockout of 2002/3.[120] On those two occasions, constituent, not constituted, power was the protagonist. The same thing happened with the occupation of factories and businesses by their workers during and after the business lockout, while the government took more than two years to take a position.

As of 2003/4, the government launched a policy that reinforced the strategy 'from below' and focused on promoting participation in communities and workplaces, inaugurating the missions and holding debates on worker co-management and self-administration. By the initiative of some municipalities, Municipal Constituents appeared, along with forms of local governments, the Local Councils of Public Planning (CLPP), and finally the communal councils and the communes.[121] Constituent power sought its own direction while cooperating with and confronting constituted power. But also 'the state has played a fundamental role in reinforcing the sense of empowerment of the base of the *chavista* movement'.[122] This has been viewed by the majority of authors and organisations (like the National Peasant Front Ezequiel Zamora, the Urban Land Committees, the majority of the barrio collectives and the independent media) sympathetic to the process as a reinforcement of the orientation from below and of direct participation.

In this very complex situation, there still persists a contradictory relationship of conflict and cooperation. With the institutional opening and the massification of the programmes, new movements emerge; but at the same time, many leaders and cadres (referring to experienced activists and organisers) go to work in the institutions, debilitating the movements. The broadening of protagonistic participation brings with it an increase in the conflicts between the state and the base, and within the state itself, which also becomes a site of class conflict. That is not surprising, since the increasingly profound social transformation multiplies the points where the different logics of below and above come into conflict.

The *National Economic and Social Development Plan 2007–2013* (MinCI 2007) postulates organisation and collectivity, respecting autonomy and liberty, as

---

120   These were two parallel events. In one, the national petroleum industry was put back to work by the workers after being sabotaged by its high-end employees to stop production. In the other, business owners in the productive sector and services went on 'strike' and locked out the workers. In many cases, workers forced opening or production, and the population became organised to collectively overcome the problems caused by all kinds of shortages (food, energy, transport, work).
121   Azzellini 2010, pp. 261–300; 2013; Sitrin and Azzellini 2014, pp. 229–44.
122   Ellner 2008, p. 5.

the basis of revolutionary democracy. Sovereignty resides in and is not transferable from the *pueblo*, and 'given that sovereignty resides in the *pueblo*, it can direct the state on its own, without needing to delegate its sovereignty, as happens in practice with representative or indirect democracy'.[123] However, the strengthening of institutions and the presence of the state bring a growing bureaucratisation which impedes transformation and tends toward institutional administration of social processes.

> In general, what the state organisms do is show up and: this is the project, this is the Commune, that's it, ready. They lay it all out and someone says: Okay, and when did we discuss this project? That kills the essence of popular participation. Of the *pueblo* building its own history.[124]

The role of Chávez has also been ambivalent. He assumed a maximally important role, directing public attention toward little-known initiatives from below, achieving thereby their dissemination and massification. He was seen as an ally and a guarantor of a process of protagonistic, inclusive transformation on the part of the popular movements, which took him as a reference in their increasing conflicts with the institutions.

> We ask as a representative of Fundacomunal, or the Ministry of the Communes, that we receive a response because perhaps the next time it will not be a document that arrives at the ministry, but a press conference with all the communities and all the beneficiaries, so that the President will know, the way he learned that the Ministry of Health was not doing its job, that they are not doing their job and he who does not do his job opens a space for someone else to enter.[125]

The centrality of Chávez, however, also created difficulties for the organic growth of popular initiatives, given that mayors, governors, and some institutions are more engaged in artificially creating a large number of initiatives endorsed by Chávez than in supporting a qualitative growth from below.

In short, the idea of constituent power not subjected to constituted power assumes the form of councils. This is reflected in the fact that the conjectured base for a future Venezuelan socialism is in a structure of councils of different

---

123 MinCI 2007, p. 30.
124 Juan Carlos Pinto, FNCSB, in Azzellini and Ressler 2010.
125 Yusmeli Patiño, commune under construction Eje de MACA, Petare, Gran Caracas, in Azzellini and Ressler 2010.

character that cooperate and converge at higher levels of organisation, in order to overcome the bourgeois state and replace it with a communal state. Various 'councils of popular power' (communal councils, councils of workers, student councils, peasant councils, women's councils, among others) are part of that structure and are being promoted and implemented.

3.3 The Simultaneity of Foci: Resistance, Insurrection and Constituent Power

How can we understand the complex, contradictory process of struggle and construction taking place in Venezuela? Hardt and Negri are clear that counterpower cannot go on being understood as it was in the nineteenth and twentieth centuries. In the classical revolutions, the three principal elements of counterpower – resistance, insurrection, and constituent power – were thought of as separate and in chronological order. In the face of the limitless sovereignty of the empire, today each one of these moments can and must be included in the others.[126]

The three elements of counterpower formulated by Hardt and Negri can be found simultaneously in the Bolivarian process: (1) in the resistance of the popular movements against political, economic, media, and imperial military pressure, and against a bureaucratisation or institutionalisation that could lead to stagnation or even regression of the process; (2) in the class struggle that temporarily assumes insurrectional dimensions; and (3) in constituent power, which designs a new society through progressive participation and self-organisation. The concept of counterpower also explains the specific character of the Bolivarian process: the partial transference of the class struggle to the interior of the state, where at some moments counterpower emanates from constituted power while at others it functions against the state.

So although Hardt/Negri's concept of counterpower contradicts the Bolivarian process on some points, it is useful to take it as a point of departure and modify it for application to the Venezuelan process. According to Hardt/Negri, who locate their concept beyond the national state in the context of empire, the disappearance of the national state as an autonomous political sphere would annul the possibility of being able to transform social space using state instruments.[127] The Bolivarian process nevertheless moves within the framework of the national state, which, contrary to the theory of Hardt/Negri, leaves some limited room for manipulation. Venezuela's international policies also demon-

---

126 See Hardt and Negri 2002.
127 See Hardt and Negri 2000.

strate a constant effort to broaden the spaces of action beyond national boundaries, in order to be able to survive as a social transformation process, which obviously cannot be produced as a mere 'national revolution', as the enormous difficulties of transforming Venezuelan society and economy show. Moreover, in Venezuela the central role of transformation is assumed not by the state, but by the organised *pueblo*.

The fact that the Bolivarian Constitution assumes the role of a social contract on the basis of which counterpower is developed also contrasts with the focus of Hardt and Negri. Nevertheless, the national and territorial frameworks derive from real political conditions, although conceptually the content and orientation of the Constitution look farther afield: while national sovereignty is key for the possibility of developing a politics that goes beyond the power of imperial decision, there is an orientation toward a continental alliance and south-south cooperation.

Another limitation of Hardt and Negri's concept is that it does not stipulate where counterpower will lead. Negri recognises that his idea of counterpower is very Leninist, so that the concept of counterpower could be understood as what the Marxist classicists have defined as 'dual power' in a revolutionary phase and/or transition to socialism, although without resolution but rather prolonged eternally. So although the concept is useful for analysing the complexity of the Bolivarian process at a certain stage, it is not helpful in indicating the directionality of the movements. To understand the intentionality and the perspective of the process of construction and search, it is more useful to refer to the Latin American concept of popular power (*poder popular*).

3.4 Popular Power: The Knowledge of Resistance

> Popular power is not something distinct from socialism, although it alludes to a singular form of conceiving and building it.[128]

∴

The idea of *popular power* is closely related to the concept of constituent power. The two emerged forcefully from below in the early 90s, and in the early years did not have many repercussions at the governmental level. Since

---

128   Mazzeo 2007, p. 29.

2005, however, popular power has been connected in official discourse with the building of participatory and protagonistic democracy, and later of socialism. The reinforcement of popular power was declared by Chávez as the most important point in the transformation process in Venezuela, assigning a central role to the communal councils.[129]

Popular power refers to the capacity of the marginalised and oppressed to change power relations by means of processes of organisation, formation, and coordination for administering and determining their own lives. The building of popular power signifies the construction of social relations contrary to the logic of capital. The model is not a finished concept, but is continually in development and renovation; it is a process of search and creation that draws on centuries of popular experience, forms of organisation, and struggles by subalterns (marginalised, indigenous, formerly enslaved, etc.). By its own logic, popular power refers to the basic grassroots democratic forms: self-organisation and councils.

> The subject of popular power has to do with the people's capacity to take the reins. The 'power' is the capacity that one has to do something. And 'popular' because it belongs to the *pueblo*, to the base. The only way forward is for the comrades to participate, empower themselves, and assume this new institutionality. Ultimately it means the democratisation of the state. It is popular democratisation, in which the *pueblo* assumes and builds this new institutionality. In order for us to be able to build socialism it is necessary that the *pueblo* take control of those instruments.[130]

In this reading, popular power is based in 'doing' and is the only way toward socialism. In previous historical cases, popular power has been understood as the need for a parallel power in a revolutionary process, creating a situation of dual power. After the consolidation of the new structures of the 'true' power, the party and/or the 'revolutionary state', popular power has been subjected to them. In Venezuela, unlike in previous revolutionary processes, popular power is not conceived of as an intermediate link, but rather as a path and a goal. And unlike other revolutions, in Venezuela there was no taking down or destruction of the old structures in promoting the creation and dissemination of the structures of popular power.

---

129 Lander 2007, p. 79.
130 Juan Carlos Pinto, Simón Bolívar Communal National Front, FNCSB, in Azzellini and Ressler 2010.

Neither can popular power, by its own logic, be awarded from above. Popular power cannot be conceived of by the state, nor can it be conceived of without the state. The question of sovereignty, or control of resources, puts on the table the question of the relation between the state and popular power.

In the Venezuelan case, Chávez and part of the government knew that it would be a central task to reinforce and consolidate popular power in order to accumulate strength and survive as a process of change. This would not be limited to the power of formal government, as was Allende's Unidad-Popular government in Chile. 'The popular government of Chávez did not assume itself to be the consummate expression of a duality of powers … and instead developed initiatives that tried to build it'.[131] In this way, the state itself has also become a battlefield.

Owing to institutional logic and the internal dynamics of the process of change previously described, the spaces of popular power have to be built with and against constituted power, which – although it may formally support the building of popular power – tends to co-opt it, imposing the norms of constituted power and administering it, sabotaging as it does so the creation of a new institutionality from below and the transformative potential of popular power. One of the measures that best illustrates this contradiction was the renaming of all the ministries as 'Ministries of Popular Power'.

---

131 Mazzeo 2007, pp. 141–2.

CHAPTER 3

Movements and Alternative Construction in Venezuela

> People, when organised, have enormous power, more than any government. Our history runs deep with the stories of people who stand up, speak out, dig in, organise, connect, form networks of resistance, and alter the course of history.[1]
>
> ∴
>
> Revolutionary dreams erupt out of political engagement; collective social movements are incubators of new knowledge.[2]
>
> ∴

This chapter offers a reading of the development of the Bolivarian process since 1998, seen through the optic of two-track construction. Offering a critical discussion of the term 'social movements', it proposes a more suitable concept for the analysis of Venezuelan movements. In a historical summary, it applies the concept to Venezuelan reality in order to present an analysis of the new framework for movement action in Venezuela. Subsequently, it analyses some of the principal popular movements beyond the movement for workers' control, and analyses the composition, orientation, autonomy and relation to constituted power of the Bolívar and Zamora Revolutionary Current (CRBZ), the Settlers Movement (MDP), and the National Network of Communards (RNC).

The political, social, popular, and cultural forces that converge in the Bolivarian process come from different socialist, communist, libertarian, and revolutionary traditions and experiences. The confluence of state-centric and anti-systemic orientations delineates new paths of social transformation, different from strategies previously proposed by the same currents. Social transforma-

---

1 Zinn 2007, p. 11.
2 Kelley 2003, p. 8.

tion is developed as a two-track process. According to the normative orientation that guides the Bolivarian process, the central agents of creating the new are the popular autonomous movements, not the state. The state is the guarantor of the material conditions so that the movements can develop and build the new social model, but in reality the asymmetry and the different logics of constituent and constituted power make for a contradictory, conflictive relation between the two.

Since 1999, a great variety of mechanisms for participation have been tried. The search for a framework for participatory and protagonistic democracy, postulated in the 1999 constitution, has arrived at popular power and socialism. Assumed to be anti-neoliberal at the outset, the Bolivarian process proposed strengthening human and civil rights and the building of a 'participatory and protagonistic democracy' that represents a supposed third way beyond capitalism and socialism – an economic transformation that looks toward a 'humanist economy of solidarity'.

2003 saw the beginning of the building of parallel structures (especially by means of the social programmes called 'missions') with broad participation from below. The impossibility of carrying to fruition structural changes in the prevailing political and economic system; attacks by the opposition, the bourgeoisie, the Venezuelan oligarchy, national and transnational capitalism, and the US in the face of a reformist social project; the organisational processes; and the radicalisation of the movements: all combined to push the process further to the left.[3]

The assumed socialist orientation (as a process of searching, not as an existing truth), the idea of popular power, and the councilist initiatives connect with the historical line of the commune and not with that of the state. The normative orientation of the transformation process proposes the overcoming of the state (and its gradual substitution by the communal state), since it is considered an integral product of capitalism. Following this analysis, the state is not a neutral instrument (as in the Leninist focus) or an autonomous entity (as in the bourgeois or social-democratic focus), and thus cannot be the central agent of transformation in building the new model of socialist society. The central role as agent of change, of creator of the new, falls to constituent power. The mechanisms of transformation, the structures of self-government, and the solutions to prevailing problems, have to emerge from the popular movements and the organised *pueblo*. The state is responsible for lending technical and economic support to constituent power and guaranteeing the

---

[3] Azzellini 2007a; Wilpert 2007.

material conditions that the realisation of the common good requires, in order that constituent power can develop the new society.[4]

The two-track approach, from above and from below, is based on the building of structures parallel to the existing institutions and mechanisms, and ultimately refers to councilism and the building of the communal state. This focus was declared by Chávez to be the normative orientation for the transition to socialism. It is shared by some governmental sectors and by a number of the organised movements that propose a protagonistic role for constituent power in redefining state and society, thus opening up a perspective on how to overcome the logic of capital. Among the popular forces that have adopted this perspective are the strongest movements, like the MDP, the CRBZ, the movement for workers' control, the RNC, and many communal councils. President Maduro assumed the centrality of communes during his 2013 electoral campaign.

This official normative orientation does not prevent the many institutions and proponents of the from-above strategy from trying to impose themselves on constituent power and reproducing the prevailing system instead of trying to overcome it. While the from-below strategy rejects representation and representative democracy, and proposes instead the exercise of autonomy and auto-government, the from-above approach can coexist with representative democracy and considers the state as the most important agent of the ongoing transformation. Following this logic, supporters of the from-below approach have accused institutional forces of promoting partisan interests and of promoting a bureaucratisation with demobilising effects. Because of the asymmetry existing between constituent and constituted power, there is a tendency on the part of the institutional bureaucracy and the parties to monopolise decisions and ignore corruption.[5]

The concrete strategy for the transformation toward socialism is based on the building of communal cycles of production and consumption, following the idea of a communal socialism. The central theoretical reference for the building of the 'communal system' is Istvan Mészáros, who delineates strategies for the transition to socialism in his book *Beyond Capital: Towards a Theory of Transition*.[6] Mészáros differentiates between capital and capitalism, and considers capitalism to be only a historical variant of the realisation of capital. The challenge facing the movements toward socialism, in Mészáros's analysis,

---

4 Azzellini 2010; 2013.
5 See APPP 2005; Ellner 2008.
6 Mészáros 1995, pp. 739–70.

lies in overcoming the 'metabolic reproduction' of capital (which has not been done in 'actually existing socialism').

The tradition of communal or communitarian socialism, with its characteristics of local self-administration, workers' control, participation, direct democracy, and horizontality, also connects with Latin American currents of Marxist thought, such as, for example, the Peruvian José Carlos Mariátegui and the ideas of the philosopher and educator Simón Rodríguez, teacher of Simón Bolívar and central reference of Bolivarianism, who in 1847 proposed a form of local self-government that he called toparchy. It also shares visions and practices with historical experiences of organisation by indigenous people and Afro-Venezuelans (for example, organisation into *cumbes*, drawing on the *palenques* or *quilombos* of Venezuela).[7]

As of 2007, protagonistic popular participation was officially located in a context of popular power, revolutionary democracy, and socialism, with the goal defined as twenty-first-century socialism (as opposed to the 'actually existing socialisms' of the twentieth century) in full development and debate. The process of search and construction is oriented principally toward such values as collectivity, equality, solidarity, liberty, and sovereignty.[8]

During the 2006 presidential election, Chávez called for the electorate to decide if Venezuela should take the route leading to socialism. After an overwhelming victory for Chávez, the new presidential term brought the broadening of participation mechanisms and councilist structures, along with a vision of twenty-first-century socialism that picked up proposals and plans from antisystemic, councilist and libertarian currents. The Venezuelan socialist project is based on the building of 'councilist structures' from bottom to top, in different sectors of the society (Socialist Workers' Councils, CCs, communes, and communal cities), with the intention that these councilist structures of self-government and control of production, together with higher-level cooperation and coordination, will gradually lead to replacing the bourgeois state with a communal state. The council form looks also toward overcoming the split between the supposedly autonomous economic, social, and political spheres, which split is seen as the foundation of the bourgeois state and capitalism (and is constantly reproduced by them). Overcoming the split between the social and the political means overcoming the difference between governed and governors, and the difference between civil society and political society. In order

---

7 *palenque, quilombo*: names for communities of self-emancipated (or 'runaway') slaves, some of which continued as communities after the end of slavery.
8 MinCI 2007, p. 30.

to avoid the state then becoming central and without a counterweight as in the countries of 'actually existing socialism', the Venezuelan project suggests that even the future communal state must itself be subordinated to popular power, which supplants the old bourgeois civil society.[9]

The central problem is an asymmetry of power in favour of constituted over constituent power. The question then becomes how the movements of constituent power can maintain their autonomy and have a fundamental influence on the transformation process without losing the initiative to the state or reproducing its forms and structures. The great challenge of the Bolivarian process is to create practices from the institutions that support, accompany, and reinforce the 'from below' without co-opting or limiting it. If constituent power is not the driving force of the process of change and the source of creation of the new, it is not possible to create a structure of co-existence opposed to the logic of capital. The centrality of the autonomy of the movements has proven to be fundamental for the social transformation process in Venezuela, as for example in the mobilisations against the coup in April 2002 and during the oil lockout.

In this context, it is important to remember that, although Venezuela's political, economic, and social system may be in transformation, and although the functioning of the state and the relation between state and society may have experienced substantial transformations since 2000, it is still fundamentally a representative political system (albeit with various elements of participatory democracy) in a capitalist society. With the deepening of the process, points of conflict have proliferated between the social transformation process and antagonistic sectors at both national and international levels; this has also occurred within the forces of the process of change, between constituent power and constituted power.

Especially since 2007, the government's capacity to reform has collided ever more frequently with the inherent limits of the bourgeois state, the capitalist system, and rentier logic. Recent years have seen a strengthening of movements and self-management initiatives that seek to overcome the bourgeois state and replace its institutionality with popular power. But at the same time, there has also been a strengthening and bureaucratisation of the institutions that, out of their own inherent logic, try to control the social processes and reproduce themselves. The process of social transformation is complex and contradictory, since constituent power is both strengthened and restrained by the institutions of constituted power. The struggles expressed in various movements of constituent power to impose themselves on the institutions are a class struggle,

---

9   See AN-DGIDL 2007; *Aló Presidente* 290 (19 August 2007), in Chávez 2008, p. 67.

with the creation of another system as the goal. In this context, it is interesting to observe that some state-initiated or state-promoted mechanisms of grassroots organisation managed to develop a relative autonomy (of organisation, debate, and decision), which is a necessary precondition if they are to transform the state.

1 Social Movements or Popular Movements?

Before we can define the role of the movements of the base in the Venezuelan transformation process, it is essential to redefine the concept of movements. I will take as a point of departure a critique of the concepts that began to be disseminated in the late 1970s and early 80s, when the study of movements was established as an academic discipline, principally in the US and Europe. This happened in the context of Marxist theories having lost their strong influence following the crisis of the Fordist model of accumulation and regulation.

The new model of production and its accompanying neoliberal policies changed the subjectivities and the parameters of organisation and struggle. Especially in Europe, one part of the new movements converged in new party organisations. The emergence in the 60s of new social movements provoked movement theorists to speak of New Social Movements (NSM), which were defined in opposition to the 'old' labour movement.[10] A central argument is that the new movements act in specific fields and, supposedly, lack the previous labour movement's clear goal of total social transformation or a socialist society. In contrast to the hierarchical structure of the labour movement, the NSM share a more horizontal, democratic internal function and do not have a binding organisational structure. In other words, NSM participants (individuals, groups and organisations) are more autonomous than those of the worker movement, though as a consequence, strategic planning is harder.[11] The NSM are 'networked social structures of people, groups and organisations, which express protest with collective actions, to change the social or political reality and oppose changes that are being made'.[12] They are considered indicators of malfunctioning political systems, or of growing differentiations in modern societies, and are based on constructed identities.[13]

---

10 See Rucht 1994.
11 Neidhardt and Rucht 2001, p. 541; Della Porta and Diani 1999, p. 14.
12 Neidhardt and Rucht 2001, p. 540.
13 Castells 1997; Luhmann 1991; Rucht et al. 1998; Castells 1997.

According to the most common definition, social movements are protest groups constituted in a more or less lasting manner, acting outside of partisan politics and directed at situations that are considered a threat. They are 'involved in conflictual relations with clearly identified opponents; are linked by dense informal networks; share a distinct collective identity'.[14] The way NSM are organised and function has a certain democratising effect. They draw public attention to topics that are marginalised or ignored by institutional politics and majoritarian society, formulate collective interests of certain groups, and develop collective practices; their activists are informed and practice alternative politics.[15] The more critical approaches in the social sciences identify the new movements as a laboratory and incubator of participatory democratic practices.[16]

Certainly, many of the new social movements have a democratising effect. We can also concur with the schematisation of characteristics in their organisation and mobilisation. The problem with most social movement theory, nevertheless, is that it reduces the movements to an intrinsic role in the system, whereby they are only able to push changes in the frame of liberal democracy but not to overcome it, and are shunted off into the social sphere, which is separated from that of the political. According to these approaches, movements are all about contentious politics, and are always constituted in opposition to an existing or future menace.

But while that might be the case for various movements, the condition cannot be generalised. The new global movements that have emerged since 2010 have further demonstrated the inadequacy of academic interpretive models. As principal participants and actors in the creation of a new social, political, and economic order – one that questions the separation of spheres – the Venezuelan movements do not fit these definitions. Another difference with the definitions of the NSM is that in Venezuela (as generally in Latin America, but also, for example, in India) many social movements are organised movements, with clear structures. These can even be more democratic and participatory in many cases than the informality of the NSM, given that the absence of formal structures tends to favour the development of informal hierarchical structures.[17]

In the Venezuelan context (as in other cases), it is necessary to understand the movements as central actors of society that have been formed by the social

14   Della Porta and Diani 2006, p. 20.
15   See Nolte 2002; Kaltmeier et al. 2004.
16   Müller-Plantenberg 2001, p. 26.
17   See Freeman 1972–3.

conditions and relations in which they were born, as much as they also form them.[18] The fundamental idea of Bolivarianism, understood as a movement of movements, is found in its divergent experiences of local, regional, national, and continental struggles of emancipation and resistance. The Venezuelan left's rich political, social, and cultural history is little known. Following Marxist historians like Eric J. Hobsbawm, George Rudé, Edward Thompson, and Howard Zinn, who envisioned a 'history from below' and who attribute a clear rationality to the movements, the development of the Bolivarian process can be described as the formation of a historical current for change, composed of different left currents coming together without homogenisation to converge in a common project of searching.[19]

This historical current for change was constituted by means of various historical events that, following Walter Benjamin, can be considered ruptures in the continuum:[20] the popular uprising of the 1989 *caracazo*, the 1992 civic-military uprisings, and the 1998 electoral victory of Chávez. The historical current for change is not a closed, hermetic, homogeneous characterisation. The Bolivarian process is characterised by the great political and historical diversity of its actors and their forms of organisation.

An important element in the creation of paths to emancipation is, as Benjamin emphasises, awareness of past generations.

> Not man or men but the struggling, oppressed class itself is the depository of historical knowledge. In Marx it appears as the last enslaved class, as the avenger that completes the task of liberation in the name of generations of the downtrodden ... Social Democracy thought fit to assign to the working class the role of the redeemer of future generations, in this way cutting the sinews of its greatest strength. This training made the working class forget both its hatred and its spirit of sacrifice, for both are nourished by the image of enslaved ancestors rather than that of liberated grandchildren.[21]

In Venezuela, it is easy to observe the importance of history in creating the identity of struggle. The ability to define the focus of the common vision of history, to create a popular hegemony in its interpretation, is central for the

---

18 See Hobsbawm 1995; Thompson 1991; Zinn 2007.
19 Bonilla-Molina and El Troudi 2004, p. 104.
20 Benjamin 1968, p. 262.
21 Benjamin 1968, p. 260.

transformation movement. In the popular struggle of Latin America, tradition and myth have a persistent function.[22] The Bolivarian imaginary connects the popular with a revolutionary interpretation of the republican heroes Miranda, Rodríguez, Bolívar, Josefa Camejo, Ribas, Manuela Sáenz, etc.[23] Moreover, at their side it places anti-systemic strugglers and revolutionary heroes (the heroines are still few in number) that emerged from indigenous and African-descended Venezuelans, peasants, and the poor, marginalised, excluded and persecuted: the Cacique Guaicaipuro, the Negro Miguel, José Leonardo Chirino, the peasant general Ezequiel Zamora, etc.[24] The transformation of past struggles against the established order into the flags of contemporary movements can be observed in all of Latin America.[25]

This recourse to the past, which always requires an update, should not be confused with nostalgia or folklore. It is, rather, the 'secret rendezvous between

---

22 Mazzeo 2007, p. 56.
23 *Francisco de Miranda* (1750–1816): revolutionary, precursor of the struggle for Venezuelan independence. Miranda fought in the American and French revolutions. In 1806, he failed in his attempt to unleash an independence war in Venezuela, after establishing a short-lived beachhead on the Venezuelan coast with a small army of liberation. *Josefa Camejo* (1791–1862): independence heroine, joined the revolution in 1810. In 1811, she organised in Barinas groups of women to participate in the armed struggle. In 1821, she led 300 slaves in an unsuccessful attempted rebellion against the royalists in the region of Coro, though in early May 1821 they achieved a declaration of independence in the peninsula of Paraguaná. *José Félix Ribas* (1775–1815): hero of the independence war in Venezuela. *Manuela Sáenz* (1797–1856): Ecuadorian, independence heroine. Over the centuries her role was reduced in the historiography to being Bolívar's companion, but today she has been restored to memory as a combatant and independence heroine, and is considered a precursor of Latin American feminism.
24 *Cacique Guaicaipuro*: Indigenous leader of the pre-Colombian era in the Spanish province of Venezuela in the sixteenth century who organised a ferocious, successful resistance against the Spanish colonists, expelling them from the region of de Los Teques in the valley of Caracas and the neighbouring coastline for almost a decade (Azzellini 2009e). *Negro Miguel*: African slave who in 1553 directed the first rebellion of African slaves registered by the Spanish colonial authority. The revolt interrupted a gold rush in the mining region of Venezuela Burla. El Negro Miguel established a maroon colony. Today he is remembered as a leader in the struggle for racial justice in Venezuela (Azzellini 2009h). *José Leonardo Chirino* (d. 1796) is recognised as a precursor to the struggle for independence and abolition of slavery, and as a symbol of African heritage of Venezuela (Azzellini 2009f).
25 To name only a few: Tupac Amaru, Tupac Katari, José Martí, Farabundo Martí, Flores Magón, Augusto Cesár Sandino, Emiliano Zapata, Pancho Villa, etc.

past generations and our own'.²⁶ And 'each update contributes to a collective, historical composition of a utopia that, in this way, has folds and layers superimposed'.²⁷ It is what Benjamin described as 'a *weak* Messianic power, a power to which the past has a claim'.²⁸ So it is completely out of place for bourgeois historians to contradict the Bolivarian revolutionary interpretation of the struggles of the past. On the one hand, history has no objectivities and is subject to interpretation; on the other, the revolutionary interpretation has lessons for the present: only when Bolívar integrated his movement to include those from below and recognise some of their claims did the movement triumph. In the face of opposition accusations of *chavistas* of being *chusma* (rabble), Chávez answered, 'yes, we're the same *chusma* who followed Bolívar'.²⁹

As Walter Benjamin wrote, the past – the memory of the exploited, oppressed, and assassinated – is fundamental in creating the path to liberation. Nevertheless, it is also the hope for, and the envisioning of, a different, achievable future, which is a necessary basis for a critical praxis of liberation. This future emerges and becomes tangible in struggles. Bloch calls it the 'not-yet'. Utopia is not a rootless fantasy, but is fundamental and necessary. As Marx noted in a letter to Arnold Ruge, in 1843:

> It will then become evident that the world has long dreamed of possessing something of which it has only to be conscious in order to possess it in reality. It will become evident that it is not a question of drawing a great mental dividing line between past and future, but of realizing the thoughts of the past. Lastly, it will become evident that mankind is not beginning a new work, but is consciously carrying into effect its old work.³⁰

In the Venezuelan and Latin American context, the most adequate term for 'social movements' is 'popular movements'. The Venezuelan movements have not been limited to a merely social role, but have entered forcefully into politics, becoming active agents in the construction of the future. Since the late 1980s, it can be observed how movement struggles in Venezuela are not limited to obtaining compliance with specific sectors' demands, but are driven by the

---

26 Benjamin 1965, p. 88, my translation.
27 Mazzeo 2007, p. 57.
28 Benjamin 1968, p. 254.
29 Herrera Salas 2004, p. 124.
30 Marx 1975a, p. 144.

desire for profound systemic changes. A fundamental aspect of these struggles consists in postulating popular participation in the reformulation of all policies and of a new political system. The electoral victory of Chávez was based on his postulating the impossibility of a political, social, and institutional continuity; being the candidate most outside the ruling system, he formulated the necessity of a rupture with it, as well as declaring the urgency of refounding the republic.

2 The Historical Current for Change and the Ruptures of the Continuum

> The popular movement becomes stronger when the political movement understands that the idea is not to intervene in the popular movements. We want instead to make their work easier, to give them the tools so that the population organises.[31]

∴

The left – the Communist Party, the unions, the youth organisation of Democratic Action (AD), and a large popular mobilisation – played a fundamental role in the 1958 overthrow of the Marcos Pérez Jiménez dictatorship. But it was subsequently marginalised by the bourgeois parties URD, AD and Copei by means of the Pact of Punto Fijo (PPF 1958), which was followed by various other pacts with businesspeople, the Vatican, and the unions that built a repressive democracy with no other channels for mediation than those of the parties in power and the unions tied to them. As a consequence, armed organisations began forming, and the Venezuela Communist Party (PCV) participated in armed struggle. Between 1960 and 1962, there were military uprisings in coordination with organisations of the left and with guerrillas.[32]

The guerrilla movements did not manage to create a base of support in the population, and they failed.[33] Nevertheless, they left an important legacy: the Venezuelan Revolutionary Party (PRV), born of a schism in the guerrillas of the

---

31 Alfonso Tovar, Fundación Cultural Simón Bolívar, Caracas, in Azzellini and Ressler 2004.
32 See Azzellini 2009b.
33 See Azzellini 2009c.

PCV in 1965, which declared itself Marxist and the follower of an emancipatory and revolutionary Bolivarianism. The central references are: Simón Bolívar; his philosophy teacher Simón Rodríguez (1769–1854), who frequented utopian socialist circles in early nineteenth-century France; the peasant general of the federal war, Ezequiel Zamora (1817–60);[34] and indigenous and Afro-Venezuelan resistance.[35] The revolutionary left began to postulate alliance with a civic-military uprising as the way to a Venezuelan revolution, and various currents began to infiltrate into the army or recruit soldiers clandestinely. There, in connection with the history of the Venezuelan army and its social composition of lower classes that reached up into the ranks of the officers, one finds the cause of the unusual positions and politics that emerged from the army at the beginning of the 60s and re-emerged in the 80s.

During the 60s and 70s, the political and military defeat of the armed struggle in Venezuela created a highly critical debate about the *foquista* concept,[36] the authoritarianism of the Communist parties, and the simple transference of revolutionary experiences. This caused the different organisations to orient themselves more toward social movements, most of them recognising the autonomy of the movements, and they began a work that was scarcely visible for many years.

The historical current for change was thus comprised of many diverse political, social, and cultural movements that converged in the 70s and 80s. Many declared themselves to be anti-authoritarian and anti-Stalinist, and were tied to the councilist tradition of socialism and the dissident voices of party Communism, both Soviet and Chinese. Others were influenced by Guevarianism, Mariateguism,[37] Trotskyism, Workerism,[38] and European autonomism. They read and discussed Anton Pannekoek and Antonio Gramsci. Autonomous popular and worker movements appeared at the base. The currents of liberation theology were present, along with ideas from national liberation movements and indigenous and African resistance currents. There were insurrectional

---

34 See Azzellini 2009g.
35 See Azzellini 2009d; Denis 2007.
36 *Foquismo*: the theory, advanced by Régis Debray and derived from the experience of Ernesto 'Che' Guevara, that relied on the notion of small bands of guerrillas, whose example was supposed to be followed by others.
37 Named for the Peruvian socialist José Carlos Mariátegui.
38 *Operaismo/obrerismo*: 'Workerism', a Marxist current originating in 1960s Italy around Raniero Panzieri, Antonio Negri, and various journals and organisations like Potere Operaio and, subsequently, Autonomia Operaia. Workerism postulates worker autonomy, assemblyism, direct democracy, and mass violence as a base for change.

movements in different social sectors. Over time, the concept of emancipatory Bolivarianism was adopted by many organisations and movements with distinct origins and histories.[39]

At the beginning of the 1980s, Venezuela entered a deep economic crisis that became a political crisis. The *puntofijista*[40] system was in decline. Its rejection by the population, especially the poor, was directed not only at the traditional parties but also at the concept of representative democracy in general. In 1988, the situation was dramatic: inflation was at 100 percent, there was hoarding and speculation of foodstuffs, and those with scarce resources were not eating. When in 1989 president Carlos Andrés Pérez implemented a programme of austerity and structural readjustment that, following International Monetary Fund guidelines, raised the price of public transport, the accumulated discontent erupted on 27 February in a popular rebellion known as the *caracazo*. The poor came down from the hills of Caracas toward downtown, looting everything they found along the way. As the uprising extended to almost all the cities in the country, the government ordered a military repression that caused between 3,000 and 10,000 deaths, depending on the source.

Investigators and activists agree that 1989 was a critical point of change, a rupture in the continuum of Venezuelan history that was also, to refer to Benjamin again, an 'emergency brake'. Responding to Marx's affirmation that revolutions are the locomotive of world history, Benjamin suggests it might be otherwise, and that revolutions are humanity's attempt to pull the emergency brake.[41]

Referring to Foucault's concept of effective history, Iturriza explains:

> If February 27 has any relationship to June 1848, the Paris Commune, May '68 in Paris, or the Argentine *cordobazo*,[42] it is that they are events that, having drastically altered the existing power relations, changed the course of historical events.[43]

The middle ranks of the army were those who, ordered by the superiors to turn their weapons on the *pueblo*, principally committed the *caracazo* massacre, and the events accelerated the conviction among them that it was necessary

---

39 See Azzellini 2009d; Denis 2007.
40 *Puntofijismo*: the power-sharing arrangement among Venezuela's three major parties, signed at Punto Fijo in 1958.
41 Benjamin 2003, p. 402; Ellner 2003, p. 19; López Maya 2003, p. 102.
42 *Cordobazo*: the May 1969 uprising in Córdoba, Argentina.
43 Iturriza 2007, p. 5.

to act fast to stop the regime. In February and November 1992, there were two civic-military uprisings that failed, the first of them led by Chávez. These, together with the *caracazo*, became constitutive for the Bolivarian process. In the midst of a crisis of traditional power, the popular movements took more and more of an autonomous stance; they gradually shifted from making specific, timely demands about concrete problems to demanding control, self-determination, self-management, and constituent power.[44]

The movements of the 80s and 90s were characterised by their great diversity, their adherence to direct politics, their rejection of representation and their limited territorial reach.[45] This development took place within the context of experiences with the party left, from the PCV to the Movement toward Socialismo (MAS) and the Radical Cause (Causa R), the latter two of which were formed in 1971 after a rupture in the Communist Party.[46]

Other ruptures of the continuum that were constitutive for the Bolivarian process were the 1998 election of Chávez and the following constituent process with broad popular participation in 1999, which created for the first time a provisional framework for the transformational process. The great diversity of the components of the process became visible:

> [T]oday one must understand that popular participation, in a myriad of forms not reducible to parties, movements, or associations, has been incorporated in a determinative manner in the political reconfiguration of the new century. The neoliberal scorched-earth policy generated integral social antibodies, so that responses are in all the reaches of society (economic, political, normative, identitarian, and cultural). The principal characteristic of the political changes in Latin America has to do with this renewed participation.[47]

This is also the foundation of the Bolivarian process:

> The extraordinary revolutionary potential of *chavismo* derives from its multiplicity of actors. This multiplicity implies the multiplication of fronts of struggle, the diversity of strategies put into action to struggle for the radical democratisation of Venezuelan society, and the capacity

---

44   See I-AA 2009.
45   It was and remains common to find organisations at all levels of the community, even politico-military organisations, which rarely extend beyond the local area.
46   Azzellini 2009a.
47   Monedero 2007, p. 5.

to mobilise to defend the revolutionary process when it has been endangered. These multiple singularities brought millions into the streets to restore democracy on April 13, 2002.[48]

3 The New Framework of Action

After these changes, social movements will not be able to continue operating as they have been, especially in the countries where the presence of leftist and progressive governments forces them to refine their tactics and discuss strategies for confronting unexpected situations. The challenges that these changes pose have been debated for some time, and are not only political in character but also theoretical or conceptual, since previous forms of analysing and comprehending reality are showing themselves to be often incapable of accounting for new situations.[49]

∴

The context of organisation and struggle in Latin America has changed fundamentally during the last decade and a half. The most favourable conditions for popular movements are found in Venezuela, with contradictions and dangers that include the financial availability and co-optive capacity of its institutions. This aspect is reinforced by a tradition of paternalistic assistance in Venezuela and by the limited experience of popular organisation and local independence (in comparison with other Latin American countries), although there have been many experiences of popular struggles.[50] Andrés Antillano of the CTU describes the problem:

> [I]n La Vega, on my street, we had assemblies every 15 days where 100, 150 people arrived and we deliberated over our different problems. [But] there was no formal organisation. Surely we ought to have resolved this tension within an organisation that is an administrative mechanism. We

---

48 Iturriza 2007, p. 6.
49 Zibechi 2006, p. 226.
50 Parker 2006, p. 92.

had an organisation that did not mobilise and a mobilisation that did not organise.[51]

To overcome that contradiction and create a broad popular self-organisation as a basic necessity for the proposed transformation process (something that, for obvious reasons, cannot be decreed by the state), the government connected its initiatives and social programme to the activation and strengthening of forms of popular self-organisation. As of 2004, social programmes, especially missions in the sectors of education, health, and production, propose the active participation of the organised community as a basic element. That was necessary, given that Venezuelan political culture and the political system have a clientist and paternalistic character, which has its origin in the rentierist economic model. The strong representative culture foments expectations of representation, rather than protagonistic agency.[52]

The approach that has been widely used in public policy since 2004–5 has been enormously effective: hundreds of thousands of volunteers organised themselves across the length and breadth of the national territory to work in the CTU and in the missions or in local popular organisations. The mechanism is visible in the Barrio Adentro Mission, which creates a new healthcare system: the state assigns a doctor to the communities if the population organises health committees that support the doctor's work. The success of the mission is rooted in the complementary nature of the two elements.[53]

While the state has played and continues to perform a fundamental role in the transformation of consciousness that, in the long term, contributes to a cultural change and to the scope of organisational autonomy, the process of 'two-track construction'[54] is faced with the contradictions inherent in the relation between constituent and constituted power. Consequently, the relation between movements and popular organisations, on the one hand, and the state and its institutions on the other, is marked by conflict and cooperation. The role of the state is ambivalent. The state disseminates and supports the popular processes, and *chavista* discourse strengthens the self-confidence of the poor and of the popular movements. But the centrality of the state and its role as a

---

51 See E-AA 2008.
52 Azzellini and Ressler 2004.
53 With the growing institutionalisation of the missions (and the partial transformation of compensated activism into salaried labour relations), their role as a mechanism of self-organisation and emancipation diminished.
54 Zibechi 2006, p. 227.

distributive entity for financial resources promotes the self-limitation of movements. Moreover, since many state institutions continue operating under a logic and with bourgeois structures that do not respond to the necessary transformations, the persistence of paternalistic and welfarist institutions threatens to distort popular autonomous organisation.

Although the majority of the popular movements and organisations are part of the Bolivarian process and make reference to Chávez, they were not and are not controlled by the president, by the United Socialist Party of Venezuela (PSUV), nor by the state; the ascent of Bolivarianism in the government has had complex consequences for them. Not all the movements managed to position themselves within the contradictory context or adapt their policies to the new circumstances.[55] Political orientations favourable to the new government and the institutional opening brought many activists from different movements to work in institutions, debilitating some movements in the process.[56] Many other movements, meanwhile, strengthened as a consequence of the new institutional policies. The indigenous movement, for example, integrated many of its demands into the 1999 Constitution, achieving more than in any other Latin American country in this era – even though in Venezuela the indigenous population is only around 2.1 percent of the total population.[57] However, given the strong persistence of developmentalist visions among the Bolivarian forces (especially the institutional forces) and the continuation of previous powers' interests and structures (especially on the local level), points of conflict exist with the indigenous populations, including the slowness with which indigenous territories are being demarcated, open-pit coal mining in the Zulia region, and local issues with cattle ranchers.

The most controversial case is that of women's movements. There is no doubt that these movements achieved the inclusion of many of their demands in the Constitution, including the historic feminist demand of recognition for housework as the creation of surplus value and the factoring of it into retirement calculations (Art. 88). The Bolivarian process, however, transformed the structures and the orientations of the women's movements. Prior to 1998, the women's movement had a more feminist cast, and while on rare occasions it mobilised some hundreds of principally middle-class women, it was more oriented toward interparty lobbying. The new women's movement is much broader-based, and is principally composed of poor women. Many of the goals

---

55   Zibechi 2006, p. 222.
56   Ellner 2006, p. 82.
57   Van Cott 2002, p. 43.

of the feminist movement, however, are reflected in the transformation process, though in a less specific way.[58]

The events linked to the rivalry that began as of 1999 between opposing models of society led to a rupture of interparty cooperation in favour of interests supposedly specific to women. Many women who had previously been activists in leftist women's organisations were integrated into the new institutions, orienting their work in the new politico-social framework toward the masses of women in the poorest social strata – for example, by institutional mechanisms such as the Women's Bank and the National Women's Institute, or the Barrio Mothers Mission, which financially supported more than 300,000 single mothers and organised them as workers and politically.[59]

Although many self-organisation processes are institutionally promoted, the great majority of women are not organised, whether in state-affiliated mass organisations or within the principal party in power (as has been the case in revolutions in Nicaragua or Cuba), nor did they organise in independent women's movements (as the 'traditional' feminist movement postulates). The majority of Venezuelan women in the barrio are organised in the context of community organisations, work in local spaces undertaking struggles outside the state framework, and are also strongly identified (despite their sharp criticisms of the institutions) with the ongoing process and especially with Chávez.[60]

These circumstances, together with the absence of a discourse and defined objectives, have prompted some researchers (who identify with a more 'traditional' feminism, if we want to call it that) to maintain that ties or connections are lacking between women of the Bolivarian popular movements and 'authentic' feminism. According to Rakowski, for example, women activists in the barrios 'have no understanding of the history of women's struggle in Venezuela'.[61] Fernandes writes: 'popular women's organising contains its own unique history, struggles, and trajectories, which cannot be reduced to the history of feminism in Venezuela'.[62] We could therefore rather accuse partisans of traditional feminism of not understanding barrio women's expressions of gender-oriented struggles.

However, the fact that women's movements have not maintained (or built) a structure for organisation and autonomous discussion means that certain

---

58 See Ellner 2008.
59 Kron 2004, p. 63.
60 Fernandes 2007, pp. 100–1.
61 Fernandes 2003, p. 99.
62 Ibid.

of their most controversial issues are being under-prioritised nationally, and enter into the national agenda only with difficulty. The paradigmatic case in this sense is the question of abortion, the legalisation of which is supported by grassroots organisations (especially collectives and feminist organisations, and some representatives of state women's institutions), but is rejected by the church, the opposition, and even by part of the Bolivarian forces – by political representatives, as well as some within the social base of the process. Those Bolivarian forces who are favourable to abortion rights and women's self-determination have not been able to introduce the subject into the present political agenda.

At election time, the popular organisations and the Bolivarian partisan and institutional forces downplay their criticisms and differences, and appear much more homogeneous than they are outside of electoral situations, when the organisations' criticisms of the government increase. In the liberal camp, this has been interpreted as subjugating the movements to outside interests. García-Guadilla, for example, maintains that the mobilisation of CTU members in the 2004 referendum in favour of the continuation of Chávez's mandate meant that the CTU was 'politically penetrated and temporally mobilised as Units of Electoral Battle'.[63] A similar argument was proposed by the human rights organisation Provea with regard to the electoral mobilisations of the FNCEZ.[64] This interpretation implicitly denies the popular movements their political rationality. Electoral mobilisations of the movements and popular organisations, on the contrary, demonstrate the advanced level of strategic rationality of the popular base. The movements see themselves as an integral part of the transformation process: in strategic moments there prevails the defence of the legal and political framework that permits the continuation of the transformation process, despite all the contradictions and problems it poses. In fact, as García-Guadilla notes, in the case of the CTU, 'once the processes were terminated, they returned to their organisational spaces'.[65]

4   Popular Actors and Autonomous Construction

The autonomous popular movements include indigenous and Afro-Venezuelan movements and organisations; gender-based and LGBT movements;

---

63   García-Guadilla 2008, p. 135.
64   Provea 2008, p. 55.
65   García-Guadilla 2008, p. 135.

alternative, independent, and community media; and many others. Given the impossibility of analysing them all, this section will concentrate on the largest ones.

The most consolidated and organised of the great movements are the peasant movement, the settlers' movement, the workers' control movement, and the more recent movement of communards (about the workers' control movement, see Chapter 6). All are part of the process of change, but nevertheless, their structures are self-organised and their debates and decisions are autonomous. All exist in a relation of cooperation and conflict with constituted power. It is interesting to note in this context that two of these movements, that of the settlers and of the communards, have their origins in state initiatives (the CTU and the CCs/communes), which have been appropriated from below and have gained spaces of autonomy.

4.1   *The Bolívar and Zamora Revolutionary Current*

The Bolívar and Zamora Revolutionary Current (CRBZ) is composed of: the peasant organisation FNCEZ; the Simón Bolívar National Communal Fornt (FNCSB), which regroups communal councils, communes, and communal cities; the Simón Rodríguez Centre for Training and Social Study (CEFES); and the Workers Popular Power Movement (MPPO). The construction of the CRBZ is the result of an autonomous focus of the FNCEZ that postulates the building of a revolutionary current with organisational autonomy within the Bolivarian movement.[66] The FNCEZ is defined as Marxist, has within its constitution a clear class orientation, and supports the government and the Bolivarian process,[67] but seeks a deepening of revolutionary transformation and more resolute action against corruption and bureaucracy. The organisation collaborates with the Ministry of Agriculture, the National Institute of Rural Development (INDER), the National Institute of Lands (INTI), the National Institute of Integral Agricultural Health (INSAI) and other institutions related to agriculture and the development of the rural environment, and also has some institutional responsibilities, especially in regional dependencies of various state institutions. Since 2010, it even has two representatives in the National Assembly, elected on the ticket of the largest government party, the PSUV.

---

66   For more information about the CRBZ, available at: http://www.crbz.org/.

67   In the face of the murders by landowners and their hired assassins of more than 250 peasants since the land reform law was passed in 2003, it can be said that the peasants literally defend the transformation process with their lives.

At the same time, the FNCEZ has organisational, political, and formative autonomy:

> We are an autonomous organisation, we have our own school, we organise it ourselves, we help the *pueblo* organise ... [A]lthough we are with the process and with the president, we are an autonomous organisation, born out of the base.[68]

In almost all the states of the country, the FNCEZ has successfully taken advantage of the new political framework for organising peasants. The Peasant Front grew rapidly, and consolidated to become the largest, most active peasant organisation in Venezuela and one of the strongest popular movements. This growth was possible because of its strategy of organisational autonomy combined with intense institutional cooperation. The FNCEZ's organisational autonomy permitted it to confront and pressure officialist powers and local, regional, and national institutions. It organised the occupation of institutions (like the regional dependencies of the INTI or the FONDAFA, the Development Fund for Agriculture, Fisheries, and Forest), which it accused of failing to respond to peasants' needs, blocking highways as a form of pressure, and occupying lands to work them. In 2005, for example, the FNCEZ organised the occupation of a part of the hacienda La Marqueseña that had been expropriated by the state, with the intention of pressuring the state to deliver part of the land to landless local peasants. In this way the FNCEZ obtained 500 hectares, machinery, and financing to put together a cooperative of local peasants.

Like the FNCEZ, the CRBZ is also an integral part of the transformation process and cooperates with governmental institutions. It too takes its own positions, which do not always agree with those of the government.[69] Its strategy is based on the building of alliances with other revolutionary sectors of the transformation process, above all with the other large movements and autonomous organisations, like the CTU/settlers' movement, the National Network of Communards (RNC) and the movement for workers' control.

Although they collaborate with the government, the focus of all the organisations that make up the CRBZ is that of the autonomous creation of a project for a socialist society:

---

68 Luz Mery Bermúdez, FNCEZ, in Azzellini and Ressler 2010.
69 To cite one example: the CRBZ forcefully condemned the illegal April 2011 rendition of Joaquín Pérez Becerra, the director of the agency ANNCOL, to Colombian authorities.

Within the Commune we talk about what communal or self-governments, as we call them, consist of. [We talk about] what [functions of] government the *pueblo* exercises in order to administer, manage, and plan the policies of the Commune and of the communal councils. We want to strengthen from the base how we ourselves conceive political, economic, cultural, and military popular power. The topic of security and defence is important for our Bolivarian process, because of threats to the revolutionary process.[70]

In July 2011, the Simón Bolívar Communal National Front started participating in the meeting of the National Network of Communards. At the international level, the FNCEZ is a member organisation of Vía Campesina and has close relations with the Brazilian MST; indeed, the CEFES was created with the support of the MST. There are also intense contacts with popular organisations in Argentina and Honduras.

4.2 The Settlers' Movement

The Settlers' Movement (MDP) is a network of urban movements composed of the Urban Land Committees (Comités de Tierra Urbana, CTU); the tenants network, which struggles against eviction and in favour of the expropriation of apartments and their delivery to those who live in them; the pioneer encampments of homeless families, who mobilise for the right to urban land and organise for the building of new collective settlements; and the janitors' movement, formed by families who work as janitors, which links the right to work to the right to have a home. Like the organisations that comprise it, the MDP emerged by the initiative and with the support of the CTUs.

The CTUs were born through state initiative, but nevertheless they rapidly created an autonomous structure and became a central pillar of popular organisation in the barrios. According to statistics from the National Technical Office for the Regularisation of Urban Lands (OTNRTTU), in 2009 there existed 7,332 CTUs. Their origins go back to a 4 February 2002 presidential decree, which – in response to the barrio residents' long struggle to legalise urban lands – officially recognised the barrios as part of the city and regulated the process of regularisation and legalisation of urban lands. Each CTU includes 200 families at most in a territory self-defined by the CTU during the process of self-constitution. The CTUs received legal status and were empowered to map the territories they organised (receiving the support of engineers and

---

70 Melisa Orellana, FNCSB, in Azzellini and Ressler 2010.

cartographers from the state) and to define land ownership in those territories. They deliver land titles and have the legal power to shape public spaces. This modus operandi has been decisive in the success of the CTUs, given that

> [t]he high degree of informality of land possession in the barrios impedes the creation of a trustworthy mechanism to determine the titleholder of an occupied parcel. In this scenario the only source to establish legitimate possession (which determines the property right) is the historic social understanding of the barrio and its residents ... [T]he CTU permits a transparent, equitable process in the regularisation of property.[71]

In 2006, an urban land law was approved after the institutional proposal was discussed in depth, revised, and widened by the CTUs in the communities.[72] Shortly after the law was passed, the CTU began to discuss how to reform it, and a reformed law, which included their proposals, was passed by the National Assembly in 2009. The forms of legalisation of lands and popular protagonism made possible the delivery of more than 500,000 individual and collective titles between 2004 and 2011. The focus of the process of legalisation of urban lands in Venezuela prioritises the collective and social, and contributes to the strengthening of the communities. That marks a fundamental difference from past neoliberal processes of legalisation of urban lands, promoted by the World Bank and others, which in the 80s and 90s in Latin America faced the challenge of commodifying urban lands that had remained off the market, in the hope of making possible the obtaining of credit and mortgages, thus dynamising the real estate market.[73]

Unlike the neoliberal process, regularisation of urban lands in Venezuela gives the communities an instrument with which to safeguard their collective interests against the pressure of the real estate markets. The ability to define land as public prevents unused land from ending up as the object of real estate speculation. In some CTUs, collective forms of urban land tenancy have emerged that assure the residents their homes, but subject to collective decision the permission to sell or rent them. The CTUs' familiarity with the

---

71 See Antillano 2006a, p. 204. In 2001, Antillano was, together with María Cristina Iglesias and Iván Martínez, one of the authors of the 2002 decree. Antillano and Martínez came from the movement for the legalisation of urban lands.
72 Antillano 2006a, p. 202; Ellner 2006, p. 86; I-AA 2008.
73 Parker 2006, p. 91.

territory and its organisational forms has made them a decisive actor in emergencies, as in the case of collapses and slides from heavy rain in the barrios of Caracas.

The CTUs rapidly widened their field of action beyond the legalisation of lands, responding to the necessities that emerged in the process of collective organisation depending on the habitat. The CTUs at first, and then all the MDP, developed proposals and projects for the democratisation of urban land ownership and struggle against the 'urban *latifundio* [large estate]', against speculation, and against the commercial centres.[74] They have produced proposals for habitat management for construction of new urbanisations, participatory urban policy, and the 'right to the city' (a proposal of the CTU to that effect was included in the constitutional reform rejected by popular vote in 2007), for the struggle for a 'socialist city', and against the use of living space and land as merchandise.

The most important institutional counterpart to the CTUs since the majority of urban lands in the barrios have been legalised is the Ministry of Popular Power for Housing and Habitat. The relation of the CTUs with the ministry has been in large part conflictive. The focus of the ministry's residential policy prioritises in a traditional manner the simple search for residential solutions. The CTUs' integral focus derives from the active participation of the communities in planning, and includes issues of habitat and quality of life.[75] Andrés Antillano notes that the problem is not access to resources. The ministry has been willing to finance projects of the CTUs, but nevertheless, this is not central to the CTUs' approach:

> We have told the ministry of housing that our fundamental problem is not that they give us resources and that they finance our projects, but that we want to define housing policy ... We have always said that we must advance in the building of a new society with the state, without the state and against the state. The relation with the state is not defined by us but by the willingness of the state to subordinate itself to the interests of the *pueblo*.[76]

This focus is shared by the MDP. In January 2011, around 100 MDP spokespeople presented and discussed their proposals with Chávez and some ministers in an

---

[74] The Caracas MDP, for example, in July 2011 signed 11 agreements for the management of residential complexes. The measure benefited 2,000 families who were renting there.
[75] See E-AA 2008; MDP 2007.
[76] See E-AA 2008.

encounter that lasted almost seven hours and was broadcast live on television, pursuant to which Chávez accepted almost all their proposals. A reform of the Organic Law of Labour was agreed upon to improve the janitors' rights, along with a new law to regulate rentals. It was decided to allow collective titles in the law of land ownership regularisation, and to provide for collective credits to finance the construction of new communities pursuant to decree. Chávez also decreed a prohibition on forced evictions pending a new law of urban land ownership and rentals, which was passed in 2011.

4.3 National Network of Communards

The National Network of Communards (Red Nacional de Comuneros y Comuneras, RNC) has been the most important autonomous movement in pressing for the construction of communes. A self-organised network that began in 2008, it brings together communes, both existing and under construction, from all over the country. The intention of this self-organised network is to build in a democratic manner from below a communal state based on councils; to continue developing a constituent popular process; and to deepen the constituent character of the *pueblo*. It was created as an institutional initiative after Chávez called for the formation of a team to analyse the existing experience of the communes that had been formed autonomously from below. Atenea Jiménez, a central activist of the commune members' movement since its beginning, says:

> A mapping was begun, identifying 21 pilot experiences. But since everything is complicated at the bureaucratic level, that took a year. It made for a very interesting project, since the communes were substantially advanced. The Ministry of Communes was created, and they kicked us all out and we decided then and there to begin a process of articulation by popular power. There were 16 communes at that moment. We articulated the idea of not working from within the state but from ourselves ... that we could speak for ourselves, learning, self-teaching, supporting the idea of endogenous development. We worked with popular education, with the interchange of knowledge ... We started out in 2008 with 16, and right now there are more than 80 experiences at the national level in the Network and we add more experiences with every activity. The process of building the commune without subordination to any kind of power outside the community brings us together.[77]

---

77   See I-AJ 2012.

The communards' Network continued growing, with about 500 communes participating in 2015. There are regular encounters of regional spokespeople, in regions agreed to by the Network, and at least twice a year national Network encounters are organised. There are also work commissions – in communications, for example – and thematic meetings, like those on 'socialist communal productive economy' or the 'organisation of the National Network of Commune Members, the organisation of the National Communal Council, and the organisation of the communal state'. Another thematic meeting worked on the project of a communal school, self-organised by the communes for their benefit. Based on the experiences of popular, liberatory, and in practice revolutionary education, it was proposed

> to develop a popular formative model to press for the birth of the new man and woman with class consciousness, contributing in this way to the transformation of the present education system, which is still conservative in nature and reproduces the logic of capital.[78]

In July 2011, it was agreed to continue the structuring process by means of a National Council of Commune Members and of national, regional, and local commissions of organisation, communication, formation, communal project planning, and defence. With respect to the latter, the intention was declared to 'assume territorial security and defence, composing the militia with combatants from the communes, with the intention of safeguarding the strategy of occupy, produce, and defend'.[79]

In the Fourth National Encounter of Commune Members of 29–31 July 2011, in the Torres municipality of Lara state, some 300 people participated, from approximately 70 communes and *cumbes* (as the Afro-Venezuelan communes in the zone of Barlovento call themselves, referring to the communities of fugitive slaves during slavery times). There were also some 15 spokespeople from the more than 80 FNCSB communes, many of which exercise collective planning in various fields, principally agriculture machinery, formation of productive cooperatives, highways, electricity, health, education, housing, and in some cases even defence. At that time there were also two communal cities in the FNCSB: the Simón Bolívar Communal Peasant City in the state of Apure, composed of 39 CCs and 10 communes, and another communal city in Portuguesa. Despite their advanced organisation, the Ministry persisted

---

78   See RNC 2011.
79   Ibid.

until 2013 in classifying them as communes 'under construction' and they did not officially exist (although they continued receiving resources as communes).

The Network is completely autonomous, although it has specific institutional supports. The encounter in Torres was supported by the mayoralty of Torres, which under the leadership of mayor Julio Chávez has been a pioneer in building popular power.[80] The local institutions only saluted the participants of the encounter at the opening assembly and did not otherwise intervene. Normally, however, relations with institutions tend to be conflictive. All the communes participating in the encounter told in their presentations of conflicts with the institutions and of how they had to pressure the institutions to support, rather than restrain, the process of popular construction. After years of experience, the general understanding is that the problem is structural, and not an issue of whether the officials in charge are good or bad. Many institutions see the Network of Commune Members as a threat or a nuisance – although not officially, given that such a stance goes against the normative orientation, and especially against the declared position of Chávez. Nevertheless, the self-organisation of the communes represents a threat in the institutional logic of inherent control, especially to the Ministry of Popular Power of the Communes, given that without resources the Network has done more to link, coordinate, and stimulate debate in the communes than the ministry itself.

Some events around the Fourth Encounter gave clear evidence of the complicated relations between institutions and popular self-organisation. Before the encounter, high representatives of the government called, unsuccessfully, on local authorities to try to obstruct it. Although the Ministry of Communes was criticised heavily at the encounter, Minister of Communes Isis Ochoa attended the closing event on instructions from Chávez, who considered the activity promoted by popular power highly important for the construction of the new communal state. The minister proposed to seek points of correspondence between the government and the communes, without giving much detail or presenting concrete proposals. Before the discourse, Ochoa attended the cultural programme of the congress, in which a theatrical work was presented about negative experiences with the Ministry of Communes. When she spoke, many participants went away to eat.

This does not mean that there is no interest or will on the part of the Network and its members to work with the Ministry or with institutions; quite the

---

80   Azzellini 2010, p. 266.

contrary. So the Network, for example, also proposed 'to participate actively in the creation of new revolutionary laws and regulations required by the popular movement'.[81] But the Network decides its agenda autonomously, based on its debates, interests, and decisions. It hopes for an institutional response to its agenda rather than the imposition of the institution's agenda. So the final declarations of the Fourth Encounter call:

> To propose to the Ministry of Popular Power for the Communes that, from the existence and reaffirmation of the communes articulated in the National Network of Commune Members, it recognise their existence as a social and political force of the revolutionary process that develops a unitary policy, based on the principles of the Bolivarian Revolution, the leadership of comrade President, Comandante Hugo Chávez Frías, and mutual respect and trust.[82]

The building of the communal state and the abolition of the existing state are on the Network's horizon, so it proposes:

> To progressively dismantle the bourgeois liberal state and construct from the *pueblo* a new form of government, the Socialist communal state, which resembles and recuperates the historic project truncated in 1498 with the arrival of the Spanish conquistador. To develop self-management capacity as a central element in exercising revolutionary communal self-government, the government of the *pueblo*, in which decisions are made in a collective, democratic manner.[83]

This challenge is not being proposed by the majority of institutions on account of their inherent logics of power, although it is the official normative orientation. In the debates during the encounter, it became clear that one could not ask the bourgeois state and its institutions to build popular power, autonomy, and the communal state. Either socialism will be constructed from below, or not at all. This represents a major change in comparison with similar encounters years earlier, when it was common to compile wish lists to deliver to the institutions, hoping they would comply. Today the communes work to

---

81 See RNC 2011.
82 Ibid.
83 Ibid.

[a]ssume the planning of the productive cycle (production, transformation, and distribution, thus promoting the cultural change of the models of consumption and consumerism) …

Accumulate the technical and organic force for the means of production to pass progressively to workers' control (councils of workers) and of the communes in their various levels of aggregation, to develop the communal economy, in transition to Bolivarian socialism.[84]

---

84   Ibid.

CHAPTER 4

The Communal Councils: Local Self-Administration and Social Transformation

> Constituent power can be an element of law, i.e., an institution that must constantly create new institutions. Nevertheless, it needs a place to do that.[1]

∴

> All pretense of construction that separates theory from the popular sectors' aspirations, expectations, and values will contribute to installing a new domination. This does not mean reneging on theory. The problem is not confusing theory or science or philosophy with consciousness. Consciousness can never come from outside.[2]

∴

This chapter deals with the communal councils (CCs), the most important initiative in creating self-administering communities and popular power in Venezuela. First, it presents a picture of the various initiatives of local participation – failures, in part – considered as background experience in the process of building the CC, then describes the mechanisms of creation, structure, and functioning of the CC. It follows the experience of the communes, of which, in June 2015, 1,169 were constituted throughout the national territory. It analyses the development and the contradictions of the CC, examines problems within the CCs and in their institutional relations, and finally presents concrete experiences of some CCs in Caracas.[3]

---

1 Negri 2008, p. 10.
2 See Soto and Ávila 2006.
3 One CC in a barrio of Caracas was visited, observed, and interviewed several times over a two-year period. Another, in a residential zone of the impoverished middle class, was visited and interviewed intensively during a shorter period. Smaller numbers of interviews were carried out in five other CCs.

Since 1999, a large variety of participatory mechanisms have been tried. Constituent power has sought a way between its own initiatives and institutional ones – between autonomy and co-optation – and any new structure is the result of this field of tension. The search for a framework for participatory and protagonistic power has led to popular power and socialism. Both are connected with the historic line of the commune, not with that of the state. The idea of local self-administration connects with the histories of indigenous people and of Afro-Venezuelans, as well as with Latin American Marxist currents, like the ideas advanced by the Peruvian José Carlos Mariátegui.[4] Chávez made a connection with the early socialist Simón Rodríguez:

> Look at what Simón Rodríguez said, he spoke in 1847 of toparchy. In a document directed to Anselmo Pineda, February 2, 1847, Simón Rodríguez said: 'The true utility of the creation of a republic, is to see that the inhabitants have an interest in the prosperity of their ground. In that way provincial privileges are destroyed.' (Bolívar said that in the towns there was a caste, and he called it that of the doctors, military, and priests, which was the caste in each place). I wish that every parish would be erected in toparchy [*toparchía*]. You know, *topos* means place ... and *arquía* is the authority or the government, like monarchy, oligarchy, in this case it is toparchy, which is the government of the place, of the inhabitants of the place, it's the popular government, it's the communal government.[5]

After the failure of the Local Councils of Public Planning (Consejos Locales de Planificación Pública, CLPP) – the first initiative at the national level of local participation – Chávez redirected his attention to the CCs that had been created from below, disseminated awareness of them, and gave them a significant boost. In many places, CCs were created as a consequence of publicising the legal initiative. Chávez's commitment to the CC strengthened the council form in general, so that, as of 2006, councilist logic can be said to have begun to expand.[6]

The CC had wide repercussions in the model of the state, whose providentialist function is no longer assumed by a specialised bureaucracy, but is realised by transferring financial resources and public technicians to the communit-

---

4 See I-HV 2007.
5 Chávez 2008, p. 43, Annual message to the National Assembly. Federal Legislative Palace, 13 January 2007.
6 See I-RD 2006.

ies.[7] Nevertheless, local autonomy is neither isolation in the face of state power, nor a counterweight to it, but instead is a networked self-administration that surpasses the divisions among political, social, and economic, and renders the state in its known form partly superfluous.

Chávez defined the CC as constituent power.[8] While the CCs have the potential to be an institution of constituent power, the place where they take form is the community (as a social relation, not as an administrative entity), and not, as Negri supposes, the metropolis.[9] In urban or metropolitan regions, the greatest popular protagonism is found in the marginalised zones.[10] However, the experience of the metropolis has demonstrated that political conflict, social fragmentation, and divergence of interests are greater there. This has complicated the situation for urban constituent processes, and has slowed them down in comparison with rural zones.[11] The percentage of the population organised in CCs tends to be higher in rural zones – where the first communes were created – rather than in urban zones.[12]

Based on historical local experience, there are various conditions for successful participation that can be catalogued – among them, the decentralisation of the services of public administration, of finance, of initiatives and of decision-making power. If only the first step is made, as in the case of neoliberal models, then we cannot speak of participation.[13] The necessity of creating spaces for participation is in view, but it is also necessary to create and promote forms of organisation and to materialise participation, since they do not appear by themselves. Finally, the population must have sufficient access to information in order to enable protagonistic participation and autonomous decisions.

In the face of the experiences of different models of local participation in Latin America, we can affirm that 'democratic governance requires respect for people's organisational and cultural traditions'.[14] It is fundamental to take as a point of departure the 'concerns that people perceive as immediate, and not what local administrations believe are their immediate interests'.[15]

---

7   See FCG 2008, p. 6.
8   Chávez 2008, p. 15.
9   See Negri 2008, p. 10.
10 Lacabana and Cariola 2005, p. 29.
11 See Parada 2007.
12 Romero Pirela 2007, p. 136.
13 Even the decentralisation of institutions of urban public administration into small, local offices can be helpful, but nevertheless it changes nothing in the citizen-state relation.
14 See Harnecker 2003.
15 Ibid.

Equally necessary is organisational autonomy for the population in the face of constituted power. This does not mean that the population cannot support the government or the transformation process, but that its decisions are really its own without having to be subordinated to the interests of others. Although constituted power has the normative orientation of promoting the autonomy of popular organisation, the inherent, inherited logic of its institutions is not conducive to widening participation and promoting autonomy. This means that constituent power must constantly put pressure on constituted power. The autonomy of constituted power is also important in reducing the risk that constituent power reproduces structures and functions of constituted power, and also in identifying and correcting errors more rapidly.

1 The Origins of the CCs and Their Antecedents in Local Participation

> Participatory and protagonistic democracy expresses itself in permitting us to organise ourselves in communities that, by generating citizen assemblies or other associative organisational forms, allows us to make binding decisions, and allows us to self-govern or go toward the possibility of self-government as a *pueblo*.[16]

∴

Forms of local self-government have been discussed since 2000 by various popular organisations and communities under different names: Local Governments (GL), Communitarian Governments (GC), and others. The method is practically equal to a constituent assembly. Germán Ferrer, member of the National Assembly for the PSUV, active in the National Association of Social Networks and Organisations (ANROS), originating in part in networks of the ex-guerrilla Revolutionary Party of Venezuela-Armed Forces of National Liberation (PRV-FALN), explains:

> In my particular case, before being a member of parliament I was discussing with communities through ANROS, and with a very similar meth-

---

16   See I-HV 2007.

odology. I believe that the CCs, which are communitary governments, go back to that. We go to the communities, we call citizen assemblies, we make regulations for neighbourhood coexistence, we establish goals and objectives, and then you can see what the strengths and weaknesses of the community are.[17]

The GC initiatives are so similar to the CC that one might say that the Executive simply put another name to it,[18] although the GCs were on a smaller scale.[19] In Caracas, the building of Local Governments (LG) began in November 2005 during the mandate of Mayor Juan Barreto (2004–8), and in November 2006 the LG were transformed into CCs. All these initiatives have been based in self-administration; grassroots activists from different left currents took advantage of the possibility contained in the Constitution of neighbourhood assemblies with binding decisions to construct local self-administrations.

As of 2004, different attempts were made to construct forms of 'local government', in the sense that the population participates in making decisions. Some of these models of local government had been discussed already in 2000–1, though their implementation was interrupted by the coup and the oil lockout. The majority were specific local initiatives, some of them limited to single towns, barrios, or municipalities. Nevertheless, failed or less successful initiatives also represent an important experience. All of them are part of a set of experiences that inform the search for forms of local self-administration. Some of these mechanisms of local participation that preceded the CC will be presented in the next section.

1.1   *Participatory Budgeting*
The model participatory budget, known at the international level principally for its application in Porto Alegre (Brazil), was previously introduced in Venezuela in 1990, and was applied in a similar way, by Clemente Scotto (LCR), the mayor of Caroní (Bolívar) (Scotto, 2003).[20] As of 1999, models of participatory budgeting were introduced in the municipalities of Guacara and Libertador (Carabobo), Iribarren and Torres (Lara), Páez (Portuguesa), Libertador (Caracas) and Libertador (Mérida), although the budget was not really participatory in every case: the municipality of Torres is generally considered

---

17   See I-GF 2006.
18   One difference is that in the local governments, the minimum voting age was 18, whereas in the CC it is 15.
19   See I-ED 2007; I-HV 2007.
20   Scotto 2003.

a positive example, while the administration of Carlos León in Libertador (Mérida) is considered negative.[21]

The participatory budget is provided for in Article 62 of the Constitution and specified in the Organic Law of Municipal Public Power.[22] The law regulates the conditions for the integration of community proposals into the municipal budget (art. 234), and defines the participatory budget as a means for the *pueblo* to exercise its sovereignty (art. 261) and as the instrument with which the neighbourhood collaborates, discusses, and decides on the definition, application, control, and evaluation of the annual municipal budget (art. 271). In the law of the Local Councils of Public Planning (2002), the participatory budget is part of the municipal development plan (art. 35) and the participatory diagnostic is an important part of the planning of the participatory budget (art. 26). The CCs go far beyond that, in that they not only place budget decisions in the hands of the population, but also hand over the planning and execution of projects, as well as a part of the finances. The participatory budget in Venezuela, therefore, must be considered in a broader way than in other cases. A central difference between participatory budgeting and the CC lies also in the methodology. In participatory budgeting as carried out, for example, in Brazil, the communities participate in deciding what should be done with a very limited amount of money for which different projects must compete; but in the CC, institutional financing is sought only after the communities have discussed their needs and desires, and the neighbourhood assembly has set priorities.

1.2   *The Failed CLPP Initiative*

The CLPP are named in Article 182 of the 1999 Constitution as a mechanism for participation in planning and decision-making of local policy and expenditures, although without specifying their tasks or their composition. On 16 May 2002, the National Assembly ratified a specific law about the CLPP.[23] Influenced by the model of participatory budgeting in Porto Alegre, the law made possible the participation of the population in local political decisions, to fix the priorities for financing and, going beyond the Brazilian model, to undertake an analysis and participatory planning and direct financing of community projects. The CLPP had the responsibility for 20 percent of the financial resources of the

---

21   On participatory budgeting in some of the municipalities, see http://www.participatorybudgeting.org/.
22   See LOPPM 2005.
23   See LCLPP 2002.

decentralisation funds (FIDES), which, according to the law, are at the disposition of the 'organised local civil society'.[24] Participation nevertheless remained mostly a pretence; instead of becoming a participatory democratic mechanism, the CLPP reproduced the representative logics of the institutions.[25] The construction of the CC, contemplated in the law as a body of the base, was practically left undone, since the initiative remained in the hands of the mayors.

With the Law of Communal Councils, in April 2006, the CLPP lost importance. When the CLPP law was reformed on 14 November 2006, the CCs were taken out of the area of the CLPP and became autonomous.[26] Although the CLPP in some cases continued to exist, they had almost no functions, since the CCs had superseded them as a form of local participation.[27]

The CLPP were composed of the mayor (as president), the councillors, the presidents of the parish juntas,[28] representatives of the neighbourhood organisations of the parishes and of the *pueblo* organised by sectors, with a majority representation for organised society in the vote.[29] According to the law, they were to analyse the necessities of the municipality, collect the proposals of the population – giving greater weight to the organised communities – systematise them, participate in the planning and orientation of the local budget; formulate proposals for the municipal development plan and focus it toward necessities and capabilities of the population; monitor and control the putting into practice of the development plan; and promote and organise the transfer of skills and resources from the municipal administration to the organised communities. They were also to promote organisation in the communities by means of integration into CLPP, which, according to the law, were to be built in all the municipalities no more than 120 days after approval of the law.[30]

Originally, the CLPP were thought of as an element of a system of planning with subsequent higher levels. For planning at a higher level it was envisaged, and was specified in Article 166 of the Constitution, to create in each state a State Council of Planning and Coordination of Public Policy (CEPP).[31] These

---

24 Ellner 2008; Lander 2007, p. 74; MPD 2002; Wilpert 2007, p. 56.
25 Parker 2006, p. 92.
26 Diniz and López 2007, p. 193.
27 Ellner 2008; I-LC 2007.
28 The *parroquia* (parish) is the smallest administrative entity. The parish juntas, local representative organs, did not have many powers and were eliminated in 2006.
29 LCLPP 2002, art. 3.
30 See LCLPP 2002.
31 See LCEPCPP 2002.

were to be made up of representatives from different levels of the state institutions and of representatives from the popular organisations, the latter to be a minority.[32] And finally, at the national level it was planned to construct a Federal Council of Government (CFG), made up only of representatives from different levels of constituted power.

However, not much happened after the approval of the CLPP law. In May 2002, various initiatives began to constitute the CLPP, but there was little active interest, either from above or below. Neither the *pueblo*, nor the different levels of administration, knew how to approach the CLPP; besides, government support was scarce and local authorities were disinterested and even resistant. The few CLPP that were formed were motivated principally by the desire to comply with the law. The coup and the oil lockout also had responsibility in the relegation of the CLPP to a secondary priority.[33]

With increased organisation of the grassroots in mid-2003, demand grew to constitute the CLPP. In the centre of attention from below were the possibilities, contained in the law, of setting aside up to 20 percent of the financing of the FIDES for organised community projects, as well as a clause specifying that municipal budgets must be approved by the CLPP. Nevertheless, the majority of the mayors – opposition as well as Bolivarians – continued avoiding, or even impeding, the creation of the CLPP, but more and more of them began to be formed after 2004.[34] For lack of will to share decision-making and financial power with the base, the majority of the mayors instrumentalised the CLPP and manipulated them in such a way that they were composed principally of their followers, or the financing of approved projects was ignored or delayed significantly. Some political factions tried to guarantee themselves political quotas of power by usurping the supposed representation at the parish level, to which the clientist mechanisms of the municipalities were extended. Many CLLP were controlled by mayors through the 'reproduction of representative roadblocks'. This also demonstrated the lack of a tradition of movements from below influencing public policy.[35] The political instrumentalisation of the CLPP made them unattractive to the base, which was already exercising political participation through other mechanisms. Here we see clearly that participatory and protagonistic democracy is a socio-cultural process that cannot be decreed from above. If participation is not the result of demand emerging from struggle,

---

32 LCEPCPP 2002, art. 6.
33 Bonilla-Molina and El Troudi 2004, p. 231; Lander 2007, p. 76; Wilpert 2007, p. 57.
34 FCG 2008, p. 11; Lander 2007, p. 76; Wilpert 2007, p. 58.
35 Parker 2006, p. 93.

then those responsible for governmental institutions need only to resist, and nothing will happen.

The failure of the CLPP was foreseeable, given that most urban municipalities have between 200,000 and 500,000 residents, and the municipality of Libertador, in Caracas, has more than 2 million. A model of direct democracy with municipal assemblies and spokespeople cannot function at these levels.

In summary, there were three principal reasons for the failure:[36]

(1) institutional representatives outweighed popular delegates, although they were formally the minority;
(2) a popular delegation at the highest level is almost impossible if there does not exist a communitary organisation to undertake a selection process at the base; and
(3) the scope of the CLPP was too large to permit direct participation by the population. As a consequence, higher levels of planning were never formed or did not function.

1.3 Metropolitan Council for Planning Public Policies (CMPPP)

According to the March 2000 Special Law of the Metropolitan District of Caracas, which created the Greater Mayoralty of Gran Caracas, the CMPPP must assume strategic planning and produce the budget for the Gran Caracas district. However, the first Bolivarian mayor of Caracas, Alfredo Peña – who moved over to the opposition during his term – did nothing to shape the CMPPP. The subsequent Bolivarian mayor, Juan Barreto, began structuring the CMPPP in 2005. A decree of the same year changed the composition of the CMPPP; as in the CLPP, the organised *pueblo* took over the majority from the representatives of constituted power. The mechanism of the delegates of the parishes, nevertheless, was very indirect and required much organisational work. First, there were elections in neighbourhood assemblies for delegates from parish assemblies, who in turn elected spokespeople for the CMPPP. Two-thirds of the delegates from organised society came from the communities; the rest were representatives of unions, businesses, professional associations, and organisations of sports, culture, and human rights.[37]

The CMPPP never achieved real importance. Like the CLPP, they were submitted to partisan logic and were in practice dysfunctional. In the few sessions

---

36 Harnecker 2009, p. 25.
37 OCMPPPC 2006, art. 5–8.

that were realised, there was rarely the necessary quorum, and they typically ended in confrontations between government and opposition partisans. Nevertheless, an interesting structure was developed at the institutional level through the CMPPP. To bring together social, economic, and infrastructural information as a base for planning, the Sala Técnica (ST) was created in March 2005, in accordance with Article 23 of the CMPPP law. The ST supported the production of projects of the organised communities, though in general its work was not well defined, so that between employees and department heads there was no unanimity regarding duties. The majority of ST employees were grassroots activists who worked *ad honorem*, receiving minimum-wage compensation. At the beginning of 2006, the ST had 230 employees. At first, it concentrated on building networks of activists in the barrio and the CC, before the CC law was passed. In this way, it did important pioneering work. At the beginning of 2006, the work was assumed by the new administration of the Greater Mayoralty and the ST concentrated on its other tasks. The number of personnel of the ST was gradually reduced, with the majority of employees moving over to work in other institutions.

1.4 The Municipal Constituent

The Municipal Constituent is a local constituent process that emerged after the approval of the Constitution, and is derived from Articles 62, 70, 132, 158, 182 and 184.[38] In the wake of the Vargas Mudslide,[39] with local elections coming up, the CNE argued that it would be impossible to organise a referendum on Municipal Constituents, and the process was forgotten; but in 2004/5, it was restarted from below and took shape in a few municipalities.

The Municipal Constituent represents a specific approach to territorial self- and co-government:

> It is an experience of collective creation, where the residents of a given municipality, appealing to the methodology of interchange of experiences, debate, and consensus building, through assemblies, workshops, meetings, workdays, forums, conferences, and other activities, establish agreements on integral development of the municipality, determining the normative, organisational, institutional conditions and the common concepts for a bettering of the quality of life, for optimizing the levels of

---

38 Guariguata 2004, p. 13.
39 The Vargas Mudslide, 15–17 December 1999, caused between 10,000 and 20,000 deaths and left 100,000 homeless.

citizen coexistence, and to make possible the democratic functioning of the Local Council of Public Planning (CLPP).[40]

The Municipal Constituent's point of departure is the analysis, accomplished together with municipal officials, of the problems, priorities, and potentials of the organised population, with the goal of producing guidelines for urban policy and administration and, in this way, to go beyond the old, exclusive administrative structures. During this process, municipal officials' and experts' positions are listened to, but the *pueblo* makes the decisions. This transformation of municipal administration is oriented toward changing its way of functioning – its methods, its styles, its institutional organisation, and its employees' ideological-conceptual profile, as well as their position and their action.[41]

The concept has been applied by very few municipalities (including Torres in Lara and Páez in Portuguesa, in 2005), and although President Chávez and other members of the government explicitly praised the model, it found few imitators. In 2007, it was done in Urdaneta (Miranda) and in the local elections of 2008; Municipal Constituents were organised in José Félix Ribas (Aragua), Morán (Lara) and Simón Bolívar (Miranda) in 2009; others were announced by candidates but not carried out. Compared with the 277 of 326 municipalities that the PSUV and its allies won, the number must be considered small. Here once again is an example of the lack of will of constituted power to undergo a transformation and really understand its function as 'public servant'.

The largest, best-known Municipal Constituent was organised in the municipality Pedro León Torres (Lara), which belongs to the city of Carora and vicinity, with some 100,000 inhabitants. After the election of Julio Chávez as mayor in 2004, he and all the institutional department heads discussed and produced, together with the organised population of the 17 parishes of Carora, a revolutionary municipal constitution. The first participatory budget was approved by the CLPP in the 17 parishes.[42] One year later, the base could participate in budget decisions in an even more direct way: all the finances of municipal administration, the money allocated by the state, the financing from the FIDES, and the special allotments, were divided entirely among the 17 parishes, and its use was decided by the communities.[43]

---

40 Guariguata 2004, p. 12. For a detailed description of the stages of the Municipal Constituent, see Guariguata 2004, pp. 16–17.
41 See Guariguata 2004; Hartling 2007.
42 Harnecker 2008, pp. 33–6.
43 Harnecker 2008, p. 34.

Julio Chávez, who in the early 90s collaborated as a civilian with the MBR-200, did not receive the support of the local MVR for his candidacy, running for mayor on the Homeland For All (Patria Para Todos, PPT) ticket instead, which was supported by popular organisations and other small parties.[44] The first year, the population did not take into account the construction and maintenance of highways, so that during the course of the year he had to ask all the parishes and mayoral departments to return some of the money so that some streets could be asphalted.[45] Despite various problems, the process in Carora can be qualified as very successful; some 525 CCs had been constituted by 2009 there, and some of the first initiatives for the building of rural and urban socialist communes emerged there.[46] Today, the CC is the central pillar of the participatory system.

1.5   The Local Work Cabinets in Caracas

Local Work Cabinets (GOL) were established in 2003, and only in Caracas (Libertador). The first budget with popular participation was made in 2004.[47] The GOLs were a mechanism for a participatory analysis of necessities and for a participatory budget from the Administration of Works of the Mayor's Office of Caracas, which is responsible for small infrastructural works and has at its disposition around 1 percent of the mayoralty's total budget. Through the GOL, contracts for work were assigned to community cooperatives. The history of the GOL reveals many of the problems inherent in the two-track construction process. Its failure, or rather its replacement by the CC, demonstrates how the social transformation process is in continuous motion and how its experiences are produced.

The GOL was proposed from below after the 2002 coup, when a network of various popular organisations and independent media directed a letter to Chávez, calling for a radicalisation of the process and promising him full support. Chávez invited the signatory groups to meet with him and proposed that they create a concept to promote participation. The groups, which had debated together about popular power in 2001–2, formulated a concept, and then were called together by the mayor of Libertador, Freddy Bernal, to develop a concrete project within the framework of municipal administration.[48] In May 2003, five

---

44   Harnecker 2008, p. 9.
45   See Hartling 2007.
46   'Comuna Popular Socialista Dr. Hermes Chávez', available at: http://sites.google.com/site/comunasocialista/.
47   See Harnecker 2005b.
48   Harnecker 2005b, p. 7.

people from popular organisations assumed the Administration of Works, and the goal was announced of presenting a 2004 budget formulated from below by the GOL.

The parishes of Caracas were subdivided into six sectors, in each of which speakers for a GOL were selected in open assemblies. An average of 200–300 people participated, many from popular organisations. The weekly meetings of the GOL were open to everyone.[49] From the GOLs of each sector, the Cabinet of Parish Works (Gabinete de Obras Parroquial, GOP) was founded. At the beginning of 2006, there were GOPs in 22 of the 23 parishes of the municipality Libertador.[50] In spite of the low budget, projects were created, priorities were set, and the participants learned about planning a budget; they based their plans not on available finances, but on the needs of the parish.

The GOLs had a certain tendency toward 'self-government of squalor'. This impression was reinforced by the fact that the mayor's office decided, in part arbitrarily, not to finance projects created and approved from below, which had a negative influence on participation: 'when it began it was pretty good, but the projects they came up with started to be thrown out, and the community asked itself, "what are we doing in these spaces, if they don't respect us?"'[51] Participation at the level of the GOL, which in many cases included territories with tens of thousands of inhabitants, was too indirect for the majority of the organised communities, and in 2006 the GOLs supported the formation of CCs, proposing to serve as the coordinating body for CC infrastructure committees. However, the CCs were created, among other reasons, to avoid direct dependence on local administrations, and once they were financed, they took the planning and execution of projects into their own hands. Since the GOLs were already integrated into and subjugated to constituted power, no new function for them emerged.

2 The Communal Councils

> The communal councils … were born in the locale but transcend the locale. We must not limit the communal councils, the communal councils are instruments or tools of constituent popular power … They must confederate or federate to cover a much larger space, so that they can make deep analyses of their communal area, their parish, their area, their ter-

---

49 Harnecker 2005b, pp. 12–15.
50 Ramírez 2006, p. 12.
51 Ramírez 2006, p. 14.

ritory; so that they can make – based on analysis – a plan, a participatory budget and so that they can develop projects of greater reach to elevate their economic, social, and political quality of life. And at the national level, I imagine a confederation of communal councils.[52]

∴

The CC law went into effect in April 2006. Informed by past experiences, especially the CLPPs' failure, CCs were defined as smaller entities and independent institutions. They rapidly became the central mechanism for participation; as such, the CCs were the organisational form on which the greatest expectations were placed, especially by the popular sectors.[53] In June 2015, there were 44,794 CCs in Venezuela.[54]

It is especially interesting that although the CCs emerged from the grassroots, their leading role and their exponential growth were due to the fact that the state supported and disseminated them at the mass level. Chávez presented them publicly at various times before promulgating the law, explaining how they were made up and how they functioned. In concordance with the local actors, he attributed to the CCs and to their autonomy a special significance:

> One of the elements that has to be worked on in depth this year is the popular organisation and the transfer of power to the *pueblo*, and now we have a clear map, which five years ago we did not have ... Constituent power overflowed its space, there was almost no popular, massively deployed organisation. Now there is, we are creating the communal councils ... We have been working up a necessary modification of the Law of Participation ... because in it a grave error was committed, the communal councils cannot be converted – according to the Law – into extensions of the mayoralties, no, that can't be, that would be to kill them ... before they were born.[55]

---

52   Chávez 2007, p. 6.
53   Provea 2008, p. 33.
54   Ministerio del Poder Popular para las Comunas y los Movimientos Sociales (22 June 2015), available at: http://consulta.mpcomunas.gob.ve/.
55   Chávez 2008, p. 19, *Aló Presidente* 246. Hospital Julio Rodríguez, Cumaná, Sucre. 5 February 2006.

The CCs are self-government mechanisms that, by maintaining the pressure of constituent power on constituted power, play an important role in what as of 2007 was being called the 'new geometry of power',[56] referring to the formal geography of, and the form of power relations in, Venezuelan democracy.[57] This concept is based on the recognition that the country's geometries of power are highly unequal and anti-democratic, and that its territorial geopolitics need to be reorganised.[58] With the advent of the CC, those who previously had no say, like rural and urban marginal communities, now have more of a voice, and the form of participation has changed from individual, representative, and passive to collective, direct, and active.

The CCs were created principally in popular sectors. Many in the opposition, doubtful about the CCs' participatory content and decentralising effect, have supposed that they serve for political control and for the dismantling of liberal-democratic institutions. However, the idea was picked up in some middle-class opposition circles; in Caracas, Maracaibo and Valencia, CCs emerged from the old Citizen Assemblies formed by the anti-Chávez opposition.[59]

The questions that are thus outlined for analysis of the local council forms, and especially of the CCs, are:

- To what point is wide participation really being promoted by the CCs?
- What effect have the CCs had on communities, coexistence, and the conditions of life?
- Are the CCs the seed of a potentially new structure of social organisation parallel to the state, or are they subordinate to it?
- Can the CCs emancipate themselves from constituted power?
- Do they have the potential for that in their constitutive process and in their way of working?
- Where do we find the problems and conflicts between constituent and constituted power?

---

56 The 'new geometry of power' is a concept supported in the debates of radical geography or social geography, as it is called by Anglophones and Francophones, respectively. It was the fourth of the five 'motors' proposed by Chávez to relaunch the dynamic of the transformation process in 2007 and considered as basic axes of the Simón Bolívar National Project. For more on the new geometry of power, see Di Giminiani 2007.
57 Massey 2009, pp. 20–1.
58 See Di Giminiani 2007.
59 García-Guadilla 2008, p. 129.

2.1   The Genesis of the CCs

The founding of CCs began in some regions in mid-2005, although without an authorising law.[60] The need for such a law emerged through 'street parliamentarianism', a term for the MEP practice of organising participatory public assemblies to discuss and draft legislation. Eduardo Daza, in 2005–6 a worker at the Sala Técnica of Caracas, tells how that institution began to support the founding of CCs as of 2005 and how those experiences influenced the law:

> It's not that the president said, 'here's a new law, from now on it's going to be like this.' It wasn't like that, we went all the way to the National Assembly to fight for the law of communal councils and though many of the demands we made were not incorporated into the law, nevertheless, the law let us take the first step.[61]

Shortly after the law was approved, a debate developed over it, which led to a reform proposal by the Permanent Commission of Citizen Participation, Decentralisation, and Regional Development of the National Assembly in May 2009. After intense discussions with the CCs, the new law was approved, with changes, on 26 November.

The April 2006 law specified that CCs were to be autonomous bodies of popular power:

> The communal councils in the constitutional framework of participatory and protagonistic democracy, are bodies of participation, articulation and integration between the various community organisations, social groups, and citizens, which permit the organised *pueblo* to exercise directly the detailed work of public policies and projects oriented to respond to the necessities and aspirations of the communities in the building of a society of equality and social justice.[62]

The CCs were empowered to develop and execute projects, receive and administer finances directly from the state and its institutions, avoiding in this way economic dependence on local administrations.[63] Participation and self-

---

60   For example, in the municipality of Sucre (Zulia) with 60,000 residents, where 32 CCs had been formed by the end of 2005 (Romero Pirela 2007, p. 126).
61   See I-ED 2007.
62   LCC 2006, art. 2.
63   The creation of a specific CC law made it necessary to change other laws in effect. With the reform of the law of municipalities (LOPPM 2005) on 6 April 2006, the Parish Councils

government were limited by law to a very reduced local level. The only possibility for greater reach that was contemplated was the formation of commonwealths (*mancomunidades*) by a few adjacent CCs. In practice, nevertheless, much more extended coordinations occurred; in the state of Falcón, for example, a network of some 400 CCs was formed based on a pre-existing network of Water Committees.

The CCs skip over all the intermediate levels between central government and communities. To support, register, coordinate, and finance them, the Presidential Commissions of Popular Power (CPPP) were created at the national level and in each state soon after the passage of the law.

> In very few months a dynamic of changes and expectations was generated that had an important organising and mobilising effect. Both the mechanisms for their constitution, as well as the procedures for the formulation of projects and obtaining of resources, have been simple and fluid, with few bureaucratic mediations.[64]

Many communities began to discuss their problems and needs, formulate their own solutions, and administer their projects. This strengthened the social networks and the culture of participation in the communities.[65] The acceleration of the processes, however, also favoured the manipulation of CCs, which were subjected to individual and group interests or received financing without obtaining sufficient training or support.

In January 2007, Chávez convened a special high-level commission to coordinate the work of various ministries in order to further promote the creation and development of the CC. The National System of Training (SNA), which organised training courses for public employees, developed a modular training course for CCs and a system of technical support for the formulation of projects. In July 2007, the National System of Technical Support for the CC (Sinatecc), which belonged to FIDES, began offering consultancy and support for CCs in all the stages of their work, installing a telephone information service and an internet discussion forum.

---

were eliminated, along with the reference to the CCs as bodies of the CLPP. The CLPP law was reformed on 14 November 2006, eliminating Article 8, which defined the CCs as bodies of the CLPP (Diniz and López 2007, p. 193).

64 Lander 2007, p. 77.
65 Lander 2007, pp. 77–8.

2.2 Makeup and Structure

The base of the communal council is the community, defined as:

> the social conglomerate of families, citizens who live in a given geographical area, with shared history and common interests, who know and interact with each other, use the same public services and have similar needs and possibilities: economic, social, urban, and others.[66]

The territory of the community can thus be decided only by a constituent assembly. The CCs are formed in urban zones with 150–400 families;[67] in rural zones they are made up of around 20 families, and in indigenous regions 10 families. In reality, the numbers are flexible, and some CCs are larger or smaller.

The basis of the CC, and its only decision-making organ, is the citizens' assembly, to which all residents over the age of 15 belong.[68] Its executive organ is made up of a spokesperson from each community work committee, five members of a financial procedures entity, and five members of a social auditing team.[69] Work at all levels of the CC is *ad honorem*. Candidates can only be elected to a single organ of the CC for a term of two years, and can be re-elected or revoked at any moment by the community. Spokespeople cannot make decisions. The only decision-making organ, the assembly, decides what committees make up the CC, which can vary according to community needs. There could be, for example, the health committee, the MTA, the CTU committees for environment, culture, sports, youth, seniors, popular economy, education, social development, food supply, housing, infrastructure, habitat, justice of the peace, security, defence, community radio, or whatever else the community decides. The executive organ is tasked with planning and articulating organised community participation. The financial entity is the administrator and executor of resources (and of the communal bank, a structure by which the community can offer credit on favourable terms, according to its priorities). The community social auditing group, on the other hand, is tasked with revis-

---

66 And 'indigenous communities: human groups formed by indigenous families associated among themselves, members of one or more indigenous pueblos, which are located in a given geographical space and organised according to the appropriate cultural norms of each *pueblo*, with or without modifications coming from other cultures' (LCC 2006, art. 4).

67 See LOCC 2009.

68 Passive and active electoral privileges for the CC, with the exception of candidates for finance and comptroller's office, who must be 18 or older (LCC 2006, art. 6; 13; 14).

69 Social auditing (*contraloría social*): control of the proper use of finance and execution of projects by organised society.

ing and supervising the management of income.[70] The structure of the CC is also supported and promoted by different governmental institutions and popular organisations.

As a first step in the makeup of a CC, a provisional promotional team of community volunteers is organised. This team convenes a citizens' assembly to elect an official promotional commission and an electoral commission, conducts a demographic community census, and convenes (in a lapse no greater than 30 days after its founding) a citizens' assembly, which – with the minimum participation of 10 percent of the population above 15 years of age in the respective community – elects an official promotional commission and an electoral commission.[71]

The promotional commission informs the community about the reach, meaning, and goals of the CC. It produces a map of its geographic zone, collects information about its history, and conducts a demographic and socioeconomic census. No more than 90 days after its founding, it convenes a community constituent citizens' assembly to elect CC committee spokespeople, members of the financial entity, and the social auditing team. This step also confirms the territorial definition made during the previous process. Once the CC is constituted, the promotional commission is dissolved.[72]

The electoral commission organises and conducts the election of spokespeople and other members of the CC organs. It is made up of five community residents, elected by the community with a quorum required of 20 percent of community members over 15. Members of the electoral commission cannot be CC officers. Indigenous communities elect CCs in accordance with their practices, customs and traditions.[73] Each CC has its own by-laws and as of 2009 must register with the Regional Office for Citizens' Participation of the Ministry of Communes, delivering its by-laws and constitutive act as approved and signed by its citizens' assembly. (Prior to that, it had to register with Fundacomunal, and prior to 2006 before the Local Presidential Commission of Popular Power).[74] Once the CC is constituted, the electoral commission is dissolved, and the 'communal power cycle' begins.

The first step in this cycle is a socioeconomic analysis of its area, to detect problems, needs, and strengths of the community. The committees collaborate to create a communal plan that defines the communal projects for which the

---

70 See LCC 2006.
71 See LCC 2006, art. 15.
72 See LCC 2006.
73 Ibid.
74 See LCC 2006; LOCC 2009.

CC will solicit financing, with proposals for the short-, medium-, and long-term that have to be approved by the community assembly. The debate over priorities continues in the participatory communal budget. Immediately the execution of works begins, or, when there is external financing, as soon as it has arrived. Projects are supervised by the social auditors during execution and after termination.[75]

During the first year, the support of the Presidential Commissions of Popular Power (CPPP) were important to the CC. The national CPPP, appointed by Chávez, was responsible for orienting, coordinating, and evaluating the CC at the local, regional, and national levels. It channelled necessary technical, financial, and non-financial support to the CC and trained promotional teams. Its members included representatives of the ministries and institutions that had the most contact with CCs, representatives of the president, intellectuals, political activists, and a representative of the CC.[76] The national CPPP appointed the regional CPPP. The local CPPP, contemplated by the law, were never created.

The CPPP were dissolved in 2007. Their tasks were assumed principally by the Ministry of Participation and Social Development (Ministerio de Participación y Desarrollo Social, Minpades), and, as of 2009, its successor the Ministry of Communes, Fundacomunal (Foundation for the Development and Promotion of Communal Power), Safonacc (National Autonomous Fund Service) and Sinatecc (National System of Technical Support for the Communal Councils). Although the CPPP did not come from the bases, and were not structured in a democratic way, they indisputably opened spaces for the bases, making possible what the CLPP did not. Without it, the massive support for the CCs would probably have remained entangled in institutional bureaucracy, partisan interests, and political power games.

2.3   *Rigid Law and Flexible Praxis*

Although the rush to pass a law authorising the CC made for errors,[77] the communities nevertheless appropriated the CC concept and adapted it to their needs, in the process of which several of the concerns expressed with respect to the law were shown to be exaggerated. Though the steps for forming a CC and its duration are fixed precisely by law, they are managed more flexibly in practice. Especially in urban sectors, more assemblies had to be organised, and

---

75   See FONDEMI 2007.
76   See I-MU 2006; I-AD 2006.
77   See I-ED 2007; I-EL 2007; I-MH 2007; for a presentation and detailed critique of the law, see Romero Pirela 2007.

the process of creation took longer, than the law contemplated.[78] The temporal extension of the processes often leads to a more solid base for the CC, but not if it is caused by external factors – of bureaucratic origin, for example – in which case it can lead to frustration. The communities' more flexible approach is often accepted by the corresponding institutions, although questions of complying with formalities are also a cause of widespread conflict.

The practice clearly departs from what the law specifies. This was confirmed by Luz Carrera, director of the Political Secretariat of the Mayor's Training Commission in 2007–8, and I could verify it during my work in a support and training programme by community activists of some 150 CCs in Caracas. In most cases there is usually more than one information assembly for the community, and it can take up to ten assemblies to consolidate even a small group. The promotional commission generally continues working, given that it has been structured as a team and has some experience, and also prepares the electoral phase, while the electoral commission often limits its work to preparing the specific election. The candidates are not presented on election day, but are sought and chosen from the community beforehand. The urban CCs elect almost no spokespeople in assembly, but have election days, with ballots and urns.[79] Not only does this achieve a higher electoral participation, but it also increases the legitimacy of the CC in the community; the election assumes importance for the population and frequently becomes a social event for community participation, with food, music, and drinks.

The CC reform law was passed by the National Assembly on 26 November 2009 after being publicly discussed in many CCs, which contributed their observations. The minimum number of families needed to create an urban CC was reduced from 200 to 150. The communal banks, which had to be formed as cooperatives, were replaced with a communitary administrative and financial entity, composed of five elected people;[80] the entities of the CC, which previously had no coordination, now form a community coordination collective (art. 24–6); and the spokespeople coordinate in the executive entity (art. 27–9). Clear rules are defined for revoking spokespeople (art. 38–40). The manner of elections did not change in the new law, but the electoral commission now has a term of two years and organises all electoral processes as well as those of revocation of the CC.[81]

---

78 See I-LC 2007; Parada 2007.
79 See I-LC 2007.
80 LOCC 2009, art. 30–2.
81 LOCC 2009, art. 36.

Many of the weaknesses of the 2006 law were overcome with the new law, but some problematic aspects continue to be in force. Contrary to the Constitution and to the first draft that was discussed, the decisions of the citizens' assembly are not explicitly binding on the authorities in general. Moreover, the law is unclear whether some level of government might have the ability to reject CC projects. The quota of financing not obtained is approximately one third, often without a clear reason. (This is especially the case with projects financed by local government and other non-central government institutions). The new law establishes that state organs and entities must privilege CCs' demands and the satisfaction of their needs. This includes taking the CCs into account during formulation, execution, and control of all public policies, privileging their allotment of public finances, and giving them preference in the transference of public services.[82]

2.4 Financing and Financial Administration

A way to finance CCs by means of mobile cabinets was created in 2004, with a maximum of 30 million bolívares (approx. US $14,000).[83] This small amount, intended for urgent measures in the communities, was raised to 120 million bolívares in June 2007. For these mobile cabinets, Chávez mobilised ministers and representatives of different institutions in certain regions to whom CC delegates could present their projects directly. This provided some interesting encounters, since the grassroots then had the possibility of directly criticising the work of the ministers, governors, and mayors, counting on the support of Chávez and the government.[84] But because of the large logistical effort entailed, it was clear from the outset that mobile cabinets would only be a temporary solution.

For direct financing of projects, the CC law created the national fund Safonacc, assigned to the Ministry of Communes in 2009, and tasking the state foundation Fundacomunal with the operative administration of finances.[85] In 2008, the Safonacc financed 11,752 CC projects nationally, for a total of 4.74 billion BsF, and the Mission 13 of April financed 46 projects for a total of 305 million

---

82   LOCC 2009, art. 59.
83   The rate is fixed: 2,150 Bs = US $1; as of 2008, the new bolívar fuerte (BsF) was fixed at 2.15 BsF = US $1. In 2013, the bolívar fuerte was devalued to 6.30 BsF = US $1 (for importations of primary necessity) and a higher second exchange rate (for the rest), with a third, free-floating rate added in 2015.
84   See I-MH 2007.
85   See LCC 2006, art. 28–9.

BsF.[86] Other financing, which could not be quantified with statistics, came from municipalities, regional governments, ministers, and the PDVSA. CCs received two billion bolívares (about US $930 million) for projects in 2006 and about six billion (about US $2.79 billion) in 2007.[87]

Communal banks were also set up by means of the Developmental Micro Fund (FONDEMI), created via a 2001 law, which advises communities on the construction and administration of communal banks, and on the creation of projects and structuring of cooperatives. These banks do not exist as physical institutions, but as exercised functions. In general, they were administered by several CC units grouped in commonwealths (*mancomunidades*), receiving from 300,000 to 600,000 BsF to deliver credits, with favourable conditions, in support of socially productive projects in the community. Projects must emerge from the community, which evaluates them and makes decisions in assemblies about the urgency and utility of the projects presented and the creditworthiness of the recipients. The first two months of credit is interest-free, after which a rate of interest is charged at a much better rate than commercial banks offer, though the majority of those who request credit from FONDEMI are not in any case eligible for commercial credit for want of sufficient collateral. The decision about projects rests with the communities, but nevertheless, FONDEMI is oriented toward productive projects and does not finance, for example, hair or cyber salons or the sale of lottery tickets. If FONDEMI does receive proposals of this type, it does not simply reject them, but tries to advise and reorient the presenters. The control of execution of the projects is in the communities.[88]

Resources for the CC come from the Republic; regional governments and municipalities; the FIDES (decentralisation funds); the administration of public services that have been transferred pursuant to the Law on Special Economic Allocations for States and Municipalities and the Metropolitan District (LAEE); and from private resources coming from private activities or donations.[89] All decisions about financial resources have to be approved by the citizens' assembly and reported in a protocol that has to be signed by a simple majority of those attending the assembly. Social auditors and other community members have to be able to have access to financial documents at any time.

To make possible a direct, obligatory funding of the CC, the laws regarding FIDES and LAEE were changed in March 2006. The FIDES law, passed in

---

86   Prensa Safonacc: '11.752 proyectos financiados a Consejos Comunales en el 2008', available at: http://190.202.111.174/index.php?option=com_content&task=view&id=32&Itemid=28.
87   Romero Pirela 2007, p. 150.
88   See I-MU 2006.
89   LCC 2006, art. 25; LOCC 2009, art. 47.

1993 and reformed on various occasions, serves to achieve decentralisation and solidary interterritorial financial balance among the states, municipalities, the district capital, the Alto Apure district, and – after the reform law – the CC. 15 articles were annulled and almost the entire text was rewritten. The distribution of finances was re-established: 42 percent (previously 60 percent) to the states, 28 percent (previously 40 percent) to municipalities and districts, and 30 percent to the CC. For additional monies not foreseen in the budget, 30 percent goes to the states, 20 percent to municipalities and districts, and 50 percent to the CC. In the LAEE, the sums were adjusted to the law of FIDES.[90] This signified a decisive rebalancing of public administration in favour of protagonistic participation of the organised *pueblo*.

For financial administration, the old law contemplated the creation of a communal bank, which was not identical to the communal banks promoted by FONDEMI. It could also be formed by various CCs and had the legal form of a cooperative. As could be quickly confirmed, compliance with all the requirements in the law of cooperatives was made very difficult for most of the communal banks.[91] In practice, monies were also transferred through other legal cooperatives and persons. With the new law, the communal banks were replaced.

Moreover, the possibility exists of transferring functions and services from municipalities and regional governments – including necessary resources – to the CCs, if they desired and were in a condition to assume them. The state telephone company CANTV, renationalised in 2007, builds 'technological platforms' from which internet and landline connections are brought to communities. The state-owned PDV chain of filling stations is passing the administration of single gas stations to CCs. MERCAL (the state company for subsidised food and basic goods) began, at the beginning of 2008, to build 'Mercalitos' administered by the CC; PDVAL (the national food supply network) did the same with its 'PDVALitos'. PDVSA (the state-owned energy company) transferred to the communities the administration of new filling stations and distributors of liquid gas for cooking. With this measure, PDVSA delivered directly to the communities, removing commercial intermediaries and lowering the end-user price to at least 20 percent of the old price.

---

90   Diniz and López 2007, pp. 194–7; The name was changed to the 'Law of Special Economic Allotments Derived from Mines and Hydrocarbons', after formerly being the 'Law of Special Economic Allotments for the States and the Caracas Metropolitan District, Derived from Mines and Hydrocarbons'.

91   See I-MH 2007.

2.5 Projects

A distinction is generally made between infrastructural, socially productive, and social projects. Infrastructural projects consist of such works as remodelling or building houses, stairs in the barrios, water mains and sewage, or sporting or other facilities for common use. Socially productive projects aim at initiating a productive enterprise in the solidarity economy. Social projects are culturally oriented or are directed toward groups with specific needs.

In the initial phase, the communities took advantage of the CCs to solve immediate problems, principally those of infrastructure and basic services. These projects provided fast, visible successes, which increased the momentum of collective participation.[92] Over the course of 2008, there was an increasing tendency toward socially productive projects.

Of the 6,822 projects financed in 2006 by mobile cabinets, 4,890 were for infrastructure.[93] Of the 1,138 CCs that filled out the Foundation Centro Gumilla (FCG) questionnaire in 2008, 33 percent had developed projects to fix or build homes. 21 percent had projects for drinking water and sewage, 15 percent road building or repair, 14 percent electrical grid projects, 13 percent construction of sports facilities, 12 percent the construction or purchase of a communal house for the CC and the repair of schoolhouses, 10 percent (especially in the barrios) projects to repair paths and stairs connecting houses, and 4 percent for plazas and parks. 13 percent had not created any project. 4 percent presented microcredit projects, and 3 percent for support of the disabled, *casas de alimentación*,[94] and educational courses; 6 percent declared 'other projects'.[95]

In the 73 percent of the CCs questioned by the FCG, the projects emerged from an agreement between the CC and community; 8 percent had come exclusively from the CC.[96] In general, the CCs seemed to be well rooted in the communities and the interest in their projects was great. 66 percent of the projects were approved by the communities unanimously; in 27 percent of cases, a part of the community disagreed.[97] In 69 percent of cases, the concrete formulation of the projects was the committees' responsibility, and

---

92 FCG 2008, p. 32.
93 Romero Pirela 2007, p. 142.
94 *Casas de alimentación* are houses where free food is cooked for distribution to poor people. Through government programmes, almost one million people get free balanced food from Monday to Friday.
95 FCG 2008, p. 32.
96 FCG 2008, p. 33.
97 FCG 2008, p. 34.

was generally assumed by small groups, made up of the most active people in the community, who in general were the same people who also held offices in the CC.[98]

According to the law, all the CCs were required to have a social auditor as an elected body, to inspect their projects. In reality, only 78 percent of projects were reviewed by social auditing. 15 percent declared that there was no social auditor. Nevertheless, given that 42 percent of them did not execute projects either, only 8 percent of projects did not have social auditing. Other motives cited were lack of organisation (5 percent), lack of community participation (6 percent), lack of awareness (6 percent), accounts were not presented (4 percent), there was no social auditing (3 percent), other reasons (23 percent), and no answer/don't know (13 percent).[99] It would appear that problems existed in the community control of projects, although given the short time that the CCs had been in existence, 78 percent under social auditing could be considered high.

The CCs demonstrated a high level of reliability and responsibility in relation to projects carried out. 73 percent were executed according to the community's plan. Given the scale of activities and the number of people involved, the percentage is high (and probably superior to the rate of compliance of institutional projects). In 16 percent of cases, the projects were not executed as planned, and 12 percent of those polled did not respond.[100] 58 percent of the CC had already received financing and 35 percent had not yet. The FCG poll confirms another frequent complaint of the CCs: of the 656 CCs that had received financing, only 54 percent obtained it on schedule.[101] The slowness or non-delivery of the money has various causes, which ranges from institutional inefficiency to intentional sabotage.[102]

In Caracas, for example, the Greater Mayoralty in 2008 offered financing for socially productive projects and issued a call to the CCs to elaborate projects. After the CCs had discussed the projects in their communities, the Mayoralty limited the financing to certain classes of projects. This provoked much disgust in the CCs, and many had to reformulate their projects. Finally, various projects that corresponded to the Mayoralty's guidelines were not financed.[103]

---

98 FCG 2008, p. 35.
99 FCG 2008, p. 44.
100 FCG 2008, p. 53.
101 FCG 2008, pp. 37–8.
102 Harnecker 2009, p. 33.
103 This was the case with at least three recycling projects in the 23 de Enero barrio.

Some CCs reacted by presenting compliant projects, while others negotiated a redirection of financing after having obtained it.

Some authors warned that CCs with oppositional orientation would have more difficulties obtaining financing.[104] In the face of the large number of cases of delayed or non-delivered funding, and the small number of CCs analysed by these authors, their conclusions are questionable. Although in the polarised political situation of Venezuela one cannot exclude the possibility that oppositional CCs would be obstructed or denied, the contrary is also possible.[105] The CC in the well-off neighbourhood of El Hatillo, for example, had difficulties with an opposition mayor. In the rural and poor zones of the municipality, there were already 17 CCs with socially productive and infrastructure projects by the end of 2006.[106] The FCG emphasised in its survey that it could not find any difference in financing between different socio-economic areas (which also tend to correspond to different political preferences).[107] After the December 2008 regional elections, there were several institutional and street attacks against CC structures in states where the opposition won. In Miranda, the new opposition governor tried to strip several CCs of their infrastructures.

The experiences of planning, application, and implementation of projects were mostly positive, although – especially on the institutional side – there could be serious problems. In particular, the delay and withholding (for whatever reason) of financing represented a disregard that could lead to frustration and decreased participation. But it also demonstrates how the conflict between constituent and constituted power has migrated into the institutions, within which projects are developed for funding at one institutional level, but thwarted and rejected at another.

2.6 Decentralisation or Centralisation

The CCs' independence from local institutions has been criticised from the liberal point of view, which sees CC independence as an interruption of the communication channels between communities and municipalities.[108] As the CCs

---

104 Córdova 2008, p. 38; García-Guadilla 2008, p. 141.
105 Opposition-oriented CCs frequently do not have enough participation to meet the official registration requirements, because that is not part of their political orientation. In several cases, neighbours' associations of AD tried to recycle themselves as CCs. Opposition-oriented CCs also show less willingness and persistence in the pursuit of government support, while for local and regional opposition administrations the CCs are not a priority.
106 See I-ED 2007.
107 FCG 2008, p. 54.
108 Lovera 2008, pp. 115–16.

do not depend on municipal administration and funding is awarded without mediation by local and regional administrations, decentralisation is not promoted, but instead the autonomy of the municipalities is reduced.[109] According to liberal critics, the decentralisation contained in the Constitution has been abandoned in favour of a new centralisation.[110]

Lack of coordination also represents a danger, because although the needs of the city's fragmented spaces are legitimate, communities may not be aware of the influence they have at a wider territorial level. Moreover, communities cannot address other needs that go beyond the community space. Therefore, according to the liberal critique, multiple administrative levels like those of liberal democracy are needed.[111]

Observation confirms the existence of competition between CCs and local administrations and that the formally non-existent level of mediation makes coordination difficult. However, this criticism ignores the fact that local and regional levels of public administration are the levels where client relations are most widespread, because of a strong link to power factors and local and regional interests. The CLPP experience demonstrated the difficulties of strengthening participation when it remains under the control of local government, and in other programmes it can also be seen how the mechanisms of local participation implemented by the central government work better than those under the responsibility of local and regional authorities.[112] The municipalities belong to institutions that most try to influence the CCs and present the greatest obstacles to their development.[113]

2.7   *Development, Situation, and Contradictions*

The CCs have been defined as a body of popular power, though assessments vary as to whether they can realise that status. The CCs are very different from each other, depending on local historical experiences of organisation, activism, education, access to information, and political orientation.[114] However, the fact that in 2015 there were more than 44,000 CCs demonstrates that with the community, the appropriate dimension to promote participation has been found.[115]

---

109 García-Guadilla 2008, p. 143; Lovera 2008, p. 118.
110 Banko 2008, p. 178; Lovera 2008, pp. 108–9, 112.
111 Lovera 2008, p. 120.
112 Lacabana and Cariola 2005, p. 28.
113 See I-AD 2006; I-ED 2007; I-MU 2006.
114 Lander 2007, p. 73.
115 With numbers based on an average, Romero Pirela calculates the following numbers for CCs across the country: 23,800 in urban zones, 22,000 in rural areas, and 5,300 indigenous

The social dynamic unleashed by the CC is enormous. Even the human rights organisation Provea, which tends to be very critical of the government's initiatives, affirms that:

> In practice, even when they reflect the polarisation of the country, they seem to be a space for greater plurality ... It is a fact that as a result of them, a larger number of people debate community problems and collectively build possible solutions. While weaknesses can be detected in the citizen assemblies as regards meeting the legally required quorum, in the communities deliberations and decisions are made, as well as advancing oversight processes.[116]

The FCG summarises that in spite of deficiencies and criticisms:

> communities are not only demanding services and satisfaction of needs, but are proposing and realizing solutions. It is the communities themselves who are finding answers to historical necessities ...
>
> Participation in popular social spaces through communal councils permits the maintenance of a local-territorial identity, turning it into a generative epicentre for new forms of participation ...
>
> An emerging change is seen, led by the popular sectors, who are increasingly assuming higher levels of social responsibility while at the same time constituting themselves as citizens.
>
> In the process of obtaining concrete achievements based on the organisation and mobilisation made possible through the communal councils, they are overcoming their lack of confidence in their own abilities, which will allow the retention of these organisational forms over time. This same process will increase the level of political consciousness.[117]

The CCs' strength is in their flexibility. They can be what the community makes of them, though this automatically leads to a very uneven development. In

---

CC (2007, p. 131). At first, it was planned to continue prioritising the constitution of new CCs in 2008. After the defeat of the 2007 referendum for a constitutional reform, it was decided to concentrate on the consolidation of existing CCs.

116 Provea 2008, p. 33.
117 FCG 2008, p. 5.

about half of the country's communities, there is no CC; in other regions, however, communes and even communal cities have already emerged. The process of participation needs to be learned and exercised, while collective and solidarity practices take time to unfold. It is also necessary to overcome old cultural habits, especially that of welfare culture. Public information and debate undoubtedly contribute to the dissemination and successful formation of CCs. Cadres and training are needed in the communities, so advice and support is of great importance, and this is offered by different institutions.[118] 77 percent of the CCs have had some type of advice from institutional officials.[119] Advice is given in all areas, for structuring and registration, participatory project planning, and project formulation, and training centres for popular power are being built with and in the communities.

However, the institutions do not only promote CCs, but also thwart them at the same time.[120] The greatest criticisms from outside the CCs concern the danger of co-optation, bureaucratisation, or a motivation that is primarily economic. The FCG divided the problems facing the CCs, according to the CCs themselves, into three blocs:

(1) Internal dynamics and weaknesses: 34%. Only 9% are problems between members of the CC and only 1% are political differences.
(2) Problems caused by government institutions: 24%.
(3) Lack of community participation: 18%.[121]

It may be noted that the criticism in the literature prioritises different points from those highlighted by the CCs themselves. Also, the emphasis on institutional problems in the talks and interviews would lead one to think that that problem is more central than it is according to the survey. This is mainly due to the fact that internal problems can be resolved by the communities themselves, while problems with institutions tend to produce more anger and frustration, and convey a feeling of helplessness and dependency.

Marta Harnecker summarises the experiences shared by the successful CCs:

> *First:* they have created a collective to set in motion community work that brings together representatives of all community forces who are willing to work for the community. A mainstay of this collective has been

---

118   See I-AD 2006; I-MH 2007; I-ED 2007.
119   FCG 2008, p. 40.
120   Diniz and López 2007, p. 204; I-ED 2007; I-EL 2007; I-LC 2007; I-RD 2006; I-SV 2007.
121   FCG 2008, p. 46.

the natural community leaders, those who stand out for their ability to mobilise. But also those people who represent activities and services to the community have been part of it: the school principal, the Mercal administrator, the doctor, and so on. And also representatives of political and mass organisations.

Second: They have taken into account the cultural traditions of the community, its language, its forms of expression.

Third: They have had a place within the community to assemble.

Fourth: They have expended a minimum of resources to begin their activities, and often the community itself has provided them.

Fifth: Their first meetings have been based on the immediate needs of the people.

Sixth: They began by analysing the situation of the community and the resources it has, both material and human. Some have decided to take a census to see what and whom they can rely on.

Seventh: They have prioritized the problems in accordance with available resources.

Eighth: They have stimulated the creative initiative of their neighbours.

Ninth: Their leaders have been willing to listen to people and take their views into account.

Tenth: Their leaders have avoided falling into paternalistic attitudes and have tried to have the people themselves resolve their problems. They have not imposed guidelines from outside, but have supported local initiatives. This has broken with the political culture of doing only what comes down from on high.

Eleventh: They have created a single work plan and then evaluated how well the plan has advanced and what results can be expected.[122]

To become part of popular power and form the base of a system of councils, as is supposedly the aspiration, the CCs must go beyond their local areas. They must, so to speak, not only be able to fix and build houses in the neighbourhood, but also participate in the debate and decisions about housing policy.[123] With the communes and communal cities, an important step has been taken regarding the potential of participation, one in which the capacity is not limited to the local micro-level.

---

122   Harnecker 2009, p. 22.
123   See I-AA 2008.

2.8 Relationship between CCs and Institutions

One of the most controversial issues is the degree of CC dependence on, or independence from, the central government and the state, implying a danger of co-optation of participation mechanisms that has also come up in other countries.[124] The question of autonomy is central to many activists; without it, there is a great danger of reproducing the state and its practices that prevent the creation of new institutions.

At the centre of the liberal critique we find the direct relation between the CC and the presidency.[125] This, however, must be seen in the context of the contradictory strategy by which the transformation process has been repeatedly deepened. Since there is no mediation of a vanguard, in the sense of a party or other mass organisation, and all possibility of a revolutionary advance by that route is annulled, Chávez assumed that function with a direct connection to the bases.[126] Liberal critics conclude that the CCs only seem to broaden participation, while in reality they signify a co-optation of local organisation by the central state, the effect of which is not to decentralise, but rather to introduce a hierarchical and clientist dependency of the grassroots organisations in relation to the presidency.[127] In this analysis, the CCs become the 'fulcrum of a delegative democracy'[128] and promote exclusion by means of political polarisation.[129] For Córdova, the matter is even simpler: 'For the state to fund directly the implementation of national policies to authorize said participation simply converts these organisations into government structures'.[130] The FCG, which investigated the CCs, verified the contrary: 'The data obtained show a low level of state interference in the dynamics of the com-

---

124 Goldfrank 2001; Schönwälder 1997.
125 Banko 2008, p. 176; Lovera 2008, p. 119.
126 See I-RD 2006.
127 Banko 2008, p. 178; García-Guadilla 2008, pp. 146–8; Lovera 2008, pp. 112, 118.
128 Lovera 2008, p. 108.
129 García-Guadilla 2008, p. 146.
130 Córdova 2008, pp. 33–4; Córdova analyses the CC with a neo-institutional approach, in the context of endogenous development of the CCs in the opposition municipality Lagunillas (Zulia), where different opposition currents and government partisans would have tried to instrumentalise the CCs, even as the lack of organisational culture impeded their creation. Many of the spokespeople were from groups of unemployed men, who brought their problems forward but neglected to build a collective agenda and develop community projects, reproducing the logic of Neighbors' Associations (Córdova 2008, p. 37). It seems strange that Córdova does not consider that these latter could be the reasons for the lack of success of the CCs and not the structure itself.

munal councils, a very positive element that ensures the true independence of these community mediations'.[131]

The risk of a dependent relationship that calls into question the CCs' autonomy has been considered by authors who share a positive evaluation,[132] as well as by institutional promoters of popular power;[133] the relationship, nevertheless, is perceived in a much more complex and contradictory way. In the CCs, various attempts at political and bureaucratic control cross paths. But the CCs, in their majority, have learned to maintain their independence. In the cases where they have not, the fault is mainly due to weaknesses such as the lack of a participatory organisational culture.[134]

The construction of popular power through the CC is an open process. All actors interviewed are optimistic about its development,[135] an evaluation shared by many analysts.[136] Only Antillano is more pessimistic, noting that tension between popular power and state power tends to be resolved in favour of the latter. The problem is in the centrality of the state to Venezuelan society owing to its high capacity for intervention.[137] In fact, state funding is ambivalent: it brings with it the danger of transforming the CC into an administrative body, makes processes of influence-brokering and institutional manipulation easier, and has also led to financial abuse, although the prospect of financing is also a dynamic force in the establishment and development of the CC.[138] Much of the organised population has its own proposals for solving their problems, but does not have the resources, which it therefore requests.[139] And although economic resources might not generate popular power, one cannot give up on decentralising and socialising them; otherwise, any talk of popular power would be mere farce. There is a risk that getting funds could become the main reason for having the organisation. Precisely for that reason, it is necessary to emphasise the whole process, that the 'struggle is for direct democracy of popular power and not for access to sources of funding that can create client relations with the old state'.[140]

---

131 FCG 2008, p. 51.
132 Azzellini 2007a; 2008b; Diniz and López 2007; FCG 2008, p. 10; Harnecker 2009; Lacabana and Cariola 2005; Lander 2007; Lerner 2007; Romero Pirela 2007.
133 See I-ED 2007; I-LC 2007; I-SV 2007.
134 See I-RD 2006.
135 See I-AA 2008; I-AD 2006; I-CLR 2006; I-ED 2007; I-EL 2007; I-LC 2007; I-SV 2007.
136 Azzellini 2007a; 2008; Diniz and López 2007; FCG 2008, p. 10; Harnecker 2009; Lacabana and Cariola 2005; Lander 2007; Lerner 2007; Romero Pirela 2007.
137 See Coronil 1997; I-AA 2008.
138 I-EL 2007; I-MH 2007; Romero-Pirela 2007, p. 129.
139 See I-ED 2007.
140 Soto and Ávila 2006.

The tendency for CCs to be understood as an executive administrative body is stronger in middle-class areas than in barrios or rural areas. In middle-class areas, the CCs sometimes conceive of themselves as technical structures that only deal with implementing projects to improve the quality of life of the community – although, according to García-Guadilla, this is also the case for the majority of the CCs in popular sectors.[141] In her research, García-Guadilla differentiates between the work content of the CCs in popular and middle-class sectors, without preferring one over the other. The difference, however, is crucial, since for the popular sectors, the challenge is to establish basic services collectively and to overcome marginalisation through their own initiative. The opportunity that is presented to them for the first time of a comprehensive, collective improvement of quality of life and future prospects, is inseparably linked to the existing political project. So even a 'technical' use has a different meaning for them, and there exists a different development potential than in the middle-class CCs, for which a technical approach means community improvements that do not concern overcoming marginalisation and which tend not to require collective community participation, nor do they depend fundamentally on the continuation of current policies.

Frank Parada, CC member in the Antímano parish of Caracas responded, on the movement webpage *aporrea.org* to an article by Margarita López Maya that criticised the CCs' supposed dependence on the state and their supposed economicist orientation. The article was debated in the CC to which Parada belonged, where it was noted that 'ours, in particular, does not depend on the state but on the community'.[142] Parada's CC emerged from the community and was based on popular power, so it is one of the CCs that frightens the representatives of the existing inefficient, bureaucratic state. Its institutional experiences have been widely varied. According to Parada, the autonomy question cannot be answered unidimensionally:

> It is very easy to say that everything depends on the Executive, but hard to say that we from our organised communities have the same right to take advantage of our resources and manage them, creating organisational and participatory results, and not only economically, because we did social auditing of other programmes in the community, and this works. We have restructured the urban land committee, the committee of health,

---

141 García-Guadilla 2008, p. 138.
142 The simple fact that an academic article about the CCs was read, debated, and commented on by CC activists in a barrio is evidence of the self-empowering process.

literary workshops are coming. In a population of about 1,400 people, who make up our council, we have delved into the historical origins of our community, and people from ... other countries have come to visit us. Which tells us that if this is not an embryo of popular power, not at all based on economicism, we ask you to please come and explain to us what it is.

When Chávez says the only way to end poverty is to give power to the people, anyone with common sense knows that what the president says ultimately translates into resources. How are we going to advance in building whatever century's socialism if we ourselves are accustomed to having others decide, that is to say, if others manage the money for us? The issue of power is revealed in who manages funding sources.[143]

Another danger lies in political co-optation, insofar as the CCs are understood as structures of the *chavista* base, instead of being understood as an expression of the whole community. These exclusionary dynamics may arise from the community itself or come from outside. According to Garcia-Guadilla, for example, in some cases spokespeople have been pressured to enrol in the PSUV.[144] If the CCs are subjected to the logic and mobilisations of the party, they cannot be community self-government.[145] The problem, however, is smaller than the strong polarisation might lead one to assume. FCG research revealed that 80 percent of CCs admit differing political positions, while 18 percent do not.[146]

More common are attempts at institutional co-optation as political capital; that is, because institutions, mayors, governors, ministers, etc. help constitute, support, and fund CCs, they gain political weight. This is not a widespread or stated policy, but an old practice linked to personal clientist relations.[147] These are in turn partly linked to political currents; however, personalised relationships predominate. Such manipulations are facilitated by the fact that institutions, because of continuous change, are exposed to great pressure to produce results, which also leads to interagency competition.

---

143 See Parada 2007.
144 Garcia-Guadilla 2008, p. 142.
145 See Lander 2009.
146 FCG 2008, p. 26.
147 Some institutions, for example, pressure their employees to participate in governmental mobilisations, including with attendance sheets. In others this does not happen. The practice of different institutions in this regard depends on their directors.

In October 2005, the Greater Mayoralty of Caracas, the government of Miranda, the mayors of the municipalities of Libertador and Sucre (all *chavistas* at the time), and Minpades, formed the 'quadripartite', in which the different actors in Gran Caracas were to agree on common criteria for supporting the CCs, according to which all CC promoters should shape their work. In reality, all the institutions continued to work on their own and with their own criteria, focusing on different elements of the councils and with some promoters looking to create CCs that would be loyal to their own institution.[148]

The competitive relationship between different institutional actors is also a cause of criticism in many interviews with CC advocates and activists. Luz Carrera reports how, as she was working on the formation of a CC with a team from the mayoralty, sometimes promoters from the Libertador mayoralty came around offering workshops to link the CC to them. In the mayor's office alone, between 2006 and 2008, there existed six departments that supported CCs. Some promoters even tried to 'steal away' CCs from other supporting institutions, and this 'crushes the communal council, they lie, they offer things they don't deliver'.[149] This has led to some divisions within communities.[150]

Nevertheless, 58 percent of CCs described their relationship with government institutions as good, and 16 percent as excellent, while 16 percent evaluated them as bad, and 5 percent as very bad.[151] Among the CCs that described them as bad or very bad, 52 percent (and in the Capital District, 65 percent) cited lack of institutional response as a cause. 7 percent criticised the lack of dialogue, and another 7 percent cited institutional obstruction. Only 5 percent indicated poor organisation of the CC as a reason.[152] The question, however, is too general, since given the number of institutions with which the CCs must deal, most have had both positive and negative experiences.

Two main options for the future development of the CCs are outlined: Will the popular organisational processes be able to gradually increase their autonomy and self-organisation, or will their relations with funding institutions be vertical and clientistic? Within this tense field, it will be decided whether the transformation process in Venezuela will be vertical and state-centric or plural, democratic, and autonomous.[153]

---

148   See I-MH 2007.
149   See I-LC 2007.
150   See I-ED 2007; I-LC 2007.
151   FCG 2008, p. 18.
152   FCG 2008, p. 19.
153   See I-EL 2007.

2.9   CCs and Popular Movements

The relation between the CCs and the previously existing forms of popular organisation (for example, CTU, MTA, and others) is complex. These organisations often played a central role in creating the CCs, although initially some organisations feared a loss of autonomy because resources would be channelled mainly to the CCs.[154] There exists the danger that the CCs would be seen as the only local organisational body, leading to attempts to subordinate them to the other organisational forms.[155] Such a development would be fatal, given that the plurality of the popular organisation cannot be forced into a single model. But so far this has not happened; the CC committees cooperate with other popular organisations in the areas of work and beyond.[156] Moreover, the possibility exists of funding not tied to the CC, to popular organisations of some other type (community media, for example). In some isolated cases, the contrary problem exists: a strong popular organisation assumes representation of the community, which it does not constitute as such; this has been the situation of some well-organised barrios of Caracas. In some situations, there were problems early in the development of self-organisation processes that did not pass through mediation by existing organisations in the territory.[157]

For liberal critics, 'the Health Committees, the Technical Water Boards, and the Security Committees became dependent on the CCs'.[158] But attachment to the social/political dichotomy while the movements are consciously transgressing the limits of that dichotomy leads to a simplified and erroneous interpretation of the relations between constituent and constituted power. If the community is understood as a whole – as a totality to which also the CCs' activities are directed – then the argument can only be in favour of coordination and democratic decision-making. The committees are only 'dependent' on the assembly with respect to financing their projects. But what could the argument be in favour of the community's not deciding its priorities collectively? The CC is a coordinating body for the community. The danger of co-optation by other entities exists in any coordination and cannot be an argument to reject it, especially when it comes to issues of interest to the entire community.

Like Provea, Lovera warns of a risk of 'wanting to unload on the communal councils ... responsibilities that belong to the state, over almost everything

---

154   I-AA 2008; Lander 2007, p. 78.
155   I-AA 2007; I-EL 2007; I-MH 2007; Romero Pirela 2007, p. 149.
156   Harnecker 2009, p. 30.
157   See I-AD 2006; I-ED 2007; I-LC 2007.
158   García-Guadilla 2008, p. 136.

that has to do with the daily life of people: health, education, environment, defence of sovereignty, control speculation, public safety'; this is decontextualised and wrong. This approach does not consider that the state lacks the ability to provide all these services and jobs, nor do the communities want the state to assume all of that. There is also a fundamental difference between services lent by the state and collective community administration and organisation.[159]

This is not only because of self-organisation and decision-making autonomy, but also with respect to the results, given that nobody knows the communities' needs and circumstances better than they do. There is a risk of the CCs becoming mere administrators of external government and state responsibilities – indeed, that risk is inevitable, given that they are engaged in re-organising state tasks for self-administration.

In the framework of the building of a new society, preserving the separation between political and civil society is explicitly rejected. This can also be observed in the popular movements, and, for example, in the records of the first meeting of the CC belonging to the FNCSB and the FNCEZ:

> We share with comrade President, Commander Hugo Chávez Frías, that for the first time in the history of the republic real power is being placed in the hands of the people ... [A]t the same time, we warn of the dangerous tendency to assume the communal councils as simple planners and executors of works, castrating their real potential as builder of the new society and the new communal state.
>
> We believe that, given the development of class antagonisms that run through the government and the process itself, the right way for us as a *pueblo* of combatants is to build an independent revolutionary current of the base that will conscientiously accompany the President in any initiative tending to build Bolivarian socialism and defeat reformism and counterrevolution.
>
> We as communal councils believe that the most expeditious way to build the communal state is to assume power at the local level, from an economic, political, military, cultural and social perspective; therefore, we must act in a bloc, giving us higher levels of organisation and coordination, it being essential that we constitute a movement that gives us voice,

---

159 Provea 2008, pp. 33, 119.

body and face as communal power, throughout the process of building socialism in Venezuela.[160]

García-Guadilla cites part of the same manifesto and uses it as an example of small groups that existed before the Chávez government, which 'propose the vision of empowerment of the CC and whose objective is to become popular power in order to supposedly build 21st-century socialism'.[161] In this, she underestimates and exhibits little understanding of the role that these groups can and have assumed in the dynamics of the process. Just as the FNCEZ supported the building of the FNCSB for the coordination and support of CCs, communes and communal cities, there are also many other activists and organisations looking to strengthen the CCs. Among them is ANROS, from which several training cooperatives have emerged, which, funded by different institutional sources, are engaged in support tasks for CCs, like the development of and support for productive projects, training, etc., but which continue to be organised outside the institutions. That also gives them the possibility of working without pay in the support of other communities.[162]

The work of ANROS has been important as a previous step to the CCs and is, like the work of FNCSB, very important for their development. In mid-2010, the FNCSB was giving support to some 100 communes under construction; several had even begun to work in a coordinated manner as communal cities. As can be seen in the history of the Bolivarian process, from its origins in the 1960s, the work of the movements, networks and popular organisations has always had a central role.

2.10   Relations between CCs and Communities

From my observations, I conclude that the CCs – and participation in them – develop best in poor, but not highly pauperised, communities. Especially in the popular sectors, most activists are women, and almost no one had social or political organising experience before Chávez's first election in late 1998, and, in most cases, not before the coup of 2003. Most had never participated in elections before 1998.

In the CCs one can observe the participation of so-called 'neither-nors' (*ni-nis*, those neither with the opposition nor with Chávez), who had not participated in previous mass organisation initiatives such as Bolivarian Circles

---

160   See FNCSB and FNCEZ 2007.
161   García-Guadilla 2008, p. 139.
162   See I-SV 2007.

or UBEs (Electoral Battle Units), which were clearly aimed at supporting the Bolivarian process. Some CCs have elected *ni-nis* as community spokespersons, even in areas where Chavismo gets between 55 and 70 percent of the vote. Their active participation in community affairs outweighs their political preference. The political participation of hardcore oppositionists, in contrast, is practically non-existent, which should not be surprising, since their position is adverse to popular power.

The formation of CCs does not always happen smoothly. Especially during the first two to three years, several CCs were formed without real popular participation. At times the community showed little interest in participating, and at best the CC was made up of an active nucleus, acting in the interests of the community, and in other cases by a group that made the CC an instrument for their personal interests. In a barrio of Caracas, I observed a CC, emerging as if by metamorphosis from the former Neighbours' Association of the former governing party AD.

The building of the CC from the community's needs is essential:

> That is: first the functions, then the institutions. This prevents creating institutions *a priori* and then finding functions for them, which gives rise to bureaucracies which, without clear objectives, become an end in themselves, serving only their self-preservation.[163]

The pressure toward bureaucratisation is also evident in the contradictions between social processes and institutional mechanisms of evaluation. The institutions prioritise economic categories, since they are easier to quantify and compare, over socio-political categories, which are central to self-organisation and the transformation process.[164] In other words, a paved road fits better into a chart than a collective process of discussion and decision-making.

The FCG survey reveals that the CCs are understood as an expression of the community. 51 percent described their relations as good, and 20 percent as excellent; but 26 percent also described them as limited, and 2 percent as non-existent, which might indicate a tendency toward the separation of levels: CCs, community, and reproduction of representative mechanisms.[165] Whether the CCs reproduce social polarisation and lead to exclusionary practices in non-homogeneous social spaces cannot be confirmed with the present investiga-

---

163 See Soto and Ávila 2006.
164 See I-HV 2007.
165 FCG 2008, pp. 20–1.

tion, nor with others; quite the contrary. What can be found is exclusion on behalf of economic interests of more or less stable groups (for example, family networks, the former neighbours' associations).[166] With more than 40,000 CCs, it is difficult to avoid having a certain number inoperable in their early stages. In general, this type of usurpation has no success after a while. At the level of the CC, as has been demonstrated, it is much easier for the community to confront these practices, and it can be observed how, over time and with increased activity and interest, new CCs are constituted to replace the old ones.

The 20 percent quorum for community participation in crucial assemblies may seem limited and problematic. Although experience shows that a 20 percent direct participation is a very high rate, higher participation is clearly desirable. In the CCs studied, participation hovered around 40 percent.

For liberal critics, here is a reason to demand the principle of representation. Making binding decisions in assemblies, in which not everyone wants to or can participate, practically compels presence and

> violates the principle of representation. It is the mayors, councillors, and representatives of the *juntas parroquiales* [parish representation] elected in an election of universal suffrage who ultimately must respond to the interests of citizens at the local level and not an assembly that can be minoritarian if there is apathy.[167]

This argument denies any possibility of structural change. Building popular power or self-governing communities becomes impossible, given that participation is reduced to matters that do not fall under the authority of constituted power, or CCs would also have to constitute themselves as representative bodies.

Liberal critics typically do not consider the CC to be autonomous against constituted power, but rather see it as a participatory annex of representation.[168] As a result, the alternatives are strengthening participatory democracy as a complement to representative democracy, or the automatic strengthening of a delegative democracy.[169] The supposed defence of movement autonomy becomes a farce. To build a model of non-representative democracy through CCs, communes, and communal cities, which will replace the existing state

---

166 See García-Guadilla 2008, p. 137.
167 García-Guadilla 2008, p. 144.
168 Ibid; Lovera 2008, p. 121.
169 Lovera 2008, p. 122.

with a new figure, one must overcome the division of the social sphere and the political sphere. In the liberal critique, however, that division is not questioned; it is the parameter for the critique. Thus, its evaluation of the transformation process can only be negative.

2.11 The Appropriation of CCs by Communities and the Question of the State

The communities have appropriated the figure of the CC.[170] The initiative for their creation emerges in 85 percent of cases from the community, with only 7 percent being proposed by institutional representatives.[171] In 84 percent of cases, the community participates in CC activities, and in 81 percent it is the community that approves the projects; while 'approval' by an institution – which is against the law and indicates a total failure of autonomy – happens only in 5 percent of cases.[172]

Many communities have the capacity to defend themselves against takeover, influence, or co-optation, if necessary, including with active resistance:[173]

> We had the experience of a military guard who wanted to form a communal council, but he wanted to choose the members, and peasants came here to denounce him, and there was a confrontation in Maracaibo with stones, sticks, and bottles … The community, the people are not going to let this process be uprooted.[174]

The communities see the CC as their instrument. According to the FCG, 22 percent describe their relations with the CC as very good, 26 percent as normal and only 4 percent as bad or very bad. 55 percent say there are no conflicts in the CC; 43 percent say there are. Of the latter group, 63 percent resolve their conflicts through dialogue, small and large assemblies, and consensus-seeking, 16 percent through more communication, 7 percent through voting, and only 3 percent do not resolve them.[175] With the existence of conflicts and mechanisms to solve them, we can conclude that the CC can be the base entity for participatory and protagonistic democracy and for popular power. Communities use democratic mechanisms of conflict resolution that

---

170   FCG 2008, p. 22; I-AD; I-ED; I-LC.
171   FCG 2008, p. 22.
172   FCG 2008, pp. 23, 36.
173   See I-ED 2007.
174   See I-AD 2006.
175   FCG 2008, pp. 28–9.

they are familiar with. The FCG concludes that the CCs do not in any way strengthen welfarism or paternalism, but that 'on the contrary, and the data speaks for itself, there is a progressive process of protagonisms and popular responsibility in the building of collective responses in the search for a better life'.[176]

The appropriation by communities of the CC form can be seen also from the way they form communes and communal cities by their own initiative. A new institutionalism is being born, whose limits and relations with old institutionality are flexible and are being constantly redefined.[177] The state, which is not external to the process, is involved and pushes the process along, but it coexists with the long-time community demand for self-government. This signifies a profound change in hegemonic power relations and has a direct influence on the state. Iturriza explains:

> If we are truly going to deepen this with a 21st-century revolution in mind, a revolution that does not look like the experience of what we know as actually existing socialism, that necessarily implies a resizing not only of the concept but also of what the state really is ... We may be witnessing the beginning of an experience that implies in large measure a resizing of the state, redistributing its relationship with the popular movement along the way.
>
> There is a phrase of Boaventura de Sousa Santos that I paraphrase, which seems to me fascinating, enigmatic, something we should sit down and think about. He develops the concept of the experimental state and even launches the idea of the state as one more social movement. Could that be possible?[178]

The contradiction between constituted and constituent power is also registered.[179] The strategy is not to oppose popular power to constituted power, but to reach a point at which the latter respects the decisions of the former.[180] The experience of the CC does not necessarily have to be successful, as underlined by Carlos Luis Rivero:

---

176   FCG 2008, p. 6.
177   Lander 2007, p. 78.
178   See I-RI 2006.
179   I-AD 2006; I-CLR 2006; I-ED 2007; I-LC 2007; I-SV 2007.
180   See I-AD 2006.

However the conception tells us that the theme of the New State is linked to the issue of popular power ... Without participation there is no popular power. The state cannot replace people. And you do not replace people at will, it's the relations that lead to replacing people. So that has to be overcome from a practical, concrete point of view.[181]

3   The CCs as a Means of Participation in the Barrios of Caracas

Political and social polarisation is more marked in the complex, complicated space of Caracas than in rural areas and many other cities. Socially, economically, politically, and institutionally, Caracas is a fragmented metropolis; its fragmentation is expressed in unequal access to resources, security, public transport, and many other issues. The changes provoked by the economic and government restructuring of the 90s have had a direct impact on how the city lives with its many uneven territories, and the neoliberal decentralisation has left a Greater Mayoralty that has no competence to implement coordinated policies in the city's five municipalities, which themselves are also totally unequal with respect to area, population and socio-economic status.[182]

The largest municipality, Libertador, officially has 2.1 million residents; not part of any state, it includes the historic centre of Caracas with the central government's administrative structures, as well as the city's west, where the great majority of the city's poor live. The other four municipalities are part of the state of Miranda. Sucre, with 650,000 residents, is situated in the far east of the city and is inhabited mainly by the middle and lower middle class, although it also includes Petare, the city's largest barrio. In the south of Caracas, Baruta has some 320,000 habitantes, with some 80 percent of them belonging to the middle and upper class. Chacao in the northeast and El Hatillo in the far southeast of the city, each have approximately 70,000, most of them middle and upper class. Most of the headquarters of the powerful financial, commercial, and economic companies are concentrated in these latter three municipalities. In the municipal elections at the end of 2008, Sucre and the Greater Mayoralty went over to the opposition. The municipalities governed by the opposition do not see themselves as part of the city and follow their own policies, so that there is practically no cooperation with the municipality of Libertador.

---

[181]   See I-CLR 2006.
[182]   For a detailed analysis of different aspects of Caracas in transformation, see Azzellini, Lanz and Wildner (eds.) 2013.

A high density of CCs is found almost entirely in the barrios and (almost always with more difficulties) in some sectors of the impoverished middle class. The transformation process

> highlights the greatest popular protagonism with social responsibility and citizenship-building within a framework of intense poverty that, despite the precarious living conditions, allows the popular sectors to live not only on the edges of the city but also, in their collective imagination, at the edges of hope. Hope of improving their quality of life and their status as citizens.[183]

The constitutional processes of the CCs, their work, and their effects for the community in two barrios of Caracas are described in what follows.[184] The analysed CC Emiliano Hernández in Los Magallanes de Catia and the CC Unidos por el Chapulún in Baruta are typical of many urban CCs in terms of their social situation and precarious infrastructure, the lack of any organisation prior to 1998, and with the majority of activists being women. In places where the CCs are more advanced, there exists at least a previous experience of popular organisation. Previous organisational experience, however, does not guarantee a more successful CC. If the CCs continue forming as expressions of popular power and with the intention of being foundational for the new communal state, it is of central importance how they are perceived by the

---

183 Lacabana and Cariola 2005, p. 29.
184 In my research, I analysed a total of seven CCs. In addition, I studied a CC in an impoverished middle-class area, and four more CCs in the barrios. The conclusions draw on the results of 25 interviews with spokespersons from 7 CCs. All CCs analysed are, intentionally, not in sectors that had a wide experience of popular organisation before 1998. All those interviewed also provided socio-statistical data via a questionnaire. Respondents lived in households of three to eight members, 15 of them in households of four or five people. The gender division of respondents more or less corresponds to the rate of perceptible participation: 18 women and 7 men. The youngest was 28 and the oldest 63 years of age. The majority, 17 out of 25, were between 36 and 50 years old. It is noteworthy that six of the seven men are either married with families or are single parents. Only five of those interviewed had any political activity before 1998, two in the MBR-200, one in the MAS, one in the Socialist League, and one more as a *chavista*. Most of the other 20 had had no political interest or experience previously. One respondent had attended the Robinson Mission (elementary school), five women had attended the Ribas Mission (middle school), and four women and one man had begun university studies with the Sucre Mission. Three people affirmed that for them life was better ten years ago than today, while for 22 it is better today.

previously not very active majority of poor communities, and what changes the CCs provoke in them.

3.1 The 'Emiliano Hernández' Communal Council, Magallanes de Catia, Caracas

The 'Emiliano Hernández' Communal Council is located in the hills of the popular part of western Caracas. Near the Plaza Sucre metro station, in the zone of Catia, is the stop from which Jeeps loaded with nine passengers set out up the steep roads. At the end of 2006, the community had 438 residents over the age of 15, in almost 200 families. Of the six CC activists I interviewed, only one had any interest in politics before 1998. The community is poor. Before 2002, it was essentially apathetic and had a very bad infrastructure. In 2003, the most serious problems were the lack of a health service, irregular drinking-water service, bad sewage lines, bad sanitary infrastructure in the homes, lack of childcare, practically no access to education beyond elementary school, precarious public transport, and lack of space for community activities. Some of the residents suffered from malnutrition and eleven families had no stable homes or lived in cardboard houses. Average household income was very low. Of six respondents, four lived in households that in 2006 had less than one million bolívares at their disposal. Two were living with a partner and three children, and two more were single mothers with two and four children respectively. Only the two households with men, both with more advanced formal education, one with a small workshop for cars and the other an insurance agent, earned between 2 and 4 million bolívares per month, in households of 4 to 5 people.

Before creating the CC in December 2006, the community achieved the installation of five *casas de alimentación* in their sector.[185] The Robinson Mission was brought to the community, and there existed a CTU, a health committee, a social security and justice committee, and a media users' committee.[186] But the work was mainly carried out by a few activists who participated in various initiatives.

The health committee, founded in 2003, was central for organising the community. The principal promoter of the local organisation, Jacqueline Ávila, was involved in that. Elected as a member of the finance committee with 203 of

---

185 *Sector* describes a territory larger than the CC community, but smaller than the barrio.
186 The users' committees are an element of control of participatory media. Financed by a fund from the National Telecommunications Commission (Conatel), they exercise social control over content, and also organise workshops to increase the capacity for media analysis by the popular strata.

213 votes, Ávila, a single mother of two, left primary school after six years to go to work. She finished high school by attending the Ribas Mission, and in 2007 began to study social management. Before 2002, she had no social or political activities or interest.

The community consists mostly of *chavistas*, and only one of the interviewees was not registered to the governing party MVR in 2006, although none had a positive assessment of the party. The community is politically active beyond specific neighbourhood issues: the users' committee organised in 2006 a community demonstration outside the offices of the private television channel RCTV, against the one-dimensional, anti-government stance of its coverage. There was a massive mobilisation for Chávez's re-election in 2006 and constitutional reform in 2007, which was explained and discussed in the community. These activities are not organised as a CC; nevertheless, almost all the principal activists participated. Even so, one cannot speak of co-optation, but of a rational community decision to support certain government mobilisations. A counterexample is that the community did not mobilise for the 2008 local and regional elections.

Despite its location up in the hills, the community has no security problem – not thanks to the police, who are mistrusted by the community, but because of community social networks. Described as unpredictable and corrupt, the Metropolitan Police (PM, of the Mayoralty) and the Policaracas forces (Libertador) have been accused of attacking, threatening, and even murdering barrio residents. The police betray the community to criminals, with whom they spend time and share interests. In the security committee of the CC, however, are two retired ex-policemen who enjoy the trust of the community. There is close cooperation on security issues with other CCs of the neighbourhood who also have ex-policemen as members of the security committee, and there are direct contacts with the highest levels of security agencies.

Transportation is a major community problem. The Jeep drivers – the so-called *yiseros* – work for a private company. Their service is unreliable, and apart from four *chavistas* among them, the yiseros refuse to transport students for half price and retirees without charge, as prescribed by law. The community also reports that most yiseros participated in opposition 'strikes' and paralysed transport to the neighbourhood. Because of the conflict, the CC refused to endorse the transportation line and its president to receive new vehicles at favourable conditions from the National Fund for Urban Transport Foundation (FONTUR). The possibility of forming a transportation cooperative was discussed in the community from the beginning, but it was not until 2009 that it began to work on the first concrete project.

The first part of this chapter will consider formal and material organisational initiatives of the CC as a body of self-administration, as well as its experiences with institutions, the community, and other CCs. The second part focuses on the process of participation as democratisation of community and social relations, including gender relations, self-empowerment and development of social actors. Finally, the autonomy of the CC is addressed. These points allow, beyond the material improvements, the analysis of the transformative potential of the process.

3.2 *The CC as a Body of Self-Administration*

Even before the CC law was passed, Jacqueline Ávila informed herself about CC, but even so, the preparation process in the community was very long and the election was not held until December 2006. An informal, temporary promotional team centred around her informed the community in turn, with good support from the Fundacomun (later renamed Fundacomunal). The first citizens' assembly was organised with the support of promoters from the Greater Mayoralty, as well as from the mayor of Libertador. Only in the second meeting was the quorum reached, and a promotional committee of five people was elected. For the next 90 days, they undertook a door-to-door census and prepared a proposal in relation to the territory of the community. The community soon perceived a competitive relationship between the two mayoralties, which affected the work on the ground, so after attending a National Assembly workshop on CCs, Ávila headed back to Fundacomun for support.

In another assembly (not in the same one, as the law stipulates it cannot be), on 12 November 2006, with the participation of 100 neighbours, the territory of the CC was approved, and an electoral commission of five members was elected (from 12 candidates) with the sole task of preparing the elections. Existing committees and those yet to be formed were discussed in the assembly and decided on the basis of the community's needs. The CC has committees of health, housing and habitat, sports, education, CTU, seniors, culture, social security and justice, food, MTA, and social auditing and finance. Mobilisation for assemblies and elections was done door-to-door and by walking with a megaphone through the neighbourhood. With teenagers, personal conversations were sought, which proved very effective: they participated because they felt they were being taken seriously. Candidates for the election of spokespeople were proposed by the community weeks before and were known to everyone.

In the elections of spokespersons on 16 December 2006, 213 of the 438 members of the larger community (aged 15 and over) participated. The election was not held during an assembly, but organised as an election day, with ballots that had photos of each candidate. The large turnout surprised activists, and the elections became a community event:

> There were people who never go out of their houses – who don't participate so one thought they were opposition – showing up and asking what do you need, bringing water to people, cookies, sandwiches, leaving a thermos of coffee on the table, many of them made *guarapo* [sugar cane juice] at 3 in the morning, it was such a beautiful participation, so much so that I love the communal council, and I've told everyone, I'm impressed with the enthusiasm that you can see all around.[187]

A spokesperson was elected for each committee, along with five administrators of finance and of social auditing. There were 41 candidates for 20 slots; only eight of them were men, of whom seven were elected. Later on, committees of tourism and communication were also formed. An evangelical church in the community made its house available for small CC meetings, while larger assemblies were held in the open on the street. The community's story is not one of competitive relationships with previous community organisations; rather, those organisations were crucial in founding the CC. Because they all emerged from the framework of the community organisational process, the CC proved to be a later development of what its predecessors had done, at a higher level. The only conflicts were with the sector's youth organisation, Frente Francisco Miranda, whose activists acted arrogantly and wanted to impose ideas of how to organise community work, arguing that they had been trained in Cuba. After a long phase of conflict, the relationship improved.

Relationships among community members as well as with adjacent communities are marked by collectivity and solidarity. If their neighbours have no CC, Emiliano Hernández assumes tasks on their behalf and integrates them actively – as in the case of a community located in the hills above, in which the formation of a CC has been actively prevented by a small group of the opposition party Primero Justicia, who have tried to provoke fights and physical confrontations during assemblies and have threatened activists. The Emiliano Hernández CC made a new census of disabled people in order to integrate a new member of their community and especially the members of the other community. 20 cases needing attention were identified, and support was channelled to them in early 2008.[188]

---

187 See I-JA 2006.
188 See I-JA 2008a.

In its first two years, the CC realised two major projects funded by Fundacomunal, and a number of smaller initiatives financed by different institutions. Fundacomunal did not reject any project, although the approval and delivery of financial support were delayed heavily. On the other hand, the project of a small sports court was rejected by the Greater Mayoralty as too costly after evaluation by an engineer. The CC got the approval of the mayor of Libertador, but then the support never materialised. In late 2008, the first steps were taken to set up a CANTV technological platform,[189] although the first informational assembly took place only in August 2009. The social auditing of works projects is a functional process, and together with other CCs, it even extends over municipal administration projects in the barrio; as, for example, with the repairing of a main street that had partially sunk. The repairs were taken charge of by a cooperative from another nearby CC, commissioned by the municipal administration, which also made available an engineer.

The community lacked a space for collective activities. As in most barrios of Caracas, the houses are small and attached to each other on the steep hills, gaps hardly exist, and public buildings are non-existent. In addition to the main road, the neighbourhood is interconnected with stairs and paths. For this reason, the acquisition of a community house was a priority. The community wanted to buy a house for sale at 70 million bolívares from a family that moved away in 2006. They requested funding from the mayor of Libertador, who would neither pay more than 45 million nor accept the proposal of the community, which wanted to put the rest under its own power.[190] In late 2006, the community invited the director of Fundacomun, which declared its support. After another eight months, the community received 124 million bolívares, three more than it had asked for. Meanwhile, the price of the house had gone up to 90 million bolívares. The community bought the house and fixed it up with voluntary work, putting in new doors, chairs, computers, and a photocopier.

In April 2008, the CC asked Fundacaracas (the infrastructure fund of Libertador) for construction materials to build a second floor to the communal house, with the intention of using it as a cultural salon for children's dance groups, a musicians' rehearsal and presentation space, and other cultural activities. For the cultural work, they linked to the National Culture Commission (CONAC).

---

189 Connection point for household telephone and internet service provided by the state-owned telecommunications company Compañía Anónima Nacional Teléfonos de Venezuela (CANTV).

190 See I-JA 2006.

They brought Cuban artists to the community who developed various activities together with the residents. The money for construction materials was approved by Fundacaracas, although subsequently after the institution's director changed, the funding was not awarded; instead, it was communicated to the CC in 2009 that it had to resubmit the project for review.

In early 2007, the CC presented to Fundacomunal a project for the renovation of 100 houses and the construction of 11 to replace an equal number of unstable houses made of cardboard or other precarious material. In August 2007, a mobile cabinet of the presidency approved 3 billion bolívares (about US $1.4 million), which took until June 2008 to arrive. Of this sum, 5 percent is for operating expenses and 2 percent for administrative expenses. 1 percent remained in the Communal Bank as an emergency fund. The assembly prioritised replacing the cardboard shacks. Construction plans contemplated an area of 70 square meters, but in consultation with the project architect, the houses were built a little larger, depending on the space available. The CC agreed at a meeting to buy all necessary remodelling materials collectively (rather than delivering individual checks as in other communities) and to pay a bricklayer in the same community. In this way, it managed to renovate 170 houses instead of 100.[191]

Half the money is delivered to the inhabitants as a grant; the other half is awarded as a credit to be repaid in monthly instalments over five years. The spokespeople of the CC were the last to receive material, by their own decision in order to avoid talk. After having finished all the renovations and replacement of houses, there was still money left over. At the end of 2008, the balance sheet was presented to the community by the social auditors and everyone was satisfied. Then, however, rumours surfaced that Jacqueline Ávila wanted to buy a house with the remaining money. The CC responded by convening an assembly, which after several meetings decided to buy a four-story house under construction in the community and deliver one floor of it to each of the four most active spokespeople of the CC (among them Ávila), who did not have homes of their own.

During those two years, the community made important advances in resolving its basic necessities:

> The biggest problems were in the health sector. There were many people with deficient health, many with arthritis who could not walk, children who didn't have prosthetics, people who needed kidney operations ...

---

191   See I-JA 2008b.

people with vision problems, there were many cases of dengue, much diarrhoea, malnourished children, and thank God for the work of Barrio Adentro, though it did not end the problem, but things did improve. Now these children are not malnourished, now they eat in the dining room [of the *casa de alimentación*], they get their vitamins from the doctor, who goes from house to house, pregnant women get their exams, their vaccinations. Most of the disabled people have the devices their problems called for.[192]

Having the communal house made it possible to install a doctor's office through the social programme Barrio Adentro, and in December 2007, a Cuban doctor came to serve in the community. Through PDVSA, necessary operations and prostheses were resolved, the Misión Milagro ophthalmology programme delivered 200 lenses, and those who needed eye operations received them. The need for education is constantly emphasised by all respondents. And despite some negative experiences with the Robinson and Ribas missions, everyone believes that access to education is guaranteed in general. At the end of 2007, the CC installed in the communal house a PDVALito, a community post for sale by the food distribution network of PDVSA. According to the merchandise it receives, it sells food at regulated prices up to four days a week. Since the transportation of the merchandise is also organised by the community, it retains 4 percent of the income instead of 2 percent.

In mid-2008, the CC contacted the public service Electricidad de Caracas to renovate or install public illumination in the streets and paths.[193] Two months later, lights were set atop poles that were already in place. The sunken street further downhill was repaired, as were the clean water lines, though the problem of sewage leaks continued. The problem of irregular supply of drinking water is being addressed at the citywide level with participation of the communities. In cooperation with institutions, various cultural activities for children were organised; among them, workshops for working with clay, painting, music, and dance; clowns came to the community, and at Christmas the sector received presents for – according to the census – 377 children. The seniors' club organised excursions for the community's elderly.

---

192   See I-PR 2007.
193   The neighbourhood's houses, built on a hillside, are connected through walks and stairs and cannot be negotiated in a vehicle.

3.3 Participation as a Process of Development and of Social Recognition

The result of participation is not simply the sum of measurable improvements, but is empowerment in the form of dignity, as barrio residents become recognised as members of society with the same importance as others, and whose needs become rights. Recognition is also expressed in the quality of services they receive, and is understood that way by them:

> We received 350 school uniforms and pairs of shoes from the Fabricio Ojeda Endogenous Nucleus Cooperative, very good quality. Before, when they gave out uniforms, [the students] wouldn't put them on because they were given a pair of pants marked with a size it was not, one shoe was one size and the other was another ... I was surprised on Monday to see all these kids here, going to school with their uniforms on. I felt such satisfaction ... that is the difference of what was and what is now.[194]

Empowerment also occurs when barrio residents become political actors and protagonists of transformation by means of their experience of overcoming marginalisation through their own activity. The experience of being an integral part of society with full rights is central for them:

> Here the people lagging behind have never mattered, people who only studied from first to sixth grade. That was like a law here, you went to first through sixth grade, and you already knew that when you leave sixth grade you go to work ... This government cares that the *pueblo* is educated, because [we weren't] for 40 years, because it wasn't convenient to them that we know what's going on ... and when this man [Chávez] showed up, I saw the difference, I saw that this man was for real, that there's a connection between him and the *pueblo* ..., many people of the opposition, they had us like we say here, stomped on. We've been called the dirt people, the badly spoken, the toothless, the hordes ... I went to the Teresa Carreño Theater now, at the age of 42, because entering the Teresa Carreño was a dream of many, and those who could go in there were very few, it was only those who had, those who could, and now thank god the president commanded the doors be opened to the people, today we go into the Teresa Carreño.[195]

---

194   See I-JA 2008a.
195   See I-JA 2006.

On the other hand, the complaint is common that institutions are not available for the communities, or only in a very limited way. Officials leave the communities hanging, they make promises they don't keep, or suddenly they can no longer be contacted or found. Often the lack of continuity in the institutions creates many problems, delaying or obstructing proceedings. During the process of constituting the CC, the community promoters' impression was that some institutions were more interested in registering the CC as receiving support from them than with actually providing an efficient consultancy. Negative experiences with institutions provoke a strong feeling of frustration. What encourages them to continue is confidence in their own forces:

> I love this process, this is something incredible. Sometimes I say that I'm going to stop doing this because the institutions don't function like they're supposed to, it's incredible their lack of ability, they're dysfunctional ... Those who really hold this process in their hands are the bases.[196]

As positive experiences, respondents cite their contacts with PDVSA, the support of Fundacomun in founding the CC, and the cultural work of Fundacaracas. Their criticisms of institutions are rarely about specific employees, and mostly concern institutional logic and structure. Nor do they see as a solution that institutions employ good collaborators, since, as in some cases the respondents knew from their own experience, these then assumed institutional logic instead of changing the institutions.

Despite the great importance of the Robinson Mission, several problems arose within the framework of government policies for the Emiliano Hernández. A community census of 2006 revealed the existence of 96 illiterate people, almost a quarter of them over the age of 15. A first literacy course was successfully completed by 14 people. The second course, however, did not finish, since the instructor stopped receiving institutional funding, without which she had no means of support, so she had to stop teaching the course. By community initiative she was contacted again and wound up teaching another group of 10 people. A course of the Ribas Mission also failed to finish. In April 2008, registration began again for the Robinson and Ribas Missions, which began in September 2008. The classes were at last successfully organised.

In interviews, sharp criticism of FONDEMI stood out. During a year and a half it had not offered the obligatory courses on how to found a communal

---

[196] Ibid.

bank, so the community could not create one. Another criticism was that institutions make decisions with little or no transparency to the community, which represents a lack of respect for the processes of self-empowerment and are seen as a hindrance. Thus, for example, the community decided to install a Mercal, and was informed that there cannot be funding for a PDVALito and a Mercal in the same community, notwithstanding that the community had already decided in assembly to install a Mercal, and a woman had declared herself ready to lend her house and administer it. This limitation had not been previously communicated or explained to the community, nor had the community been consulted.

To solve some problems, direct contacts are needed in institutions, given that otherwise they will often delegate their responsibility. The community had such an experience with Hidrocapital in regard to the drinking water supply, when in 2006 there was water only every other week. The community tried without success to get Hidrocapital to fix the problem, but in April 2008, the problem still existed. According to the community, the reason for this was the Hidrocapital official responsible for the sector, a member of the opposition who was boycotting the work. Halfway through 2008, the community managed to establish through a contact in Fundacaracas a direct link to Hidrocapital, which replaced the pipes soon after.

Bad experiences with institutions have not led to a decrease in participation. On the contrary, now that the community considers it a right, they demand that the institutions make it reality:

> In the institutions they don't pay you the attention you deserve, they always treat you like you don't know anything, that you're ignorant. It's what we always tell people, that the president signs the Constitution not so people will know that that is the Constitution, but to be read, so that when we go to an institution, we say, look, here's article such-and-such, what does it say? That nails it: I have my rights, you have your duties, you feel powerful because you're sitting at your desk there, but no, I also have power because I am from the *pueblo*, I'm a Venezuelan of voting age with an identity card and I also have the right to participate. I struggle so that people can study, can prepare themselves to have weapons to fight with, not knives or bottles, but intellectual arms with which to dialogue and to go up against an engineer.[197]

---

197   See I-PR 2007.

> The struggle here has been hard, but within all the bad stuff that goes on, we have our satisfactions too. You have to be insistent, because if you wait for the institution to come to you, that's not going to happen.[198]

The CC developed its own strategies to put pressure on institutions. They seek out ministers or mayors at public acts or events and 'ambush' them, asking for the funding that was promised but not delivered. Another effective strategy is the collective action of several CCs asking for compliance with their demands.[199]

The Emiliano Hernández sought cooperation with other CCs, including with those they did not 'get along with'.[200] In early 2008, delegates from 14 CCs began meeting weekly to exchange information, discuss common initiatives, and divide up tasks. The number of participating CCs rose rapidly to 32. But an employee of the Greater Mayoralty, who participated in the meetings, provoked fights and divisions and assemblies of delegates did not continue. At the end of 2008, coordination resumed among the CCs. As a first common project, 10 CCs took on a cleanup in sectors of the local administration.[201] But the cooperation ended after only a week. The communities were not disposed to assume externalised services with very low salaries. In 2009, the new administration of the Libertador municipality centralised the urban cleanup once again; this time, truck routes were decided jointly with the communities.[202]

There is a strong desire to link up at a higher level, not only in order to take on other kinds of tasks, but also as an expression of popular power. Organised efforts in this area come from the community or from other communities without institutional support. Linkage does not just occur around material-type projects, but also happens for political purposes. There is, for example,

---

198   See I-JA 2008a.
199   Ibid.
200   Ibid.
201   Sanitary service, largely privatised, has long been one of Caracas's most urgent problems. The private sanitation companies themselves created artificial emergencies, forcing the municipal government to contract them for the cleanup, paying exorbitant prices for their 'special services'. Such 'emergencies' are also provoked for political reasons to destabilise the situation, showing the 'ineffectivity' of the government. The neighbours of the Emiliano Hernández tell how a mountain of trash was regularly piled up beside the Hospital of Catia. The adjacent CC posted guards at night and detained a driver who arrived nightly to empty a truck of garbage by the hospital. According to the driver's account, he was paid by oppositionists to do it.
202   See Azzellini and Ressler 2010.

an emergency network of activists from several CCs, a lesson learned from the experience of the coup, that was once mobilised to (peacefully) block the political opposition's Leopoldo López from coming to the barrio with television crews.[203] This act does not have to be seen as undemocratic, but as a self-defence mechanism because of bad experiences with the opposition, which made community members fear for their lives. At the community level, the oppositionists are integrated.

3.4 New Social Relations and Community Transformation

In a few years, the community created a rich collective and participatory community life. Several CC activists described how bad experiences with the old Neighbours' Associations of the AD, who worked for their own interests and for their party, and had a hierarchical structure, generated at first a negative feeling about participating in local organisations. At first, Jacqueline Ávila was alone:

> When I started here … I had no idea what community work was, and I heard that some places had health committees and I was like, okay, so why doesn't my community get anything … and I began to see where I got all that. I started going out every day and I started making institutional contacts. They started to know me in the institutions. I wrote my letters the best I could; now I can more or less hold my own writing a letter, but not then, I put down more or less what was on my mind. And little by little I got results.[204]

The immediacy of the issue of healthcare led many to participate actively. In the barrios, most people knew of cases of lives saved by Cuban doctors. In the Emiliano Hernández, this also convinced a fervent 88-year-old oppositionist, who had wanted nothing to do with the Cuban doctors. After a heart attack, the Cuban doctor of Barrio Adentro gave her first aid, saving her life. From then on, she accompanied the doctor on her preventive visits in the barrio.[205]

Before the constitution of the CC, some collective work actions (known as *faenas bolivarianas*, or Bolivarian tasks) had been successfully accomplished.

---

203 See I-JA 2008a; Leopoldo López was mayor of Chacao, from the right-wing party Primero Justicia. In 2002, he participated in the coup against Chávez and 'arrested' the interior minister Rodrigo Chacín.
204 See I-JA 2006.
205 See I-HM 2007.

Fundacaracas's programme makes available construction materials for small repair jobs and the community contributes days of collective work. In this way eleven stairs and roads were repaired, and a sports facility for children was built. The rapidity of the results made it possible to integrate many neighbours into the work, and interest and participation increased. During the founding of the CC it had been difficult to convince the community what participation meant and that they had to take their interests into their own hands. The neighbours had lacked the custom and a reason for assemblies and, especially during the first ones, they had difficulty concentrating.

It was constantly necessary to encourage the community to participate, since otherwise the danger that they would not participate was great. Many residents expected the CC to represent them. But the number of activists grew constantly. Before the elections there were between ten and twelve; at the end of 2006, 20 were elected to the CC; at the end of 2008, the number of active participants had grown to 35, and at the end of 2009 to 45, of whom about half demonstrated great enthusiasm.

Work for the community is highly valued and is not restricted to social, family or political networks. Not all 20 members of the CC previously knew each other. Two of those I interviewed had named themselves candidates for tasks they originally had not wanted to take on, since the community needed them most urgently there. Participation is not simply exercised, it has to be learned and developed. This process has changed relationships within the community and it has also changed the actors themselves.

3.5   *Participation as a Process of Democratisation and of Building Collectivity*

Solidarity among community members, and also with others, has grown. Social relations in the community have improved considerably. With the CC there was a jump that made possible a development of a new quality of collectivity: a community that before 2002 was described as apathetic and in which many people did not know each other closely became a community in which it was possible to decide collectively that four women of the CC, who had no house of their own, should receive one with community money. With that, the community somehow balanced the problem that the activity of all four corresponded to one full-time job. The work of the CC has a collective livelihood and activists are supported by the community in different ways:

> I don't get a salary for community work. But the people here in the community don't leave it at that ... I feel that many people here in the community care about me and are watching out for me, for my children.

One way or another, they let me know I can count on them, that they will help me, not to be embarrassed. That's important, it strengthens one.[206]

The social nexuses of the community multiply and strengthen:

> Last night we exchanged Christmas gifts and many people even cried because living so many years here we had never greeted or dealt with each other, and last night it was incredible how we all knew each other, we all spoke, we hugged ... [T]he participation that is going on in this community is incredible, because it was too apathetic, it made me angry, I called meetings and assembly and ended up crying.[207]

In the space of two years, the participatory culture took root in the community. There were neighbours that no one expected to see, participating in committees.[208] Participation is understood as democratisation and equality of rights:

> Participatory and protagonistic democracy is that we all participate, it's something horizontal, no one has ranks, and it's protagonistic because we are the ones who set the standard ... We all participate in a voluntary manner, not because we're directed by someone, we have no chiefs.[209]

Collective activity increased. On one occasion, 10 children were baptised; on another, seven couples were married. Oppositionists are not excluded: conversation with them is sought and they are invited to participate. In the remodelling and housing construction project, oppositionists participated from the beginning. Only six families of active oppositionists did not participate in any community activity, by their own decision. In 2006, the seniors' club (*club de abuelos*) had a Cuban therapist who gave therapeutic dance and gymnastics. Libel Espinoza, who worked on behalf of the community with the club, attended training in therapeutic dance, gymnastics, and assistance for seniors. Together with the ministry of tourism, the club also organises free trips for the elderly to different places, like to beaches or mud baths.

A successful integration of seniors was achieved by means of the *club de abuelos*, which is very large. The seniors are extremely enthusiastic, they

---

206   See I-JA 2008b.
207   See I-JA 2006.
208   See I-JA 2008b.
209   See I-WM 2007.

go to parties, it's amazing their participation ... Here we put on an event for them in October, we brought in a salsa band, we made a meal and everything, there were many of them that started to cry, saying that it was the first time in their lives that someone had paid them a tribute like that.[210]

The community makes an effort to develop in a collective way and without excluding anyone. A dense social network of mutual collective responsibility has been formed. The perceptible changes for children and the opportunities it has brought them have meant that they, unlike their parents, can have a plan to improve their lives. This is basic to human dignity and the possibility of being able to create another culture:

> Before, we did not enjoy that freedom to speak their minds that they now have. They have a life plan, my child says, 'Mami, I'm going to be a doctor,' whereas when they asked me that, I said I wanted to reach the age of 15 fast so I could go to work to help my dad. We did not have a life plan. The children now do because the government that has given the most attention to the people has been this.[211]

The culture of participation has also influenced the community's children, who appropriate the mechanisms they observe. In 2006, two demonstrations of children were organised in the community, one demanding that Alexander – who moved away – should not leave, with the slogan ¡Uh! ¡Ah! ¡Alex no se va!,[212] and another asking for a sports facility. On presidential election day, the children also asked to vote, so an election was organised for them. In general, the men commit less to working with the base than the women do; in 2008, only six men in the Emilio Hernández were stable and reliable supporters of the CC. As an explanation, both the women and men I interviewed said that men are lazier, place little value in community work, are erratic, and have no continuity. Even most of the new members and collaborators of the CC are women. Many housewives especially, who previously did not leave their homes, have joined the health committee.[213] The health committee also deals with specific problems of women; for example, it organised in 2006, together with INAMUJER (National Institute for Women), a workshop

---

210 See I-LE 2007.
211 See I-JA 2006.
212 A play on the 2002 anti-coup slogan: ¡Uh! ¡Ah! ¡Chávez no se va! (Chávez is not going away).
213 See I-JA 2008b.

day for adolescents, young women and mothers about sexuality, contraception methods, birth, and motherhood. It was at once agreed to organise more such events. For many, the health committee is the primary link to local participation:

> I met Jacqueline, I started working with her and with the Cuban doctors ... [L]ater we started to work with aid for the neediest people, take a census, then I got into the social protection committee that also worked with that, disabled people, sick people, sick children, single mothers, extreme poverty; after we finished that work I was more steeped in it and I signed up for the Rivas mission, I signed up, I had the good luck of coming out in the first scholarships in the first list, thank god I graduated, and when I got out, I signed up for the UNEFA [University of the Armed Forces, which is open to the public].[214]

Women are more active in all areas of community work; even in finance, where there are two women to three men, Jacqueline Ávila occupies the central role. That conflicts with patriarchal models. According to women interviewed, the idea that women have to take care of the home and care for children leads to the idea, even in some institutions, that women should not be relied on as much to fulfil certain tasks and are discriminated against.[215] That, however, cannot stop the transformation process of gender roles:

> Venezuelans say they are *machos*, now they are realising they need to participate more. And thanks to the laws we have equality. They try to make an effort more now, and participate more in order to achieve what we want. Women demand more of men, both at home and in the institutions, and we propose to demand more.[216]

> This revolution goes farther for women, men are mad because women are like, 'look, now I go, I come, I'm off to a march, I have to do such-and-such a thing.' Women are going to the streets and men are at home.[217]

Women take more advantage of the training missions than men do. Many of the women of the community study, especially social pedagogy and social

---

214   See I-PR 2007.
215   See I-LE 2007.
216   Ibid.
217   See I-PR 2007.

management, among other careers. The role of women as backbone of the community grows, not following familiar patriarchal models as an invisible task, but publicly, in a collective, recognisable way. The transformation process catapulted some women literally from the oven into the city, to a role of active builders of the new society. And that has been accompanied by an interest and a conscience with respect to history, politics, and the world.

The politicisation of the CC participants happened because of the changes they observed. Of six respondents, five had no social or political activity or interest before 1998. In many cases, a particular event drove their participation. Jacqueline Ávila lived through the death of a friend's infant and of the mother of an acquaintance during the oil lockout of 2002–3, when, because of a lack of fuel, they could not get medical help on time. In some cases, the emergency situation drove the poor to burn their furniture in order to cook. Libel Espinoza says about herself that until 2005 she was practically focused entirely on her own person, without any interest in something more. She began to participate actively after having visited a workshop about the 'inclusion of older adults' in the community. There she realised immediately the connection with her own experiences, her deceased grandmother and her own life, and the importance of solidarity and collectivity. She participated 'for my community, for my *pueblo*, for the future of my children, even for myself'.[218] Her impulse to participate immediately found an adequate response that led her to continue integrating herself into the community.

Respondent Arquímedes Rodríguez had been part of MBR-200 in the 90s and had a longer history of activism:

> I was always a revolutionary. My father was a soldier, and he was always against the government of Carlos Andrés,[219] he was a *guerrillero* with Eloy [Torres], Douglas Bravo, [Teodoro] Petkoff,[220] ... and when Chávez arrived, whom I met on one occasion in Yare, I got motivated. This man can be the change ... I have always had that motivation. And it's not about me, it's about those who come after me, my children, my grandchildren ... And yes I am seeing changes.[221]

---

218 See I-LE 2007.
219 Carlos Andrés Pérez, president of Venezuela from 1974–9 and 1989–93.
220 They first organised from 1957 on the infiltration of the Venezuelan military on behalf of the Communist Party, from the early 1960s on, they led the guerrilla connected to the CP and were involved in the military uprisings between 1961 and 1963.
221 See I-AR 2007.

Rodríguez has no key role in the local work; however, his story is important for the community because he offers direct access to the history of the struggles in Venezuela, which is in turn connected to pictures, stories and speeches that are publicly claimed as historical links in the framework of the transformation process. Through him, the history of change comes alive.

The conditions allowed them all to develop rapidly. This happens especially through education, whether institutional offerings or private initiatives:

> I'd rather read than play computer games or watch TV, I set myself a schedule, okay, from 7 to 10 I'm going to read, the more you read the more you keep yourself busy, and at some point you learn a lot.[222]

It is not unusual that the effort to grow as a person is understood as a debt connected with Chávez, not as a burden but as an incentive: 'if Chávez fights for us, for the poor, and opens all possibilities, then we have to do everything we can to grow, excel, and take matters into our own hands'. Everyone talks about a transformation to socialism that has to be developed, and they see themselves as participants in this construction through the CCs. The idea of socialism is not precisely defined, but oriented in terms of values. Everyone underlines the need for a profound cultural change. Venezuelan society is seen as too individualistic and oriented toward property. The common notion of revolution is of a long process of construction.

Often respondents summarise their own personal change as having become 'more human' and having grown through knowledge, like Jacqueline Ávila:

> The main thing I've learned from this was human feelings. It fell to me to conduct the census house to house with those people who were being classified as high risk. There were cases where I took the census in a house and left weeping, seeing the human misery that was there ... My life has changed because I think I have grown a lot.[223]
>
> My life has changed 100%, ... I have changed much ... More than anything, we have humanised, because before it was from your front door to inside your house. You didn't know what was happening with your neighbour, or to that neighbour woman whose husband you saw drinking all night while she had no food. And we integrated ourselves, we spoke with the

---

222   See I-WM 2007.
223   I-JA 2008b.

woman, look, study, we're going to bring you in here, look at your husband, speak up, don't let him mistreat you, this is the woman's house, go to the prosecutor.[224]

Most of the women named the future of their children and other generations as the principal motivation for their participation; a 'maternal' responsibility.[225] However, activist men argue in the same way, and also highly value their commitment to the community: 'I'm excited because it's the first time I am participating this way with my community, it's an experience I had not had'.[226] A sense of 'maternal' responsibility, reasonable from a social point of view, seems to be in the ascendant.

The importance of external institutional stimulus to the organisational process is great. But the community outgrows it, manifesting itself as autonomous and measuring institutions by how they handle their needs, which have been internalised as rights, and by how they relate to the construction of another society. The CC Emiliano Hernández leverages many different possibilities of support and funding, and maintains contacts with a variety of institutions. CC activists see state funding neither as a problem, nor as a gift, but as a legitimate, unquestionable right:

> Many people say: 'The communal councils are organised so they can get money.' Of course, because when they give us money we solve problems. It makes me angry to hear that, because they're saying that you just built the communal council to grab money, as if the money is for yourself. As if we did not deserve it. Then they want that someone going to Fundacomunal should thank them for the favour, for the alms they are giving. That's where they're wrong, because we are clear that it belongs to us.[227]

The autonomy of the CC and of the community is beyond question:

> For me, participation is the maximum popular power ... because the decisions come from below, from the assemblies, who really decides are the bases, the community, the *pueblo* ... We ourselves are assuming power,

---

[224] I-PR 2007.
[225] Fernandes 2007, p. 122.
[226] See I-WM 2007.
[227] See I-JA 2008a.

the communal council is a local government, we ourselves are going to manage our own resources.'[228]

The CCs are not seen as an appendix of constituted power, but as autonomous bodies that depend neither on any institution nor on the president. 'This is a state of beginning, but eventually you're going to see pure communal councils, because we already have autonomy. We're going to make this go well'.[229] The community imposes its will in the face of the institutions and defends itself against any attempt to co-opt it, which, in most cases, comes from the municipal level. The participation of the community in certain governmental campaigns does not follow the expectations of the government or of the PSUV, but is a rational decision made by the community.

3.6 The CC 'Unidos por el Chapulún', Parroquia Nuestra Sra. del Rosario, Baruta

The municipality of Baruta (Miranda), part of greater Caracas, has 317,288 residents; 79 percent of them live in middle- and upper-middle-class sectors, and 21 percent in barrios, which are located in the hills and have a very precarious infrastructure. The CCs, which have been constituted in almost all the barrios, receive no support from the oppositionist municipal government.[230]

In the community of the CC 'Unidos por el Chapulún', there was an MTA before the CC was constituted, which resolved most of the problems of drinking water and sewage. Shortly before the CC was constituted, a CTU was also formed. Evangelina Flores and her husband were central figures in community work and in building the CC; they had promoted the CTU in early 2006 and did the same with the CC after having seen something about the CC on television. The community formed a precursor to the CC, with several elected officials. Next it informed the Greater Mayoralty, which sent promoters, although ultimately the most useful aid came from Fundacomunal. In the first large assembly, the community was informed about the CC and a promotional committee was chosen by direct election, which made the census. The census showed 200 families; another 42 who followed a neighbourhood oppositionist did not want to register in the CC, but after they saw that the CC got results, almost all of them joined, a few at a time. The CC was officially constituted on 26 May 2006. More than 70 people participated in the assembly and elected,

---

228   See I-JA 2006.
229   See I-WM 2007.
230   Echenique, Torres and Zorrilla 2003, pp. 103–4.

by a show of hands, 10 spokespeople and five people for social auditing and finance. They work together as a group and share tasks.

The CTU and the MTA continue functioning, and there is a new committee on sports, as well as a participant in Madres del Barrio (Barrio Mothers, a social programme for poor mothers) and an aide from the Misión Negra Hipólita (a programme for homeless support, named after the Bolívars' nanny), which coordinates with the social security and prevention committee. But the CC does not want to form too many committees. For each project an assembly is convened and it is noted who participates. Participation in the assemblies is more or less 30–40 people, who change frequently. The tendency is toward an increase in participation. Mobilisation is done with signage, displayed in the community.

14 of the 20 elected members of the executive committee continue to be active; three are men, and one of them is 'principal spokesperson'. The CC is aware that such a figure does not exist in the CC law and the structure of the CC will be accommodated to the law in the next elections, a few months away. Nor does the CC have by-laws. The community does not see it as necessary to have them and no one asked for them when the CC was registered. When the CC began its work it met twice a week, then the frequency dropped to once every two weeks, and when necessary, additional meetings are convened. During the week many members of the CC stay in contact with one another and attend institutional meetings in small groups. Community projects and matters are discussed by the executive committee; when it has reached a consensus, it convenes a community assembly, where the decisions are made. The first community project was the rehabilitation of a small abandoned school to install a day care centre. The opposition, which did not participate in the CC, was against the project. The CC contacted the government, which at that time was all Bolivarian, of the state of Miranda, which approved the project. Three months later, the government of Miranda began work and then installed a day care centre. The community also received credits for repair of homes. A hill that put some houses at risk from landslides under heavy rains was partly planed and secured. The social audit followed up on all the activities of the institutions and of the community.

Additionally, the CC received from the government of Miranda funding for a playground and 104,000 bolívares from the Greater Mayoralty for three socially productive projects: a hairdressing shop, a bakery for bread, and an information centre. Given that land for the playground was not yet available and there was no place for the socially productive projects, the community decided to use the funding of the playground to buy a community house that would also house the socially productive projects. These, the community decided, would be owned collectively through the CC. The workers are also chosen by the community. In the next assembly, the community decided to reorient the bakery project and change it to a textile production business.

The experiences with institutions are, as with other CCs, mixed. From the oppositionist municipal government of Baruta, the CC has never received any support, not even functional street cleaning in the barrios. With the government of Miranda (when it still had a Bolivarian governor), the experiences were mostly good; with the Bolivarian Greater Mayoralty and its institutions, they were bad. On one occasion the mayor Juan Barreto came to the barrio, promised support, and the community never heard from him about it again. The Mission Madres del Barrio in Caracas denied any responsibility for Baruta, since it was a supposed middle-class municipality, and delegated the responsibility to the mission office in Miranda, where the community received little response. After a while, some women were integrated into the programme. Fundacomunal, on the other hand, dismissed three employees who had mistreated and offended the CC members, three days after the complaint was made. The critique of the institutions is not limited to demanding that they function better. The respondents see the basic contradiction between constituent and constituted power: 'It is not convenient to the institutions that we communal councils should direct the local, municipal, or state government. For that reason we are blocked by many institutions and by the bureaucracy that we continue living in'.[231]

No CC member had organisational experience before 2002. The participation process has totally changed the life of the neighbourhood, and has influenced gender relations. Evangelina Flores describes how she spent 12 years of her life waiting for her husband to come home from work to serve him dinner, until she realised that she had to get involved and organise if she wanted a positive change in her surroundings.[232] Achieving for the community is a great source of satisfaction to the activists. For the residents of a community that was previously marginalised in several ways, the participation process signifies enormous personal growth. The great emancipatory, creative force is rooted in the fact that the process benefits not individuals but the collective: 'I have learned a lot, I've learned to have better relationships, to have a good group of friends. I've learned to be more organised, to have more participation, to lose the fear of being told no. Now I'm not afraid'.[233]

---

231   See I-EF 2008.
232   See I-EF 2008.
233   Ibid.

The respondents declare unanimously that Chávez motivated the participation. The CC's economic committee is entirely made up of *chavistas*, which facilitates organisation. The respondents emphasise that the CC is open to everyone regardless of political orientation; nevertheless, the attitude of some residents who refuse participation is reinforced by the oppositionist municipal government. Although various oppositionists refused at first, they wound up integrating into the CC and with time they all became supporters of the process of change.

The CC is understood as an autonomous body of community self-organisation and every attempt at co-optation is rejected: 'We work very quietly but we get things done, and we're not going to accept someone coming to make a political platform of the work we've done'.[234]

During the early phase, the community was sceptical as to whether the CC would really function or whether the resources would really reach the community; today, the majority considers them the best form of organisation. The community has successfully appropriated the CC model and adapted it to its own requirements. Although the structure and makeup of the CC do not correspond to the law at all points, there is no doubt that the community has built an operative democratic self-administration. This fact has been recognised by the institutions involved. The community aspires to financial independence, and to that end is working on building a community economy responsive to its needs, starting with socially productive projects that have received funding.[235]

Out of the need for coordination with other CCs for matters beyond the community, a network sprang up. Along with seven other CCs, the 'Unidos' CC participates in a commission with the state company CANTV to install landlines and internet. The CCs also discuss together how to solve the problem of poor public transportation, and achieved the removal of the Metropolitan Police and the arrival of the Miranda police. The eight communities also together discussed security and tried to regulate the sale of alcohol, though the sale of drugs remains an unresolved problem in the community.

3.7 CCs in Caracas: Conclusions

Of the examples presented and five more CCs that I have studied, I conclude that locating the CC initiatives at the community level was a correct step. The dimension of community corresponds to an existing self-identification with a barrio, a sector, and as a nucleus, with a community, which tends to be the

---

234 See I-MLH 2008.
235 See I-EF 2008.

centre of social life. Identification with the community tends to be stronger than with an office, a job, or other identifications. The minimum size of 200 families established by law has proven to be too large in several cases. In the new law, the minimum number has been lowered to 150 families.[236]

By means of the mechanisms of participation, and especially with the CC, the community changes profoundly. 'Needs that until recently were resolved at the domestic level of each household, now come to have a collective character and are seen as problems that the community should participate actively to solve, thus enhancing the *collective space*'.[237] The class constitutes itself as a community. Its construction is an active process. From the community, barrio residents project themselves into the city and for the first time begin to be part of it. Public space is conquered in three dimensions: 'collective space, living space, and institutional space'.[238] These forms of participation break with the social segregation imposed on the territory.

In general, communities were able to solve their most pressing problems, such as food, education, and healthcare. In this context, the experience of being an actor in overcoming one's own marginalisation has been of primary importance. To be taken into account by the government, to have one's own opinion heard and counted, to deal with institutions that should explicitly be of service, brings a sense of dignity, even though many institutional experiences are negative ones. The communities' self-confidence has grown enormously and they confront institutions more decisively once they know that the law and the guidelines of the transformation process are on their side. Participation makes it possible for the communities and their residents to develop perspectives and plan their lives with more self-determination and not limit themselves merely to survival.

3.8 *Participation*

The possibilities of participation offered by the CCs began mobilising many people. Out of 25 interviewees, only five had some social or political activity before 1998, though three of those were key figures for the development of the work in their community and the creation of the CC. With the arrival of the CC, there was a qualitative and quantitative leap in participation in all the communities, and the nucleus of activists, which in most cases had been six to eight people, grew to 15–30. The CC's variety of tasks makes it possible for the initi-

---

236 LOCC 2009, art. 4.
237 Lacabana and Cariola 2005, p. 37.
238 Ibid.

ators to approach other people, and to assume tasks for the community. Since the CCs are thought of as an instrument of self-administration for the entire community, it is important that participation brings visible improvements to the community. Although all lament the levels of apathy in their communities, a strong will to participation can also be seen. Everyone relativises their complaints, and people also tell of unexpected participation, of processes of political and social awareness, and of emancipation:

> No, the communities are not apathetic, none of them ... The communities' way of thinking in general is different now. I say this from what I see and what I live constantly. So I think that participation is to be there, at every one of the things we do ... and when I go to Baruta, I go to the Candelaria, we're there doing politics because we are for all, we are no longer on our own. The participation is there, as a principle.[239]

The CCs work better in the barrios than in middle-class or impoverished-middle-class areas, even in cases where the participation in the assemblies is less. Communication structures and social contacts are more intense in the barrios. The middle class is also much more susceptible to the opposition's anti-CC propaganda. For the diffusion of the CC model, state television played an important role.

The communities appropriate the CCs, adapting them in form and content to their needs and abilities. They base themselves in the law of communal councils, which for many with no previous organisational experience represents an important grounding; however, no one understands the law as a fixed rule. With the creation of an effective community structure in the foreground, the majority of the communities organised more assemblies than the law contemplated. The activists explain why: when participatory experience is lacking, more explanations and discussions are needed. In most cases, the timeframe was longer than the law specifies. In only two of the seven CCs was the executive committee elected in an assembly, while the other five organised election days that represented important community social events.

The community as such exists beforehand, but it is also produced through work with the CC in an act of social construction. Barrio residents 'have retaken the public spaces of the popular barrios, filling them with life and with activities ... now living together has a different dimension and redefines the relation

---

239 See I-CB 2008.

between private and public'.²⁴⁰ The communities change, and collectivity and solidarity assume a growing importance. Internal conflicts tend to be resolved by the communities themselves, without need of institutions. Competition and selfishness are not to be found either within the community or in relation to other communities.²⁴¹ On the contrary, a great solidarity and willingness to aid the poor and weak can be noted. Even in communities that do not have a high level of participation, there is a strong solidarity with those with fewer resources.

Two of the seven CCs reach collective dimensions that have clear characteristics of a solidary society oriented toward community needs, as in the case of the Emiliano Hernández, where homes were bought with community money for the four CC spokeswomen who had no homes, or, for example, the decision by Unidos por el Chapulín that the businesses to be founded would be community property under community administration. But the work of the central activists is often full-time. Many are supported by family and friends, and some by the community and the CC. Only one communal council discussed a proposal for economic compensation for its spokespeople.

Women participate more than men. In six of the seven communities, 70 percent of the activists are women, and in the executive committees the participation by gender is similar. In only one community is the participation of men and women described as more or less equal. Almost all the CCs have great difficulties integrating adolescents into their work. In different activities of the CCs – workshops, encounters with institutions, assemblies in the community, and also in the concrete work of the CC – it is rare to see people under 25. This does not mean that youth do not participate in general, only that they do less in the community, though more elsewhere, for example in the areas of media and communication.

For activists, participation is the 'action of a collective, by means of organisation, the planning of different fronts and community social groups'.²⁴² Almost all say that they have grown personally through participation. The personal process is often described as 'humanisation' or sensitivity, and is considered an important sign of how the community's social relations have been transformed. Despite some reversals, almost all underscore that they feel realised

---

240   Lacabana and Cariola 2005, p. 38.
241   There are reports of singular cases, like the case of a woman in the Emiliano Hernández who secretly sold her repaired house and disappeared. Relevant cases of competition or selfishness that might threaten the CC's functioning were not found in the CC under study.
242   See I-WP 2008.

by their work in the CC. The majority see their work in the context of a socialism under construction.

It is not unusual to connect socialism with love of neighbour. A participation influenced by religious feelings is common. One woman I interviewed had before 1998 been active for 30 years in an evangelical church;[243] another, in a Catholic homeless aid association.[244] Typical for the Latin American context is the case of a man who came to MBR-200 in the 90s who was a catechist.[245] Nevertheless, one must underscore that such behaviour is very differentiated, and that while it is common to make reference to and orient oneself by Christian values, the Catholic Church as an institution does not enjoy much prestige among the popular classes.

Although participation is high, it cannot be said that it is consolidated, and it depends, in most cases, on the initiatives of individuals who act with inciting and coordinating force. Without the continual initiative of the central actors, the participation of the majority of the others would probably drop off considerably. Another problem is the culture of representation, which is profoundly rooted in Venezuelan society. In the communities there is a strong expectation that the CC activists will act as representatives.

3.9 Relationship between Communities and Institutions

The relationship between communities and institutions is controversial. The state initiative has proved to be basic to the spread of the CCs, making it possible to reach many communities, which otherwise would not have had other networks or experiences with which to launch self-organisation for self-administration. In the concrete work, nevertheless, state institutions tend to rein in and hinder the processes, with demoralising consequences. Often the same institution will give support and workshops on how to advance to self-administration on the one hand, but impede the putting into practice of it on the other. The former case indicates how the class struggle has moved into the institutions, while the latter indicates how the same institutions are structurally incapable of creating the new.

All the CCs analysed have had bad experiences with institutions. The most frequent complaints concern the slowness of the processes, setbacks because of

---

243 See I-MV 2007.
244 See I-AL 2007.
245 See I-PRI 2007; In Chiapas, México, many catechised indigenous people joined the liberation theology movement EZLN; in Nicaragua, El Salvador and Colombia, liberation theology played an important role in revolutionary struggles, see Camilo Torres.

incomplete information, poor accessibility, broken promises, lack of coordination and competition between different institutions, insufficient support and attempts at co-optation.

As a consequence of institutional inefficiency, some new participants became discouraged and dropped out. However, there were also cases of rapid financing without sufficient preparation. Very similar projects delivered to the same institution could be delayed by three to 18 months before being financed, making community planning and development as a self-administering body difficult. The communities tend to have relatively clear ideas about what they want, but they lack the methodological as well as the financial resources. Despite the problems and contradictions, the institutions are asked to lend necessary support to the communities and subject themselves to the autonomous bodies of the CC. Nevertheless, while the communities see access to services and support as a right, within institutions they often encounter disparaging attitudes and expectations of subordination and gratitude. Because of this, the majority of representative offices do not have a high reputation in the communities and the contrary case occurs to what is common in other countries: the closer the level of representation, the less the level of confidence. Local and municipal administrations have the highest number of negative mentions, although different CCs had positive and negative experiences with the same institutions and all also mentioned numerous positive experiences as well, but the latter tend to be tied to personal contacts and individuals. This demonstrates that the institutions have not come to a new understanding about their tasks and their way of working.

Almost all of those interviewed indicated, in one way or another, the fundamental contradiction between constituent and constituted power: 'These gentlemen who are already comfortable in office will not want to give up their benefits, they live on the needs of the people. It's like a small business, you understand?'[246] So the solution is not simply to employ better workers, but a new institutionality that abolishes the separation between the institution and the 'object' of its procedures.

In various internal contradictions within the institutions described here, it can be clearly seen how they intersect with class struggle. In spite of all the criticism, the institutions are not seen as the central problem. All the communities develop strategies to impose their will. For constituent power, institutions do not represent a limit but merely an obstacle that has to be overcome. All the respondents emphasise that the principal problem is in the

---

246 See I-TE 2008.

population itself, in the lack of a culture of participation, given that the process of self-empowerment opens all the doors. In this context a central role is played by education.

The CCs understand themselves as autonomous community self-organisations and they vehemently reject any attempt at co-opting them, whether partisan or institutional, as well as rejecting the accusation that they were formed only for money. Access to resources, and having control over how to use them, is seen as a right. This is reinforced by the experience that the work of the CCs is more efficient than that of the institutions. In all the analysed committees, a transparent, conscientious management of the finances could be observed, along with a great effort to bring projects to fruition. This corresponds to the results of the research by the FCG.[247] Although the majority of respondents knew of cases in which CC funding was diverted into private pockets, this does not bring into question the delivery of resources. Moreover, this always involves one or at most two CCs of the minimum of two dozen that the majority are in contact with. Here again community responsibility is indicated, since the abuse of funding is only possible if the community permits it.

The communities are understood to be totally independent of the institutions. In several communities there were attempts at institutional co-optation that was not allowed. The CCs rebel against any subordination. If the CCs do not feel competently supported, or sense that the institutions or their employees have other interests, they often go to different institutions in search of support. Given that the institutions are permeated with class struggle, the CCs manage to find support for the development of their own ideas and forms of organisation at the highest level. As we have observed several times, support for self-determined community building can come from within the same governmental body as a concurrent attempt at co-optation.

The direct link with the presidency from the beginning, and the strong effort by Chávez on behalf of the CCs even after the change of institutional responsibilities, does not create co-optation or dependence. For the majority of respondents, Chávez was the undisputed leader of the process, adored and at the same time seen as an equal, a member of the *pueblo*. It was not about obedience or blind following, and neither was it a personalised relation. Chávez is seen as the initial impulse and most important supporter of the process, but the CCs are understood to be independent. Respondents opine differently about the institutions, the government, and Chávez himself, about whom the most frequent criticism is that he chose his officers badly.

---

247 See FCG 2008.

It is also the case that no partisan co-optation can be observed, even though 21 of the 25 respondents are members of the MVR/PSUV and only four belong to no party. Not one of the 21 party members gave the party a positive evaluation; several gave a negative one; they criticised internal power struggles and competition, social climbing, careerism, and in some cases attempts at co-optation by political representatives, who met with sharp rejection in the communities and are seen as careerists who want to appropriate the work of others. The community mobilisations in governmental campaigns are not due to any co-optation; on the contrary, they are rational decisions made within the framework of the politicisation process. The communities do not support all the mobilisations; they only support those that they consider strategic. All see the continuation of the present government in office as a guarantee of continuation for the process in progress. This is recognised even by one *ni-ni* respondent who does not consider himself a *chavista* or an oppositionist.

At the community level, one can witness, in general, a great opening to the oppositionists. Five of the seven communities made active efforts to integrate them into community work, especially by means of direct conversation and invitations. One part of the opposition and the *ni-nis* in these communities participate in community activities. These people see the CCs as less connected with the government than any other mechanism of participation, understanding the CC rather as a community instrument. In this spirit, the president of an opposition apartment building assembly in Candelaria put a large room at the CC's disposition to organise the first community assembly.[248] The opposition's perception of the CC depends largely on the national political conjuncture. When political confrontation sharpens, many tend to distance themselves from the CC. This is reinforced by the fact that in decisive elections, the majority of the CC activists dedicate more time to the electoral campaign than to the work of the CC.

Tendencies toward political exclusion can be perceived in two CCs, without having been openly declared. Even in those two CCs, the oppositionists were integrated into the census and the programmes, whenever they did not refuse. That the two cases are located in the opposition municipality of Baruta is surely not coincidental. In the majority of the communities, there is a small nucleus of oppositionists who reject any community participation, and in municipalities with opposition governments they receive direct support that is denied to the CCs in the barrios. This increases the number of those who refuse to participate and reinforces the polarisation in the communities. That

---

248 See I-PRI 2007.

is the origin of the stronger tendency toward exclusion in those CCs; in the municipality of Libertador, with a Bolivarian government, this tendency is not found.

Beyond the rejection of participation by the opposition, which tends to reduce to a minority of them, two CCs in high-opposition sectors report active sabotage attempts by some oppositionists. Despite that, CC activities have shown themselves disposed to integrate the opposition into the community work. Other CCs know as well of cases in adjacent communities in which the opposition has tried, including through the use of physical violence, to hinder the forming and functioning of the CC. At the community level, those who practice intolerance and sabotage are clearly a minority among the opposition.

The majority of respondents see the CC as the lowest level of a system of councils in construction, that over the long-term redefines and in many ways also replaces the institutional complex – and along with it the existing state, its tasks, and its division of labour. It is an open, complex process whose success is not guaranteed. The contradiction between constituent and constituted power, perceived also by the communities, has not been decided in favour of the former. On the contrary, constituted power continues to occupy the stronger position. But the CCs have the potential of being an institution of constituent power, something that can be seen in the networks that emerged among CCs. The CCs also appropriated the concept of communes, which are seen as an instrument of overcoming the old institutions and for self-administration.

CHAPTER 5

New Collective Business Paradigms

> Capitalist enterprises work for themselves alone, and we are trying to do exactly the opposite, work for the community. To work for society, so we all get the profit. Not only workers that are here in the business, but the people outside, around us, the population.[1]

∴

> Rank doesn't exist, here we're all equals. We depend on an assembly that directs the cooperative in any moment of doubt, anything, we go to the assembly to discuss things. It approves or not. This is practically the owner of the company, the assembly.[2]

∴

Since 1999, a great number of policies have been put into practice in Venezuela with the aim of democratising the administration and the ownership of the means of production. With the passage of time, different models of self-management and co-management have been introduced and tried. The first basic orientations for democratising the administration and owning the means of production were formulated in the 1999 Constitution:

> **Article 70.** These are the means of participation and protagonism of the *pueblo* in the exercise of its sovereignty ... in social and economic matters, bodies of citizen service, self-management, co-management, cooperatives in all forms including those of financial character, savings banks, communitary business, and other forms of association guided by the values of mutual cooperation and solidarity ...

---

1   Aury Arocha, laboratory analyst, Tomates Guárico, in Azzellini and Ressler 2006.
2   Rigoberto López, coordinator, spinning department, Textileros del Táchira, in Azzellini and Ressler 2006.

Article 115. The right to property is guaranteed. Everyone has the right to the use, enjoyment, and disposition of his or her assets. Property is subject to contributions, restrictions, and obligations that the law establishes with the aim of public utility of general interest. Only because of public utility or social interest, by means of firm sentence and payment of a just indemnisation, can the expropriation of any class of assets be declared.

Article 118. The right of workers is recognised, as well as that of the community, to develop associations of participatory social character, like cooperatives, savings and mutual associations, and other associated forms. These associations may develop any type of economic activity, in conformity with the law. The law recognises the specifics of these organisations, especially those relative to cooperative action and associated work, and its generative character of collective benefits. The state promotes and protects these associations destined to better the popular alternative economy.

Article 308. The state protects and promotes small and medium-sized industry, cooperatives, and savings associations, as well as family business, microbusiness, and any other form of community association for work, savings, and consumption, under a collective property regime, with the aim of strengthening the country's economic development, sustaining it in the popular initiative. Training, technical assistance, and opportune financing is guaranteed.[3]

The protagonism of the workers and popular sectors in promoting the defeat of the 'business strike' in 2002/3 and the previous failure of the coup by the opposition in April 2002, also largely due to popular mobilisations, paved the way for legislation, measures, and social practices that look to a structural transformation of the economy and are drawing the framework of a new economic model. During the business strike, several factories closed by their owners were taken over by their workers.

The new orientation of economic policy after 2003 included many elements from below, like an increase in the promotion of cooperatives and co-management models, as well as an anti-imperialist orientation from above, like limitations to international investors and an orientation toward food sovereignty.[4]

---

3   See RBV, 1999.
4   Ellner 2006, p. 84.

The government concentrated more on building a state productive sector and organising the distribution.

The economy to be strengthened has been called, variously, solidary, social, popular, or communal economy. A clear definition or distinction of the term does not exist. The basic tendencies were summarised by Roland Denis (in August 2002, when he was vice-minister of social economy planning), as social economy:

> 1. The social economy is an alternative economy. 2. Democratic and self-managing practices thrive there. 3. It is driven by associated, not salaried, forms of work. 4. Its means of production is collectively owned (except in the case of microbusiness). 5. It is centred on the egalitarian distribution of the surplus. 6. It is in solidarity with the social setting in which it develops. 7. It is committed to its own autonomy in the face of monopolist centres of economic or political power.[5]

These plans and ideas were not realised in 2002/3. The systematic implementation of means of support for them only began in 2004 with the creation of the Ministry of Popular Economy. In 2005, the Venezuelan government officially adopted a socialist orientation and began the nationalisation of industries, companies of strategic importance, and unproductive businesses, and began to expand the productive sector of state or collective property.

The strategy for constructing an economy beyond capitalist logic and democratising economic cycles is based on the expansion and consolidation of the popular economy by means of self-administered productive entities promoted by the state, which assumes an important role with respect to general planning.[6] This orientation emerges from a strategy of radical, sustainable, endogenous development based on existing resources and potential, on collective management of the means of production, and on a more active state role in the economy.[7] Several collective business models of co-management and self-

---

5 Denis 2005, p. 233.
6 See I-CL 2007; I-CLR 2006.
7 Azzellini 2010, pp. 220–2; Valles 2004; Endogenous development has its roots in the first proposals of the CEPAL in the 1950s and was developed by Antonio Vázquez Barquero and Oswaldo Sunkel (Sunkel 1993). As an alternative to neoliberal concepts and to overcome the failed strategy of import substitution, the concentration on one's own possibilities was promoted, with a state that actively intervenes, corrects 'errors of the market', and promotes the dissemination and massification of science and technology. Existing possibilities are strengthened and networked. Originally it is not an anti-capitalist concept and it was based

management have emerged and been promoted in recent years. Since 2006, the workers' councils became the official normative orientation for the organisation of workers in state-owned businesses and institutions.

Unlike, for example, Soviet-style state socialism with its state ownership of the means of production, in Venezuela, where there is no single clear plan for how to arrive at socialism, a wide variety of practices and models for administration and ownership of the means of production are being experienced at once.[8] The approaches from above and from below, which coexist in a continuous, unresolved tension within the Bolivarian process and in the government, are also found in the area of production. Moreover, private interests, corruption, the lack of mechanisms for transparent controls, and a lack of experience and responsibility all lead to frequent non-compliance from responsible institutions with respect to guidelines for forms of businesses and the participation of workers in them, leading in turn to increased conflicts within state companies and institutions.

The Ministry of Popular Economy became the Ministry of Communal Economy in 2007, and was renamed the Ministry of Communes in 2009. Since then, 'popular economy' has been the main term used, though in order to suggest building, developing and consolidating by means of and within the communities, the term 'communal economy' has also been used and has gained more weight with the constitution of communes. To promote it, Chávez signed a presidential decree in July 2008 that makes a legal framework available to collective and community businesses and opens the possibility of implementation of networks of barter and local monies.[9]

The idea of communal cycles of production and consumption are rooted in the work of Istvan Mészáros, who from 2005 represented an important orientation for Chávez and for Venezuelan politics. Mészáros delineated basic ideas for a transition to socialism in his book *Beyond Capital*. In the chapter 'The

---

principally on the private sector. The Venezuelan strategy proposes not only endogenous production but also endogenous distribution. Carlos Lanz emphasises the structural limits of endogenous development in capitalism, where the rate of profit determines investment and technological innovation, and free competition does not rule, but rather a tendency toward centralisation and concentration of property. For this reason, the promotion of endogenous development has to assume the perspective of going toward a transition toward overcoming capitalism (Lanz 2004, pp. 17–19). The concept transformed from a concept of alternative capitalist development to one of an alternative logic to that of capital (Lebowitz 2006, p. 99).

8 See Lander 2009.
9 'Law for the Promotion and Development of Popular Economy', in *Decreto N° 6.130, Extraordinario de la Gaceta Oficial N° 5.890*, 31 July 2008.

Communal System and the Law of Value',[10] he details, with reference to Marx's *Grundrisse*, the idea of a communal system (communitarian and cooperative):

> Accordingly, in striking contrast to commodity production and its fetishistic exchange relation, the historically novel character of the communal system defines itself through its practical orientation towards the *exchange of activities*, and not simply of *products*. The allocation of products, to be sure, arises from the communally organised productive activity itself, and it is expected to match the directly social character of the latter. However, the point in the present context is that in the communal type exchange relation the primacy goes to the self-determination and corresponding organisation of the *activities* themselves in which the individuals engage, in accordance with their need as active human beings. The products constitute the subordinate moment in this type of exchange relation, making it therefore possible also to allocate in a radically different way the total disposable time of society, rather than being predetermined and utterly constrained in this respect by the primacy of the material productive targets, be they commodities or non-commodified products.[11]

Since 2008, models have been favoured that aspire to transform small and medium-sized business into direct social property, that is, so that they are managed completely by their workers and by the communities. The principal reason for integrating the businesses into the communities was to avoid the errors of Yugoslavia, where businesses under workers' control had to operate in a market system, socially isolated and competing among themselves.[12] By integrating and democratically planning with the communities, it is also hoped that it will be easier to evade or overcome the logic of mercantile relations.

This chapter examines the different initiatives of administrative models and collective ownership of the means of production in Venezuela. Beginning with the cooperatives (1), it then covers the new business models of the Social Production Companies, co-management in private businesses and socialist factories in state companies (2).

---

10 Mészáros 1995, pp. 739–70.
11 Mészáros 1995, pp. 759–60.
12 Lebowitz 2006, pp. 102–3.

1   Cooperatives

Through this cooperative model we seek to not enrich people but neither that they earn less and are exploited, that we get to a better quality of life, that our associates have decent housing, their children have decent education, and then under that parameter create the growth and see what we call or what the president calls, what we are building, the socialism of the 21st century.[13]

...

To work in a cooperative is much better than working for another. Working for other people is like being a slave to them. Not in a cooperative, because one works in his or her own way. Obviously this doesn't mean that you can do whatever you like in a cooperative, no, you do what you have to do without anyone needing to tell you to.[14]

∴

Before the government of President Chávez, the social or solidarity economy was an undeveloped, marginal sector. In February of 1999, there were only about 800 registered cooperatives, mostly in the sectors of finance and transport, with about 20,000 members.[15] The cooperativist culture was little developed even in the cooperatives, and the majority followed capitalist logic and a reformist orientation.[16]

A central approach of the Chávez government with respect to the construction of a solidarity economy was to promote the creation of cooperatives, launching a set of support measures for the cooperativist sector that led to a boom in the creation of cooperatives beginning in 2004. By mid-2009, accord-

---

13   Luis Alvarez, manager of administration, Textileros del Táchira, in Azzellini and Ressler 2006.
14   Carmen Ortíz, coning operator, Textileros del Táchira, in Azzellini and Ressler 2006.
15   See Melcher 2008. The figures vary between 762 (Melcher 2008) and 877 (Piñeiro 2007). In an interview, Juan Carlos Baute, director of Sunacoop in 2008, gave a figure of 800–900 cooperatives (I-JCB 2008).
16   See I-LP 2006; I-SV 2007.

ing to Sunacoop, there were some 274,000 registered cooperatives.[17] According to statistics from Sunacoop, 27 percent of them, 73,968, were in operation and were officially certified as cooperatives.[18]

Of the cooperatives operating in 2008, 49.38 percent worked in the service sector, principally tourism, business services, cleaning, industrial maintenance, and beauty shops. 25.3 percent were productive cooperatives, mostly in agriculture, cattle, fishing, manufacturing, and industry. Another 11.48 percent were transport cooperatives and 7.64 percent communal banks.[19] Without counting the communal banks – the financial entity of the communal councils that assumes the legal form of a cooperative without creating any jobs – in 62,000 cooperatives there were 2,012,784 people working, around 13 percent of the economically active population.

1.1 Roots of Cooperativism in Venezuela

Beyond collective forms of production and work deriving from indigenous or Afro-Venezuelan traditions, the cooperative movement in Venezuela began in the early twentieth century. Several agricultural cooperatives emerged in the early 60s, receiving support from the state during the 1961 agrarian reform. Nevertheless, most of these cooperatives rapidly became businesses in which peasants received salaries but did not participate in or influence the decision-making. State support was given from the perspective of 'pacification' of the popular movements of the era, in the framework of the concept of the US's 'Alliance for Progress'.[20]

The first Law of Cooperatives in 1966 created the National Supraintendency of Cooperatives (Sunacoop) and regulated state support.[21] During the 70s, a cooperativist tendency was manifested, influenced by young Catholic community activists who 'adopted cooperativism as a tool for social transformation'.[22] There also emerged several successful peasant and artisanal cooperatives, especially in the states of Lara, Trujillo, Falcón, Táchira, Mérida and Barinas, which in part had their roots in the politico-cultural work of the PCV and of the PRV-FALN guerrillas.[23]

---

17   Baute 2009.
18   See Baute 2009.
19   See Sunacoop 2008.
20   Díaz 2006, p. 151.
21   Sunacoop was the institution tasked with registering and supervising cooperatives in Venezuela.
22   Bastidas 2003, p. 23.
23   Díaz 2006, p. 152.

The cooperatives created during this time achieved the greatest coordination, establishing 18 Central Regional Cooperatives in 1967, and the National Central Cooperative (CECONAVE) in 1976. The Central Cooperative of Social Services of Lara (CECOSESOLA) in Barquisimeto, which began in 1967, is considered the most successful traditional (i.e. pre-Chávez) cooperative of Venezuela. It has a network of 80 cooperatives of producers and consumers with some 20,000 members, of which some 300 work in cooperatives.[24]

1.2   Governmental Policies of Support for Cooperatives

The 1999 Constitution assigned to the cooperatives a special importance as a means of economic inclusion, democratic participation (article 70), and decentralisation (article 184). The Constitution established the legal responsibility of the state to 'promote and protect' the cooperatives (articles 118 and 308), with the idea that they would receive massive state support in order to reach a social and economic equilibrium.[25] It was thought that the cooperatives' culture of solidarity work would radiate outward from them.

The creation of cooperatives was facilitated as of 2001 with passage of the Special Law of Cooperative Associations, which eliminated the feasibility study contemplated by the previous law for the creation of cooperatives, removed fees for the official registration of cooperatives and other red tape, reaffirmed that they were exempt from the Rent Tax, and highlighted the state's obligation to support them.[26] Under these favourable conditions, registration of cooperatives increased massively as of 2004.

At first, institutional support was focused on family cooperatives or those with a small number of partners. The work of the various institutions was uncoordinated and the creation of new cooperatives was not yet massive. But after defeating the destabilising manoeuvres of the opposition, the Venezuelan government has since 2004 dedicated itself to promoting domestic production and to a more systematic restructuring of the Venezuelan economy.

Two presidential decrees in 2003 and 2004 required all state institutions and businesses to prioritise small businesses and cooperatives over other private contractors. In many institutions, employees of private businesses with whom there were service contracts (cleaning, security, food, etc.) were incited to form their own cooperatives so that they could be contracted directly by the institutions without having to resort to private businesses.

---

24   See Fox 2006; Melcher 2008; Piñeiro 2007.
25   Díaz 2006, pp. 160–3.
26   See I-JCB 2008.

In 2004, Minep was created, which, along with other institutions, promoted the cooperatives more actively.[27] Sunacoop and different ministries and institutions began to offer workshops about cooperativism (values, principles, basic organisation, rights and responsibilities under the new law, etc.) and supported the forming of cooperatives by workshop participants.

A programme of labour training, the Vuelvan Caras Mission, was created under the responsibility of Minep. Although the initial goal was 50 percent higher, until late 2007 (when it was restructured and renamed the Ché Guevara Mission), Vuelvan Caras trained some 800,000 people and funded 10,122 small and medium-sized entities of production, the vast majority of which were cooperatives, and in which 680,000 people worked.[28] Additionally, many cooperatives appeared spontaneously, stimulated by state discourse and policies.

The cooperatives received credits with preferential conditions and more flexible requisites through microcredit programmes according to the Law of Microfinance, under which very small cooperatives can even get interest-free loans. Access to credit is organised through the state banks established for this purpose (Women's Bank, Bank of Economic and Social Development, Bank of the Sovereign People, Bank of Regional Promotion for the Andes – Banfoandes) and through other financing organisations.

Minep, PDVSA, and other institutions, companies, and banks of the state, as well as local and regional administrations, supported the creation of cooperatives with financing, support, training, and guarantees of purchase.[29] All these entities of the state between 2003 and 2008 have invested more than a billion dollars in the construction and support of cooperatives.[30]

1.3 Limitations of State Support for Cooperatives

State support has been basic to the massive creation of cooperatives. Most Venezuelans who have formed cooperatives come from the most marginal sectors of society, and usually do not have capital to invest, nor do they have access to credit. Moreover, their generally low level of education and lack of experience in dealing with institutions make it harder still for them to do the administrative work necessary for forming a cooperative.

At the same time, many cooperatives under construction have been harmed by the ineffectiveness of financial institutions and state services. Financing,

---

27 Renamed Ministry of the Communal Economy (MINEC) in 2008 and Ministry of Communes in 2009.
28 Azzellini 2010, pp. 220–4; Minec 2009.
29 Ellner 2006, p. 84.
30 See Baute 2009.

once allocated, takes months to be delivered, and the same goes for machinery or promised inputs. There are also cases in which the inputs delivered are below the value set in the institutional contracts with the cooperatives. Moreover, in many cases the institutions often do not provide the cooperatives with the requisite technical assistance.[31] In the case of agricultural cooperatives, it has not been unusual for them to be forced to resort to agribusiness companies to plant, compromising their harvest because the government funding did not arrive on time. Thus, many of the agricultural cooperatives that were formed under the Vuelvan Caras Mission framework went for months and even more than a year without receiving land, even though they were well prepared and ready to go to work.

There have also been deficiencies in the cooperatives themselves: 'the non-requirement of training prior to the creation or as a requisite of the association, detracts from the principles, values, and democratic practices, making the cooperatives just like any other capitalized business'.[32] Cooperative values and principles, organisational plans, internal cohesion, and inter-cooperative integration were lacking in many new cooperatives. A considerable number of cooperatives were registered simply because doing so did not involve expenditures, with some people listed as participants in several cooperatives; others were really family businesses; and still others were formally registered as cooperatives to gain access to state aid. Thus, some cooperatives only existed on paper, and there was misappropriation of funds.

The unprecedented growth in the number of cooperatives outpaced the creation of efficient state mechanisms to support them, inspect them, and monitor the proper use of government resources. Sunacoop, for example, had only eight auditors, and each audit required two days or so.[33] Nor were sufficient expert personnel available to conduct support workshops, especially in the case of technical materials and accounting. Even the workers in the ministries and institutions recognise that the accountability of many cooperatives and the Sunacoop inspections have been insufficient.[34] Moreover, in many cases the institutional personnel sent to support the cooperatives were insufficiently prepared or totally inept, although with full institutional authority. Many institutional interventions in cooperatives increased problems and conflicts instead of resolving them.[35]

---

31 See Piñeiro 2008.
32 Bastidas 2003, pp. 54–5.
33 See Piñeiro 2005.
34 See Ellner 2008.
35 See Melcher 2008.

Beyond the institutional deficiencies, there were also many problems within the cooperatives. Among the greatest obstacles to their successful functioning were the 'capitalist' orientation of members and the lack of worker consciousness about administrative labour practices.[36] Social coherence was debilitated by internal conflicts originating principally in lack of experience with respect to social relations and administrative tasks. Moreover, these shortcomings and conflicts were exacerbated by the lack of collective supervisory mechanisms.[37]

1.4   Internal Organisation of Cooperatives

Notwithstanding the problems and shortcomings described above, the new Venezuelan cooperatives generally have a democratising effect on the world of work and a liberating effect for the working population. Participants generally know that without bosses giving orders, everyone has the same rights and obligations. The absence of a vertical hierarchy, together with the democratisation of the organisational structure, contributes to workers having a more complete vision of the processes of production, augmenting their responsibility and commitment, and creates a more satisfactory, agreeable work environment. Dulfo Guerrero, Plant I coordinator of the cooperative Textileros del Táchira, explains:

> In the workplace the employer is always looking for a way to intimidate the worker. Certainly we have noticed that they did great psychological harm to the vast majority of workers who had more than 30 years of service to the company. Today, no, on the contrary, when we visit our production manager, our sales manager, we feel a great joy, why? Because we know they are the people that are somehow moving the interests of the cooperative for the well-being of all.

> We want to ask those who have administrative responsibility to please be clearer, more precise, and not hide information, in order to avoid a disagreeable experience. Because we are all totally clear that if the administrators here don't satisfy the aspirations of the members, then they are the ones who would be at risk of leaving the cooperative as such.[38]

---

36   Ibid.
37   See Piñeiro 2007.
38   See Azzellini and Ressler 2006.

The decision-making participation of workers in the cooperatives is generally direct. Because of its democratic character, cooperative management is substantially different from that of private capitalist enterprise and conventional state companies. According to the law of cooperatives, the supreme organ and body of decision of the affairs of the cooperative is the assembly of all members, although for lesser questions decision-making power can be delegated.[39] The assembly generally decides at least the most important aspects like the election of its directors (at least five: general coordinator or president, treasurer, secretary, social auditor, and education coordinator); production targets based on sales commitments; workers' monthly income or 'advances'; the distribution of surplus; the taking on of debt; and the inclusion or exclusion of members.

According to the law, decisions are usually made by simple majority, although changes in rules, or dissolving the cooperative or fusing it with another, require a three-fourths majority (Art. 17, 70, 71). The voting mechanism is proposed and decided by the assembly itself. In general, officers (directors, work coordinators, etc.) are elected by secret ballot, while other decisions are made by a show of hands.[40] All cooperatives must deliver the minutes of the assemblies in which the most important decisions are made to Sunacoop, which verifies that the cooperatives comply at the minimum with requirements to have an annual general assembly at the end of the fiscal year, to decide what to do with surpluses, and to affirm that they have the minimum quorum.[41] With respect to the latter requirement, it can be noted that in the cooperatives that function best, the modality prevails of looking for consensual solutions, or at least with much more than a simple majority.

The process of discussion, collective management and decision-making assemblies with democratic participation by all is a learning process that helps develop workers' skills and tends to improve production processes, which nobody knows as well as the workers. They begin to know other areas and contextualise their own specific knowledge of certain phases or stages of production. With this broader vision of the production process, they also acquire the ability to make more general decisions. This helps to overcome the social division of labour (the basis of bourgeois society), the division between manual and intellectual work, and therefore the separation of areas of work and the decision-making work entails. That obviously does not mean that specialisa-

---

39 LEAC 2001, art. 21, 26.
40 See Piñeiro 2007.
41 Ibid.

tion is suppressed; especially in advanced and complex production processes, it is necessary. On the contrary, it signifies giving everyone the possibility of an overview that will facilitate general decision-making and prevent privileges arising from the division of labour.

Collective democratic practice and self-management of work also make workers grow personally. This is especially the case with cooperatives that have sprung up as worker initiatives and that have had to fight and keep fighting to obtain the necessary support. Many workers describe, with satisfaction, how their lives changed through the process of protagonistic participation in cooperative management. Generally, beyond learning about all areas of the cooperative, they also deepen their education, both scholastic and political.

1.5   The Problematisation of Cooperativism

In an empirical analysis of 15 cooperatives, Piñeiro establishes that democratic practice is weakened in them by internal conflicts that principally have their origin in the workers' scarce professional and administrative experience.[42] The majority are women without work experience, not even in the informal sector. Internal conflicts are exacerbated by the absence of collective supervisory mechanisms that ensure that everyone complies not only with their rights but also with their acquired obligations and responsibilities. Moreover, in some cooperatives, most often in the newly constituted ones, democratic management is also affected by the fact that only a small circle of directors, or even only the president, make decisions, without consulting the assembly.

Most of the cooperatives studied by Piñeiro followed the logic of capital; it was a mistake to think that cooperatives would naturally produce 'for the satisfaction of social necessities' and that the internal solidarity of the cooperatives, based on their collective management, 'would spontaneously extend into local communities'. Instead, they concentrated on maximising their earnings without supporting adjacent communities. In order to have higher income, many declined to integrate new members into the cooperative, and some cooperatives even concentrated on producing for export in place of satisfying local and national needs first.[43]

Although reducing vertical hierarchies did generally signify an improvement of working conditions, the fact of having many owners rather than one does not by itself produce fundamental changes in the form of operating a capitalist enterprise. Many Venezuelan cooperatives continued resorting to competition,

---

42   Ibid.
43   See Piñeiro 2010.

exploitation, and capitalist efficacy, adopting the capitalist logic of profit maximisation while leaving aside solidarity and social aspects. Even the majority of the cooperatives, including those formed by Vuelvan Caras, have been integrated into or assimilated by the capitalist market. Some authors attribute this to a 'capitalist' orientation;[44] to this, however, one must add lack of experience in the development of alternative markets, lack of support, and the pressure of the capitalist market.

The 100 Nuclei of Endogenous Development (NUDES), created as part of Vuelvan Caras with the goal of creating networks of cooperatives that could contribute to overcoming capitalist logic, for the most part did not comply with that initial objective. The expectation was that socially productive chains and networks only materialised in a few cases, generally when some previous social organisation already existed and the state had specially promoted the creation of such networks.[45] Instead of forming a new social or solidarity economy, most of the cooperatives ended up at the service of the monopolies that controlled distribution and the national markets.

The legal status of cooperatives has also been applied to some cases of companies taken over by workers and/or nationalised by the government. Company co-ownership by workers and state institutions furnished the justification for co-management, or shared administration. Factories were re-founded as joint stock companies (*sociedades anónimas*) with 51 percent state ownership and 49 percent ownership by a worker cooperative. All important decisions affecting the factory were made in the weekly assembly of the cooperative, with larger-scale decisions having to be approved by the state. In the large companies of mixed ownership by state and workers, however, the workers rejected that model and proposed that all shares in the company become social property; that is, even though the workers managed the enterprise democratically by means of a workers' council, they saw that being co-proprietors with the state pushed them toward capitalist logic. This model has also been abandoned by the state.

There is also the risk that cooperatives might be used by capitalist enterprises for subcontracting workers, thus evading the guarantees and rights established in labour legislation, making working conditions more flexible. This even occurred with some state institutions, which tried to oblige certain employees to form cooperatives in order to contract with them afterward. In the region of Táchira, the personnel of the Vuelvan Caras Mission labour train-

---

44   See Melcher 2008.
45   See Piñeiro 2008.

ing programme had to defend themselves against the attempt of mission directors to require them to form Cooperatives of Integral Assistance, with the intention of then subcontracting them.[46] However, there are still many workers, especially the more qualified ones, who prefer to work as a cooperative in institutional projects since it gives them more leeway, provided that the work is not totally predefined.

Some labour sectors also fear that the massification of cooperatives could obscure the employer-employee relation, diminishing their respective responsibilities and, in this way, obscuring the class relations that continue to exist in the Venezuelan capitalist system.[47]

The fact that out of 274,000 cooperatives registered in 2008, only 73,968 were operative and certified, and that some of those were badly managed or were not really cooperatives, has provoked strong criticism of the policy of promoting cooperatives in Venezuela.[48] The index of success of the cooperatives might appear low, but the total number of operating cooperatives actually represents an enormous increase compared with the 800 that existed in 1998. The creation of a large number of small businesses, even though they do not ascribe to the cooperativist philosophy, in and of itself represents a certain 'democratisation of capital' in the framework of the Venezuelan economy, which has long been characterised by an extremely monopolistic and oligopolistic market.[49]

Many who sympathise with the Bolivarian process believe that the cooperative sector will consolidate in the medium term. Moreover, the government underscores the high value of experience, and because of that, it does not consider the efforts to have been a bad investment. From the experience thus obtained, Sunacoop restructured its training for future cooperativists, strengthening especially the social and political aspects of the training. In addition, it began to work more closely with the organised communities, from which there emerged the model of community-administered cooperatives. The communal enterprises, which have spread rapidly, form the base of the economy of the communes, as I will discuss (see Chapter 7).

---

46 See Aguirre 2006.
47 See Ellner 2008.
48 See Baute 2009.
49 See Ellner 2008.

2 New Entrepreneurial Models

2.1 *Private Enterprise and Co-Management*

At the end of 2005, the government created the Factory Within programme (*Fábrica Adentro*), assigned to the Ministry of Popular Power for Light Industries and Commerce (MPPILCO as of 2010, previously MILCO), for private enterprises with economic problems and low production levels. Factory Within offered credit at very low interest, subsidies, technological support, and worker training. In order to participate in this programme, employers must reach an agreement with their workers about how to implement a model of co-management that allows the workers to participate in administration, in the board of directors, and in the business's profit. In addition, the business has to transfer part of its earnings (5–15 percent) to an Industrial Transformation Fund, is not permitted to lay off workers, and must create new employment.

By the end of 2006, 1,520 businesses had entered the programme, of which 847 had their projects approved, received credits, and began to implement the agreements. Of these businesses 69 were previously closed down, while the others increased their production capacity. In total, 268 new projects for substitution of imports were presented.[50]

The measures, however, did not bring about the desired democratisation of labour. The quality of the supposed co-management varied from factory to factory, without ever achieving a true participation of the workers in managing the enterprise. In several cases, the modality of a minority co-ownership was adopted, transferring a portion of the property to the workers, through individual shares of property or through the minority participation of a workers' cooperative in the enterprise. This pulled workers into a business logic without giving them any real participation in decision-making. Thus, although they shared the principal owner's interest in producing more added value, they had no opportunity to make decisions affecting work or production.

As a consequence, Factory Within changed its orientation. Though it continues to support private enterprise, it has expanded its action to socialist state enterprises and cooperatives, providing important technical support. In 2010, there were 1,200 companies attached to the programme.[51]

---

50 'Compañías entregarán 10% de las utilidades al Fondo de Desarrollo Endógeno Industrial', in *VTV* (20 December 2006), available at: www.aporrea.org/actualidad/n88173.html.

51 Programa Fábrica Adentro acompaña el trabajo de las cooperativas, Prensa MCTI/Amazonas, available at: http://www.cntq.gob.ve/.

2.2 Co-Management in State Businesses

> We cannot say that co-management failed, because co-management was never put into practice. Some attempts were made, some things were done, good experiences ... We have to take from those experiences and go past them, go deeper.[52]

∴

'Co-management' refers to a mode of business management shared between the state and workers. But no co-management law was ever passed; a proposal advanced by a union sector in 2007 was rejected by many workers given that the debate and the existing practice were more advanced than the law, meaning that co-management had no legal basis. Consequently, different models have been discussed and applied. In Venezuela, it was planned to implement co-management in state enterprises and in companies in which the state participates or provides important support. The models usually give more participation to the workers in theory than co-management does in different European countries (Germany, for example), although in many cases in practice the real participation of the workers has proved to be more limited.

Co-management is rooted in the experiences of the 2002 lockout, when the directors and many officers of the state oil company PDVSA stopped oil production. The PDVSA workers took command, elected their superiors collectively and restored the basic operations of the petroleum industry, which had been reduced almost to zero. This enormous collective effort nevertheless was maintained only during the extreme situation of the business lockout. Initiatives of workers to introduce some kind of co-management in PDVSA were rapidly rejected and boycotted by the directors. The first steps of co-management from below were taken during the oil lockout at CADELA (Electricity Company of the Andes, Limited) and CADAFE (Electric Administration and Promotion Company, Limited) state electrical companies. CADELA created a co-management with the workers and communities early on, while at CADAFE there were problems until 2010, when a new initiative was successful.[53]

---

52 See Carlos Agüero, worker, Inveval, 2008.
53 See Gómez 2005a, 2005b; Harnecker 2005a; Lebowitz 2006, pp. 102–3.

The greatest governmental impact on and support for co-management occurred in 2005–6, when the latter was introduced in some state enterprises and others of mixed property (state/workers' cooperative). While the lack of a co-management law caused conflicts about the type of co-management, it also opened a space for experimentation with a wide variety of different models that might otherwise have been victims of regulation.[54]

Companies that were considered "strategic" were excluded from co-management, as in the case of PDVSA, officially a 'strategic business' that could not be 'left' in workers' hands. The partisans of workers' control, however, argued to the contrary: that strategic importance is one more point in favour of broad co-management. During the oil lockout, PDVSA was abandoned by the administration and put back into action once again by the workers, demonstrating that it has been the workers who have remained faithful to the process of change, defending their enterprises and guaranteeing the recovery of industries.

Despite the political orientation toward co-management, at many state companies there was no co-management because of the contradictions inherent in functioning within a bourgeois framework and a capitalist environment, and also because of the resistance to change on the part of many state institutions and companies whose business and political culture is (despite the rhetoric) vertical, not horizontal. Democratising company structures, then, is not a harmonious process at all, but a very conflictive one.

In the case of co-management, this also can be due to diverging understandings and expectations. While workers usually see it as an intermediate step toward workers' control and the construction of a new socialism from below, many officials see it more as a mechanism for reducing conflict at work and improving the processes, thus taking advantage of the labour force's subjectivity without allowing it true participation. This experience has also been repeated in the creation of the Socialist Workers' Councils (CST) in state enterprises and institutions since 2008. The deeper the process of change and/or popular mobilisation, the greater the contradictions. Conflicts over co-management and problems in its practice emerged especially in the firms taken over and expropriated, and in state enterprises where there was a worker initiative for more workers' participation or control. The first two businesses to be expropriated – the paper factory Invepal and the valve factory Inveval, both of which had been taken by the workers – exemplify this situation, as does the case of the state aluminium smelter Alcasa.

---

54   See I-EL 2007; I-RI 2006.

As a consequence of co-management experiences and the resulting conflicts with the state and its institutions, the politically active workers' sector of small and medium-sized enterprises rejected co-management models that turned them into owners of the means of production, given that the condition of proprietors in the still-capitalist environment was in contradiction with the intention of building a socialist model; this move was, without a doubt, an expression of class struggle. Instead, the workers favoured models that turned the enterprise into direct social property, managed completely by workers and communities.[55] This is also the position of the CST (Socialist Workers' Councils),[56] which proposed a model based on councils of multiple administrations mixed with workers' councils, resource producers, communities, and, in the case of very large factories, the state.[57] In a document resulting from a national encounter, the co-management implemented in Venezuela was criticised as unsuitable for building socialism.

> The co-management that has so far been applied ... has corresponded more to a reformist concept within capitalism, than to a truly socialist concept ...
>
> Thus it recognises, incorrectly, that ownership of the means of production – capital – is what generates the right to participate in decision-making. In the socialist conception, it is labour in all its forms: material or intellectual, simple or complex – recognised as a source of social wealth – that empowers participation in the management of companies ...
>
> If shares are the private property of some workers and/or capitalists, they cannot at the same time be the property of other workers, nor of the communities, nor of all the *pueblo*. And in consequence, neither can be the surpluses that are generated in the productive process ... That is, with the property of actions, workers end up converted into new capitalists.
>
> Historical experience with co-management does not generate a positive balance. Its application in the disappeared Federated Republic of Yugoslavia signified worker alienation, capitalist anarchy, and competition between workers of some enterprises with others. And in the end, it reproduced capitalism.[58]

---

55 Lebowitz 2006, pp. 102–3.
56 Before they were officially introduced in 2010, the CST already existed and were the largest forum for workers' councils and pro-worker initiatives.
57 MinTrab 2008, pp. 15–16.
58 MinTrab 2008, pp. 13–14.

This position should not be confused with the critique of co-management expressed by traditional or Marxist labour unions, which reject the participation of workers in businesses as a neoliberal strategy. There is always a risk that co-management can be used as a neoliberal strategy to generate better earnings, increasing production through worker integration while mitigating worker demands. Like almost all cultural, social, and political innovations, co-management has been absorbed into capitalism and has contributed to its modernisation. However, in a serious project of social transformation with a socialist perspective, the workers cannot remain salaried and dependent. They have to assume responsibility for production and for their workplaces; otherwise there will be no social transformation. This position has been expressed as well by workers at factories like Alcasa, Sidor, Inveval, Invepal, and obviously by the movement for workers' control.

2.3 Social Production Companies

In 2005, the idea arose of creating Social Production Companies (EPS) as the base of a transition toward a socialist model of production. With this model, the Venezuelan government assumed that companies (cooperatives, state enterprises, mixed enterprises, and even private companies) could be socially responsible regardless of their form of ownership, and accordingly tried positive incentives to promote socially responsible behaviour on the part of companies. It was hoped that the EPS, incentivised by state aid (credit on preferential terms, technical assistance, purchase contracts), would place a higher value on social than on private benefit (and the accumulation of capital) and would orient their production toward social necessities instead of being guided by capitalist logic, thus prioritising use value over exchange value.[59]

Nevertheless, no official, universally valid definition of an EPS was ever created. Different state institutions have implemented different concepts. For example, the EPS formed by or with the aid of the state petroleum company PDVSA had to pay a portion of their profits to a PDVSA fund, with which PDVSA financed projects in the communities. This seems more an additional tax than an integration of the cooperatives into the communities. Many companies that in reality did not comply with the criteria registered as EPS for the advantages offered by the state.[60]

Faced with only partially successful experiences, and in expectation of new collective business forms that were to be created through constitutional re-

---

59 See El Troudi and Monedero 2006.
60 Díaz 2006, pp. 157–8.

form,[61] the EPS model stopped being applied as of the second half of 2007. It was concluded that in order to direct company activities towards the satisfaction of social needs and not only maximising their private profit, they should be controlled by the workers together with society, and in particular by the communities they affect.

The term EPS has been used since 2008 in the absence of precise criteria for defining it, but by this time referring not so much to Social Production Companies as to Social Property or Socialist Production Companies. These new EPS can be companies of 'indirect social property', which are administered by the state; or companies of 'direct social property', administered directly by communities and workers.

All the (non-strategic) state companies and especially the new companies built in the framework of the broad state programmes should gradually transform into direct social property. The workers of these factories are supposed to be chosen by the communal councils, while the institutions contribute only skilled workers necessary to train others. To the extent that workers are trained, management and specialised positions will be transferred gradually to the hands of workers and organised communities. However, in many cases the institutions and company managers do not make much effort to organise this process or prepare the workers. Given that the workers are fighting for participation in the control of the companies, this increasingly leads to conflict.

---

61 This was rejected in a referendum in late 2007.

CHAPTER 6

Workers' Control, Workers' Councils, and Class Struggle

Workers' councils do not possess any secret quality which makes them by virtue of their form, revolutionary. They do, however, have several characteristics which make them different from unions. First, they are based on the power of workers who are together every day and exercise continuous power over production. Second, they are directly controlled by the workers themselves, who can recall their delegates at any time. Third, they follow the actually-existing organisation of the working class in production, rather than dividing it along lines that quickly become obsolete, as has happened over and over again in the history of unionism.[1]

∴

A thought from comrade Che: 'The worst enemy of all revolution is bureaucratism and corruption.' This is why we propose that the workers without bureaucracy or corruption are the only ones who can develop and establish the base of socialism, promoting the communal councils, the student councils, the peasant councils, together with the integration of the new being, of the new worker, of the new socialist being.[2]

∴

Throughout history, under every form of political system and government, everywhere in the world, workers have struggled for participation in decision-making processes at work, and have tried to develop forms of co- and self-management, or workers' control. Even without previous explicit experience of forming councils, collective administration – whether by means of assemblies or other mechanisms of direct democracy and horizontal relations – has often

---

1 Brecher 1973, p. 106.
2 See Nelson Rodríguez, worker, Inveval, I-NR 2007.

appeared as an inherent tendency of the worker base. What clearly emerges in the legacy of partisans of workers' control, both historic and contemporary, is the liberating character of workers' control in transforming a situation of capitalist alienation and authoritarian control into one of democratic practice.[3]

The struggle for greater participation in the administration of business, the takeover of companies, and the struggle for workers' control in present-day Venezuela within the framework of a growing class struggle: these are not new phenomena. Worker initiatives for control of their companies have historically appeared in situations of economic, political, or social crisis, in socialist, national and democratic revolutions, under governments proclaimed socialist and in capitalist contexts, at times of peak production and in stages of restructuring or decline.

Nor is it a new phenomenon that Venezuelan workers in struggle find themselves confronting not only private entrepreneurs, capitalist structures, and company administration, but also union sectors and governmental institutions. Almost all the historical experiences of workers' control, especially workers' councils, have inevitably collided with political parties, unions, and state bureaucracies, whether in the Russian Revolution, Italy in the 1970s, Poland in the 1950s and 1980s, or in present-day Argentina, South Africa or India, to name only a few examples.

The common criticism that workers' councils have historically been paralysed by profound challenges and have confronted serious institutional obstacles cannot be denied. However, seeing that everywhere there are also successful examples of worker self-management, the most pertinent question is: how have these challenges been confronted in the most democratic work organisations? In many cases, moreover, the obstacles have been imposed by the state or by parties, although there is no doubt that the inevitable interactions with the capitalist environment have provoked severe contradictions and complications for companies under self-management.

In spite of the ups and downs of the struggle for workers' control in Venezuela, it has become stronger and taken on more concrete forms of organisation, forming an important part of the historical legacy of workers' worldwide struggles against alienation and exploitation for gaining control of their companies and of their lives.[4] Without a doubt all historical experiences are different, but the essence of these struggles remains the same: opposing oneself to

---

3   See Azzellini 2015; Cormenzana 2009; Korsch 1977; Lanz 2007; Lavaca 2004; Mandel 1974; Ness and Azzellini 2011; Pannekoek 2008, Rebón 2004; 2006; Ruggeri 2005, 2010; Sitrin 2006, 2012; Trabajadores de CVG and Alcasa 2009.
4   Azzellini 2015; Ness and Azzellini 2011.

the form of the process of production – the backbone of any society – and building, by means of councils and self-management, elements of a future classless society free of exploitation. In Venezuela, however, a combination of characteristics makes for a special case. On the one hand, the declared intent of the government is to introduce workers' control, even though in practice the logics of bourgeois institutional power and control work against it; on the other, unlike most historical cases, in many companies the struggle for workers' control is not the result of a situation of production collapse that somehow obliges the workers to assume production as an emergency measure.

When in 2006 the workers' control proposal was assumed by the government, principally by Chávez, it was supported only by small nuclei of workers. But since that time, public debate and workplace experiences have contributed to the growth of a workers' control movement. Although workers' control forms part of the government's discourse, and although Chávez himself launched the proposal to form Socialist Workers' Councils (CST), there is nevertheless strong institutional resistance to transferring control of the means of production into workers' hands and to their having a decisive role in the administration. The resistance is even greater to workers' participation in the institutions themselves.

In an interview, Vice Minister of Labour Elio Colmenares defined workers' control as the mechanism by which workers control the bureaucratic administrative structures in order to guarantee the materialisation of the state's policies, which are supposedly generated by a common interest and in favour of common benefit.[5] This vision, which recalls aspects of the failed 'state socialism', represents an important tendency in various ministries, which after the failure of co-management have concentrated on promoting medium-sized factories under institutional administration. That focus, however, is not shared by all of the ministry, and even less so by the government as a whole, the National Assembly or other institutions.

There is no common position in the government on the characteristics of workers' control; because of the different positions on the left with respect to the subject, and because the government and its institutions are permeated with contradictions and class struggle, there are different approaches in parallel, and the situation is changing on an ongoing basis. So on the one hand, the government issues calls to the workers to take over unproductive or badly administered factories. The government's official discourse is in favour of workers' control, and expropriations and nationalisations demonstrate its political

---

5   See I-EC 2010.

will to undertake structural transformations. On the other hand, the institutions leave very little space for post-nationalisation initiatives by workers, and they tend to maintain control of administration and production.

This chapter will analyse the emergence and development of struggles for workers' control in Bolivarian Venezuela, concentrating on specific cases to exemplify the routes, conflicts, and contradictions in the process. The intention is to show how the struggle for workers' control is framed by class struggle and the struggle for another system, although in Venezuela it takes place within the complex context of cooperation and conflict with the state and its institutions.

1   Recuperated Companies and Nationalisation

> They didn't meet payroll, the employees went a month without getting paid. So we took the initiative, because we had already said: we're going to take the company. But we had no one to back us. When they missed payroll we got together and took the company, and on the 7th at 8 a.m., we didn't let the administrators enter. And until today they haven't been able to enter and they're not going to enter, because we're here, the revolutionary workers, and we continue with the revolution so that all the companies that are taken or are badly administered, pass into the hands of the workers, since the businessmen, the so-called businessmen, are unable to run a company.[6]

∴

Recuperated companies (*empresas recuperadas*) are commonly understood to be those that have been taken out of private capitalist control by their own workers. In Venezuela, because of the specific modes of the process of change, the term generally refers to companies under control of workers or the state that were acquired after being closed by the owners, or acquired from banks (in the case of bankruptcy), or expropriated for national interest (so the term does not always refer to companies that have been occupied by workers). These companies are either direct social property (under control of the workers and/or communities) or indirect social property (administered by the state), and some

---

6   See Zulay Boyer, worker, Tomates Guarico, in Azzellini and Ressler 2006.

have assumed the legal form of cooperatives. According to the declared will of the government, they must have collective or mixed forms (state and workers) of management, although in many cases there is not a true participation of the workers in making the company's decisions, and in the majority of state enterprises there are labour conflicts and struggles for greater worker participation.

Although the possibility of expropriation forms part of the 1999 Constitution, there were few expropriations before late 2005, concentrated principally in the petroleum sector, to renationalise the petroleum industry that in spite of being supposedly national had been in part privatised in the previous decade through the policy known as the 'petroleum opening'.

During and after the lockout of 2002/3, workers took over several small and medium-sized enterprises, demanding payment of unpaid wages or to prevent closure. At first, the government delegated the cases to labour courts, until expropriations began in 2005.[7] Until 2007, however, the expropriation policy was not systematic, except for the petroleum and agricultural sectors, in the latter of which the 'war on the *latifundio* [large estate]' was declared in 2005.[8] Expropriations in other sectors were usually the consequence of pressure from workers who had taken over the companies and demanded expropriation.

Systematic policy expropriations began in 2007, affecting some strategic sectors: the principal cement companies; Sidor, the largest steel mill in the country (after a long struggle by the workers); four refineries of heavy crude in the Orinoco Oil Belt, which were operated by international petroleum companies; CANTV, the largest telecommunications company, which had been privatised in the 1990s; and electrical utilities, banks, and various food companies. From 2007 to the end of September 2011, some 988 companies were nationalised, 402 of them were in 2011.[9] Among these were many large agricultural estates – between 2002 and 2011 more than 2.5 million hectares were recovered from the *latifundio*[10] – and various nationalisations in the financial sector, in 2009 and 2010, of small fraudulent banks that were at the point of bankruptcy or had defrauded their customers. Given that the former proprietors were indemnified according to the market value of their property (if it was legally their property, which especially in the case of the *latifundio* is not the norm), some proprietors of large estates and medium-sized companies were not opposed to nationalisation, which signified a good deal for them.

---

7   Ellner 2006, p. 85.
8   Azzellini 2007a, pp. 198–221.
9   'Fedecámaras: El Gobierno ha expropiado 402 empresas sólo en 2011', *El Universal* (27 September 2011).
10 INTI, available at: http://www.inti.gob.ve/quienes.php.

The first expropriation of a private business outside the petroleum sector was the paper factory Venepal (now Invepal), in January 2005, and at the end of April there followed National Valvemaker (CNV, now Inveval), which principally produced for the petroleum industry; both had been taken over by their workers. In July 2005, the government began a policy of expropriation of several businesses that had been closed and taken over, after more than two years of pressure from below and the takeovers. The opposition found itself weakened after having failed with all its grand mobilisations from the coup of 2002, to the petroleum sabotage and business lockout in 2002/3 and to the recall referendum against Chávez in August 2004. The decisive factor in all these victories of Bolivarianism has been popular mobilisation.

National production was hurt by the coup, the petroleum sabotage and the lack of investment. On the one hand, there was the need to increase production in the country; on the other, the stalled enterprises taken over by their workers. The Executive took advantage of the favourable political climate and began expropriations.

State support was basic for most occupied companies. Very few companies taken over could produce on their own account, like the National Hardware Industry (INAF), a factory of faucets and pipes in Aragua, or the textile factory Gotcha of Maracay, both of which were taken over by their workers in 2006. INAF was producing under workers' control, without credit or state support, from the time of takeover in June 2008, and its 60 workers tried for more than two years to find an institutional response to their situation, delivering petitions, plans and analysis of the business, without ever getting an answer. In November 2009, Chávez saw by chance an interview with one of the workers on the state television channel VTV and followed up on the case immediately, signing and ordering nationalisation a week later.[11]

Almost all the companies recuperated by their workers, however, either had obsolete machinery or had been stripped by their owners after closing down, and needed large investments to get production going. Beyond the private sector, which obviously will not invest in a factory taken over by its workers, only the state has such quantities of capital. Although these companies managed to start up production, few had the productive and administrative capacity to survive capitalist competition on their own, so without the support of the state they would have been totally exposed to the capitalist market.

---

11   'Presidente Chávez ordenó la expropiación de la Industria Nacional de Artículos de Ferretería (INAF)', *Aporrea.org* (09 November 2009).

In late July 2005, on his television programme *Aló Presidente*, Chávez read a list of companies in the process of expropriation or under examination for expropriation, and of companies partly paralysed or closed – a total of 1,149 companies nationally, of which 136 were in the process of evaluation or expropriation. Chávez issued a call to the *pueblo* to report other closed companies and, speaking of a fish-processing plant, announced: 'If the owners don't want to open it, we will have to expropriate it and open it ourselves'.[12] María Cristina Iglesias, Minister of Labour, issued a call for the unions, workers, and ex-workers of abandoned or unproductive companies to take them over and recover them with state support. The initiative was received with enthusiasm by the union confederation UNT (National Workers' Union), which declared full support for the government's measures and announced the occupation of 800 closed companies.

The National Assembly joined the initiative and declared a 'national interest' – a legal mechanism that proceeds to expropriation – in the sugar plant of Cumanacoa and the pipemaker Siderorca in late September 2005. It had been more than two years since Cumanacoa was taken over by its workers, after its capacity had been reduced gradually to 20 percent. Siderorca had also been stopped for years. In the following months, several food companies that had been taken over by their workers were nationalised, among them the slaughterhouse Fribasa; a tomato plant belonging to the US company Heinz; and Promabasa, a corn flour processing plant belonging to the Venezuelan industrial group Polar. In most cases, the former owners did not receive indemnisation since over the years they had accumulated labour, social, and tax liabilities; some had even pocketed government credits and support, so there was no balance to pay them after the state expropriated them.

Nevertheless, the total number of businesses taken over, expropriated and acquired by the state was much below the 800 that had been announced. Not counting companies already expropriated or acquired by the state, the number of companies taken over in Venezuela, in 2006, came to around 40. Not even the UNT followed the announced policy of taking 800 businesses and neither did CCURA, an important left current within the UNT that plays a central role in many labour struggles.[13]

---

12   RNV (18 July 2005).
13   With a Trotskyist background, the Classist, Unitary, Revolutionary, and Autonomous Current (CCURA) was one of the largest, most active currents of the UNT, until it split in 2007. The minoritarian current kept the name CCURA; very worker-centred, rejecting the government as bourgeois, it founded its own party. The majoritarian current, which took the name 'Socialist Tide' (*Marea Socialista*), supports the government critically and even

There are several reasons why there were not massive takeovers of companies in the face of such apparently favourable conditions. Many of the companies had been closed for years; the ex-workers were not in contact with each other, and some had other work. In a few cases, as in the now Agroindustrial Cooperative Cacao Union in the state of Sucre, it happened that a sufficient part of the previous labouring mass returned to the factory.[14] The shuttered companies had in many cases been stripped of any usable pieces, or the machinery was obsolete, so that a rapid relaunch of production was unthinkable. In addition, the union tradition in Venezuela focuses on economic struggles, mainly wages.

Nor did state institutions show a strong commitment to promote and support the announced measures. In spite of Chávez's initiative, the government developed neither a clear modus operandi for the taken-over companies, nor a systematic, defined policy for productive sector expropriations. At the regional level, most governors did not support the implementation of Chávez's ideas with respect to expropriations and workers' control, and either did not support taken-over companies or opposed the expropriations. Without massive pressure from below, the President's initiatives remained stuck in the bureaucratic apparatus.

Workers' struggles to take over companies continued to provide the majority of the expropriations. Most of the recuperated companies and the struggles in favour of nationalisation remained very isolated and did not incentivise a local or regional dynamic.[15] During the first years, there were few contacts between recuperated factories, so there was little linkage of struggles and experiences. The occupations were born out of defensive situations, primarily motivated by the preservation of jobs. Radicalisation of the practices, and deeper reflection, usually occurred after the takeover, although it can be observed over time how the organisation of recuperated factories, subsequently accomplished within the framework of the movement for workers' control, has taken several qualitative and quantitative leaps since 2006.

---

forms a current in the PSUV. After being marginalised by the Maduro government, it decided to run with other groups on a platform critically supporting the government for the 2015 parliamentary elections, while several historical figures of Chavismo, who have also been marginalised by the Maduro government, are now close to Socialist Tide.

14 See Azzellini and Ressler 2006.
15 Lebowitz 2006, pp. 100–4; One exception was the workers' struggle for nationalisation at the steel plant Sidor in 2007–8. Despite the negative attitude of the Bolivarian governor of Bolívar state, a deeply rooted movement developed, with massive mobilisations, until Chávez ordered Sidor's nationalisation (I-OL 2008).

A more systematic policy of expropriation from mid-2008 has sought to build productive chains and give to the state and communities more control over the production and distribution of food, with the aim of guaranteeing the communities' food supply. More *latifundios* were expropriated; the company Agroisleña, which produces agricultural inputs, was nationalised, as were the Owens-Illinois glass bottle factory, several food production companies, and the supermarket chain Éxito/Cada. Although several companies for different reasons lowered their production volume or their efficiency after nationalisation, others, especially in food production, increased production considerably. Aceites Diana, for example, was out of production when it was nationalised in June 2008.

> As of that date, the workers produced initially 8,500 tons of product which has risen now to 20,000 among oil, vegetable shortening, and industrial margarine ... Jobs increased 50%, reaching 300 employees who worked in three shifts.[16]

However, the low level of institutional effort in preparing the workers to control the processes of production and administration, along with the institutional opposition to workers' protagonistic participation, occasioned more and more conflicts. In general, it can be affirmed that although working conditions and pay improved in the companies nationalised by the state, the institutions resisted the workers taking control of the businesses or of the decision-making; instead, state bureaucratic control predominated. Gustavo Martínez, the complaints secretary of the Café Fama de America union, nationalised and administered by the state, declared: 'This company increased its production 20 percent since the government expropriated it. Workers' pay improved, and and we even got Cestatickets, but we still are not part of company management'.[17]

As the case of Sanitarios Maracay demonstrates, contradictions and different points of view run through the government and its institutions. The company was closed by its owner, the oppositionist businessman Álvaro Pocaterra, on 14 November 2006, and was occupied the same day by 550 workers.[18] The plant began the production of sanitary equipment under control of workers who demanded expropriation and nationalisation. They wanted to incorporate its products, which were being sold at solidarity prices in the neighbourhood

---

16   '2010 ha sido el año de las expropiaciones', *Ultimas Noticias* (19 December 2010).
17   Ibid. Cestatickets are prepaid food vouchers distributed by employers in all workplaces with more than 20 employees that do not have a free canteen.
18   See *Aporrea.org* (19 November 2006).

for the bathrooms of newly constructed houses, into the framework of state programmes and housing. At the beginning of 2007, the first workers' council in Venezuela was formed at Sanitarios Maracay.

In spite of the organisational capacity of the workers to administer the company and the strong mobilisation of the Revolutionary Front of Co-managed and Occupied Companies (Freteco), the then minister of labour, Ramón Rivero, a declared Trotskyist coming from the FBT,[19] announced publicly that the company was not of 'national interest' and for that reason would not be nationalised. The UNT-CCURA in Maracay then organised a day of strikes and highway blockades on 22 May 2007, with the participation of some 3,000 workers from 120 companies, interrupting the principal traffic arteries of the city from 5am until 11am, in solidarity with the struggle for Sanitarios Maracay. When the Social Commission of the National Assembly learned of the actions, it issued a petition to President Chávez and to the Minister for Light Industry and Commerce (MILCO) to expropriate, by decree, Sanitarios Maracay and transfer management to the workers.[20] At the same time, minister Rivero signed a separate contract with the company's owner and employees. The factory, however, remained abandoned by the owner.

The workers, together with the CC of the zone, continued struggling to reopen the factory under workers' control. In 2008, they tried to manufacture some plastic pieces, but the initiative was unsuccessful because of the deplorable condition of the machinery. Surprisingly, Chávez announced in December 2008 that Sanitarios Maracay would be nationalised and a pact made with the workers.[21] Nevertheless, it was not until 19 December 2010 that this happened, when Chávez personally signed the expropriation decree. With the participation of workers' spokespeople and representatives of the Ministry of Science, Technology, and Intermediate Industries, an intervenor board was formed, which entered the company on 20 December.[22]

The workers began receiving their salaries again and began to work with the support of teams of engineers to restore the electrical lighting, which had been ripped out by the former owner. There were important investments in

---

19 FWB: Bolivarian Workers' Force, a moderate union current, later renamed Bolivarian Socialist Workers' Force.
20 'La Asamblea Nacional de Venezuela pide la expropiación de Sanitarios Maracay', available at: http://www.controlobrero.org/content/view/134/30/.
21 'Trabajadores de Sanitarios Maracay exigen el pago de pasivos laborales y que se concrete la nacionalización de la empresa', (22 December 2008), available at: http://www.aporrea.org/trabajadores/n125948.html.
22 *Correo del Orinoco* (21 December 2010).

machinery, and the company was reactivated in late 2011 producing bathrooms for the Vivienda Mission, a state housing construction programme.[23] The question of workers' control has not yet been resolved. A Socialist Workers' Council was formed, but its participation in decisions is limited.

2   Workers' Control and Workers' Councils

The democratisation of management is essential, it is the spirit of the constitution, the spirit of protagonistic participation. This can have different names. We speak of a horizontal organisation … that's the idea, the thick line, later we have to give form to how this horizontal line is going to function.[24]

...

From the beginning, we proposed direct management of the company and how we would organise it at the executive level and the administrative level but … beyond that, I believe the most important thing is to discuss the executive and administrative arrangements. We are creating political management by the new worker.[25]

...

The above testimony of Inveval and Alcasa workers reflects the growing demand for 'workers' control'. The issue has been raised more and more by striking workers demanding nationalisation of private companies, as well as in state-administered nationalised companies and in state companies and institutions. The demand has been reinforced especially in nationalised companies and in new state companies, whose workers from the beginning had the expectation that the management of the state would solve existing problems – something that was often not the case.

---

23   'VENEZUELA: Gobierno Nacional y trabajadores resucitaron a Sanitarios Maracay', Correo del Orinoco (09 August 2011).
24   See Carlos Agüero, worker, Alcasa, I-CA 2008.
25   See Nelson Rodríguez, worker, Inveval, I-NR 2007.

> The so-called 'Interventory Juntas' are generally integrated by technocrats, who apply the same general criteria that private companies apply against the labouring mass, the majority of these juntas 'are incoherent in their decision-making' because they follow a counter-revolutionary political line.[26]

Administrative officers installed by state institutions mostly do not have a political understanding of worker participation, are marked by capitalist business culture and hierarchical logic, and do not have a real interest in changing the relations of production and organisational structures. In many cases the institutions have not changed the companies' administrators or middle-level management. They were left at their posts in order to supposedly guarantee better functioning of the companies. But like their counterparts in the institutions, these employees often reject workers' control, seeing it as a threat to their privileges, and are convinced that the company administration requires chains of command and hierarchies.[27]

> Vertical structures continue being maintained, and 'lead by obeying'[28] becomes 'lead by submitting'; in practice, the alternative proposals are mechanisms of participation but not of decision-making, so that in many cases they become anti-crisis structures with no real possibility of breaking with the capitalist way of life.[29]

Corruption among directors continues to spread, and companies are used for personal enrichment, something that would be more difficult under workers' control. Or people are

> appointed to positions of responsibility ... who do not believe in the socialist project, who are not with the Bolivarian revolution, and therefore are always betting on the failure of our companies, delaying and obstructing the workers' organisational forms.[30]

Now that building workers' control is the normative orientation in Venezuela, there is the contradictory, almost Kafkaesque situation that when a company

---

26 See ENCO 2011.
27 See I-AR 2011; I-ES 2011; I-RE 2010; I-RE 2011.
28 This refers to the Zapatista slogan 'mandar obedeciendo'.
29 See ENCO 2011.
30 Ibid.

has been recently nationalised, the workers first receive several months of socio-political training about the history of Venezuela, Bolivarianism, co-management and Socialist Workers' Councils, the Simón Bolívar National Plan, and other political topics. But when the workers want to put into practice what they have learned and ask for more participation, the administrative structure, installed by the same institution that organised the training, denies them participation. This situation has strengthened the movement for workers' control.

Conflicts with respect to working conditions, workers' rights, participation, co-management, or workers' control have emerged in many of the nationalised factories, like Café Venezuela, Fama de América, Fetraelec, the cement companies and many others. It can be affirmed that the class struggle has been strengthened or has emerged where it did not exist. Conflicts with respect to co-management also emerged in recuperated and expropriated companies. Many businessmen, and administrators of state companies as well, see co-management as a social pact to avoid conflicts, create jobs and increase production, whereas workers tend to see it as a step in the transformation to workers' control of the companies following a socialist model.[31]

> I think that in order for co-management to work, the three parts that I mentioned earlier must be strengthened – each worker must have socio-political preparation, for all the workers to know exactly in which direction we are going. We can't just come and focus solely on production. No, we have to get into the administrative areas, too. We have to give ourselves the training necessary in order to be able to have total control of the company.[32]

One of the sharpest conflicts is over productivity. Apart from better, more dignified working conditions, one of the central motives of workers fighting for control is that they see it as the only guarantee of eliminating corruption, raising production, and producing efficiently to satisfy the needs of most of the country. Their experience with the state bureaucracy has shown them that the majority of administrators sent to companies by the institutions are unqualified, causing production to drop. This could be because they are really incapable, or are responding to certain groups' political interests, or it could be due to networks of clientism and corruption of which they are part. Meanwhile,

---

31   'Nuestra lucha estratégica no es la cogestión sino avanzar hacia el socialismo', in: *Rebelion .org* (26 April 2005; Internet version: 12 August 2009).
32   Rowan Jimenez, worker, Invepal, in Azzellini and Rressler 2006.

among the workers the firm intention grows of building a different socio-economic project, at the same time that the feeling of responsibility grows with respect to their role in this process of building.

2.1 The Movement for Workers' Control

The movement for workers' control has developed slowly but steadily, taking some qualitative leaps. As could be seen with respect to the development of recuperated companies in Venezuela, there was not a movement of takeovers at the level, for example, of Argentina.[33] For a long time, occupations were isolated. The first coordination that was born was the Revolutionary Front of Workers of Co-managed and Occupied Companies (Freteco). Freteco began in 2006 as a Marxist alliance of factories and combative workers, among them Inveval, Invepal, Invetex, Siderorca, Tomatera Caisa, INAF, and activists at Venirauto, General Motors, Alcasa and the Cumanacoa sugar plant. Freteco served as a forum for debate about the socialist organisation of production and the mobilisation for struggles, and maintained a solidary but critical position toward the government.[34] The workers organised their own training with respect to the history of co-management and workers' control:

> Through Freteco and all the co-managed companies we are studying the socialism of Yugoslavia and of each of the countries where there have been experiences of co-management or workers' control. This is for us to do ourselves, this work of sociopolitical training, so that the training is not reformist, but is about the changes this country really needs.[35]

The first workers' council was formed at Sanitarios Maracay. Then, in 2007, councils emerged at the INAF and at Gotcha in Maracay, both of which formed cooperatives. The workers of Inveval introduced councils at the beginning of 2007. Some other factories, mostly those taken over by their workers, also introduced councils. The search for an organisational model with an anticapitalist perspective led the workers to organise councils.

> The class has had to educate itself in the absence of an institutional framework. The workers initiated some four or five years ago processes of self-training and research, which allowed them to make a cumulative history, even of Venezuela as a historical reference point, with a rich discussion

---

33 See Rebón 2004; 2006; Ruggeri 2010; Sitrin 2006; 2012.
34 Freteco 2007.
35 José Quintero, worker, Inveval, I-JQ 2006.

about the workers' councils of the 70s. In this process of research, they arrived at the sources of the Marxist classics, Rosa Luxemburg, Antonio Gramsci, [Anton] Pannekoek, among others, and they also began to build their own experience, their own critique of representative democracy and participatory and protagonistic democracy at the company and a series of very interesting experiences occurred that, because of their systematisation and critique, are the source that nourishes our present training process.[36]

In 2008, a broader initiative emerged: the Socialist Workers' Councils (CST), which regrouped existing workers' councils and proposed initiatives in their favour.[37] For two years, the CST were the central forum for discussion of models of horizontal councilist organisation in companies and of issues of socialist economic administration.[38]

From the process toward workers' control of the basic industries of Bolivar state by means of the Guayana Socialist Plan 2009–19 and in reaction to strong attacks on the process of workers' control, activists of Alcasa, Sidor, and other companies organised the First National Encounter for Workers' Control and Workers' Councils in Ciudad Guayana 20–22 May 2011, in the theatre of the production unit Sidor. The encounter brought together more than 900 participants from a number of workers' councils, CST, occupied companies, and unions, who held 30 panel sessions.[39] The panels worked on three generative questions:

(1) What are the fundamental contradictions present in the political experience and practice of the Venezuelan working class for the construction of workers' control and workers' councils, why do they emerge, and what should the workers' role be in overcoming them?
(2) What ideas or principles are necessary to orient the political action of the Venezuelan working class toward proposing workers' control and workers' councils?
(3) Taking into account that building socialism in Venezuela is conditioned by the anticapitalist and antibureaucratic struggle, what are the political, organisational, programmatic, legal, economic, social, and other proposals?[40]

---

36 See Richard 2011.
37 See CST 2009.
38 MinTrab 2008, p. 15.
39 See ENCO 2011.
40 Ibid.

The discussion centred on: (a) analysis of the present situation; (b) theoretical contributions; (c) specificities; and (d) plan for struggle: strategies (action criteria), actions, and organisational proposals.[41] Three great obstacles to workers' control were identified: first, the opposition attacks everything that has to do with revolution; second, the sectors of the process 'that hide their true interests with a supposed revolutionary discourse, whose idea is not to eliminate definitively the capitalist way of life, but to change its personification' and as a consequence the sabotage of workers' control in the same Bolivarian process and that there is not a legal basis for proposing workers' control or workers' councils. And finally, the problems of workers – depoliticisation, apathy, scepticism, individualism, and consumerism – as well as the dismantling and fragmenting of the labour movement at the regional and national level and the lack of criteria for strategic worker planning.[42]

In spite of all 'the contradictions, obstacles, and deficiencies' in the process of building workers' control that were identified in discussions during the encounter, there were positive evaluations, such as:

> The conjuncture of forces is still favorable to the workers ...
> The working class has decided to change the old model, we want to participate in management.
> The call that has been made to us, to organise ourselves into workers' councils and fight for workers' control, has come from the President of the Republic.[43]

The movement for workers' control is connected to the peasants and the communities, and supports the building of communes on the way to the communal state.

The operative proposals of struggle and organisation take the following as a point of departure: 'If one of the principal obstacles to workers' control is the bureaucracy, then we should declare bureaucratism as one of the principal problems to be attacked'.[44] Among the many proposals one finds: 'To realize actions of categorical rejection of the persecution and harassment by the bureaucracy against the working class, social sectors, and peasantry'. There are proposals to strengthen the autonomous organisational structures, create a network of self-training, disseminate and discuss the project of the CST law, define

---

41 See ENCO 2011.
42 Ibid.
43 Ibid.
44 Ibid.

new forms of property, radically democratise the administration, and much more. Organisationally, it is proposed to make individual and regional thematic meetings, create a working parliament, promote various types of worker organisation to address problems of advocacy, society, politics, and ideology, and the

> [c]reation of multiple directors' commissions for decision-making in factories. The commissions should be composed of organised workers, organised communities, the state, and suppliers of raw materials, to fight bureaucratism and corruption.
> Creating workers' councils by production branches in the different municipalities and states, to strengthen the national and regional organisations that defend the project of [workers'] control.
> Holding regular worker meetings for the evaluation and permanent follow-up of what has been done and to continue organising ourselves to enhance the experience of workers' control.
> Creation of a fund for the self-management of working-class encounters.[45]

While the positive points were few in comparison with the large number of contradictions and obstacles, the tenor of the meeting was not pessimistic. Quite the contrary: the National Meeting for Workers' Control and Workers' Councils was a success that marked an important step in the struggle for workers' control. The movements for workers' control came to be coordinated by the National Collective for Workers' Control and, together with the Socialist Workers' Councils, organised in July 2011 the first national demonstration for workers' control, attended by thousands of workers from all over the country. Other events followed: mobilisations, regional meetings, and in June 2013 the First Workers' Congress, subtitled 'Assessment and Challenges to Workers' Control and Workers' Councils in the Building of Socialism', at the Alfredo Maneiro Steel Mill of Orinoco (Sidor), Ciudad Guayana, with the participation of 450 workers from 81 companies. Prepared through a sequence of meetings with 215 spokespeople, the congress advanced the political debate and the organisation and coordination of the movement for workers' control, and agreed on new initiatives for struggle.[46]

---

45   See ENCO 2011.
46   See PCTT 2013.

2.2   The Socialist Workers' Councils

In 2007, Chávez publicly launched the idea of Socialist Workers' Councils (CST). These are not union organisations, nor do they replace that function: 'The purpose of labour unions is to help workers sell their labour power as advantageously as they can. Unions will always be needed for this purpose. But while unions are necessary, they are not sufficient'.[47]

At the beginning, only a few factories (Invepal, for one) answered Chávez's call. A CST forum was created for interchanging experiences and discussing possible models of socialist management.[48] With time, there was a massive initiative from below to form Socialist Workers' Councils (CSTT),[49] as they began to be called. Pressure from below brought some institutions to begin to permit or even promote the creation of CSTT as of 2010, although there is still no law to that effect. Even though the call to form the CSTT came from the president himself, the initiatives were obstructed and attacked in many state institutions and companies. In most of the institutions, there is still an effort to impede the creation of CSTT, and in others and in the state companies the responsible institutions attempt to assume the protagonistic role in their creation, taking away their meaning and reducing them to a representative body of workers to deal with the governmental bureaucracy about complaints. This has turned the CSTT into a new space of conflict, which in several cases has resulted in the struggle to create them becoming a new struggle for workers' control.

As Stanley Aronowitz summarises:

> Workers' councils or committees can only become serious expressions of working class interests when they challenge authority relations in the enterprise, are based on some understanding that the prevailing division of labour reinforces these relations, and when they possess the power and the desire to transform the workplace in accordance with a new conception of the relations between work and play and between freedom and authority. Workers' control demands that are instruments of trade union and bureaucratic institutions merely reinforce the powerlessness of workers because they sow the seeds of cynicism concerning the possibility of actually achieving the vision of a self-managed society.[50]

---

47   Lynd and Lynd 2000, p. 1.
48   See CST 2009; MinTrab 2008.
49   [Translator's note: the Spanish name is specifically gender-inclusive: *Consejos Socialistas de Trabajadores y Trabajadoras*].
50   Aronowitz 1991, pp. 426–7.

Until 2015, there was still no law to regulate the CSTT and their participation in company administration, although there already existed hundreds of CSTT, most of them without a real participation in decision-making. However, some CSTT do important work to create workers' control, developing struggles out of their demands with respect to salaries, loans, and working conditions, as well as demanding to have social auditing and participation in the companies.[51] The first proposal of a project of 'Special Law of Workers' Councils' was proposed by the PCV in July 2007 and is supported by the Bolivarian Socialist Workers' Front (FSBT, previously FBT), the most officialist of the unions. Like the 'Organic Law of Labour' (LOT), the CSTT law has been discussed and postponed by the National Assembly for several years. Obviously there are strong political interests that have managed to paralyse the forward movement, even though there is a power relation favourable to the passage of laws.[52] The proposed law has also been criticised as insufficient and adjusted to the interests of the unionists.[53]

In March 2011, by popular initiative, a new 'Project of Special Law of the Socialist Workers' Councils' proposed by the Platform for Struggle of the Socialist Workers' Councils of Gran Caracas was discussed before the members of the Permanent Commission on Integral Social Development of the National Assembly.

The mobilisation and discussion in favour of the two laws have massified in the time since 2011 and the commission of the National Assembly responsible for laws has held several meetings with CSTT, groups of workers' control, and unions, to integrate their observations and proposals into the LOT. Finally, it was President Chávez who on 30 April 2012 decreed the new 'Organic Law of Labour and Labourers'.[54] In article 297, the law establishes that:

> The workers' councils are expressions of Popular Power for protagonistic participation in the social process of work, with the end of producing goods and services that satisfy the needs of the *pueblo*.
>
> The forms of participation by workers in management, as well as the organisation and functioning of the workers' councils, will be established in special laws.[55]

---

51 Martín 2011a; 2011b.
52 See Richard 2011.
53 See León 2013.
54 See LOTT 2012.
55 Ibid.

It also clarifies in Article 498 that the CSTT have 'their own attributes, distinct from those of the union organisations contained in this Law'.[56] In July 2015, still no special law on workers' councils had been passed, although the Permanent Commission on Integral Social Development of the National Assembly was discussing three proposals it received.

The absence of a legal framework to guarantee the structuring of workers' councils made creating them difficult.[57] Though workers followed a line launched and shared by Chávez, many who have promoted the creation of CSTT in public companies or institutions have been persecuted and accused by their bosses of counter-revolutionary activity.[58] This happened in the Madres del Barrio Mission (a social programme for single mothers), at the state television channels VTV and Ávila TV, and even in the Ministry of Labour and in the institutions of the Ministry for Communes (for example, in Fundacomunal and in INCES, the National Institute of Socialist Training and Education), which should be at the forefront of creating the CSTT.

Between the workers and the public administrators, Alberto Bonilla, sociologist and co-founder of the first Workers' Council of the Ministry of Labour, sees obstacles and contradictions on both sides:

> On the workers' side there is a significant vacuum in the exercise of participatory democracy and workers' control; on the contrary, individual sovereignty is frequently delegated to representatives. Our past is characterized by practices that trained us to delegate, which functions perfectly well in capitalist logic because it is rooted in private property, in the division of labour, which is to say, in the division between those who know and those who don't know ... We were trained this way, not to participate, but to delegate, to obey, and we are the product of these social relations of production that assign to us a subordinated, passive role ...
>
> And on the side of decision makers, whether they call themselves officials, chiefs, administrators, or directors, they are impregnated with the capitalist ideology, which is an authoritarian, dictatorial ideology that does not allow replies, so that for a public decision maker it becomes difficult to permit protagonistic participation of the workers when it is inconvenient to their interests.[59]

---

56   Ibid.
57   See Richard 2011.
58   See Martín 2011b.
59   See Richard 2011.

Faced with a growing number of CSTT initiatives, many institutions changed their strategy and instead tried to seize the initiative by creating them, thus controlling the process and constituting CSTT with limited functions. This of course completely distorts the original intent of the CSTT, reducing them to organs for the representation of workers before company management to discuss complaints and questions of work organisation. This has especially been the case in private companies near the point of nationalisation, and in institutions in which there has not yet been a CSTT initiative.[60]

There should not be a contradiction between the functions of trade unions and the CSTT or other organs of workers' control. Nor has the trade-union movement, which largely maintains a clear autonomy from the governing parties and the state, ruled against the CSTT.[61] Nevertheless, while the National Workers Union (UNT), an independent central union not associated with the party or the state as was the case in many other revolutionary processes, officially supports workers' control and the CSTT, many oppositionist unions, coming from the old union structure of Acción Democrática and CTV (Venezuelan Confederation of Workers), are opposed to any form of workers' control or more direct participation in the workplace. Even the FSBT opposes forms of workers' control in many workplaces in practice. This is especially the case in the basic industries of Ciudad Guayana (Bolívar state), where this union sector is linked to state governance, deputies, and ex-ministers. When Chávez named the worker Elio Sayago president of Alcasa on 15 May 2010, the M21 (the Alcasa union affiliated with the FSBT) immediately fired off a communiqué rejecting the nomination and continued sabotaging the process of workers' control.[62] The fact that unions by their logic act as mechanisms of struggle within a system has been repeatedly highlighted by Marxist theoreticians from Marx to Gramsci, as well as by activists engaged in struggles. Because of this, the union as an organisation does not usually lead the transformation process that is being pushed forward in part by its own members. As the Alcasa worker Elio Sayago says:

> What we need right now is for our union leaders to understand that they need to look for worker protagonism. How to facilitate that the workers' knowledge really guarantees control. As much as the union leaders, we of the *pueblo* have achieved a level of understanding and wisdom that right

---

60   See I-RE 2010; I-RE 2011.
61   Ellner 2006, p. 82.
62   See I-ES 2011.

now transcends traditional union demands. And right now we have the historic opportunity to build society, to define our own destiny.[63]

In Venezuela, this inherent tendency of unions is reinforced by the historical fact that many unions were a corporate structure for the private appropriation of public goods and funds during the Fourth Republic (1956–99), creating a culture of theft that in many places has remained in effect. In the construction sector, especially, many unions function literally as mafias and have armed confrontations between themselves for control of labour and construction contracts.

In summary, the CSTT are instruments that have been created and promoted from below, are accepted and assumed by government bodies, and have become a space for struggle between, on the one hand, the vision of advancing toward worker self-management and workers' control, and on the other, the institutional logic of classifying and limiting social processes in order to neutralise their constituent force, as well as attempts by some unions to use the CSTT to recycle their function as mediators between base and management. Especially within institutions, the CSTT are used to struggle against the growing Bolivarian bureaucracy.[64] These experiences of institutional obstruction lead to radicalisation and self-organisation of the CSTT.

2.3 The CVG and the 2009–19 Socialist Guayana Plan

The Venezuelan Corporation of Guayana, or CVG, is a state holding company that brings together 17 basic companies in Bolívar state, the most important industrial centre for developing the country's raw materials. This complex emerged in the 1960s to diversify the productive base of the country (although it followed the same logic of petroleum in that it principally dealt in the exportation of raw materials). The CVG produces and processes carbon, iron, steel, and aluminium. Several of these plants have been nationalised in recent years – or re-nationalised, after several companies were intentionally run into bankruptcy in the 1980s with the aim of privatising them. Lack of investment, technological backwardness, and corruption left the companies that remained in state hands running at a continual loss.

For decades, the basic and mining industries of Venezuela have been plagued with clientist networks – between foreign capital, regional ren-

---

63   See Azzellini and Ressler 2006.
64   See Martín 2011b.

tier clans, and an elite of privileged workers – operating in something like a paradise of 'free theft.' Before 1998, the oligarchic state had little interest in intervening in this situation. After 1998, the arm of the state was not sufficiently strong to turn around decisively the clientist domination of the sector ... In this context, a transition to new models of participatory management is evidently difficult to achieve.[65]

Alcides Rivero, worker at Alcasa, member of the workers' control collective, of the monitoring team of the 2009–19 Socialist Guayana Plan (*Plan Guayana Socialista 2009–19*), and of the board of directors of the aluminium company Bauxilum, says that, according to some estimates by workers, corruption in the CVG leads to annual losses of 30 billion dollars. When Rivero discovered and denounced the disappearance of up to 30 percent of raw materials during river transport between the mines and the processing plants, he received death threats.[66] In June 2011, Luís Velásquez, director of commercialisation of the steel company Sidor, was arrested. Velásquez was allegedly the head of the so-called *mafia de cabillas*, dedicated to the theft and massive diversion of steel rods (*cabillas*) used in construction. In November 2010 alone, Velásquez diverted 12 trucks with 336 tons of steel rods, valued at almost $400,000. According to investigators, Velásquez sold the rods and other materials to private companies in Venezuela, Colombia and Brazil, in which he was even partly invested as a partner.[67]

Beyond the economic harm, the political fallout of such a theft is also enormous. The steel rods, sold at subsidised prices, are basic for the government to be able to comply with its goal of constructing more than two million homes by 2018. Given that the shortage of housing presents a fundamental problem in Venezuela, which was aggravated by massive floods in 2011, compliance with housing construction is considered key for the government's credibility. Given the estimated magnitude of losses from corruption, it is obvious that the case of Velásquez is not an isolated one. Velásquez is said to be a personal friend of the regional governor Francisco Rangel Gómez and was also a member of the board of directors of the recently nationalised cement plants CEMEX and Lafargue, as well as the nationalised companies of the CVG, Orinoco Iron and Briqven.[68]

---

65 Blankenburg 2008, pp. 20–1.
66 See I-AR 2011.
67 See Martín 2011a.
68 Ibid.

That the basic enterprises have to be restructured and modernised is a given. Only workers' control can guarantee the end of corruption and the direction of production toward the public interest, so the best option for increasing labour democracy and the companies' economic viability is to transform them into a transparent network of basic industries on the way to workers' control.[69]

In May 2009, Chávez participated in a weekend workshop with more than 300 workers from the CVG's iron, steel, and aluminium companies, including the members of the Alcasa Workers' Control Collective. In this workshop, possible solutions to the sector's problems were discussed and new strategic lines were proposed for the transformation of the CVG, with workers' control of production at the head of the list. Chávez authorised a ministerial commission to produce, together with the workers, a plan for the transformation of the CVG based on the guidelines elaborated in the workshop. Thus, the Socialist Guayana Plan emerged, approved by Chávez in August 2009.[70] The Plan can be summarised as the construction of three large corporations of iron, steel, and aluminium under workers' control, which then form a single company.[71]

The structuring, as the plan's title indicates, is projected to be medium- and long-term. The workers' councils were not established by decree, for which the workers were thankful, given that if the councils are not the result of worker interest, it is unlikely that they will be successful.[72] The Workers' Assembly of the Socialist Guayana Plan created a socialist production model for the basic companies, a work plan for the transition, and norms for the functioning of work groups in the factories.[73]

In the following months nothing happened, so in April 2010, the government replaced the Minister of Basic and Mining Industries and CVG President Rodolfo Sanz with José Khan, who announced that he would work for the application of the plan. In May, saying 'I bet on the workers (*me las juego con los trabajadores*)', Chávez named workers who had participated in the workshop and in the debates to the presidencies of the 17 CVG factories, including the nine iron, steel, and aluminium plants. At Alcasa, the environmental technician Elio Sayago, a workers' control activist from the beginning who was appointed by the collective for workers' control, was named president of the company by Chávez. The results of the new management varied from

---

69   See I-AR 2011; I-ES 2011; I-RE 2011.
70   See Mppibm 2009.
71   See I-AR 2011; I-ES 2011.
72   'Control Obrero', Publicación de trabajadores de CVG Alcasa, (16 September 2009), no. 2, in *Aporrea.org*, available at: http://www.aporrea.org/endogeno/a86731.html.
73   See I-EE 2015.

company to company, although by 2012 the majority of the worker-presidents had been removed and the workers denounced the non-compliance with the plan.

In many of the companies, especially Alcasa, conflicts were exacerbated. Unions, bureaucracy, local, regional, and national politicians, private industry, suppliers, etc. sprang into action against the Socialist Guayana Plan, which is not surprising if one considers, on the one hand, the volume of earnings from corruption and, on the other, the billions of dollars that the National Executive planned to invest in the modernisation of the CVG's industries.[74] The corporations were created 2013–14 and Alcasa president Ángel Marcano was named president of the Aluminium Corporation (while he continued being president of Alcasa). The corporations that have been created are all typical corporations with vertical structures, the opposite of what was proposed by the Workers' Assembly of the Plan Guayana. All the companies of the CVG, moreover, continue being dependent on state funding.[75]

3 Workers' Control: The Example of Inveval

> The previous organisational diagram was vertical, its functioning hierarchical. Then when we started to design the factory council, implement it here to have the workers take over the administration, we designed an organisational diagram that would be the most horizontal possible, 100%. The authority here is the workers' assembly, it's the maximum authority.[76]

∴

The National Valvemakers Company (CNV), renamed Inveval (Endogenous Venezuelan Valve Industry), was expropriated on 27 April 2005. Located in Carrizal, Miranda, it had previously belonged to Andrés Sosa Pietri, ex-president of PDVSA and a hardline oppositionist who was involved in the 2002 coup.

The CNV, which sold valves to PDVSA, was founded by Sosa Pietri while he was president of PDVSA, with PDVSA capital. Together with the foundry Acer-

---

74 See I-AR 2011; I-ES 2011; I-RE 2011.
75 See Aporrea Tvi 2014.
76 See Julio González, Inveval worker, I-JG 2008.

ven, it produced valves that were principally used in the petroleum industry and, in lesser measure, in sugar mills, the paper industry, and water systems. The plant was closed by Sosa Pietri during the business lockout of December 2002/January 2003. After the lockout, without paying the back salaries missed during the lockout and without paying severance to dismissed workers, he tried to restructure and reopen the factory with reduced wages and benefits.[77]

The workers rejected Sosa Pietri's plans, and 63 of the 120 workers took over the factory to create pressure for back and severance pay, which at first was their only demand.[78] They did not even enter the administration building or the production warehouse during the first occupation, advancing their cause via the institutional path instead. Deciding in their favour, the Minister of Labour ordered rehiring and the payment of missed wages, but the owner did not accept the decision; through his contacts in the court system, he obtained several orders of eviction, annulled each time by other judges.

There was no institutional support for the workers, and there still exists no coordination of taken-over factories or even a consciousness of the problem in union organisations. At the end of 2004, the situation seemed hopeless and the workers abandoned the company. But after they learned in January 2005 that the owner had begun removing machinery from the factory, energised by the expropriation of Venepal, they occupied the plant again in mid-February. On 27 April 2005, CNV was finally expropriated by the national Executive.[79]

3.1 *From the Struggle for Pay to the Struggle for the Factory*

With the state promising to solve all the problems, the Inveval workers' expectations were great. Their idea was to repair the factory quickly in order to resume production in August, but the ministers in charge delayed more than two months before paying the first salaries, and not until December did they officially receive the keys to the plant. Moreover, the authorities did not expropriate the foundry Acerven, located elsewhere, which supplied the raw materials it needed. Without Acerven, which also belonged to Sosa Pietri and also stopped production in 2002, Inveval could not produce new valves, but could only dedicate itself to maintaining and repairing existing ones.[80]

The company's organisational model was the first apple of discord. While the workers, animated by Chávez's declarations, proposed a model of workers' control, the bureaucracy insisted on impeding it. The first proposal from Minep

---

77 See Azzellini and Ressler 2004; I-LM 2006.
78 See Azzellini and Ressler 2004.
79 Azzellini 2007b, pp. 51–3; Azzellini 2009; Cormenzana 2009, pp. 27–43.
80 See I-JQ 2006; I-LM 2006; I-NR 2007.

did not contemplate even minimally Chávez's promise of a worker majority on the board of directors and a worker president, proposing instead that all company directors be named by the state. The Inveval workers rejected the proposal, and months of argument ensued about the company's governance. The ministerial bureaucracy proposed a typically capitalist hierarchy, while the workers proposed one of collective directorship and workers' control. Before signing a pact of co-management in August 2005, the Inveval workers went back and forth with the ministry through eight proposals that were rejected by one side or the other.[81]

The prevailing laws and the commercial code imposed serious limits on the workers' intentions, so the co-management pact was not what the workers had hoped for, but at the time it seemed the best possible solution.[82] The state agreed to put 6 billion Bolívares (some $2.29 million) to finance the reopening of the factory, and the company was refounded as a joint stock company, 51 percent state-owned and 49 percent owned by a workers' cooperative. The factory administration remained under the responsibility of the workers' assembly, which elected three of the five members of the board of directors, including the president. Besides the two ministry members on the board of directors (who in reality never showed up), no other state personnel were part of the factory. All the decisions that affected the factory were made in the weekly assembly of the cooperative. Decisions with a broader reach had to be approved by the ministry.

Inveval finally began to function in mid-2006. First, the infrastructure was repaired, and then production began, but owing to the lack of a foundry, only maintenance of already existing industrial valves could be performed. It did not take the workers long to notice that state administration, which at first had seemed the solution to the problems, had merely transferred the class struggle to the level of institutional confrontation.

At the beginning, the workers' assembly of Inveval decided on a salary increase, one single wage for all, and a 7-hour workday. After 4 pm, several educational missions entered the factory and gave the workers, as well as the residents of the neighbouring communities, primary and secondary school courses. Some workers learned to read through the missions or finished their primary school. Others participated in the Ribas Mission (secondary school) or Sucre Mission and some took afternoon courses in universities. With the passage of the years, almost all the workers received some additional education

---

81 See *Prensa INCE* 2005.
82 See I-LM 2006; I-NR 2007.

and several continued on to college, taking courses that would help them administer the company.[83]

In 2006, the Inveval workers organised themselves into Freteco. In three years, a group of workers who at first asked only for their back pay had transformed into a solid collective struggling for workers' control. Through Freteco, socio-political training workshops were held in the factory, studying historic examples of workers' control, from Turin/Italy at the beginning of the twentieth century, to Yugoslavia, to the present-day examples of Argentina and Brazil. Meanwhile, workshops in administration and technical production were organised through the National Institute of Socialist Training and Education (INCES), in which workers studied how to overcome the social division of work within the factory.

In 2006, a new labour structure was implemented at the factory. Tasks with a strict division of work were suppressed and the only ones with detailed defined tasks were the president, the other members of the board of directors, and the coordinators of the areas of production and administration. The others began to rotate tasks, although always according to their capacities.[84]

3.2 The Workers Abandon the Cooperative and Form a Council

For two years, the workers of Inveval tried to administer the factory themselves under the new cooperative model, trying to direct it with non-capitalist logic, but since the company was a joint stock corporation, the cooperative was obliged to adopt a classic management model. Not only did the form of the company mandate action in conformity with the capitalist market, but also the legal framework made direct administration by the workers impossible.[85] The separation of the areas of work and decision increased the apathy among the workers and their isolation from the board of directors.

The workers realised that to be owners was pushing them toward capitalist-entrepreneurial logic. The cooperative was not only a partner in the factory, but was also co-responsible for its debts. The workers describe how they began to adopt a logic of living to work and pay debts:[86] 'The cooperative promotes capitalism because it's created precisely in this capitalist system and that's what we don't want here ... [I]n other words, we did not kick out one capitalist to replace him with 60'.[87]

---

83 See I-JG 2008; I-LM 2006; I-NR 2007; 2011; I-VU 2006.
84 See I-JG 2008; I-LM 2006; I-RA 2008.
85 See I-LM 2006.
86 See I-NR 2007.
87 See I-JG 2008.

In January 2007, the workers of Inveval took up Chávez's proposal to deepen the revolution by forming workers' councils.

> The President said that we should form factory councils. That it should be the workers who organise management. Otherwise we wouldn't be doing anything to break up the social division of work, to democratize knowledge and all these questions, and from there pass to a true socialist stage, because we are all in transition.[88]

The workers of Inveval decided to elect, immediately, a 32-member factory council, and no longer updated their status as a cooperative. The general assembly of 61 workers – the factory's highest decision-making organ which gets together monthly and additionally as necessary – is followed by the factory council, made up of spokespeople from all the departments and other voluntary workers, which discusses all questions that were previously discussed by only five members of the board of directors. Spokespeople are elected for a year, and can be removed at any moment. Several council commissions – socio-political, finance and administration, responsibility and oversight, discipline, technical aspects, and services – present work summaries and proposals to the council.

Inveval proposed to MILCO that it abandon the cooperative and transform the company into direct social property; that is, that Inveval be state property, but fully controlled by its workers in coordination with the communities.[89] This proposal was presented to Chávez, who endorsed it, along with Inveval's proposal for studying mechanisms to transfer valves without payment and that Inveval in return would present an annual budget, to be financed by the state.[90]

From mid-2008, the factory has been 100 percent social property under workers' control. Tasks and responsibilities in the factory rotate, and are revocable by the workers' assembly. Julio González explains:

> In the workers' assembly we began to assign responsibilities, not posts, responsibilities in each instance for good management within the organisation. Look, we're going to assume these responsibilities with this purpose, with this ideology, to break up the social division of work and democratize knowledge, and each of us is preparing for that. So we have to

---

88   Ibid.
89   See I-NR 2007.
90   See I-JG 2008; I-NR 2007; The valves are, in large part, for the petroleum industry and in lesser part for water companies, all of them state-owned.

rotate in succession. When we worked for the previous owner we saw that our merits were appropriated by the managers but the innovator was the worker, the one who worked the machine every day, right? Now we are the ones who know how the company and the productive process are evolving. That's why we did all this.[91]

Inveval now is moving toward the development of a socialist factory model. At the same time, its workers are coordinating and integrating with surrounding CCs to build a communitary government from below. Nelson summarises the process and the vision of the future:

> Participatory socialist management, factory council, socialist company, revolutionary government, and communal council. What this slate represents is how we have gone about structuring and how the way of governing companies has transformed, creating administrative and productive policies, and we have concluded that through the factory council we have made a qualitative leap in terms of how to manage this socialist model.[92]

Attempts to produce basic valve parts at other private foundries were mostly unsuccessful. The private companies – against the logic of revenue – formed a front against Inveval and refused production or delivered defective valves.[93] The expropriation of the foundry Acerven, signed by Chávez in August 2008, was finalised only in February 2011, but institutional problems continued. There were months-long delays in paying allocated funding and there were problems with getting the PDVSA to buy valves, though it came to them for repair and maintenance of some of its existing valves.[94] Acerven should have been supplying raw material to Inveval, but in 2014 Acerven stopped operating and was tied up in bureaucratic proceedings to keep it from being handed over to the workers of Inveval. Inveval continued producing at only 30 percent of its capacity, and needs an annual state subsidy. The ministerial and PDVSA bureaucracies seem to have decided to make Inveval fail. A company self-managed by its workers and with such political clarity and will to struggle is a threat.

In January 2014, a branch of the Jesús Rivero Bolivarian Workers' University was launched in the Inveval plant. This initiative sought to systematise the

---

91 See I-JG 2008.
92 See I-NR 2007.
93 See I-JG 2008; I-RA 2008.
94 Cormenzana 2009, pp. 203–4.

knowledge and experiences of workers or make it possible to take university courses within the company.[95]

Thus, in spite of institutional obstruction and resistance by private capital, the Inveval workers' tenacity, organisation, and political training made it possible for them to maintain their factory under workers' control.

4 Alcasa: Class Struggle for Productive Transformation against Bureaucracy and Corruption

The company CVG Aluminio del Caroní S.A. (Alcasa), in Ciudad Guayana, Bolívar state, produces raw aluminium and its derivatives. It began operations in 1967, and its capacity was increased several times, but in the mid-1980s incomplete modernisation and disinvestment made it inefficient and sank it in debt. Since then, the plant has produced losses consistently. In 2005, President Chávez decided to implement a model of co-management in Alcasa that proposed a path toward workers' control, and the Marxist Carlos Lanz assumed the presidency of Alcasa. In spite of important advances, the initiative encountered resistance and occasioned sabotage at all levels of the company, of the CVG, and of the regional and national administration. After Lanz left Alcasa in May 2007, his successors were opposed to workers' control.

The process of co-management and restructuring was halted in mid-2007, and Alcasa's productivity deteriorated until a new process of workers' control and restructuring was initiated in May 2010 under the framework of the Socialist Guayana Plan 2009–19. With the new worker-president Elio Sayago, Alcasa began to develop a model of workers' control, while recovering its productivity and struggling against the same governmental bureaucracy, but in February 2012, Sayago was replaced by an ex-deputy of the PSUV who was close to forces opposed to workers' control, and with that, the process that began with him was terminated.

The events at Alcasa reflect the class struggle in the Bolivarian process. The class struggle is expressed in the attempt to build the new in the face of all the resistance of the old, which remains embedded in the ranks of the transformation process, so the resistance to attacks on various union factions from certain sectors of government is also class struggle. Like the different factions inside union organisations and governmental institutions, the different factions at Alcasa represent differing economic, social, and political interests that con-

---

95 See Lucha de Clases 2014.

tinue coexisting in the Bolivarian process. Only a minority want to transform the basic industries of the CVG into productive industries within the framework of new relations of labour and production, leading to the overcoming of capitalist relations.

4.1   Revolutionary Co-Management

> Look at the contradiction we have. President Chávez's intentions are very good, but those in charge retain the same vision as before of who directs and who obeys. Since it is not directed from below by the same popular sectors … it is not a problem of good will. It is a problem of construction, of how it is built, who built it and who directs the process.[96]

∴

In mid-February 2005, the stockholders' assembly of Alcasa appointed Carlos Lanz as the company's director. Lanz, a sociologist, ex-guerrilla, and Marxist who had been proposed by Chávez, began immediately with broad co-management. Besides the internal democratisation of the company, the goal was to reduce corruption, increase efficiency, and make it productive again. Lanz postulated a revolutionary co-management, which proposed a 'change in the relations of capitalist production' and workers' control at Alcasa.[97] Among the workers there was a small group in favour of co-management, while most had no idea what it was.

Lanz's first step at Alcasa was to install the workers' assembly as the highest decision-making body with respect to internal issues. The assembly decided on a salary increase of 15 percent for the workers and the replacement of all department heads with new ones, elected in the workers' assembly of the corresponding department. In addition, it decided that the department heads would receive the same salary as the other workers. Within two weeks after Lanz assumed the presidency of Alcasa, all the department heads had been replaced.

Following the new internal organisational model, departmental assemblies were implemented as the highest decision-making body of the departments,

---

96   See I-OL 2008.
97   See I-AR 2007.

and they elected a three-person directorate that substituted for individual department heads. Each department also elected a spokesperson for each ten workers. The spokespeople were responsible for the flow of information upstream as well as to the workers, and could be dismissed by the same assembly that elected them. Thus, the departments began to decide collectively from below about the organisation of labour and about productive investment.[98]

This internal change in Alcasa was reflected in the new board of directors, elected by the stockholders' assembly in November 2005. Three of its members came from the CVG, and three others (Lanz and two workers) from Alcasa. Among the alternate members of the board of directors were a professor of the Bolivarian University and an economist, in representation of the organised local population.[99]

Alcasa brought different educational missions to the plant and founded its own centre of socio-political and ideological training, the Negro Primero[100] Training Centre, within the factory itself. In this school, two-week training courses began to be given to groups of workers. The Training Centre rapidly transformed into a key centre of debate and organisation in favour of workers' control and of workers' councils. From 2007, it also offered university studies, organised together with the Jesús Rivero Bolivarian Workers' University, to broaden and systematise worker understanding generated in practice.[101]

Productivity increased 11 percent as the internal changes made themselves felt.[102] In combination with the high price of aluminium on the world market at this time, and with the reduction of the previous massive losses from corruption (now made more difficult by collective decision-making and control), the earnings of Alcasa improved in 2005–6. In these two years, Alcasa also liquidated debts owed to workers and ex-workers for back wages and pension contributions.

Alcasa became an EPS and began to support the construction of cooperatives for the further processing of aluminium and its derivatives. It created a department of cooperatives to support the cooperatives contracted by Alcasa. As a first step it began the fusion of all the micro-cooperatives into 12 large cooperatives, which, according to the long-range plan, would be gradually integrated into the fixed payroll of Alcasa. The cooperative members were made equal

---

98   See Azzellini and Ressler 2006.
99   See *Prensa Alcasa* (24 November 2005).
100 *Negro Primero*: 'First Black', the battle name of Pedro Camejo (1790–1821), black officer in the Venezuelan War for Independence.
101 See I-AR 2007.
102 See Bruce 2005.

to Alcasa's fixed-payroll workers in terms of rights: they received access to the same services within the plant, including the dining hall, transportation, and recreational structures. The department of cooperatives signed an agreement with those responsible for the other departments that they would commit to favour cooperatives when subcontracting. In this way, the cooperatives no longer had to compete openly for contracts with private companies.

In July 2006, Lanz put his presidential post up for a referendum in reaction to massive criticism of his performance and of the process of co-management by sectors from the right of the Bolivarian process and from union opposition currents. He won with 1,800 of 1,920 votes (out of a total of 2,700 workers).

At the end of that year, Sintralcasa, the union for the Alcasa plant (its composition is determined by internal elections in which different union currents present slates) signed a new collective contract with Alcasa that fixed the constitution of workers' councils in the factory. Its content was endorsed by the government and upheld in court in February 2007. In it, the creation of the transitory model of co-management was contemplated as a collective process. All sections were supposed to present ideas for debate, from which the workers were to construct a new organisational model of labour.[103]

Given the centrality of basic industries in Guayana and the leading role of the workers, the interests aimed at preventing successful control are very strong. Despite all the advances, Lanz, Alcasa, and the co-management process continued encountering strong opposition from broad sectors of the local, regional and national administration, as well as from opposition media and union sectors. All were pointing at the failure of co-management as a path to workers' control.

> The only space for participation in all the [CVG] companies was made at Alcasa, no one else has done anything. And that was only an attempt that was sabotaged, by not giving us adequate resources, because Alcasa had gone nineteen years without investment. Even our comrades in the National Assembly opposed us, so this has been difficult for us.[104]

In May 2007, Carlos Lanz left the presidency of Alcasa for health reasons, and the co-management process stopped.

---

103   See *Prensa Alcasa* (22 February 2007).
104   See I-AR 2008.

4.2 The Victory of Bureaucracy and Corruption

The new Alcasa president paid no attention to the structures he found upon his arrival and did not respect the decisions from work groups nor from other collective bodies, much less the constitution of workers' councils.

With Lanz in office, the lack of new by-laws or internal regulations for the factory had been an advantage that allowed the new co-management process to move freely without an externally defined framework. But it was a distinct disadvantage under the new president, who did as he wanted. With the bodies of debate and decision lacking information and influence, workers' active participation sharply declined. Of the 17 departments of Alcasa, only four still had work groups in 2008, all of them in the area of production.

Alcasa's productivity crashed, with company losses reaching $180 million dollars in 2007.[105] Even so, the workers did not mobilise for co-management or workers' control. Such a rapid takedown of a relatively advanced process had multiple causes, but a key reason was resistance by the economic interests involved; the proposed Alcasa co-management process found strong resistance within the company and from the CVG.

According to the testimony of several workers, one of Lanz's management errors was implementing the process of co-management while keeping the old administrative apparatus intact instead of replacing the administrators.[106] The administrative level, along with some higher-ranking posts regarding specific areas and tasks and along with union leaders, is the central node for interests and influences at Alcasa. Under Lanz, greater collective control reduced the margin of action by adversaries of co-management, who limited themselves to passive resistance. But as soon as Lanz left Alcasa, the administration returned to its habitually corrupt practices. The plan of integration of cooperativists to the fixed payroll of Alcasa was not carried out, while administrative and union employees used their influence to integrate friends and families. The fixed payroll of Alcasa grew from 2,700 to almost 3,300 workers. Of the 600 new workers, only 60 or so came from cooperatives.

Under the logic of 'steal and let steal', some departments even re-elected their corrupt previous chiefs. The new president reinstated the direct sale of aluminium below the world market price, in order to generate immediate cash flow. Once again entire truckloads of aluminium began to disappear, and production intended for subsidised national sale was diverted to phantom companies, then exported.[107]

---

105   I-CA 2008; I-OL 2008.
106   See I-AR 2008; I-CA 2008; I-OL 2008.
107   See I-CA 2008; I-LD 2011; I-OL 2008.

The members of the Alcasa workers' control collective estimate that 40 percent of Alcasa's aluminium production costs were due to corruption.[108] This corruption, deeply rooted in rentier culture, leads to Alcasa's aluminium production costs being higher than the price paid on the world market (as of 2006, aluminium prices declined), which demonstrates the non-viability of the situation (although a different system of costs should be created, since the present one is based on the capitalist economy and does not consider variables like environmental and social costs).

The situation deteriorated even further when Carlos Aguilar assumed the presidency of Alcasa in April 2008. Technical maintenance had been neglected and Alcasa's machinery had deteriorated rapidly; the direct sale of aluminium below the world market price increased, while future loss-producing sales were contracted with the transnational Glencore; Alcasa's essential machinery was sold to phantom companies and its productivity plummeted, while its debts increased. Aguilar initiated a policy of getting rid of Alcasa's cooperatives, obliging them once again to compete with private companies for their contracts, and tried to avoid putting into action the social projects of workers in four communities (for example, school renovation), financed by the Alcasa social fund, created by order of the CVG. In addition, liabilities to the workers began to accumulate again, given that mandatory social benefits were not paid. All these irregularities were confirmed in a social audit of the workers in early 2010.[109] The Alcasa union Sintralcasa, controlled by the M21, maintained silence because it is a strategic ally of the Aguilar group of interests.[110]

By October 2008, relations had broken off between the president and the workers organised in favour of co-management. However, the experiences of the Alcasa workers with co-management had not been in vain, as the worker Osvaldo León explains:

> Co-management had great lessons and benefits. The simple fact that hundreds of workers would occupy the Alcasa transformation process is extremely important. The fact that they spoke their minds in assembly

---

108 See I-AR 2011; See also: Interview with the workers of Alcasa Oswaldo León, Alcides Rivero, Cruz Barreto and Manuel Figuera (videos) 'Alcasa no es más que la expresión muy pequeña de lo que pasa a nivel político en el país', (25 May 2011), available at: http://www.aporrea.org/trabajadores/n181549.html.

109 'Colectivo Control Obrero: Sobre la grave situación en Alcasa y todas las empresas de la industria básica de Guayana', (09 January 2010), available at: http://el-victoriano.blogspot.com/2010/01/sobre-l-agrave-situacion-de-alcasa-y.html.

110 'Prensa Frente Socialista de Trabajadores', *Aporrea.org* (29 January 2011).

and that they discussed issues directly with company directors, something that had never happened in this factory, is also an important lesson.

The work groups did not function and this bureaucratic fence meant that co-management was paralysed ... but with great experiences, having made grand advances.[111]

The defeat of the Alcasa co-management process was thus only a reversal. The consciousness-raising process of struggling for workers' control continued, and the idea was relaunched later, more forcefully. The Negro Primero Training Centre managed to keep its financing from Alcasa, and kept going. Those workers who were in favour of workers' control, formerly a small minority, formed a collective that became an important force in the factory. From Alcasa they continued making alliances in the region, staging mobilisations and debates with workers from other factories, teachers' unions, CCs, student organisations, the UBV (Universidad Bolivariana de Venezuela), cooperatives, and EPs. They also made a fundamental contribution to the workers' struggle for nationalisation at the steel mill Sidor.

In May 2010, Chávez named Elio Sayago, environmental engineer at Alcasa and activist for workers' control from the beginning of the process, as the company's new president. Sayago was chosen by the workers of the Alcasa workers' control collective who participated in the elaboration of the Socialist Guayana Plan. This was the beginning of the next round of the struggle to restructure the CVG and to implement workers' control.

4.3 Workers' Control Returns

Sayago assumed the presidency of Alcasa in May 2010. Operating within the framework of the Socialist Guayana Plan, his brief was to make Alcasa into an efficient worker-controlled company that would supply the needs of the Venezuelan population. The Plan proposed the creation of two large companies – one for aluminium and the other for iron – integrating all the CVG companies.[112] In the aluminium sector, this involved eight companies from the extraction unit to the processors (Alcasa, Alucasa, Alunasa, Cabelum, Rialca and nationalised companies Alven, Alvarca, Alentuy).[113]

---

111   See I-OL 2008.
112   See Mppibm 2009.
113   See I-ES 2011.

Sayago, who was president of Alcasa until February 2012, describes the context:

> When we decided to go ahead, the President of the Republic put a question to the officials of the state: 'Are you willing to share power with the workers and the *pueblo*?' Then a dynamic began that during ten years of revolution there had not yet been, a confrontation within the government itself ... It is essential to understand that when Chávez calls for collective management under workers' control, not everybody says yes. It's here in Guayana that the contradictions within the government are exacerbated because there are leaders and mafias, who took advantage of these last ten years to accumulate power while wearing a red cap and now they like that butter and they don't want to give it away. They even become potential enemies of the revolution because what the revolution implies is a real transformation process ... It's important to understand this element from a historical point of view, because there is a theoretical discussion about what the contradiction is that the Bolivarian revolution has to resolve.[114]

The material conditions under which Alcasa began this process were not good. As Osvaldo León explains:

> When the comrades assumed the Transitory Presidencies to move workers' control forward, we affirmed that they wanted us to manage the crisis, because they left behind companies with signed contracts for future sales of aluminium and alumina, all with conditions that damage the interests of the workers and of the nation, 'sell-out contracts' in the words of one minister. At Alcasa, comrade Carlos Lanz handed the plant over to Mr. César Aguilar with more than 90% of its lines in production and functioning normally, which allowed for the paying of debts to workers. Now, in lines 3 and 4, which have an operative capacity of 406 cells, only 200 are left, and more than 60% of those have grave deficiencies. In the eyes of the workers, these men came to destroy the plant and prepare the grounds for privatioation. With a diminished cash flow, with debts to us the workers and to the suppliers, with a plan of selling only raw material at the lowest price ...[115]

---

114 See Sayago 2011.
115 See *Prensa Marea Socialista* 2011.

The support for workers' control at Alcasa, however, had grown through the experiences after Carlos Lanz, the struggle of Sidor, and the work of the Training Centre, although it encountered ferocious resistance.

In summary, the process at Alcasa has multiple dimensions of struggle. At the international level, it faces a division of labour within a neo-colonial framework. But this is not the principal contradiction, and 'it is not a contradiction between nation and empire',[116] as Elio Sayago continuously emphasises, but a contradiction between the global capitalist system, of which Venezuela forms a part, and socialism under construction. The crisis is in the model of social relations and development that go with the capitalist model. The main struggle is for the construction of new social relations, for new relations of production, and against the internal forces that for different reasons are not disposed to permit this new creation from below.

4.4   *The Organisational Structure of the New Alcasa*

The first step toward a more democratic administrative structure was to democratise information about the company's situation. Scarcely had Sayago assumed the presidency in May 2010 when discussions began in the multipurpose room of Alcasa during which the company's financial situation, cash flow, and the possibilities and limits of the existing situation were presented to the workers with video and graphics. From then on, there has been an informational assembly once a week. Every Monday, the worker-president Sayago gave an accounting of the present situation in a general assembly in front of the Alcasa gates.[117]

With respect to the transformation of the organisational structures of Alcasa, the central question was how to change the social relations of production, which are relations of power. To overcome the existing relations, workers' control and co-responsibility had to be implemented. To do that, it was necessary to generate a different consciousness, because the capitalist structure sets one worker in competition with another for better individual conditions. If we take as a point of departure the fact that, as Marx indicates, existence determines consciousness, then it is difficult for the worker to generate a solidary, collective consciousness in a capitalist, competitive environment. Thus the transformation of consciousness goes hand in hand with practice, with how ideas are made concrete.[118] For that reason the base from which a different, solidary,

---

116   See I-EN 2011.
117   See I-ES 2011; I-LD 2011.
118   See I-ES 2011.

co-responsible consciousness is generated is the exercise of participation, of working in a collective way, sharing collective decision-making, and even collectively resolving other fundamental issues (e.g. housing) that are not necessarily connected with the company.

Alcasa is divided into an area of production and another of administration. There are 17 departments in all; except for some very small ones, like the culture department, all have their own operations management. The first step in eliminating the hierarchical structure of Alcasa was the creation of work groups in each department, replacing the previous management with broad-based discussion. Each work group brings together those who execute the work with those who control the variables of the work, making decisions based on collective knowledge, respect, and complementarity about planning, logistics, finance, and environment.[119]

The functioning of the work groups, however, has not been ideal. While a group might decide something, procedures, norms, and delegation of responsibility have not changed, so that in the end, decision-making always ends up in the hands of the existing hierarchy.[120]

In late 2010, the Council of Process Coordination (CCP) was formed to integrate and direct the different areas and permit a holistic vision of the plant. Participating in the CCP, which is part of the Organised Direction Centre, are the president's office, administrators, the union, and the committee of hygiene and security.[121] The CCP makes general decisions about the company with respect to issues such as transportation, food, raw materials, commercialisation and maintenance, and drew up measures to reactivate access control and improve internal security. When the decisions in question are more sensitive or far-reaching, they are brought as proposals to the workers' assembly, so that they can be decided in that body, where plans and financial arrangements with clients are discussed.

> That's fundamental, since the workers are the ones who produce, and if we make commitments without consulting them, the transformation process makes no sense; we would be denying the very thing we want to build. To build co-responsibility, we have to confront the previous model and transform it in practice, through action.[122]

---

119 See I-ES 2011.
120 See I-LD 2011.
121 See I-AR 2011; I-ES 2011.
122 See I-ES 2011.

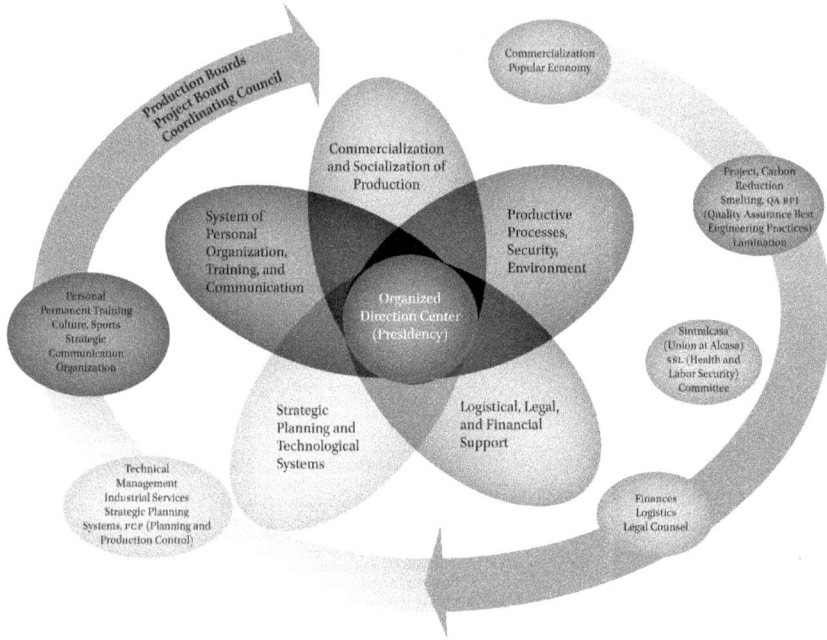

FIGURE 1   *New organisational structure of CVG-Alcasa (2010–11)*

Although according to established norms, neither the CCP nor the workers' assembly formally have the legal capacity to make these decisions, in practice the two bodies have become recognised as legitimate. Neither the union, nor even Alcasa's board of directors, have rejected the decisions they made.[123]

With the CCP in operation, the support for Sayago was extended to a group of workers who were getting master's degrees in business management from the Jesús Rivero Bolivarian Workers' University, in a programme that usefully and directly involved them in researching the restructuring process from within. Within the discussions between the professorial team and the CCP, the idea emerged of 'systems' (the areas grouped around the Organised Direction Centre, cf. the figure) with the objective of moving toward a more horizontal, more integrated management.[124] Five systems were created: Commercialisation and Socialisation of Production; Personnel, Organisation, Training, and Communication; Productive Processes, Security, and Environment; Logistical, Legal, and Financial Support; and Strategic Planning and Technology.

123   See I-LD 2011.
124   Ibid.

These systems are intermediate levels between the boards and the CCP, in which all the elements relevant to an area are brought together to share experiences, planning, capacity, spare parts, and inputs, and thereby create a holistic vision of the plant although they pertain to different sub-processes.[125] Each system has a responsible person who communicates with President Sayago, while highly skilled workers are distributed according to their fields of expertise within the different systems, forming a support team in the corresponding system. This drives the integration of workers into management, at the same time that the knowledge acquired from highly skilled workers is incorporated and applied.

The System of Personnel, Organisation, Training and Communication is directed toward the transformation of men and women, within the framework of the change of the social relations of production. Moreover, it brings together all aspects linked to the integral development of the human being, including culture and sports, with the aim of improving the quality of life of the Alcasa workers by means of a collective perspective.[126]

In putting into practice the new organisational model, nevertheless, there have been problems. The functioning has not been as fluid as proposed in the model:

> Okay, this theoretically works, but in practice it hasn't. To a moderate degree, we have been able to articulate and keep active the CCP whether Elio Sayago attends or not. In this we have advanced; now the CCP stands alone, and people are understanding that we are a collective and that it's better to make decisions collectively than separately. The problem is that although the CCP is getting stronger, the boards aren't, so we're looking for the opportune moment to relaunch them.[127]

Faced with the unprecedented task of introducing a workers' control mechanism in a plant with more than 3,000 workers, it is not surprising that conflicts arise. Under the Sayago presidency, they were dealt with collectively and dynamically in the course of the process, with an organisational model that was not monolithic, but which developed and changed through practical experience. So at first, for example, there was no plan to create the systems; the idea grew out of the weakness of the boards and the necessity for another intermediary layer.

---

125   Ibid.
126   See I-AR 2011.
127   See I-LD 2011.

4.5 *Worker Inventiveness Workshops*

Since layoffs are not permitted, the dismantling of an entire production line at Alcasa under the previous president obliged the relocation of its workers elsewhere in the company. With Sayago as worker-president, one group of workers asked not to be relocated to other departments, where there was already a surplus of labour, but to begin by their own means to develop and produce replacement parts that Alcasa until then had acquired from private domestic companies, or even by importation. Faced with Alcasa's precarious financial situation, which obliged the reduction of expenses immediately in order to keep cash flow down and maintain some operativity, the idea was approved, with spectacular success.

The idea of making replacement parts internally at Alcasa originated in 2009, when a group of cell skimmers participated in a technical-productive workshop given at the Negro Primero Training Centre.[128] The simple design of the skimmers and the possibility of improving them, as well as the fact of having access to resources and materials, gave the workers the confidence to propose a project to make skimmers at Alcasa. It did not come to fruition immediately, but in mid-2011, when the grave cash-flow deficit and the increasing price of tools made the purchase of sufficient skimmers prohibitive, the workers brought the idea up again.

The skimmers are made with recyclable material found in ferrous waste from the production process. While the moulds are made, perforated, and pressed, handles are made, which are then welded to the moulded material, and the finished skimmers are emery-polished and painted. The team tested prototypes, then in August 2011 began daily production of 12 skimmers, supplying in this way almost all the skimmers Alcasa needed, about 15 a day. With the market price of skimmers at around 512 BsF (some $120 dollars), the company saved almost $1,500 a day. One must underscore the fact that in the face of Alcasa's grave financial situation, and the limitations on the availability of equipment and inputs, these workshops were practically made from scratch by the workers in recovered spaces.

Another important replacement part produced within Alcasa is the 'top' that covers the electrolysis cells in order to keep CO_2 and other contaminants from dispersing into the environment. Moreover, by sealing off the cell, the top thereby guarantees the necessary temperature during the heating of alumina

---

128 'Skimming cells' (*desnatar celdas*) refers to removing a stratum that forms on the surface of the aluminium, which is done with a tool called a skimmer. Its useful life is about a month, after which it is discarded on a slagheap.

for its transformation into aluminium. The tops are made with 18 components, all produced at Alcasa and assembled by workers from the workshop. The Alcasa-made ones have several advantages over those available on the market; since they are made of aluminium, they weigh only 18 kg, versus 25 kg for the commercial ones. This is an important difference, since the lesser weight makes the work easier. Besides being lighter, they are more solid and have a ladder rung that commercial tops do not have. This is safer for the worker who has to climb up during the production process to attach clips.

Like the skimmer workshop, the production of tops (which involves 10 workers) has been installed in a recovered central space chosen for its proximity to the industrial equipment used in fabrication – the press, the cutter, the perforator, the welder, the oxygen equipment, etc. – which are shared with other departments.

Another replacement-parts project in the same space makes window shutters of recyclable aluminium to replace the translucent sheets that are installed in all the plant's windows so that light can come in. The commercial sheets previously acquired were very expensive, and moreover did not permit the circulation of air.

During a visit to the workshop where the skimmers and tops were being made, it was interesting to confirm that the workers at the replacement-parts projects belonged mostly to the oppositionist union, now representing the majority of Alcasa, which has historical ties with Acción Democrática. Nevertheless, these workers were enthusiastic about building workers' control and explained how their liberty, and the change in their working conditions, had encouraged their creativity as workers, permitting them to invent and construct parts that not even visiting engineers from other CVG factories thought possible. In the concrete terrain of work, the differences between parties disappeared – an observation previously noted by German council members at the beginning of the twentieth century. The base of workers' control is, as the worker Alcides Rivero explains, simple: 'Our proposal of unity is based on a programmatic point of view, a purposeful point. What proposal do we make? That we participate, that's the idea, the only proposal'.[129]

4.6 The Alcasa Initiatives and the Institutional Embargo

The framework of the Socialist Guayana Plan contemplates large investments in CVG industries from the Chinese-Venezuelan investment fund Chinalco, commonly called the 'Chinese Fund'. Alcasa, the CVG company in the worst

---

129 See I-AR 2008.

technological and financial condition, cannot perform to its full potential without massive investment. In September 2010, Chávez approved $403 million via the Chinese Fund for different projects to promote technological adequacy at Alcasa. Nevertheless, owing to the bureaucracies of the CVG, the Ministry of Basic Industries and Mining, and the Chancellor's office, as of late 2011 Alcasa still had not been able to sign the commercial contract with its Chinese counterpart that would give it access to the financing.

According to plans, the investment is directed toward recovery and technological updating of the entire plant. Alcasa would go from an annual production capacity of 35,000 tons of aluminium sheeting to 116,000. With an orientation toward the construction of housing, it also provides for development and construction of a plant for extrusion of metal framework for use in housing, with a capacity of 40,000 tons of frames annually. A major development of the manufacturing sector is planned, in synergy with Cabelum (aluminium cables), Alucasa (aluminium foil) and Rialca (wheels and auto parts). All the projects will be executed under workers' control. Plant modernisation would take some three years; nevertheless, Alcasa could be solvent with its creditors and pay its back debts to workers within a year.[130]

Although Alcasa has presented short- and long-term proposals for development, and funding has been authorised, there has been no institutional response, the explanation of which would require an analysis of the bureaucracy within the social relations of production as expressed in power relations, trade relations, and the division of labour. The struggle for transformation takes place in all three areas, and also through the transformation of the means of production and productive forces.[131]

Meanwhile, Alcasa has tried to strengthen itself and recover the company through its own efforts by means of different initiatives. After discussing the contracts for the future sale of raw aluminium to the transnationals Glencore and Noble Group signed by the previous president, the workers' assembly and the Alcasa board of directors decided to abrogate them. The union M21, which had been politically allied with the previous president, rejected the decision and declared itself in favour of complying with the transnationals.[132]

Instead, Alcasa focused on earning the trust of domestic customers. The first step was to manage the company's situation openly. In a meeting with domestic customers, a raise was negotiated of the advance payment received by

---

130   See I-ES 2011; Sierra Corrales 2011.
131   See I-ES 2011.
132   See I-AR 2011.

the company for raw materials from $20 to $150 a ton, and to add to that more than $30 million, to be paid in aluminium, to support the incorporation of more production cells. Alcasa also confronted the problem of debts that the previous administration had accumulated with its international providers of inputs for aluminium production. Since Alcasa was unable to pay its debts, it no longer received inputs and had to seek out new providers. By means of worker strategy and effort, Alcasa managed a monthly cash flow of around $10 million, enough to reassure some international providers and resume commercial relations with the cancellation of some long-standing unpaid debts.

On the morning of 9 November 2010, before the first shift, the M21 attempted a 'coup'. Two dozen unionists chained the gates shut and took the president's office, but 600 workers entered the factory accompanying Elio Sayago and took it back.[133] In November and December 2010, the dismantling of inoperative cells began, with the intention of replacing them, in a slow process of maintenance and recovery of productive capacity. After the dismantling, the incorporation of new cells was planned for February. A plan to pay off debts to the workers had been approved by the workers' assembly. Against all odds, and without government funding, Alcasa had achieved – by the force of worker management – the opening of a short- and medium-term perspective. Nevertheless, it would not lead to the incorporation of the new cells. The union M21, which had refused to participate in the workers' assembly, incited a conflict over the debts to workers accumulated during Aguilar's management, though they had never confronted him on the issue, and paralysed production.

4.7 The Attack on Workers' Control and the Negation of the Socialist Guayana Plan

In January and February 2011, the M21 executed a 34-day 'strike'. Blocking workers' access to the plant, they called for the resignation of Elio Sayago as president and demanded the payment of workers' back debts. In reality, the conflict sought to end workers' control. The outburst was not by chance: for some sectors of the government and even of the Bolivarian process, and even more for the institutional bureaucracy, the fact that Alcasa had managed to enter into recovery through its own efforts, and had materialised workers' control in the process, represented a threat to their interests and privileges.[134]

The intention of M21 and of its leader José Gil was to make workers' control fail in order to have access to the forthcoming money of the Chinese

---

133 See *Marea Socialista* 2010.
134 See I-ES 2011.

Fund.¹³⁵ While Alcasa was paralysed, M21 representatives went to China in the name of the Alcasa presidency to negotiate, and received visiting representatives of Chinalco. For that to have occurred, there had to be some complicity in government sectors.

Gil belonged to the group of power and interests of the governor of Bolívar state, Francisco Rangel, a group that included important sectors of the Ministry of Labour, the ex-Minister of Labour and then National Assembly deputy José Ramón Rivero,¹³⁶ and José Ramón López, mayor of the municipality of Caroní, where Alcasa is located.¹³⁷ They attempted with all the means at their disposal to make workers' control fail in the basic industries of the CVG and especially at Alcasa, whose work force was the most emblematic of the process and was represented by M21. Their ticket, which claimed to be socialist and Bolivarian, won union elections in August 2008 and was not legally in charge anymore when the conflict erupted, but new elections had not yet happened.¹³⁸

The activism of the opposition to workers' control is based in a network of militants 'liberated' from the Bolivarian Socialist Front of Workers (FSBT), which is to say, militants paid by the companies without working in the plant. They assume practically all the function of direct political operators on behalf of the interests of the governor's group within the plants. In Alcasa, there are 120 militants of M21 on the payroll. The situation is similar in the other CVG companies.¹³⁹ Some are even armed and threaten their adversaries.¹⁴⁰

---

135   Ligia Duerto, e-mail of 25 February 2011.
136   Rivero, also from the FBT, was Minister of Labour and Social Security from January 2007 to April 2008. Together with Governor Rangel, he was responsible for the heavy repression against the Sidor workers during their struggle for nationalisation; he also publicly supported the plans of the FSBT to form a union confederation as an alternative to the UNT. Rivera was removed as minister by Chávez because of his actions in the case of Sidor.
137   'Alcasa no es más que la expresión muy pequeña de lo que pasa a nivel político en el país. Entrevista con los trabajadores de Alcasa Oswaldo León, Alcides Rivero, Cruz Barreto y Manuel Figuera (videos)', (25 May 2011), available at: http://www.aporrea.org/trabajadores/n181549.html; see also 'Estévez, Hector: La pelea a cuchillo del PSUV en las empresas básicas de Guayana', (31 January 2011), available at: http://www.aporrea.org/regionales/a116778.html and 'Entrevista a Oswaldo León', in *Correo del Orinoco* (09 February 2011).
138   Figuera, Manuel: *Dictadura sindical en Alcasa* (28 May 2011), available at: http://www.aporrea.org/trabajadores/a124125.
139   Interview with Alcasa workers Oswaldo León, Alcides Rivero, Cruz Barreto and Manuel Figuera (videos): 'Alcasa no es más que la expresión muy pequeña de lo que pasa a nivel político en el país' (25 May 2011), available at: http://www.aporrea.org/trabajadores/n181549.html.
140   See Ligia Duerto, e-mail (25 February 2011).

In February 2011, a group of 'unionists' led by José Gil physically attacked spokespeople of the cooperatives that worked at Alcasa for having signed an agreement with the president of Alcasa for payment of accumulated debts. One of them even pulled out and fired a gun, but fortunately did not hurt anyone. The man was arrested and faces criminal charges.[141] The attacks by unions opposed to the process of workers' control in Guayana became massified; in Ferrominera there was one dead by gunshot and in Bauxilum some were wounded.

Neither the PSUV nor the government made their position clear in the face of the Alcasa conflict, nor did they intervene in support of the workers who were attacked, since the conflict was within different currents of the same Bolivarian process and because there exists an interest on the part of powerful sectors to make workers' control fail. At the same time, then foreign minister Nicolás Maduro, accompanied by other high governmental figures, went personally to Venalum to end a strike that had been organised by an opposition union.

The Alcasa lockout finally failed. M21 pulled back, and the government tried to cover them by paying a part of the workers' back debts. Workers and communities entered to retake the presidency and the installations. The economic harm caused by M21 was enormous. Moreover, the 34-day stoppage left only 172 of 396 reduction cells in operation, half of them so old that the quality of aluminium produced was affected.[142]

In the subsequent union election, the M21 lost its majority, the pro-workers' control left was divided into three tickets, and the winner was a representative from an opposition union, who despite being tied to Acción Democrática was supportive of workers' control. His election was not a vote in favour of the opposing union, but rather a punishment vote against M21. Since the left was divided, the option for many workers to impede union representation from M21 in Sintralcasa was to vote for the opposition candidate, who won the election with 400 votes more than M21 – the widest margin ever in Alcasa's union elections.[143] In Venalum, on the other hand, a union oppositionist who had paralysed the plant was soundly defeated.

After the defeat of M21's strike and in the election, the level of conflict in the plant came down. However, the attacks against Sayago and the process

---

141 'Sindicato de trabajadores de Alcasa fue denunciado ante la fiscalía' (20 February 2011), available at: http://www.aporrea.org/trabajadores/n175384.html.
142 See *La hoja de aluminio*, 49 (28 April 2011).
143 See I-AR 2011; I-ES 2011; I-LD 2011.

of workers' control did not stop. There also followed 'administrative isolation', which prevented Alcasa from accessing the funds authorised for modernising the plant.

In the months following the M21 sabotage, Alcasa slowly managed to increase operationality once again, acquire more domestic customers, and sign some contracts of cooperation.

Despite this, Elio Sayago was relieved of his post by Chávez in February 2012 without any clear explanation. Ángel Marcano, who was assigned as the new president, is an ex-worker at Alcasa, twice a deputy of the PSUV in the National Assembly, and close to the governor of Bolívar state and to the M21 leadership. His appointment was publicly rejected by collectives of workers' control at the different CVG companies, by Alcasa workers, communal councils, popular organisations, several union currents, the Communist Party, and the spokespeople of the Guayana Socialist Plan.[144]

During Marcano's tenure, the productive capacity of Alcasa was further reduced, and the old hierarchical-capitalist administrative scheme returned. The Alcasa workers denounced the deterioration of installations and cells, corruption, lack of transparency, misadministration, unjustified dismissals, debts to the workers, and much more.[145] At the end of 2014, Alcasa signed an agreement with the Italian company Presezzi Extrusión for the 'design, fabrication, installation, and startup of the second phase of the extruder plant'.[146] The contract had been initiated by Elio Sayago in 2011.

> The updating projects have been advancing at a good clip despite the problems and the lack of compliance with the plan. The updates obstruct production because one has to take cells and equipment out of action, but nevertheless it is estimated that this year the projects will conclude and production can resume. The former administrators, who have always shown commitment, are organised in the Micromission and there they are trying to get production moving forward. The present administrators, who are mostly inefficient, inexpert, and irresponsible, do not worry about anything but their personal and political benefit. There is much criticism of them, and also much disappointment.[147]

---

144 See Workers', popular, communal, and political organisations of Guayana 2012.
145 See *aporrea tvi* 2014; FTSA 2014.
146 See *Prensa MPPI* 2014.
147 See I-EE 2015.

While Marcano promised 'that in 2015 Alcasa will recover its capacity to cover the national market',[148] the workers denounced grave failings at Alcasa.[149] Considering that the workers have demonstrated with videos how the Alcasa extrusion plant was still inoperative after having been inaugurated five times, Marcano's promises lack credibility. At the beginning of 2015, production had still not taken off, and operating norms were not being complied with. Supervisors who try to impose discipline are assaulted by rightist sectors of the company union (whose representatives have the majority) and of the FBST, whose affiliate at Alcasa is the M21. However, following the union guidelines left by Chávez, the M21, the Primero Negro team, and almost all the leftist groups joined together, which did not result in a common policy.

> Well, like we Venezuelans say: together but separate. Gil's group continued anti-worker practices in the name of workers' control, appointing incompetent cronies as managers, bringing in workers with salaries above those with equal duties, making arbitrary decisions without respecting the workers' right to participation, and overriding the actions of work groups.[150]

Seeing that in Alcasa nothing was being done toward the transformation of Alcasa into a socialist company, the Negro Primero Training Centre established the Socialist Alcasa Micromission, intending to develop a management focused on the transformation of Alcasa. Marcano accepted the proposal, but he named as programme director a person without any capacity to bring a group together, so the mission was unsuccessful.

5   New Struggles for Workers' Control

Since 2013 a wave of conflicts has been observable in the state companies of Venezuela. In most cases the issue has not been wage or even strictly labour demands, but rather company management and ministerial bureaucracy. The workers have taken control of the plants in order to reclaim workers' control, effect a transformation to socialism, and re-orient production toward satisfying the needs of the popular masses.

---

148   See Soto 2014.
149   See *aporrea tvi* 2014; FTSA 2014.
150   See I-EE 2015.

In most state companies there are conflicts over questions of participation and working conditions. Protests and denunciations of mistreatment and irregularities are increasing. The most important case was the food producer Industrias Diana, a state company managed with broad worker participation by means of a Socialist Workers' Council. When on 26 July 2013 the Minister of Food Félix Osorio named David Mendoza as the new general manager for the plant without consulting the workers, they rejected the unilateral appointment. They mobilised workers, communities, and alternative press to the plant, prosecuting their struggle with determination until an acceptable new manager was named, while at the same time maintaining production.[151]

Industrias Diana is the largest domestic producer of oils and margarine, filling 35 percent of the national demand for margarine and producing mayonnaise, salsas, and soups. 80 percent of its production is distributed by means of state trade networks and 20 percent goes to the market. Besides its central plant in Valencia, Carabobo, Diana has five other production sites. The company's former proprietors had gradually brought it to the edge of bankruptcy, but it was nationalised at the workers' request before the owners could dismantle the factory, and was placed under state administration in 2008 with the promise of workers' control. At the moment of nationalisation, production was at 200,000 litres of oil a month, employing 300 workers. With a broad participation of workers through the CSTT, Diana presently produces a total of 7,000 tons of edible oils annually, with 2,000 workers. At the same time it plans to build another plant and raise production to 37,000 tons a year. Industrias Diana is one of the few nationalised companies that are widely self-sustaining; it has raised its workers' salaries, pays dividends to the state, and even has investment capacity.[152]

Besides objecting to the unilateral way in which David Mendoza was designated as the new general manager, the workers objected to his status as a private entrepreneur in the food sector, something that did not square with the interests of the revolution. The workers declared that 'the person who assumes the responsibility of directing the company must have come from it, guaranteeing the experience of production and a commitment to the political basics the factory was founded on by the Comandante; that is, under workers' control

---

151 'Trabajadores de Industrias Diana rechazan nombramiento inconsulto de Gerente General', available at: www.aporrea.org/endogeno/n233446.html.
152 'En Industrias Diana el Control Obrero fue ordenado por Chávez', señala Carlos Seijas (11 August 2013), available at: www.aporrea.org/trabajadores/n234253.html.

and for the revolution'.¹⁵³ To support the mobilisations and relay information live, a community radio station was brought to the Industrias Diana grounds.

After Mendoza and his team paid no attention to the protests and installed themselves in office, on 31 July the workers of Industries Diana evicted them, escorting them out of the plant.¹⁵⁴ Minister for Food Felix Osorio not only criticised the workers of Industrias Diana, but even went so far as to say that Chávez had been wrong about the workers' councils and that they were not capable of managing a company.¹⁵⁵ To subdue the workers, he froze the payroll.

After a 20-day standoff, on 15 August president Nicolás Maduro confirmed the designation of General Dester Rodríguez as the new general manager of Diana. Rodríguez had previously worked in the coordination of community contacts at the food distributor PDVAL (which belongs to the state petroleum company PDVSA) and had the workers' approval. Héctor Mieres, worker at Diana and part of the CSTT, declared: 'The most important thing about this achievement is the disposition that General Rodríguez has demonstrated to understand and respect the decision-making and participatory mechanisms that we the workers have achieved as part of workers' control'.¹⁵⁶ The example of Diana is important, given that in the past several processes for workers' control at other state companies had been aborted without major resistance on the part of the workers.

With the new directorate in place, and on the way to workers' control, Industrias Diana registered a new production record in March 2014, supplying 38 percent of the national market with more than 19,000 tons monthly of oil and fats (lard, oil, and margarine). Moreover, the government approved an investment of $67 million that would permit the quadrupling of production.¹⁵⁷

Another very important case is the victorious struggle of the workers of Lácteos los Andes (Landes) in August 2013. Landes produces milk, cheese, yogurt, and juices, and supplies millions of Venezuelans daily. After modernisation, it had three main plants (Cabudare, Caja Seca, and Machiques) and 37 smaller entities.

---

153   'Trabajadores de Industrias Diana rechazan nombramiento inconsulto de Gerente General' (26 July 2013), available at: www.aporrea.org/endogeno/n233446.html.
154   'Consejo de Trabajadores de Industrias Diana. Trabajadores de Industrias Diana desalojan de las instalaciones a la nueva gerencia impuesta y repudiada' (31 July 2013), available at: www.aporrea.org/trabajadores/n233774.html.
155   See León 2013.
156   'Con lucha y movilización: ¡Victoria de los trabajadores de Diana!' (15 August 2013), available at: www.aporrea.org/endogeno/n234542.html.
157   See Comisión Merco Sur Alba de Industrias Diana CA. 2014.

Landes had been nationalised by President Chávez in 2008 in response to a shortage, intentionally caused by private industry, of milk and milk products. It was supposed to become gradually controlled by workers while they prepared to assume the tasks. However, there were never decisive advances in worker participation. While the workers were preparing, they formed CSTT and commissions for all areas inside the company and also in relation to aspects connected to workers' quality of life. In March 2013, the workers of Landes began denouncing a drop in production that reached 40 percent. Maintenance of the plant was neglected, while the money allocated for it disappeared. The workers held management responsible, accusing its officers, and ultimately also Osorio, of corruption, but months of investigations and audits had no result. According to the workers, various officials in different institutions were covering up mismanagement in the company. In August, the workers intensified their struggle, demanding the dismissal of management and advances in workers' control at Landes. One worker summarised: 'We have an unresponsive management that has done nothing. The solution is to remove the management and open an administrative, civil, and penal investigation, and resolve the problems with workers' control'.[158]

After several meetings of the workers with representatives of the President of the Republic, at which they presented their complaints and proposals, President Maduro removed the directorate of Landes. The proposal to move over to a model of workers' control and to designate a worker elected by workers as manager was discussed. In subsequent weeks, a restructuring of the company's administrative model was agreed upon that moved to a model of increasing workers' control, and Landes came under direct control by the workers, who carried out a social audit. Luis Moreno, a Landes worker who was elected general manager by the workers, is also part of the 'National Political Command', the maximum authority in the company, formed of 25 spokespeople from different plants, chosen by the workers in direct, secret elections. As the term suggests, the spokespeople do not make decisions, but are merely the voice of decisions made in workers' assemblies. It was further agreed to create a workers' political command in each region and to subdivide the company's organisation into six territories with separate administrative policies in each territory. All of this was based on the experiences and decisions of the workers.[159]

---

158 'La lucha de Trabajadores de Lácteos Los Andes comienza a rendir frutos' (28 August 2013), available at: www.aporrea.org/trabajadores/n235180.html.

159 Gómez, José Ramón. 'La unidad de la masa trabajadora rompe paradigmas en la empresa socialista Lácteos Los Andes (ESLANDES)' (30 September 2013), available at: www.aporrea.org/endogeno/n237190.html.

Another state company was taken over by its workers in late August 2013, the Pedro Camejo Socialist Enterprise, located near the town of Urachiche in Yaracuy state. Its workers, acting with the support of the peasantry and of the PSUV mayor of Urachiche, accused the management of disrespect and complained of large sums of money gone missing, while much agricultural machinery went unrepaired for lack of replacement parts. Worker Carlos Gudiño affirmed that 'it's not a takeover, but workers' control as a response to bad management'.[160]

The company lends specialised machinery and transportation services to the agricultural sector; for the peasants, its services are essential, especially during the season in question, the 'winter harvest'.[161] During the takeover, the workers continued working, repairing machinery and putting it at the disposition of the peasants. At the end of 2014, the struggle continued: the workers were fighting for control of the company while confronting a campaign of threats, intimidation, and repression, and the directors were preparing to fire the workers' council spokespersons. The workers continued denouncing a series of irregularities that affected the company, like 'inoperativity, abandonment of machinery, lack of supplies, robbery, unutilized machinery from the Cuba-Venezuela pact, lack of efficient service to producers, etc.', while supporting producers' denunciations of corruption in the company, and they requested government intervention.[162]

There were half a dozen new takeovers in the private sector. Among them were the graphic arts company Azertia GC in the industrial zone of Palo Verde, in Petare, Gran Caracas, and the chicken production plant 'Aves Barquisimeto' of the SOUTO group in the north of the city of Barquisimeto, in Lara state. 'Aves Barquisimeto' was taken by 28 workers after the company announced its immediate closing on 21 August 2013, liquidating 180 workers. Characterising the closure and firings as fraudulent and illegal, the workers took over the plant, insisting that it was in perfect condition and could be started up at any moment. With the takeover, the workers hoped to prevent the owners from dismantling the plant, as well as to continue maintenance. They demanded nationalisation and transformation into a Socialist Production Company managed together with the surrounding communities.[163]

---

160 'Hablan los trabajadores de la Empresa Socialista Pedro Camejo, tomada desde el mes pasado' (17 July 2013), available at: www.aporrea.org/trabajadores/n236406.html.
161 Ibid.
162 See Consejo Trabajadores Maisanta de Guanarito 2014.
163 Radio Tamunangue Libre. 'Trabajadores mantienen toma de la empresa "Aves Barquisi-

Other companies under workers' control in Lara State are Beneagro (part of the SOUTO Corporation), Bhrama (Grupo Cisneros), Egreca (Gres), Alentuy (Aluminio) and Interceramic C.A., which produces ceramics for floors, facades, and ceilings. Interceramics's owner closed it on 31 August 2012, communicating to the workers via Skype from Spain that the factory had ceased operations and that all of them were dismissed. The workers decided to take over the factory and launch a struggle against the owner. During the struggle, the idea of reopening the company under workers' control became more and more prominent, with the consequence that production began again under workers' control on 29 October 2013, with the products to be contributed to the housing construction programme Gran Misión Vivienda Venezuela.[164]

The struggles for workers' control at Industrias Diana and Landes brought ideological and political questions out of the background and raised them to the level of national debate. Their struggles, which weave alliances with communal councils, communes, community media, and grassroots organisations, are based on unity among workers and a high level of organisation, and are profoundly rooted in territory. By means of this combination, the workers achieved what – despite the official discourse in favour of workers' control – state institutions did not.

6 Approaching the Issue of New Worker Subjectivities in the Context of Participation and Class Struggle

> No, it's not only about changing the relations of production because you can change the relations of production and that's an achievement, but you also have to change the way you think. Because if I'm going to produce in order to earn more, if I'm the owner of the means of production, I'm not accomplishing anything. I have to be the owner of the means of production not so I can be an owner, but so that I can help the communities, that's the key.[165]

∴

---

meto" por incumplimientos laborales' (14 October 2013), available at: www.aporrea.org/trabajadores/n238025.html.

164 Lara: 'trabajadores reactivan empresa Interceramica bajo control obrero' (31 October 2013), *Radio comunitaria Tamunangue Libre 95.3FM.*, available at: www.aporrea.org/trabajadores/n239076.html.

165 See José Quintero, worker, Inveval, I-JQ 2006.

Especially in Venezuela, few researchers have paid attention to individual and collective subjectivity in class struggle and social transformation. According to most of the interviews I conducted, however, it emerged as a central issue in the lives of workers in organised struggle through direct participation, horizontality, group decision-making, and control of the means of mass production and the production process.

The construction of a democratic, self-managed, non-capitalist society obviously requires a new subjectivity; otherwise, any structural change – if that is what occurs – would be superficial and therefore reversible at any moment.[166] Only when people feel that they have control over their lives, and recognise that this change is connected with their struggle, will they be able to consolidate and advance in the construction of the new. And it is precisely in the experience of collective agency, in the development of popular power, where the new subjectivities are constructed. The actors' identification and satisfaction with what they do in their lives increases and consolidates their participation.

The creation of new subjectivities and of protagonism is central to the Bolivarian process. Subjectivity cannot be transferred or conceded, but has to be formed in an active, autonomous way, because the new subjectivities are formed in and through class struggle. The Venezuelan case presents a very complex relationship, given that the creation of new subjectivities takes place there with the support of and the instruments offered by constituted power, and at the same time against that same constituted power. Class struggle emerges from this relationship.

Almost none of the workers I interviewed had any political training or militancy prior to 2002. At Alcasa, only a few had a long history of struggle. As suggested by the interviews I have quoted, and also by my research into forms of construction of local self-government, the growing class struggle in Venezuela is creating a grounding of new social subjects, who are agents of revolutionary change.[167]

This new subjectivity is manifested in multiple ways. The workers reflect it when they describe their newly assumed participation in collective administration of their jobs, which is to say, in how they take control of their lives. In many cases, they express it by means of how they have transformed into 'new people'; they have discovered new feelings and have begun to be agents of change rather than objects of social processes.

---

166   See I-ES 2011.
167   See Azzellini 2010.

Previously I was a worker in this company when it was capitalist. It had been stopped for eight years, the plant. With the framework of our Constitution and the revolutionary project, united with the government, we took the company into co-management. Now we form the cooperative. Previously we came to work on Monday and just waited for our pay on Friday. We belonged to the machines. The owner came in and said: work – and we worked – stop – and we stopped. Not now, our eyes have been opened, our minds, our hearts. Now the company is not ours either, it belongs to the communities. Here at the company, in our dining room, 40 children from the nearest community are eating, the neediest ones.[168]

As Marx wrote:

> Communism as the positive transcendence of private property as human self-estrangement, and therefore as the real appropriation of the human essence by and for man; communism therefore as the complete return of man to himself as a social (i.e., human) being – a return accomplished consciously and embracing the entire wealth of previous development. This communism ... is the genuine resolution of the conflict between man and nature and between man and man – the true resolution of the strife between existence and essence, between objectification and self-confirmation, between freedom and necessity, between the individual and the species.[169]

As Gramsci notes, during the economic and political domination of the bourgeois class, the real development of the revolutionary process cannot be seen in the development of unions or parties that belong to the bourgeois, representative system; it is hidden, 'in the darkness of the factory and in the obscurity of consciousness of the uncountable multitudes that capitalism subjects to its laws'.[170] If we take as a point of departure the fact that Venezuela continues to be a capitalist country with a bourgeois state, the revolutionary process cannot be seen in the governments' successes, in the development of union struggles, or in the actions of formal structures of representative participation.

---

168   Alexander Patiño, Unión Cooperative Agroindustrial del Cacao, in Azzellini and Ressler 2006.
169   Marx 1975c, pp. 296–7.
170   Giachetti 1972, p. 158.

Considering the peculiarity of the Venezuelan process, in which the construction of the new happens both with and against constituted power, and in which constituted power's resistance to change collides with the force of constituent power, the new subjectivities that emerge from class struggle are usually found in those points of conflict between constituent and constituted power. These new subjectivities and experiences of the capacity of 'doing', of being the agent of one's own destiny, can be seen emerging forcefully in the Venezuelan workplace, especially since 2007. At the centre of this development is the creative passion of the workers' desire to build a society free of exploitation and alienation. In all fields, this desire has been confronting the contradictions of capitalism, of the bourgeois state, of the predominant bourgeois and capitalist logic, and of the impossibility of making the changes considered necessary within the framework of the prevailing system. It also confronts strong institutional resistance to change. For constituent power, however, this crisis is not insurmountable but an obstacle; it is the engine that drives it, again and again, in search of another way out, to establish itself as the socially dominant force, as we have seen clearly in the cases of struggle presented in the previous chapters.

In their struggles, the workers create new social relations. Within the companies, the present is interrupted by messianic time, the now-time, which gives an idea of the possible future and makes everything possible and imaginable:[171]

> The workers learned that it was possible to administer and control the entire productive process. A great lesson! They told me it was impossible, no?[172]
>
> Now one feels freer, flying higher ...[173]

The ongoing Venezuelan experience of the struggle for creation of new subjectivities through control of the workplace and the production process repeats elements of historical examples from around the world.[174] But only in the twenty-first century can we find many examples of how these new subjectivities have been created through workers' direct participation in the issues that most affect their lives.

---

171   See Benjamin 1968.
172   See I-OL 2008.
173   See Ramón, Inveval, I-RM 2008.
174   See Azzellini 2015; Korsch 1977; Lanz 2007; Lavaca 2004; Mandel 1974; Ness and Azzellini 2011; Pannekoek 2008, Rebón 2004; 2006; Ruggeri 2010; Sitrin 2006, 2012.

Among the best-known examples is the case of Argentina, where in the wake of the popular rebellion of 2001, 350 closed businesses have been recuperated – taken by their workers and put to collective production, without bosses or owners. The workers appropriated the slogan of the Brazilian Landless Movement (MST): 'Occupy, resist, produce', which also appeared in Venezuela in the peasant movement FNCEZ and in some recuperated companies. More than a decade after the popular uprising in Argentina, the majority of the recuperated companies continue producing.

For Andrés Ruggeri, one of the principal researchers into recuperated companies in Argentina, and coordinator of a research project on recuperated companies at the Universidad de Buenos Aires, the two most important conclusions that can be reached from the experience of the recuperated companies derive from: (1) the numbers, production, and persistence of the companies; and (2) the forms of decision-making and the building of new social relations. As Ruggeri emphasises in a report on a meeting of recuperated companies, not only has the idea of recuperation not disappeared; in spite of the difficulties, it has become an option that workers consider valid when faced with the closing of their workplaces.

The new subjectivity is rooted in the direct and horizontal participation that usually emerges in the struggle for recuperated companies. According to research into the recuperated companies of Argentina, most WRCs maintain the direct democratic practices they introduced during the struggle in their later everyday operation: 88% of the WRCs claim to hold assemblies regularly, 44% of them hold weekly assemblies and 35% monthly assemblies.[175] The workers speak of the new subjectivity that appears in these processes of construction of new social relations. Carlos and Julián of the recuperated ceramic factory Zanón – called by its workers FaSinPat, Bossless Factory (*Fábrica Sin Patrón*) – comment:

> [Carlos] We try to make decisions using consensus. In the assemblies, we try to create a space where each person and position is heard, so that whatever decision we make is ultimately based on all of our opinions, or at least the majority. Here in the plant, we're organized into different sectors based in areas of work. Every day, each sector has a meeting. The factory-wide meetings, where each group shares what they're doing, are on Wednesdays. This is where we make decisions, including ones like paying everyone the same 800 peso salary.

---

175 PFA 2010, 47.

[Julián] Something we've observed is that each assembly is increasingly participatory. We've seen all the compañeros go through a sort of waking up process. It's not just talk – everyone is putting their all into this ...

Before we took over the factory, the only thing we had to do was work, and we didn't worry about the rest ... It's like an older compañero said: 'We shouldn't wait for the very people who tortured us to solve things for us.' We understand that now.

Every day we all participate more. We all have the possibility to speak and seek solutions, to be more active and create change together.[176]

The interesting thing about these quotes is not only the form of organisation, but that the names of the two Argentine workers could, as has been demonstrated in the course of research, be replaced with the names of workers in Inveval, Alcasa or with the name of Alexander Patiño, who at the beginning of this subchapter compared his previous condition in the factory to that of a machine. Although conditions in Venezuela are different from those in Argentina or other countries because of Venezuela's greater institutional opening, in any case its contradictions produce class struggle, whether within the state or against it, and it is precisely through class struggle that the new subjectivities are formed.

6.1 Horizontality in the Factory and Change Throughout Society

In all the interviews with workers in the process of struggle, issues of participation and democratic decision-making occupy a central position. Almost always, the new practice is explicitly contrasted with previous structures of work and decision-making. In companies where some model of self-management or deep participation has been installed, it is common for the workers to speak of liberty, like Aury Arocha:

> Our way of working now is very different, because before we worked like a dictatorship, not now, now we're free. We're free, OK, but not to do whatever we want. We're working in a unified way, we're totally spontaneous in our opinions, and we work with much more harmony.[177]

---

176 Sitrin 2006, pp. 64–5.
177 Aury Arocha, laboratory analyst, Tomates Guárico, in Ressler and Azzellini 2006.

The testimonies detail how assemblies are held, how decisions are made, and what the internal processes are. From there, they arrive at a broader context, of what workers' control means and how it is related to the rest of society, to arrive at the point of how they and their lives have changed through participation and have assumed a protagonistic role in their own lives and surroundings. They link the new individual subjectivity to the collective dimension, and in so doing they produce new collective subjectivities.

José Quintero, worker at Inveval, proudly describes in detail the decision-making process there. His testimony, echoed in interviews with workers at other companies, manifests a consciousness of his new protagonism. Workers at companies without co-management or self-management usually do not know who makes the decisions in the companies where they work, or how those decisions are made, and if they knew, it would not be an object of discussion. However, to create self-managed democratic processes is essential in the struggle for workers' control.

> Since this is a new process and we as workers are learning and building, there have been moments where it was difficult to reach agreement. There have been moments in which the differences were so great that no consensus could be reached, but we the workers are clear that this is normal in a company and that ideas are debated until there is a consensus. If we don't reach a consensus the assembly is suspended, and a new meeting is set up.[178]

Julio González of Inveval describes the form of horizontal organisation introduced by the factory council in 2007. There the general assembly is the highest decision-making body, and therefore the elected spokespeople do not make decisions but rather comply with them. The assembly can also immediately revoke any elected 'position'. These mechanisms of horizontality, which can be found in many forms of direct or non-representative democracy throughout history, are common in the new forms of democracy emerging in Venezuela. The communal councils, the communes, and the structures of the organised movements all operate with the principle of the 'spokesperson', which excludes representation. In all the interviews, as well as in other companies I visited, breaking the social division of labour and overcoming the fragmentation of the workers' consciousness is portrayed as central.

---

178 See I-JQ 2006.

> We began to design the factory council, implement it here so that the workers themselves manage the company. The previous organisational diagram was vertical, its functioning was hierarchical. The organisational diagram we designed was the most horizontal possible, 100% ... We are 61 workers and the workers' assembly is the maximum authority, followed by the factory council that comprises 32 people with a one-year term, including directors and coordinators of each body, although the workers' assembly can revoke their position at any time for demonstrated mismanagement, or can renominate and confirm them. This avoids bureaucratisation and lets us break with the social division of work. For example, I am ratified and today I'm in the marketing group, tomorrow I might be on some machine or in a different department, depending on my knowledge, obviously. Let's be clear, you can't put someone in a position that they don't understand, because performance suffers or the job is not done right.[179]

Of course, the democratic organisation of a company with 61 workers is easier and quicker than that of a bigger company, as in the case of Alcasa with more than 3,000 workers. After the interrupted experience of co-management/ workers' control at Alcasa, and two years before the new process toward workers' control, Carlos Agüero of the Collective for Workers' control explains:

> We speak of a horizontal organisation ... none of us has sufficient practice, none of us ... we come from the structure of representation, so for the culture of participation there has to necessarily be development, no? An apprenticeship ... Then our proposal really is that the company management be a democratic work group.[180]

In their jobs, the workers build relationships with other areas of organisation and struggle. The connection with the communities is vital, as is also the responsibility that the workers feel toward them, as exemplified by the words of Ubencio Valerio at Inveval:

> The community helped us much during the takeover. We asked for contributions down there in the street on Friday and Saturdays, payday. And they gave. We collected enough to buy coffee and water, and the com-

---

179 See I-JG 2008.
180 See I-CA 2008.

munity helped us a lot. Now, since we are still starting up, we haven't yet gone into the community, but our hope is that this company can move forward and help fill the community's needs. The only way we're helping right now is in the missions, there are people studying here.[181]

All the factories have community work and all have been supported by the communities. The workers of the paper plant Invepal regularly organised fairs at the beginning of the school year to sell the school supplies they produce directly into the community. They also formed voluntary community work brigades, as did Alcasa, and the communities are supported in the creation of collective production entities.[182] The connection is also political in the sense that the factory workers see their struggle for workers' control as part of a project for democratisation and self-management that extends to all reaches of society and in which they are connected with mechanisms of self-government like the communal councils and communes.[183] In this way, workers on the job project themselves as agents of change for the entire society, understanding that it is not possible to change the factory alone:

> It's still a capitalist system out there. For all we want or need for it to be different, we're going to come up against the external reality. We can get along very well here and believe in what we do, but when we face the world outside, even to talk to PDVSA, or to establish relationships with another company, we realize that we are still capitalists. If we don't go into a market and produce at a certain level, we are not competitive, and then we crash. What you want, what you work for, is one thing, but what's out there is something else.[184]

> Me? What I've learned is that life can't be seen in strictly monetary terms, there's politics in everything. They taught us that politics was for politicians, but that's not true. We've seen that if we don't go into politics, we won't have the tools to make the changes we want.[185]

Participation, then, is projected toward building a new society, antagonistic to the existing one. In the process of building, which – as we have seen – is class

---

181   See I-UV 2006.
182   See I-LD 2011.
183   See I-AR 2011; I-ES 2011; I-RE 2010; 2011.
184   See I-LM 2006.
185   See I-JQ 2006.

struggle, the will to unlimited participation, to absolute democracy, clashes with constituted power. The struggle for workers' control is also, and is frequently framed from the beginning as, a struggle against the power structures that are designed to reproduce and perpetuate what already exists.

6.2   The New Collective Self

Class struggle for social transformation demands a massive popular, protagonistic participation. To achieve that, people have to take control of their lives at both the individual and collective levels, in a dialectical process of mutual influence between the agents of social transformation and the social transformation process. Being able to find solutions to the problems of one's own life through direct horizontal participation and organisation with others transforms the people into agents and nourishes class struggle:

> The relationships between workers have changed a lot. Now there are no employees, we're all equal, and we all get paid the same. If we have to contribute something, we all contribute, and we work united.[186]

> Here we're going to come out winners. Because it's not one person's interest, but a collective interest. And that is what is most satisfying to us as a *pueblo*. I believe that this is a model to be followed. I believe this is the way out of so much poverty that we have in the state, in the country, and – why not say it? – the world. Because this way gives greater participation to a *pueblo* that had been tossed aside, abandoned. And unfortunately here we produced a lot for the benefit of one person, and for all we produced, we continued being poor. Today our quality of life is totally different, I believe that is the feeling that we can express in our own words.[187]

Workers with no experience of protagonistic political participation before 2001/2 tell how they have changed personally, becoming protagonists in their own life and in history:

> When they speak of socialism many are scared: hey, what's that? Well, socialism in a few words is love, happiness, social justice. Previously we had none of that, we didn't know anything about it. We went along because we saw the others going along. Now we're taking decisive steps.

---

186   See I-UV 2006.
187   Dulfo Guerrero, Textileros del Táchira, in Azzellini and Ressler 2006.

> Previously they wrote our history, ever since Columbus arrived history has been written by those who took our lands, our thoughts. Now ... we are the protagonists, we're doing the writing, we're going forward.[188]

They speak of having become more solidary, more content, more satisfied, freer. Meanwhile the same process of creation of the new subjectivity is going on in the barrios, as described by Inveval worker Luisa Morales:

> I've changed a lot, I've definitively stopped being a passive person, a person who simply dedicated herself to work, to study, to take care of her daughter, see that her parents were in good health, her family. No, now I think that one's mission in life must be much more transcendental. You have to contribute more, you have to worry about others more, and not only about your own. You don't know if the child next door ate, if the wife is okay, if her husband has work ... you have to stop being selfish, and I've learned that, not to think only of me and mine, I've learned to go beyond that and get involved somehow.[189]

Through her experience of struggle at Inveval, Luisa Morales went from being a non-participant to an active participant, with the perspective of changing all of society and moving beyond capitalism. This is the now-time, a window from which it is possible to have a sense of what a longed-for future society might be like.[190] This process has been repeated in Venezuela thousands of times at work and in communities, and it eventually materialises in the strengthening of the movement for workers' control and for communes.

---

188 Alexander Patiño, worker, Unión Cooperativa Agroindustrial del Cacao, in Azzellini and Ressler 2006.
189 See I-LM 2006.
190 See Benjamin 1968.

CHAPTER 7

Communes, Production, and the Communal State

At a higher level of territorial organisation, there exists the possibility of the creation of communes, which emerged from below and evolved from the communities' need to come together at a higher level than communal councils, in order to develop wider-reaching projects. Communes are formed from several communal councils in a self-defined territory, and can develop long-range projects and measures, while decisions continue being made in the communal council assemblies. The communes link the CCs, the missions, and grassroots organisations in order to plan, implement, and evaluate together.

At a level beyond the communes, Chávez proposed that larger areas, which did not have to correspond to official administrative divisions, form communal cities. This could happen if all their territory was organised in communal councils and communes following a model of administration and planning from below.[1] These communes and communal cities are understood as structures of popular power.

In December 2010, the National Assembly passed the Popular Power Law, the Social Auditing Law, the Public and Popular Planning Law, and the Law of Communes. Although there is no law that regulates them, several communal cities have emerged – so far, rural and structured around agriculture.

The debate continues about moving beyond the state by means of alternative structures created from below. As of 2000, the role of the state, as well as the relationship between state and society, has undergone profound changes. Chávez argued that the passage from a US-dominated capitalist state under the control of the national bourgeoisie to a state in transformation had already been consummated, although still within a capitalist framework. Nevertheless, the bourgeois state with its structure continued 'alive and kicking' and would have to be dismantled progressively, in parallel with the building of the socialist, communal state. In the medium term, this involved transformation into a socialist state with a regulated market, and subsequently to a 'communal state socialist system ... where indirect and direct social property predominates, and an important component of the social property would have to be communal property'.[2]

---

1 Azzellini 2010, p. 2013.
2 Chávez 2008, p. 38.

In the following section, I will analyse the communes as fundamental pillars of the communal state, and the communal companies that have emerged from the communes as a new model of collective self-management of production. Finally, I will make some comments about the communal state.

1   Communes

1.1   *Origin and Form*

The commune is seen by the social bases as the most important instrument of self-organisation for moving beyond representative democracy, the bourgeois state, and the prevailing capitalist model. Although popular initiatives to create communes increased massively beginning in 2010, the Ministry did not register any communes until 2012, when it was obligated to do so because of protests and popular pressure from communes under construction. The number of registered communes reached 1,195 in July 2015,[3] almost all of them after President Nicolás Maduro named Reinaldo Iturriza Minister of Communes in April 2013.

Shortly after the first communal councils began forming in 2005, forms of cooperation began to be established between several communal councils called 'commonwealths' or 'confederations', or simply taking the form of a network. Discussion and the search for a form of self-government in broader spaces began from below. Chávez paid special attention to the communes, which began to be created autonomously and without an 'official script' as of 2007, the year he resumed the initiative and began to speak publicly of the commune as a superior level to the communal council.

Atenea Jiménez of the National Network of Communards bears witness to the process:

> In answer to a call by Chávez in 2007, debates began in each community over what the commune should be. Several communal councils formed communes, but there were historic popular movements that were not linked to the communal council which then could not remain outside the commune. This debate happened in almost every case and it was agreed that all those movements should be organically linked in the commune as well as the communal councils.

---

3   'Ministerio del Poder Popular para las Comunas y los Movimientos Sociales' (25 July 2015), available at: http://consulta.mpcomunas.gob.ve/.

There was also the risk that the commune would replace the municipality or the parish in terms of politico-administrative organisation and our proposal is that it is not that kind of space, because otherwise it would be like in many other countries, one more body of the bourgeois liberal state. That would mean changing the name, though the function would remain the same.

We began to build in that sense and we began to study also other historical experiences of the commune. We created a space for debate and have invited international guests who have considered the subject. We began the work of visualizing the entire country in communes. It is a process of building, it is being able to resume constituent popular power, which is in the constitution, which is the creator that permits the opening of spaces and the collective creation of a number of things, then, the people started to say, let's create the communes.[4]

Communities across the country have appropriated the concept and are creating communes. These are not decreed by the government, but are created in a collective process by communities, communal councils, and popular organisations. In the area of Barlovento, Afro-Venezuelan communes call themselves *cumbes*, referring to the maroon communes created during slavery times.

From the beginning, creating communes was simpler in rural and suburban areas. In rural areas the communes are usually made up of fewer communal councils (between five and 20) and the common needs are more obvious than in urban areas (where a commune usually consists of between 20 and 40 communal councils). One of the first communes appeared in the southeast of Barquisimeto, in a suburban space: the Socialist Commune Ataroa, which draws on a high density of popular organisation and capacity for self-government. It is made up of some 30 CCs and a large number of popular organisations.[5] Alberto Moreno of the Jorge Eliécer Nieves Communal City of the FNCSB says: 'We don't believe that any process of community organisation and formation requires a law'.

By the time a Law of Communes (LOC 2010) was approved in late 2010, there were already hundreds of communes in existence and under construction. Within the Venezuelan transformation process, it is not unusual that the practice exists first, and then the experience serves as the basis of law;

---

4 See I-AJ 2012.
5 In this case, the extensive pre-existing experience was also decisive for development. Available at: http://comunasocialistaataroa.blogspot.com.

however, as Luz Carrera indicates, once the law existed, the practice advanced further.[6]

In the context of forming communes and communal cities it is important to differentiate between (absolute) political-administrative space and (relational) socio-cultural-economic space.[7] The communes reflect the latter; they do not correspond to existing political-administrative spaces, and they can cross municipal or even state frontiers, given that the population defines and models its own socio-cultural-economic spaces. The mechanism for building socialist communes and communal cities is flexible, and they themselves define which tasks will be taken on. This flexibility makes it possible to find one's own way toward self-government, which can begin with what the population itself considers most important, necessary, or opportune. An important element in creating a commune is the integration of other organisations and councils to guarantee the participation and rights of minorities, vulnerable or special interest groups in the nascent institution.

The idea of non-representative self-organisation based in councils creates a 'new geometry of power'. The concept of *power* in human or social geography, as elaborated by Doreen Massey, has been 'put to positive political use ... [recognising] the existence and significance, within Venezuela, of highly unequal, and thus undemocratic, power-geometries'.[8]

In the process of creating their self-government structure, the communities prioritise the appropriateness of the structure for the communities. To this end, they adapt the form and content of the communes to their needs and abilities. The functioning of self-government is based in democracy and participation and is opposed to the logic of institutional representation. Adys Figuera León and Delbia Rosa Avilés of the commune under construction Los 7 Pilares Socialistas described the functioning of its self-government structures:

> We make decisions in the commune and the communal councils in assemblies, and we also have planning meetings every Saturday with a start time of 9 a.m. and no finish time. During the week we plan what we will do on Saturday, when we get together to continue making decisions.[9]

> All the communal councils go. There are spokespeople from all the communal councils. Anyone can attend the Saturday assemblies – not only

---

6 See I-LC 2007.
7 See Harvey 2006.
8 See Massey 2009.
9 See I-DRA 2012.

the spokespeople, but people from the community, everyone who wants to attend the meeting is welcome to get involved and participate. There is good, active participation. Everyone likes to participate. We explain, then everyone gives their opinion and suggestions about what we're doing so that anyone can participate. You know that there are people who are a little embarrassed [to speak up], but we have managed to get people who have never participated and who are coming in fresh, to get active, go to the assemblies, accompany the others.[10]

In a workshop in a barrio of Barinas, in the Venezuelan southwest, Carmelo González, of the Autonomous Municipal Institute of the Communes of Barinas, explained:

Water, electricity, telephone, the creation of an EPS, all these are problems for the communal assembly to deal with, because it's a power you have – not us as public officials, but you who have the possibility of having the power in your hands. It's something new, created by a kind of socialism unknown elsewhere. Because when the creation of the communes becomes fully realized across the nation, [in] Barinas, Venezuela, we can try to have here a communal government transitioning toward socialism, toward a new power-geometry. And all these conversations and forums serve to enable you to take these words to your communities ... because discussion generates participation. And this participation will permit you to generate government, and the government is not who has the power. The power is in your hands in the possibility that you can create this model of socialism ... We are trying to learn collectively what you know, because it is something more than what we can know: the knowledge of the *pueblo* that is being expressed right now.[11]

It should be noted that González's focus is not the norm among institutional employees. Often they try to impose certain mechanisms and it is rare that they offer service to the communities and popular organisations, as happened in the case of Barinas. But during the last two years, the communities' growing self-confidence, experience, and determination can be seen in an inversion of power relations between communities and officials.

---

10   See I-AFL 2012.
11   Azellini and Ressler 2010.

1.2 Communes and Constituted Power

In late August 2008, the 13 de Abril Mission was created with the task of promoting and supporting the creation of communes. Three main axes were envisioned: (1) the coordination and integration of all the missions; (2) the infrastructural transformation of the habitat through the construction of housing and especially of public spaces like plazas, parks, schools, and sports facilities; and (3) the development of a communal economy by means of productive projects, based on existing resources and knowledge. The economy that would thus emerge would be mostly communal property. In the remaining months of 2008, 400 million BsF were approved for 127 projects in 47 sectors of the country.[12] The 13 de Abril Mission and some responsibilities of the social ministry were transferred to the Ministry of Communes when it was formed in 2009. In May of that year, the Ministry was working with 55 communes under construction; one year later, it was 200.

After the communes became official governmental policy, there were several cases of negative institutional interference in the organic popular processes of creating self-government. Mayors, governors, representatives to the National Assembly, and the Ministry of Communes itself – all tried to divide territories by creating supposed communes from above; the communities, however, knew how to create their own paths to the commune, even if doing so provoked conflicts with constituted power. Adys Figuera León illustrated the case of her commune under construction Los 7 Pilares Socialistas in Anaco, Anzoátegui state.

> Everything began in 2010 when the mayoralty of Anaco grouped the communal councils by sectors and 17 communes appeared. Each director of the mayoralty was the representative of one of the communes. This created a great discontent within the municipality. However, people continued attending the meetings with the directors from the mayoralty. The only commune that would not accept this imposition at that moment was ours: Number 2, not even a name ... We would not accept any of the mayoralty's directors. We began to work in the communities, in the same communal councils that they based their communes on at that moment. We took polls, we continued meeting, everyone went on contributing in work groups. We did not stay just our seven communal councils of the supposed Commune 2, but we extended at the municipal level. The geo-

---

12 'Nace la Misión 13 de Abril para derrotar la miseria y avanzar en la creación de *Comunas socialistas*' (08 July 2007), available at: http://www.consejoscomunales.gob.ve/index.php?option=com_content&task=view&id=225&Itemid=73 (last retrieved March 11, 2009).

> graphical territory of a commune is defined after integrating everyone who wants to join it. On our way we encountered obstacles continuously, communities that pulled out then rejoined. But bit by bit, the work in different sectors throughout the municipality consolidated …
>
> As of right now, our commune-in-development is made up of 42 communal councils. Each community has about 1,000–1,500 people. We have more than 50,000 inhabitants …
>
> We've had confrontations with the mayoralties … they've called us anti-revolutionaries, troublemakers, etc. At first when we began our work we asked ourselves, could we be wrong about this? But no, we weren't wrong because we believe that this is the right way to go. Not the way of the institutions, because the institutions are more of the same, whoever they are, whether a mayor of the revolution or a mayor of whatever. That's always going to be a bureaucratic institution and that's what we need to break, because the system that has the institutions doesn't work. Some people say, 'The staff there is no good.' No. It's the system that doesn't work.[13]

The relationship between the Ministry of Communes and many communes under construction continued being conflictive for several years.[14] Certainly, the ministry provided important support with workshops and funding; according to many communities, however, it did not respect the autonomy of the communes, and tried to impose itself on issues from territorial limits to specific projects. Although popular initiatives to constitute communes increased sharply as of 2010, the Ministry did not register a single commune until 2012, when it was obligated to do so. In massive demonstrations of protest and pressure from the communes, they simply 'self-registered' with the institutions by delivering the necessary documents, which principally consisted of a foundational certificate and documents confirmed by commune members about assemblies and necessary participation. Josefina Cadet of the Artesanal Eco-Tourist Commune Cacique Terepaima in Lara state tells how the communes organised to achieve their objective:

> In a struggle that began in 2012, we achieved the registry of 42 communes in the state of Lara. Several communes began to get together, to study,

---

13 See I-AFL 2012.
14 It remained conflictive until President Nicolás Maduro named Reinaldo Iturriza Minister of Communes in April 2013.

to see everything we had in common, and we came to the conclusion that for all the struggles that deserved a conjoined force, like for example that the resources of the state were not arriving to the farmers, we had to strategize how to get the communes officially recognised. We designed all the guidelines and procedures ... We didn't get a single format wrong. The work the ministry had to do, we did ourselves, complete. Those assholes didn't even have a format for receiving the documents. We read that law from top to bottom so that there would not be a single error. We got some lawyers from the PSUV who helped us draft the foundational letter that would not have a single legal error. And just in case they tried to reject us, we had the articles of the law at hand ... so we set aside a date for a grand popular *fiesta*.

We never imposed a way of structuring a commune. We projected fifteen, and we got nine. And nine went with their paperwork, with the agreement we had reached, with the same foundational charts, with the same documents, everybody with their folders. The others accompanied us, there was participation by the popular movements, and we organised a march. The communes participated – from Torres, Urdaneta, Irribarren and Palavecino in Yaracuy and a commune from Portuguesa, with the understanding that we will implement the same procedure for the state of Portuguesa and the state of Yaracuy. We announced that we were going to register the communes on such-and-such a day, we called the press, called everyone and we went to register our communes, we put up some stuff in the street, we dug in, we called, Fundacomunal had to come out to receive our document and the nine communes went out to see that they did. That made noise at the national level. That was November 21, 2011. With that action we opened up the registration of the communes at the national level. We continued monitoring and oversight, and they had to implement and activate all the proceedings. Then we accompanied the Commune of Portuguesa, there was a reluctance to register them, we blocked the place ... and they had to receive us, it was televised, and now that commune is registered.[15]

Obviously, communes existed and functioned as such and were called communes without being registered by the ministry. Principally the issue was that the communities wanted a legal basis for consolidating their autonomous col-

---

15   See I-JC 2012.

lective practice in the face of constituted power. The situation changed drastically with the entry of Reinaldo Iturriza as Minister of Communes in April 2013. In September 2013, Adys Figuera León of Los 7 Pilares Socialistas in Anáco, who at that moment had been trying to register for almost two years, commented:

> The commune is still not registered. We took the steps required by the law and that Fundacomunal solicited. We have had a tough political struggle in the municipality, but nevertheless we keep on working and organising. We are legitimized by the *pueblo*, we meet on Saturdays as a commune and we are constructing popular power. The struggle has been hard, because the old does not want to die and the new has not been born. Above all there are problems with the bureaucratized municipal government over funding. However, long-needed radical changes are being made in the Ministry of Communes. We hope to be registered and we continue working and organising.[16]

The commune was registered two months later.

Communes that developed their own initiatives and had strong self-organisation, many of which were organised in the RNC, met with institutional resistance at all levels, as Atenea Jiménez describes:

> We have had no substantial support from any level of government. It's an exception for there to be a good relationship with the mayoralty or with the regional government, or with some ministry or with some institutional body of the formal state. We have tried to speak up, but all we've gotten has been obstacles and impediments. Even with the National Assembly! We had to mobilise to stop the law of communes, when the first law was to be passed, because our critical perspective was ignored. This strengthened us and allowed us to express our level of consciousness. Material reality tells us that it's impossible to go on waiting for a minister, for an institution. It has to come from the people with the force of popular power, from their organisation, and it's going to depend on the extent to which we organise.[17]

For that reason, many communities see the socio-productive development of the communes as a necessity. Adys Figuera León explains: 'We want to

---

16   See I-AFL 2013.
17   See I-AJ 2012.

develop the communes productively so they can truly be a communal self-government'.[18] A change can be observed in the kinds of projects undertaken by communal councils and communes. During their first years, most communal councils and communes concentrated on repairing homes, roads, and common spaces, and in creating access to basic services. Then, little by little, productive projects began increasing, especially in the communes.

The perspective of many commune members is one of autonomy, though that does not signify renouncing funding or other kinds of support from the state. Quite the contrary: state support is required, along with control of resources. However, the main focus is on constructing communes through one's own effort and following one's own decisions, as we have seen, frequently confronting state institutions in the process.

2 Companies of Communal Social Property and the Construction of a Communal Economy

The necessity of forming community-controlled companies as an alternative to traditional worker-controlled cooperatives emerged in 2006 from communities that had had problematic experiences with cooperatives founded as a result of institutional programmes and incentives. Soon different governmental institutions were also promoting models of communal cooperatives, and names for them proliferated: Communal Companies, Communal Socialist Companies, Companies of Communal Social Property, Companies of Communal Socialist Production, and other variations. In these new communal companies, the workers come from the communities, and they are the ones who, through communal councils and communes, decide which companies will be needed, what organisational form they will have, and who should work in them.

Traditional cooperatives did not permit advance planning of a production cycle (production, transformation and distribution, thereby fostering a cultural change in the models of consumption and consumerism) to create what Mészáros calls communal systems (communitary and cooperative) of production and consumption.[19] Their work did not necessarily correspond to the interests of the communities, but rather to the interests of the cooperatives' members. Often they did not contribute to the development of a communal economy and were integrated (or forced) into chains of capitalist production for private enterprise.

---

18   See I-AFL 2012.
19   See RNC 2011; Mészáros 1995, p. 792.

In order to collectively advance, many communities began developing types of communal cooperatives on their own. Recognising the problem, Sunacoop began to work more strictly with the communal councils to restructure the training for future cooperativists, especially training in 'socialist values', which created a tighter connection to the communities.[20] The goal is to avoid the errors of Yugoslavia, where companies under workers' control had to operate in social isolation and competed among themselves.[21]

As of 2008, the Communal Social Property Companies (EPSC) model emerged. Institutions and state companies began to assume and promote this communal company model, and at the end of 2009 there were 271 EPSC in the Venezuelan territory, while 1,084 other companies were operating under administration shared between communities and the state.[22] The number of companies has grown since then, now that the EPSC has been demonstrated to be the most successful and promising model for a collective local company so far. With the 'Organic Law of the Communal Economic System' of 14 December 2010, a legal framework was created for the EPSC, and today there are thousands of these companies at the communal level.

While all kinds of EPSC can be found in the communities today, the principal sectors where they are located correspond with the most strongly felt needs of the barrios and rural communities: the production of food and construction materials, and the provision of transport services. Textile and agricultural production companies, bakeries, and shoemakers are common. As Pablo Arteaga from the commune Eje de MACA in Petare, Caracas, says:

> In over 40 years of democracy here, it has been proven that private companies have failed; even more so in means of service supplies: water, waste, electricity, energy, gas and other types of services. The people from the communal councils, who know the functions of these services theoretically and practically, have taken up the task of finding a solution. That is what we are doing here; it isn't easy but it's not impossible either.[23]

Some state enterprises promote the creation of direct distribution networks under community control. In most cases, this is born of workers' self-initiative,

---

20   See I-JCB 2008.
21   Lebowitz 2006, pp. 85–118.
22   Gil Beróes, Aurelio 2010, 'Los Consejos Comunales deberán funcionar como bujías de la economía socialista', *rebelión.org* (04 January 2010), available at: http://www.rebelion.org/noticia.php?id=98094.
23   Azzellini and Ressler 2010.

as in the case of several of the state's cement companies. The nationalised company Cemento Andino was the first cement company to promote community distribution for construction materials and help build community cement block production sites. As Zoraida Benítez of the 'community and environment' department of Cemento Andino notes, in this way speculation was reduced and prices were lowered by eliminating intermediaries.[24] The example was taken up by other state cement companies. The paper products factory Invepal began promoting community stores for the direct sale of school supplies in 2013, and had set up 30 communal stores run by communal councils and communes by the end of the following year.

PDVSA began to build Gas Comunal, a distribution network under community administration to supply liquid gas for home use. The petroleum company offered support to the communities for constructing a distribution centre, supplied gas in tanks, and gave training courses for the administration of the communal companies. PDVSA also developed a new model of gas cylinder, lighter than the metal model distributed by the private companies. The high gas prices charged by private companies are principally due to the abuse of the oligopolistic structure of the market, since liquid gas, which is a secondary product of petroleum production, is very cheap in Venezuela. By distributing it through the Communal Social Property Companies, consumer prices were lowered to 20 percent of the market price. By controlling the distribution, the communities can also decide collectively to give out free cylinders and gas to residents in difficult economic situations (principally single mothers, in my observation).

In the communes, socially productive projects under collective communal management are generally considered of high importance. As Adys Figuera León of Los 7 Pilares Socialistas in Anáco explains:

> If we aren't the owners of our own system of production, how are we going to be a commune? It's more of the same. We go on being dependent on the same institutions and that's not the idea. The idea is to detach ourselves from Daddy … from Mother Mayor, Mother Regional Government, and to own the means of production ourselves. In the communities where we are, none of us is developing projects to put in sidewalks, because we know that we can put in sidewalks later. The focus has been on socially productive projects.[25]

---

24   See I-ZB 2010.
25   See I-AFL 2012.

Access to the necessary financial resources for the construction of the new communal economy is considered a right by the organised popular bases, even though their perspective is autonomist. The productive projects not only have the function of improving conditions and quality of life of the communities and creating the basis for autonomous financing of the communes; they are also seen from a perspective of transformation of the relations of production and the capitalist economic model.

> No commune can be autonomous if it does not produce wealth that can be distributed among its members. If we have a commune that relies on a third party – a governor, a mayor, whoever – that does not depend on itself to generate its goods and services and wealth, then it's not a commune. How do we imagine these new social economic relationships that the commune provides? And how are surpluses distributed? What are the social relationships within these companies of social, communal, whatever property? ... In the commune there has to be workers' control of the companies that are already there and of the ones that are going to be established. And not only the workers but the commune itself decides how it will function and how it will produce and what to do with the surplus. The management is socialist because the commune decides.[26]

Generally, the communities are supported by state institutions, especially by the Ministry of Popular Power for the Communes, with workshops to design their preferred form of organisation for the communitary company. In this way, the communities themselves decide about the structure and mission of their companies through a long process of training and debate.[27] At the Eje de MACA commune in Petare, Gran Caracas, made up of some 30 communal councils, in August and September 2010 I was able to attend excellent workshops given by an employee of the Ministry of Popular Power for the Communes on how to design, together with the community, management structures for some community companies.[28] The discussion concluded that the basic lines of the companies would be decided by the assemblies of the commune, along with the companies' workers, who would jointly decide how to manage the eventual earnings above costs in order to maintain the companies in operation.[29]

---

26 See I-AJ 2012.
27 See Azzellini and Ressler 2010.
28 Ibid.
29 See I-ER 2011; I-PA 2011.

In the words of Rafael Falcón, Ministry of Communes promoter for the construction of EPSC:

> The present models of leadership, organisation and administration are made for individual interests. They are those of the capitalist companies. There is someone who decides, who enriches himself and others that are being exploited and have no influence or control over the activities. We want to finish with that! How will we finish with it? The means for this we must build here, there is nothing like it existing yet. What should our model company look like?[30]

Beyond collective decision-making with respect to the structure and the goals of the EPSC, the issues that emerge as central for the communities are the non-hierarchisation of the activities (so that differentiation according to tasks and abilities does not result in hierarchisation in importance, status or pay); permanent training and mutual learning; rotation at work (according to abilities); and a social benefit for the community and beyond, if possible.

Eje de MACA's liquid gas distributor began operations in April 2011, and immediately began generating sufficient revenues to cover operating costs and the salaries of its four workers.[31] In June 2011, the commune received six all-terrain vehicles suitable for the transport of passengers and began to run its own communal transportation line in the barrios of the upper part of the commune, which previously had no regular transportation.[32]

With the consolidation of the communes, proposals for productive projects increased in number and size, besides becoming more sophisticated. Adys Figuera León and Delbia Rosa Avilés, of the Los 7 Pilares Socialistas commune, which is part of the National Network of Communards (RNC), described their commune's central productive project:

> We have already materialized some projects. We have the resources and are in the process of implementation. The most important is the tile factory, which came about as the result of the meeting of the National Network of Communards in Carora, Lara. We visited their production site for artisanal tiles and we brought the idea back to Anaco because we have the raw material, the clay. We were developing the project of a housing factory for prefabricated panels, and the ceilings of the houses have tiles ...

---

30 See Azzellini and Ressler 2010.
31 See I-LM 2011.
32 See I-PA 2011.

We got in contact with specialists who make tiles, and went to different communities taking courses. The first funding we sought was to build the ovens. We designed gas ovens ... the ovens are built in the communities. We're bringing the raw material and what we need is a space to situate the ovens and a space to store what we produce. For the project of a housing factory, we were working with the Ministry of Science and Technology, and we worked jointly with the people in our communities: engineers, lathe operators, masons, etc., to design the plans to produce the prefabricated panels.

The waste material after the firing of clay tiles becomes a light material that can be processed into panel production. The panels we're making right now we're making artisanally, not with the moulds we need, because the financing we need to make the moulds is very high, we're talking about almost 15 million bolívares [at that time about US $3.5 million].[33]

The project of a housing factory is made up of the tile factory, the mould factory, the production of the kit of metallic structures, and ... [n]ow we're making the six ovens, which will be distributed among groups of communal councils. With the ovens we will create 1,326 jobs.[34]

The idea is to keep expanding the making of ovens and take them into other communities. It's not only for the commune, our vision is the economic transformation of the whole municipality.

In this housing factory there is also communal carpentry and a factory for sinks. It will not be private companies building the houses, but something that will be managed by the community though the communal councils or the commune.[35]

More than a year later, Adys Figuera León said:

We have created the housing factory as the Communal Direct Social Property Company 'Revolutionary Forces for Everyone.' We're installing an extrusion plant for tiles. The project has three phases and carries with it a

---

33 See I-AFL 2012.
34 See I-DRA 2012.
35 See I-AFL 2013.

connected fishery project. We have a project for controlled-environment greenhouses, which is the Communal Direct Social Property Company 'Cultivating Dreams,' where we're going to produce vegetables, peppers, onions, paprika ... right now, because of the lack of financing we've only installed four greenhouses of the twelve that we've planned ... We created the Hugo Chávez school of productive socio-political training, where we support the organisation, planning, and economic development of other communities and municipalities in the state. The facilitators and the work team come from the 7 Pilares Socialistas commune.[36]

At the RNC meetings it was also agreed to have regular interchange of products between communes, as for example of fish from one commune on the coast of Vargas for goat meat from another in the mountains of Lara. There is also a network of barter, and a network of 13 existing communal currencies associated with the RNC that can be considered an indirect form of barter. Besides strengthening local economies, since its use is restricted to a specific area, local currency supposedly generates a non-capitalist logic, since its function is limited to the interchange of value and it is not usable for accumulation. The government has promoted and supported the use of local currencies, which were also included in the Organic Law of the Communal Economic System (LOSEC) of December 2010.[37]

3 Communal State: State or Non-State?

The form of the communal state is a 'work in progress' which occurs through the creation of councils in different environments and territories and through the coordination among them. So far, the territorial council system has three levels: communal councils, communes, and communal cities. In the 'Organic Law of Communes', the communal state is defined as a

> form of social political organisation, founded in the Social State of Law and Justice established in the Constitution of the Bolivarian Republic of

---

36 See I-AFL 2013.
37 The law establishes that the Central Bank of Venezuela (BCV) will regulate everything relative to communal currency. The BCV, however, can do nothing, since it is established in the Constitution as well that the BCV cannot regulate any other currency than the bolívar, the national currency. So, ironically, there is a law that legalises communal currencies, which in any case exist, but no mechanism for regulating them.

Venezuela, in which power is exercised directly by the *pueblo*, by means of communal self-governments with an economic model of social property and endogenous and sustainable development that permits the achievement of supreme social happiness of Venezuelans in the socialist society. The basic structural cell of the communal state is the Commune.[38]

This implies a profound transformation of constituted power and a re-signification of the state. By this definition, the communal state would be more a non-state than a state.

According to the debate about the communal state, the new structure would tend toward replacing the old institutionality. However, there have also been affirmations by high representatives of the government to the effect that old institutions and territorial divisions would remain intact, and the new structures would act as a parallel power.[39] The normative orientation given by Chávez is clear: 'a communal city, a city where there is no need for parish boards, where there is no need for mayoralties nor municipal councils, but Communal Power'.[40] Chávez has also been clear with respect to the necessity of destroying the state and that this task can only be brought to fruition by popular power:

> In order to advance toward socialism, we need a popular power capable of dismantling the networks of oppression, exploitation, and domination that linger in Venezuelan society, capable of configuring a new sociality out of daily life where fraternity and solidarity run in parallel with the permanent emergency of new ways of planning and producing the material life of our *pueblo*. This will pulverize completely the form of the bourgeois state that we inherited, which still reproduces itself through its terrible old practices, and will give continuity to the invention of new forms of political management.[41]

The proposal for the communal state and the '*comunera* democracy' go back to Kléber Ramírez,[42] who was one of the founders of the guerrilla group FLN; subsequently one of the commanders of the PRV-FALN guerrillas and leader of

---

38   See LOC 2010.
39   Lander 2007, p. 79.
40   Chávez 2007, p. 6.
41   Chávez 2012, p. 2.
42   See Ramírez Rojas 1991; 1998.

the PRV Ruptura,⁴³ he became one of the central ideologues of the clandestine civil-military organisation founded by Chávez MBR-200. The communal state strategy, which corresponds to a focus from below, has become the political project of the movements:

> The question is how to begin to visualize the way to construct socialism. We as a *pueblo* find ourselves trapped at some point: we gain power, we have a revolutionary government, we have a revolutionary president, the flag of the left is raised ... but there are still many gaps in the proposals for 21st century socialism. We began working on how we visualize or believe this construction of the new state must be in order to afterwards arrive at what the construction of a communal state is, understanding that it is a non-state. The term 'communal state' is a contradiction. Some say that what we are going to construct is a communal society.
>
> The consensus of the RNC is that the existing state must be dismantled and that there must emerge a new form of organisation and order that takes as a point of departure the commune as a form and system of government, the government of the working class – the *pueblo*, the exploited *pueblo* that has to give its labour-power to be able to live. We continue to deepen the question of organization regarding what this communal state or this communal city would be like in the country as a whole, and also in respect to our internal organization as network.⁴⁴

The communal state, or, more precisely, a form of social organisation by means of councils and based on self-determination, self-management, and direct democracy, is the point of convergence for the grassroots movements in Venezuela. The CCs, the communes, and the National Network of Communards; the Settlers' Movement (MPD) and the movement for workers' control; the collectives in the barrios – all converge on the perspective of the communal state. And in the popular bases there is also great support, corresponding as it does to the ideas of the bases that have fully appropriated the idea of the communal state:

> The straight line is the communal state directed by Popular Power, that is, by the *pueblo*. What we have now is not directed by the *pueblo*. We have

---

43 In 1978–9 Chávez was also part of the clandestine leadership of PRV Ruptura, as he mentioned on his TV programme *Aló Presidente* 288 on 27 July 2007.
44 See I-AJ 2012.

> constituted power. The idea is to really arrive at Popular Power, with the *pueblo* making its own decisions.[45]
>
> The communal state is like a new Venezuela, in which the people direct all its public policies. How do we get there? We don't have it yet, but if we raise consciousness in the communities that we really do have the power in our hands, that they can exercise that power, we will arrive at the communal state.[46]

As is characteristic of the Bolivarian process, the contradictions and confrontations criss-cross through the institutions. Luz Carrera, director of the Training Commission of the Political Secretary of the Greater Mayoralty of Caracas, who conducted training for the CCs, leaves no doubt about her intentions:

> We are trying to dissolve the Mayoralty, we want to dissolve it and we want to transfer the power to the people, but really do it, not just on paper, so the people have it, all of it. That they can be organised, that they have a space where they can sit down to think, to write and moreover to become the power of the commune, and our fundamental role is to support them so that this can happen.[47]

Nevertheless, the dissolution of representative structures has to be understood as a long process. According to the liberal critique, the CCs would greatly limit the abilities of the municipalities even as the limits of institutional responsibility become blurred.[48] That is precisely the potential.

The political organisation of twenty-first-century socialist societies, as a horizontal confederation of communities or as networks of social organisations, has been formulated in a similar manner – without reference to Venezuela – by Gustavo Esteva in Oaxaca (México).[49] Esteva underscores the 'communitary impetus' from which socialism originates before becoming 'collectivism, bureaucracy and auto-destruction'. 'The communities appear as an alternative because in them the union between politics and place is re-established, and the *pueblo* acquires a form in which it can exercise its power, without need-

---

45 See I-DRA 2012.
46 See I-AFL-2012.
47 See I-LC 2007.
48 Banko 2008, pp. 177–8.
49 See Fernández Colón 2006.

ing to yield to the state'.[50] Similarly, the concepts of Popular Power and the communal state open the possibility of understanding 'state' as consisting of certain limited, democratically legitimated functions, which can co-exist with the autonomy of the communities.[51]

These concepts create a nexus with indigenous and Afro-American experiences and with the socialist tradition of communes, which were hegemonic before the appearance of state socialism. Marx, after a profound analysis of the Paris Commune, concluded that 'the working class cannot simply lay hold of the ready-made state machinery and wield it for their own purpose. The political instrument of their enslavement cannot serve as the political instrument of their emancipation'.[52] But moving beyond the state does not signify the absence of structures of social, political, and economic organisation. Chávez gave weight to the idea of a 'socialist system' and a 'communal state', not the reverse.

Is the communal state a state? Or is it rather a non-state? Whatever the term, the basic question is whether the future structure of the communal state and the path to it will reproduce domination and with it exploitation, or whether it will move toward a structural overcoming of domination. Past 'socialist states' have not resolved the problem; on the contrary, since there also was no bourgeois civil society, the state ended up being everything and everywhere, and became a repressive bureaucratic apparatus of administration. The future socialist state and the communal state must submit to popular power, which, in turn, must replace the existing bourgeois civil society.[53] In this way, it is hoped, the division of spheres can be avoided, and with it also the centrality and totality of the state, as it was the case in 'actually existing socialism'.

---

50 See Esteva 2009.
51 Ibid.
52 Marx 1986, p. 533.
53 Chávez 2008, p. 67; AN-DGIDL 2007.

CHAPTER 8

Local and Worker Self-Management, Two-Track Construction, and Class Struggle: A Preliminary Assessment

After 16 years of the Venezuelan social transformation process, the strategies from above and from below continue to exist concurrently. Two-track construction occurs in this constant tension. While the state makes many processes possible, it also makes them hard to accomplish, restrains them, and derails them. However, although constituent power may be blocked, the new initiatives that are emerging undeniably display its traces. In Venezuela, despite all the contradictions, conflicts, and dangers inherent in two-track construction, the importance of having governmental power has been demonstrated – not to make the state the actor of change, but to open spaces and guarantee material conditions so that the new can emerge from below. The government is the hybrid resulting from the encounter between movements and the state, between anti-systemic and state-centred approaches. The result is not the sum of the parts, but is the process of creation of a new governability, a new system of security and regulation: 'the new governabilities are neither a unilateral construction nor a fixed place, but a collective construction in movement'.[1]

The persistence of strategies from above and from below in the process of profound transformation has demonstrated that it is possible to practice two-track construction, while strategies that either understood the state as the actor of change, or wanted to make revolutionary transformations without taking control of the state, have failed. Besides all contradictions, governmental discourse, and many governmental practices have strengthened social mobilisation, but in this process, the relationship between constituent and constituted power is not – nor can it, nor should it be – harmonious; it is a relationship of cooperation and conflict. Even though governmental policies promote participation and contribute to an enormous politicisation of the population, there is often conflict in the interface between above and below. That is not surprising, given the structural contradiction between constituent and constituted power, nor is it negative. Driven by its contradictions and conflicts, constitu-

---

1 Zibechi 2008, p. 275.

ent power is a concept of crisis.² For this reason, the new society cannot be created in planning offices, but only in real-world practice.

Tightly connected with this is the concept of popular power, i.e. the potential and capacity of subalterns to govern themselves by means of processes of organisation and training, and thereby overcome prevailing power relations. This refers to the mechanisms of popular democracy of the base, to self-administration and councils, with an orientation toward overcoming the split between political and social spheres. As of 2005, the construction of participatory and protagonistic democracy, and as of 2007 also of socialism, have been officially connected with the strengthening of popular power. It is important to emphasise that popular power is not understood as a transitional phenomenon on the way to the ultimate consolidation of a 'revolutionary state' and/or party, but rather as the practice of creating socialism: it is both path and goal. Since in Venezuela there was no taking down of old political structures, the process of constructing popular power is much slower than in other revolutionary processes. Constituent power, which is propelled forward by a continuous process of collective self-empowerment from below, repeatedly comes into conflict with constituted power. This process is not linear, but is marked by different conjunctures, highs and lows, advances and setbacks.

In this book, I have focused repeatedly on the ideas and imaginaries of the superstructure of the Bolivarian process. A critic would object that these are chimerical, that the social being produces consciousness. This is undoubtedly correct. However, being and consciousness are not opposing poles, nor can they be equated with the base-superstructure binary. Thought and ideas are part of the social being, since there exists a consciousness 'that not only perceives nor only invents ideologies, but produces in a practical way'.³ From the beginning of Bolivarian socialism in 1964 to the communes, it has been frequently demonstrated how ideas can materialise after developing in a subterranean way not easily visible to scholars. Miguel Ángel Pérez Pirela emphasises this: 'As in a musical work, the tempo of Venezuelan thought has to adapt to the melody and the tempo of events. The tempo of a *pueblo* ... does not wait for intellectuals to think what must be done'.⁴

In the absence of a uniform ideology or a clear road map, many politico-philosophical explanations and debates accompanying the transformation process have failed to take into account key ideas about superstructure that are

---

2 Negri 1994, pp. 387–8.
3 Agnoli 1999, p. 15.
4 Sanoja 2008, p. ix.

being discussed in the Bolivarian process. This has led to an ongoing lack of contextualisation, accompanied by banalisation and wrong evaluations. An understanding of the transformation process and how it unfolds is possible only if one takes into account existing ideas that have not yet materialised. Since late 2005, the transformation process has been located in the context of a twenty-first-century socialism that is – unavoidably – vaguely defined, but which includes several elements of critical and popular socialist currents. The present model of capitalist society has to be replaced by a socialist one. This socialist model has different priorities than the capitalist one regarding investment; its development model aims at breaking with dependence on world centres of power and with the exploitation and export of natural resources. It seeks to replace the rentier model of economic capitalism with a socialist productive model, based on the logic of work, and to transform not only the model of accumulation, but also the model of development.[5] For this process of transformation to socialism, an important reference has become the work of István Mészáros, who advocates building communal (communitary and cooperative) systems of production and consumption in which labour determines the interpersonal relations of exchange.[6]

The Venezuelan search for a socialist alternative is strongly rooted in the socialist line of communes and councils, mixed with elements of popular, indigenous, and Afro-Venezuelan experience, in this way redirecting socialism toward Marx's ideas about social organisation without domination. Both in self-organisation and in the creation of a different economy, the focus lies on the commune. The state is understood as an integral product of capitalism, and as such must be overcome by building a communal state that is a network of self-administered communes.

With reference to Mészáros, ex-Minister of Planning Jorge A. Giordani lists 'socialist emancipative objectives': 'labor with meaning for the associated producers themselves'; a 'self-determined distribution of the social wealth'; and 'the creation of material and political conditions necessary to assure the gradual debilitation of the state'.[7] But there is still a long way to go.

The most difficult task so far has been the transformation and democratisation of the economy. Though qualitative changes are undeniable, up till now they have, broadly speaking, moved within a capitalist framework, so that the rentier economy could not be overcome. Oriented as it is toward capitalist

---

5   Giordani 2009, p. 22.
6   Giordani 2009, p. 792.
7   Mézáros 2009, pp. 58–9.

forms of consumption and not toward real necessities, the present model of production and consumption is still driven by capitalist parameters, and is for this reason unsustainable. The new socio-cultural framework has not yet been created that would allow the necessary broad social debate to take place about what production happens, how it happens, on whose part and for whom, and how the surplus is distributed.

Nor should that be surprising. There are fewer alternative experiences in the economy to draw on than in the field of social organisation, and they are harder to apply, because of the totality of the capitalist model and economic globalisation. The restructuring and democratisation of the economy is opposed by concentrations of enormous private interests whose networks reach deep into state institutions and companies. The huge difficulties experienced in applying the government's policies to even the basic industries of the state can be explained by the fierce resistance to change embedded in these companies by networks of clients, and by local, regional, national, and international interests.

Until now, the Bolivarian process has managed to remain plural. One achievement of the last 16 years has been to broaden the organised social base of the transformation process without homogenising it, although there have been institutional attempts to do so. Many of the popular organisations engaged in the process are autonomous and are neither subordinated nor tied organically to government or party – although especially in the PSUV and in the government, the contemporary crisis has been accompanied by the increased marginalising and silencing of critical and dissident voices within the party. This tendency, though not unusual in party structures during times of crisis, is dangerous and promotes the fragmentation of the unity that has held for so long. The *chavista* base and even the base of the PSUV have in various ways opposed attempts at control and discipline – denying support, for example, to many PSUV candidates for National Assembly in the party primaries for the September 2010 election.

In the subsequent municipal elections of December 2013, when the PSUV did not select its candidates through primaries, at least eight mayoralties were won by declared *chavista* candidates running against the PSUV. Among them were grassroots activists, candidates from the PCV or other pro-government parties, and people who had been expelled by the PSUV. These were not necessarily 'better' candidates than the PSUV's, but their election does show that the grassroots are no longer disposed to accept candidates imposed by the party's high command and that a PSUV imposition can be defeated from a *chavista* position with a popular mobilisation.

1　The Bolivarian Process and Class Struggle

Class struggle is unfolding in the interior of the Bolivarian process itself. Class constitutes as *pueblo*, which is not homogenising, but rather is constituted and enriched by diversity. Because of construction from below and from above, class struggle exists with and against the state and its institution, with an ever more marked tendency to struggle against the limitations of institutional inefficiencies and insufficiencies that block or restrain advances in the construction of popular power. This results from the inherent logic of constituted power and its systemic limits, and from the asymmetry of power between constituent and constituted power (favourable to the latter), when according to the normative orientation of the transformation process it should be constituent power that defines and develops the new.

The Venezuelan social transformation process proposes supplanting the bourgeois, capitalist state by creating popular power, a vision that in Venezuela differs from historical concepts of popular power and is closely related to the concept of constituent power. In historical revolutionary processes, popular power was seen within the framework of the concept of 'dual power' as the construction of counterpower structures from below during the revolutionary process before the 'seizure of power'. With the seizure of state power by revolutionary forces and the consolidation, the dual power structure was considered to be no longer necessary, since the state, directed by revolutionary forces, then represented the central agent of a social transformation planned and directed by itself. To achieve this task, the state had to have absolute power and there could be no parallel power, since that would limit the state's capacity to plan and direct the revolutionary transformation. As a consequence, popular power that was constructed during the struggle against the old state and system ended up subject to state or ruling-party power, whether by co-optation or repression.

In Venezuela, however, the construction of popular power was proposed after the 'seizure' of state power (or rather government), and popular power is not seen as a transitory solution on the way to the consolidation of power by the supposed revolutionary state, but as a parallel process that would gradually supplant the power of the state and its institutions with self-administration structures constructed from below and based on popular experience. In the communal state, the structures of popular power would supplant civil society, which in liberal concepts assumes the role of counterweight to the state. The construction of popular power, which refers to forms of direct democracy and to council and self-administration structures, would move forward in the construction of a 'communal state', which would be the networking of advanced structures of a democracy that is non-representative but direct in all reaches of society.

Establishing whether the development of the Venezuelan transformation process can create and maintain the potential to advance in that direction (perhaps without arriving) is fundamental to analysing Bolivarianism, along with the main popular movements of the ongoing transformation process, as a motor of change. In this context, it is important to establish whether the popular movements are spaces from which the class struggle is developed, and whether they have political and organisational autonomy, these being the essential preconditions for them to assume their proposed role in creating popular power.

The larger organised movements in Venezuela – the Bolívar and Zamora Revolutionary Current (CRBZ), the Settlers' Movement (MDP), the National Network of Communards (RNC), and the communal councils and communes, among other self-governing structures – have relative organisational and political autonomy (although in the case of the communal councils and communes, this affirmation cannot be generalised, but rather refers to a potentiality in a contested space of struggle). Class is constituted by struggle in self-organised spaces in support of a project for a different society, antagonistic to bourgeois, capitalist society. In the ongoing construction process, the central reference point is not the state, but the autonomous processes that create popular power.

The struggle takes place within and outside, and with and against, the state. Class identifies itself as a *pueblo*, as a counterpart to the oligarchy and the bourgeoisie. References made by the popular movements, and the connections that are being created between movements, demonstrate a common orientation toward the communal state. But although initiatives have been undertaken in common, the common project has not yet been expressed in a common organic organisational form among the different movements.

2   Communal Councils, Communes, and Communal State

The communal councils have become the most successful mechanism for popular participation and self-organisation in only a few years. The combination of state action and the action of the organised *pueblo* has contributed to this situation: created from below, the CCs were taken up and promoted from above, although in many cases the decisive factor was the great determination of organised communities to enact decisions and priorities in the face of institutional attempts to derail the organic processes of the base.

The community corresponds to an existing self-localisation, and represents the strongest level of social identification. Especially in the barrios, there is a strong will to organise and take political responsibility for one's own interests, so – and this has been underestimated by most researchers – the CCs enjoy an enormous potential for organising the population and unfolding constituent power. Subaltern self-empowerment has set in motion a profound process of social transformation that leaves no social relation untouched. In the CCs of the barrios of Caracas, this construction process can be observed as a collective, consciously constituted, act of the communities as they adapt the CC to their necessities and capacities. Collectively discussing geographical reach, necessary committees, and working methods, they make collective decisions about problems, propose solutions, and put them into practice.

Organised, the communities can resolve their basic problems with respect to food, education, and medical services. However, too much concentration on material results can distract from the social processes, which are the essence of the CC. Involving as it does an active process of community creation and social construction, the CC process transforms communities. Success in organisation and mobilisation creates a growing confidence by the actors in their own abilities and qualities, and with it a growing political consciousness and sense of autonomy. Internal conflicts are usually resolved by communities themselves with the aid of institutions. In general, the CCs have a record of highly efficient management of resources and projects, much better than any state institution, though funds have sometimes been diverted.

The assertion that most CCs are not in a condition to make more than small changes to their environment is mistaken.[8] Participation contributes to the rupture of 'socio-territorial segregation',[9] in that the barrio population reconquers public space on three levels: collective space, life space, and institutional space. Participation allows the communities and their residents to develop perspectives and have a more self-determined life plan, instead of focusing on mere survival. Especially in the barrios, women participate much more than men. Participation and the process of empowerment lead to a positive change in gender roles and relations.

Many of the communities appropriate decision-making power at the highest levels; the communes and communal cities are constructed from below and, at least until 2013, almost without the support of the Ministry of Communes. The construction process is facilitated by the communes' and communal cities'

---

8 See García-Guadilla 2008; López Maya 2008.
9 Lacabana and Cariola 2005, p. 37.

ability to define for themselves what their priorities are, what tasks they need to assume, and what plans they need to make, according to the aspects defined as most important or relevant by the population itself. At first, many communes, and especially the most advanced ones, were in rural and suburban zones, and were often formed around issues of agriculture, transport, and energy supply. The communes and communal cities are innovative in that they do not have to correspond to existing politico-administrative territories, but can go beyond municipal or even state limits if that corresponds to the common socio-cultural-economic territory that the population itself wants to model from below.

The process of constructing communes in Venezuela is an expression of autonomy, and represents an important qualitative leap. While state support has been important, contributing to the dissemination and strengthening of self-organisation processes, at the same time it inhibits and limits these processes, requiring the communes to struggle for their autonomy. The relationship between movements and popular organisations, on the one hand, and the state and its institutions on the other, is marked by conflict and cooperation. But in Venezuela, unlike in other countries, the grassroots position is also the supposed normative orientation disseminated by the government, which places the communities in a position of ethical advantage when institutions do not respond.

Despite the community actors' vehement criticism of the institutions, they do not see institutions as their principal problem – not because they expect them to improve, but because they trust their own capacities to overcome institutional obstacles. To enact their will, communities have developed strategies that include the activation of personal contacts, pressure on institutions by means of protest letters and alliances with other CCs, actions within institutions, occupations, and highway blockades.

The construction of communal councils, communes, and companies under workers' control is seen by many of the actors involved as part of the path toward a 'communal state'. The council system, presently under construction, is in the long-term supposed to redefine and in many ways replace the institutional complex and with it the existing state, its tasks, and its division of labour. In this process, the logic, needs, and visions of constituent vs. constituted power come into contradiction. Although the rhetorical figure of the communal state has been used more and more since 2013, and even by the government itself, it is still an undefined concept. The debate over forms of broad self-organisation and the practical building of them is in full development. Even the term 'communal state', although launched by Chávez, has been questioned; many in the base consider it an oxymoron. After the death of President Chávez in March 2013, the popular mobilisation increased, there were several conflicts over workers' control at state companies, and the process of commune building became stronger. This was partly due to the designation by the new president, Nicolás Maduro, of communes as having a central role in the transformation process and adopting in his campaign the central slogan of the grassroots, 'Commune or nothing' (*Comuna o nada*), which is seen as a legacy of Chávez. In consequence, there were changes in the Ministry of Communes, and a massive campaign to register communes got under way. Communes and their projects have a daily media presence. Meetings are being convened all over the country – regional meetings of the RNC, local meetings of communes, and encounters co-promoted by the Ministry together with the base. The greater attention paid by the government to the communes contributes to their greater spread and consolidation, but it also carries the constant threat that the government will cut off the creative potential of constituent power by bureaucratising all the proceedings and turning the communes into an administrative body subordinated to the Executive or a simple depository for aid.

3 Property Models, the Administration of the Means of Production, and Class Struggle

Many different company models for achieving a democratisation of the relations of production have been created and put into practice in Venezuela. Some potentially aim at creating the conditions to overcome capitalist logic beyond the exploitation of a salaried labour force, the separation between manual and intellectual work, and the separation between companies and the social groups they affect with their activity. Other measures have led only to a democratisation of the relations of capitalist production and of the property and administration of the means of production, but without having the potential of establishing socialist relations of production, in which society controls the productive processes in order to meet social needs.

Extensive pro-cooperative measures led to the creation of more than 70,000 operating cooperatives. However, the lack of high-quality support systems, the failure to build alternative circuits of commercialisation and commodity chains, the inability to expand the mechanisms of financial control, and the internal deficiencies of the cooperatives themselves led the majority of them to follow the logic of capital and become integrated into the capitalist market. The ideal of cooperatives naturally producing for social needs from a sense of community solidarity built from collective management was not fulfilled. We should not be surprised that establishing socially committed production processes not directed by capitalist reasoning should be extremely difficult. Real-world experience shows that in a capitalist environment, cooperatives continue falling into capitalist practice, making problematic decisions over issues like the distribution of work and earnings.[10]

However, recognising the limitations of traditional cooperatives does not mean they cannot play an important role in creating socialism. Although cooperatives may not necessarily be socialist, they can nevertheless be a useful model for small, local companies in constructing a local solidarity economy.

The state's attempt to increase worker participation in the administrations of private companies by offering companies access to low-interest credit, subsidies, technological support, and labour training did not lead to a democratisation of their administrations at all. The models adopted by the entrepreneurs varied, but none of them gave the workers a real say in company decisions. In most cases, the workers were transformed into minority co-proprietors, which gave them more responsibility without giving them more rights. This model was finally rejected by the workers and abandoned by the state.

A similar fate befell the model of co-management between state and workers, applied in some expropriated companies, by means of cooperatives that transformed them into co-proprietors. In the end, the workers themselves rejected being co-proprietors, since that induced them to assume capitalist logic.

The government also tried to promote socially responsible behaviour on the part of the companies by means of the model of Social Production Companies (EPS). Whatever the form of property (cooperatives, state companies, mixed enterprises, and even private companies), it was hoped that by means of state incentives (credit under preferential conditions, technical assistance, purchase guarantees) EPS would prioritise use value over exchange value instead of being guided by capitalist logic. The model was only partly successful; in some state companies it forced a greater orientation toward the communities, both in production and commercialisation as well as in the purchase of inputs and support in the training of cooperatives. However, unified criteria were never stipulated, the majority of the EPS did not develop any real integration with the communities, and as of 2007 no more Social Production Companies were created.

After these experiences with different models of property, the normative orientation preferred by workers and by the state (at least in official declarations, even if the practice differs) is that of 'direct social property', in which the

---

10   See I-HV 2007.

companies are administered by the workers and the communities, organised in communal councils, communes or other forms of self-government.

As of 2008, the term EPS began to refer to Socialist (or Social) Property Companies. These EPS could be companies of 'indirect social property', which are administered by the state, or companies of 'direct social property'. The term Socialist Production Companies was also used for new factories and for other expropriated and nationalised companies, which are also supposed to be direct social property and which should be on the way to worker and community management. The institutions, however, did little or nothing to train workers, or to transfer administration gradually to their hands; when workers demanded more participation or workers' control, the institutions usually opposed them. As for the internal organisation of the EPS, many of them had old, vertical structures imposed on them. Moreover, practically all the EPS, whatever the model, reproduced capitalist logic of social division of labour, of alienation, and of the maximisation of revenue by means of control of the means of production.

After the application of different collective business models, the most successful initiative turned out to be the modality of the Communal Social Property Companies (EPSC, handled at first under different names such as Communal Cooperatives or Communal Companies). These companies of local production and community service were born from below and are promoted in the communities by state institutions. The EPSC are the collective property of the community by means of the communal councils or communes, which are the local self-government mechanisms that decide what the companies' organisation model will be, who will work there, and what use the eventual revenues will be put to. The EPSC could thus achieve a better balance of costs, efficiency, and social aspects than state companies or private enterprise.

Class struggle also emerges in the application of these different models of ownership and collective administration. In several cases, the workers entered into conflict with institutions, rejecting models that pulled them toward capitalist logic, and in other cases they developed important struggles in the direction of greater participation in the management of the company and greater orientation toward satisfying popular necessities. The experiences these models furnished of the state's inefficiency or incapacity (whether structural or punctual) to guarantee efficient production or launch a change in the social relations of production have contributed decisively to strengthening the movement for workers' control. In short, class struggle has been fomented where it previously did not exist.

4   Nationalisation, Workers' Control, and the Socialist Workers' Councils

Workers' control, which in the first years of the government was supported only by small groups of workers, was launched as an orientation by Chávez in 2006/7 when he issued a call to form Socialist Workers' Councils (CST), though governmental institutions only began to propagate these councils two to three years later. In most cases, the institutions tried to impede the constitution of CST, while state companies tried to co-opt and direct the structuring of CST as representative bodies and institutions for handling complaints about work conditions or for troubleshooting, without permitting the participation of workers in the company administration or in the productive process.

Although the movement for workers' control has grown notably since 2008/9, its progress has been slow, since it often began as official state policy and did not mainly emerge from struggles. At the same time, the state is also the greatest inhibitor of workers' control, and another important factor influences its dynamic as well: in Venezuela, the productive structures were not taken down. There were no conditions under which workers were 'obligated' to assume the production and administration of 'their' companies; in fact, many of the companies taken by Venezuelan workers were those shut down by their owners after the business strike. In short, though the struggle for workers' control is directly and indirectly fomented by the state, the state also presents an obstacle to its materialisation.

It is necessary to note that no common position exists in the government with respect to workers' control. There are different approaches in parallel. One important tendency, which recalls the failed state socialism of the twentieth century, sees workers' control as the control mechanism of the bureaucratic administrative structures by the workers to guarantee the materialisation of state policies, which supposedly represent a common interest. Other sectors, however, support workers' control; meanwhile, the government and its institutions are riddled with contradictions and class struggle. The nationalisation of companies in the industrial productive sector did not begin until 2005, while systematic nationalisations, principally in the chain of production, preparation, and commercialisation of foodstuffs, began only in 2007. Most of these nationalisations, however, were under the modality of state ownership, which did not alter the social relations of production, much less overcome or abolish capitalist exploitation.

The great majority of social property companies in Venezuela are under the supervision of state institutions, not the direct administration of workers and/or communities. As a consequence, workers' struggles have arisen in most of the nationalised companies, in other state companies, and also in state institutions. The conflicts revolve around a greater participation of the labour force in the organisation of work and the administration of companies. Some struggles originate from a perspective of workers' control, while others develop that perspective during the conflict.

The CST, which the institutions in many cases use to institutionalise, limit, and control workers' struggles, has paradoxically become one more vehicle in the struggle for workers' control as the movement grows and takes qualitative and quantitative leaps. In May 2011, a national platform was at last constituted of workers from workers' councils, CST, occupied companies, and unions.

Until his death, President Chávez was the most important governmental ally in the struggle for workers' control. Besides his personal initiatives in the case of some factories (Inveval and Sanitarios Maracay, among others) and his calls for the creation of CST, he launched the Socialist Guayana Plan, which seeks to group the basic CVG industries of aluminium, iron, and steel into three big companies under workers' control, strengthening them and putting them at the service of popular interests. In May 2010, he appointed worker-presidents to the basic companies, with the now-famous words 'I bet on the workers'.

The example of Inveval demonstrates how class struggle can be developed from the contradictions experienced in a struggle. Beginning as a struggle to collect back salaries and compensation after the closure in 2002, the Inveval struggle operated at first within the framework of the prevailing system. But then it became a struggle for workers' control, the overcoming of capitalist relations in production, total social transformation, and nationalisation. After achieving nationalisation, the incompatibility of ideas developed by the workers with the model of state co-management and co-ownership led them to renounce ownership, form a council, and take over the enterprise as social property under workers' control. Notwithstanding the institutional obstacles, Inveval continues under workers' control.

The case of the aluminium plant Alcasa offers the best illustration of class struggle that pervades the Bolivarian process. Of all the CVG companies, Alcasa had made the most progress toward workers' control, and its workers had been active in propagating it, thereby provoking the most profound conflict within the government since 1999. Several governmental and CVG bodies boycotted and sabotaged all the elements of the plan related to worker participation.

Although the future of Alcasa and the other CVG industries is unknown, it can be seen that it formed a strong, determined movement in favour of workers' control. In the words of Ligia Duerto, of the department for strategic planning at Alcasa, uttered during worker-president Elio Sayago's tenure: 'we have the highest level of internal conflict that we have ever had, however, we also have the highest level of class struggle'.[11] The conflict is focused on a central contradiction, as per the testimony of the worker Osvaldo León:

> It's a hard battle between those of us who firmly believe in getting rid of the hierarchy, the division of labour, [and] market relations, and [believe] in converting this corporation into property of the *pueblo*, [versus] those who want to keep the social relations of capital and power intact.[12]

My research suggests that collective forms of administration and ownership of the means of production, and the struggles for them, must be considered as class struggle, at the same time as they open a perspective for overcoming capitalist relations of exploitation and production. Struggles for workers' control create forms and spaces of a developing self-management that aspire to overcome the division of labour and change the social relations of production.

The workers' subjectivities deepen the process of change. Clashes with reality; the permanent crisis in which constituent power moves; the barriers it encounters and its resistance to being subordinated – all these aspects of struggle spark new subjectivities. While this is not an automatic process, there is a dialectic between consciousness and real change. Direct, collective, democratic participation creates these new subjectivities, foments class struggle, and is basic to the construction of a new society that is not guided by capitalist logic.

However, the asymmetry of power between the state above and the new entity being built from below can easily lead to the from-below being politically influenced by the state and its 'representatives', rather than the reverse. There also exists the risk that the new from-below entity will reproduce the logic and forms of constituted power, such as hierarchical structures, representative mechanisms, division into leaders vs. led, and bureaucratisation. In that case, initiatives from below will not seed a coming society but will instead be adjuncts of constituted power. So, for example, administrative structures have not changed much in most of the CVG companies, and the supposed workerpresidents were almost all relieved of their posts over time. The struggles for workers' control continue.

The greatest danger is that, as has historically happened, the newly constituted power, supposedly revolutionary, will be seen as the culmination of dual power. The Venezuelan government and, especially, Chávez have not seen the state as *the* revolutionary power, as in other revolutionary processes; on

11   SeeI-LD 2011.
12   See *Prensa Marea Socialista* 2011.

the contrary, they have promoted the construction of popular power and prolonged the parallel existence of 'powers'. Despite this normative orientation, from-above logic predominates in the institutions, in which the state is seen as the actor for change and popular power is an institutionally integrated appendage. The strategy from below, on the contrary, understands the progressive government in power as a preferential framework for the construction of popular power in search of overcoming the state and its form.

New practices of organisation and popular participation have driven a qualitative change of traditional political culture and have contributed an immense variety of experiences of social self-determination. The processes of self-organisation supported institutionally – especially the CCs and the communes – have developed their own dynamic which, in spite of all the inefficiencies and weaknesses, is moving ahead of the institutions. In many barrios and rural communities, the will to organise and play a protagonistic role in the construction of the living environment is enormous. Residents, especially women, make massive use of the possibilities of training in missions, universities, courses, and workshops, and this in turn contributes to the personal growth of individuals and the collective development of the communities, which gain in competence, organisation, collectivity, and autonomy.

For 16 years, the strategies from above and from below have coexisted in constant tension within the transformation process, but the perpetuation of this process would only be imaginable if the relationship between constituted and constituent power were to change in favour of constituent power over constituted power. Unless constituted power puts a brake on constituent power, the latter's growing organisation from below and its developing popular power will crash the gates.

With the deepening of the process it becomes continually harder to implement, within the institutions of a bourgeois, bureaucratic state, a politics for which they are not structurally suited. Guidelines, announced government policies, and even enacted laws are not put into practice or are done so in a very incomplete way. Corruption and clientism continue to be disseminated and undermine public trust. To this is added the resistance of the institutions themselves, which fear becoming superfluous. The broadening of the mechanisms of participation multiplies the points of conflict between constituent and constituted power, and within the state itself, which is ever more permeated with class struggle. There is the contradiction that in order to impose sovereignty and satisfy social rights, the Venezuelan state must be strengthened, since this clashes with the normative orientation to overcome it. Moreover, this strengthening – without the adequate construction of mechanisms of control from below, and with many institutions impeding the application of the existing mechanisms for social auditing and control of institutions by popular power – has increased corrupt, corporative, and bureaucratic processes instead of overcoming them.

The expansion of institutional measures leads to greater bureaucratisation, which in turn impedes the declared process of opening and transformation, and tends toward an institutional administration of social processes. The practice of the state is not limited to supporting and promoting initiatives from below, but also demonstrates at the same time a tendency to discipline and co-opt popular organisations. In this context, the public funding of popular organisations and public initiatives has an ambivalent role. It is absolutely necessary to redistribute social resources and promote self-organisation, given that the positive effects are tangible; however, it also reinforces the danger of unequal relations of dependence and clientism. With the asymmetrical power relation between constituent and constituted power, the new institutionality from below is continually exposed to the danger of reproducing the logic of constituted power instead of overcoming it.

A discrepancy between discourse and reality does not have to be a negative – if, without losing contact with reality, the process remains open and still follows the discourse, which is bound to be ahead of reality. Without discourse, there cannot be debate, development and perspective. There are many policies that demonstrate this opening. The CCs, the communes, and the communal cities have the full potential to be an ongoing constituent process and to be institutions of constituent power. Their future development, however, is uncertain. The process of popular participation can drag on longer, stagnate, or retrogress for various reasons. It is 'a road that has not ceased to be, during a good part of its trajectory, a rehearsal'.[13]

For more than 16 years, Venezuela has been the largest social laboratory in the world, offering glimpses of a variety of possibilities and approaches to building a society 'with the categorical imperative to overthrow all relations in which man is a debased, enslaved, forsaken, despicable being'.[14] It remains to be seen whether a consciousness of the need for change will lead to a new order or only a change of elites. The decisive factors in this process will be not only the tension between below and above, as studied here, and the class struggle, but also the threats to the Venezuelan process from outside the country and from the internal opposition.

---

13   Chávez 2007, p. 4.
14   Marx 1975b, p. 182.

5 The Relation of Constituent and Constituted Power to Class Struggle

Sixteen years into a two-track social transformation process in Venezuela, constituent power continues to be its most important motor. At the same time, the contradictions between constituent and constituted power have been the greatest obstacle to the creation of a new model of society from below. Overcoming these structural conditions depends not on the good will or declared intentions of the state and its officials, nor on the integrity of individuals – although a greater ethical and political commitment would surely help. Institutions inherently tend toward controlling social processes, pigeonholing them and imposing homogenous proceedings because of the institutional need to classify in order to plan. This contradicts constituent power's creative character and inhibits organic social processes. In the framework of the construction of the communal state, many of the existing institutions have to work toward overcoming their own existence or transforming their roles completely, ceding space and functions to the organised *pueblo*. Institutions, however, inherently tend toward consolidation and reproduction, and the tendency becomes more pronounced in times of profound social transformation, when every institution is called into question.

A central contradiction is found within the competing logics of constituent vs. constituted power, or, in other words, in the opposition of the logic of class struggle for the construction of socialism vs. institutional logic. Progress in social relations does not fit into a chart, which is usually the basic institutional instrument for measuring and presenting achievements. Material results that follow capitalist logic, however, are measurable and quantifiable, and can fit into any chart, so that it can supposedly be demonstrated that 'it worked'. Whether working with companies or communities, institutional employees can thus present tangible results to the institution, which in turn can demonstrate that it is not useless.

Moreover, if the jobs of institutional employees as well as the existence of the institution are assured, if the structures receiving support (whether companies or local self-management) continue depending on institutional aid, then the possible independence of the supported structures contradicts the interests of the supporting entity. Therefore the institutions declare their support for social processes as necessary to justify their own existence.

Contradictions and conflicts regarding control of the means of production are even more marked because of the economic interests in play. The democratic control of the means of production by workers and organised communities is the strongest mechanism against corruption in the companies, and is the only guarantee of production oriented toward satisfying popular needs, besides signifying the automatic end of privileges.

Class struggle goes on within the institutions as well. In the institutions charged with supporting nationalised companies or new factories built by the state, it is common for part of the institution to train and prepare the workers in socialist values, co-management, workers' control and the founding of socialist workers' councils, while the parts of the institution tasked with implementing worker participation are almost always blocking or impeding it.

Workers' control and the issue of changing social relations of production put the government itself to the test, revealing who is part of the democratic construction of a new model together with workers and organised communities, and who basically wants to follow the old model based on capitalism and its state. The conflict between the two is an expression of class struggle. The emancipatory potential of the Bolivarian process resides in this tension.

Some sectors of the government and of the process who are adverse to workers' control attempt by all means to impede its materialisation, and when they cannot impede it, they try to make it fail. Nevertheless, although they have managed to considerably restrain the bringing of companies under workers' control, they have not been able to stop the struggle in favour of workers' control. But they have also contributed – both through their initiatives and through conflict – to strengthening the movement for workers' control and to creating and fomenting new class struggle.

After sixteen years of governmental power, the strategies from above and from below have both remained as part of the same social transformation process. Although the tension has been constant, there has been significant progress. The growing conflict over workers' control makes evident the basic contradiction that prevents this parallel existence of constituting and constituted power from being prolonged forever. The crisis that began in 2014, which hit Venezuela very hard because of the low price for oil, its main export product, has intensified conflicts and contradictions between the bases and the institutions. However, the power relations at the heart of Bolivarianism do not suggest that either of these strategies will impose itself on the other any time soon.

Interviews

Macro Actors

Antillano, Andrés – Sociologist and CTU activist.
   (I-AA 2008) 20/04/2008.
   (I-AA 2009) 25/01/2009.
Lander, Edgardo – Professor of Sociology, UCV.
   (I-EL 2007) 03/01/2007.
Denis, Roland – Philosopher, ex-Vice Minister of Planning and Development (2002), and grassroots activist,
   (I-RD 2006) 24/08/2006.
Sanoja Obediente, Mario – Professor of anthropology, UCV.
   (I-MSO 2008) 12/03/2008.

Macro Actors (Labour and Production)

Baute, Juan Carlos – Director of Sunacoop.
   (I-JCB 2008) 23/12/2008.
Colmenares, Elio – Vice Minister of Labour
   (I-EC 2010) 17/01/2010.
De Sousa, Félix – Researcher of the department of co-management and workers' control, Miranda International Centre (CIM),
   (I-FDS 2006) 21/08/2006.
Denis, Roland – Philosopher, ex-Vice Minister of Planning and Development (2002) and grassroots activist.
   (I-RD 2007) 07/01/2007.
Enciso, Rafael – Researcher, economist of the Ministry of Science and Technology. (I-RE 2010) 02/08/2010.
   (I-RE 2011) 26/07/2011.
Iturriza, Reinaldo – Sociologist, Director of Information and Public Relations, Ministry of Labour and Social Security (MINTRAB); ex-Director of the department of research and communication, Minep.
   (I-RI 2006) 14/12/2006.
Lanz, Carlos – Sociologist, ideologist of Vuelvan Caras, ex-president of the Alcasa aluminium smelter, collaborator of the Ministry of Science and Technology.
   (I-CL 2007) 4/10/2007.
Oropeza, José Vicente – Researcher of the department of co-management and worker's control, Miranda International Centre (CIM).

(I-JVO 2006) 21/08/2006.
Primo, Luis – Unionist of the UNT, Corriente Marxista Revolucionaria, and Freteco.
(I-LP 2006) 18/11/2006.
(I-LP 2011) 16/09/2011.
Rivero, Carlos L. – Vice Minister of Minep.
(I-CLR 2006) 23/08/2006.
Vega, Samuel – Director of the department of worker training, Secretariat for Endogenous Development, Political Secretary of the Greater Mayoralty of Caracas.
(I-SV 2007) 23/01/2007.
Vivas, Héctor – Socio-productive and socio-political director of the Endogenous Nucleus La Unión, Puerto Ordaz (municipality of Caroní), Ministry of Science and Technology official responsible for technological transfer to the CC.
(I-HV 2007) 22/01/2007.

Communal Enterprises, Commune 'Eje de MACA', Petare, Gran Caracas, Miranda

Arteaga, Pablo – Approx. 50 years, unemployed.
(I-PA 2011) 19/08/2011.
Martini, Lorenzo – Approx. 50 years, lawyer.
(I-LM 2011) 19/08/2011.
Patiño, Yusmeli – Approx. 40 years, homemaker.
(I-YP 2011) 19/08/2011.
Rivero, Elodia – Approx. 60 years, retired teacher.
(I-ER 2011) 19/08/2011.

Cemento Andino, Monay, Trujillo

Benítez, Zoraida – Worker, Community and Environment department.
(I-ZB 2010) 10/08/2010.

Inveval, Valve Factory, Carrizal, Miranda

Aguilar, Rolando – Worker.
(I-RA 2006) 23/11/2006.
(I-RA 2008) 09/04/2008.
González, Julio – Worker.
(I-JG 2008) 09/04/2008.

Montilla, Ramón – Worker.
  (I-RM 2008) 09/04/2008.
Morales, Luisa – Worker.
  (I-LM 2006) 23/11/2006.
Quintero, José – Worker.
  (I-JQ 2006) 23/11/2006.
Rodríguez, Nelson – Worker.
  (I-NR 2007) 07/10/2007.
  (I-NR 2011) 26/07/2011.
Ubencio, Valero – Worker.
  (I-VU 2006) 23/11/2006.

Alcasa, Aluminium Smelter, Ciudad Guayana, Bolívar

Agüero, Carlos – Worker and member of the Negro Primero Training Centre.
  (I-CA 2008) 22/04/2008.
Bolívar, Roque – Student and member of the Negro Primero Training Centre.
  (I-RB 2008) 22/04/2008.
Duerto, Ligia – Worker, member of the strategic planning team and of the Council of Coordination of Processes (CCP), previously the department of cooperatives.
  (I-LD 2011) 15/09/2011.
Erejón, Eduardo – Name changed for reasons of confidentiality, Alcasa worker.
  (I-EE 2015) 14/01/2015.
León, Osvaldo – Worker and member of the Negro Primero Training Centre.
  (I-OL 2008) 21/04/2008.
Rivero, Alcides – Worker and member of the Negro Primero Training Centre.
  (I-AR 2007) 26/10/2007.
  (I-AR 2008) 21/04/2008.
  (I-AR 2011) 15/09/2011.
Sayago, Elio – Worker-President of Alcasa.
  (I-ES 2011) 14/09/2011.
Sucre, Denis – Worker and member of the Negro Primero Training Centre.
  (I-DS 2008) 21/04/2008.

Macro Actors (Communal Councils)

Daza, Eduardo – Community participation promoter. Technical Department, Political Secretary of the Greater Mayoralty of Caracas, ANROS.
  (I-ED 2007) 24/01/2007.

Delgado, Alexis – Minpades, CC work area.
   (I-AD 2006) 14/08/2006.
Carrera, Luz – Director of the commission of political training of the Political Secretary of the Greater Mayoralty of Caracas.
   (I-LC 2007) 25/09/2007.
Harnecker, Marta – Sociologist, collaborated in the CC law.
   (I-MH 2007) 24/01/2007.
Ulloa, Mayerling – Director of FONDEMI Caracas.
   (I-MU 2006) 17/11/2006.
Vega, Samuel – Director of the department of worker training, Secretariat for Endogenous Development, Political Secretary of the Greater Mayoralty of Caracas.
   (I-SV 2007) 23/01/2007.
Visconti Osorio, Francisco – Ex-general, leader of the November 1992 military uprising, 1992, National Institute for Agricultural Research (INIA) and FNCSB consultant.
   (I-FV 2008) 15/03/2008.
Vivas, Héctor – Socio-productive and socio-political director of the Endogenous Nucleus La Unión, Puerto Ordaz (municipality of Caroní), Ministry of Science and Technology official responsible for technological transfer to the CC.
   (I-HV 2007) 22/01/2007.

Communal Council Activists

Communal Council 'Emiliano Hernández', Magallanes de Catia, Caracas

Ávila, Jacqueline – 1964, Finances, single mother of two, social promoter.
   (I-JA 2006) 22/12/2006.
   (I-JA 2008a) 20/04/2008.
   (I-JA 2008b) 16/12/2008.
Espinoza, Libel – 1973, Seniors' club, single mother of four, hairdresser.
   (I-LE 2007) 04/01/2007.
Melean, Hortencia – 1968, Social auditing, married with three children, no profession, unemployed.
   (I-HM 2007) 04/01/2007.
Moya, Wilson – 1965, Finances, married with three children, mechanic with a small workshop.
   (I-WM 2007) 09/01/2007.
Rivas, Petra – 1970, Social auditing, lives with partner and three children, hairdresser.
   (I-PR 2007) 04/01/2007.
Rodríguez, Arquímedes – 1957, Finances, married with two children, insurance agent.
   (I-AR 2007) 09/01/2007.

Communal Council 'Unidos por el Chapulín', Nuestra Sra. del Rosario Parish, Baruta

Flores, Evangelina – 1970, Finances, married with three children, secretary, social promoter.

(I-EF 2008) 03/04/2008.

Hurtado, Rosa – 1949, Social auditing, married with seven children, two still living with her, seamstress without her own machine.

(I-RH 2008) 03/04/2008.

Hurtado, Marta – 1979, Social auditing, single mother of one, kitchen helper.

(I-MHU 2008) 03/04/2008.

Group Discussion with CC Spokespeople of Six Parishes in the Municipality of Libertador

Esis, Thamara – CC in Santa Rosalía parish.

(I-TE 2008) 31/03/2008.

Communes

Avilés, Delbia Rosa – 45 years, constructor of popular power, spokesperson, La Floresta Communal Council, Los 7 Pilares Socialistas Commune, Anaco, Anzoátegui state.

(I-DRA 2012) 11/02/2012.

Cadet, Josefina – 49 years, computer engineer, taxi driver, Agua Viva Communal Council, Ecoturística Artesanal Cacique Terepaima Commune, Agua Viva, municipality of Palavecino, Lara state.

(I-JC 2012) 11/02/2012.

Figuera León, Adys – 33 years, facilitator of popular power, Las Charras Communal Council, Los 7 Pilares Socialistas, Commune, Anaco, Anzoátegui state.

(I-AFL 2012) 11/02/2012.

(I-AFL 2013) 17/09/2013.

Jiménez, Atenea – 38 years, National Network of Communards of Venezuela, Belomonte, Caracas.

(I-AJ 2012) 14/02/2012.

Rodríguez, Merzolena – 44 years, spokesperson of the Pueblo Nuevo Norte Communal Council, Los 7 Pilares Socialistas Commune, Anaco, Anzoátegui state.

(I-MR 2012) 11/02/2012.

References

Acha, Omar 2007, 'Poder popular y socialismo desde abajo', in *Reflexiones sobre Poder Popular*, edited by Miguel Mazzeo and Stratta Fernando, Buenos Aires: Editorial El Colectivo, 17–36.

Agnoli, Johannes 1999, 'Subversive Theorie. Die Sache selbst und ihre Geschichte', *Gesammelte Werke*, Volume 3, Freiburg: Cairá.

Aguirre Morales, Edwin 2006, 'Las Cooperativas de Asistencia Integral – CAI – o cómo perjudicar la Misión Vuelvan Caras I', *Aporrea.org* (11 January 2006), available at: http://www.aporrea.org/actualidad/a18844.html.

Althusser, Louis 1971, 'Ideology and Ideological State Apparatuses (Notes towards an investigation)', in *Lenin and Philosophy and other Essays*, edited by Louis Althusser, London: New Left Books, 121–76.

Anderson, Benedict 1988, *Die Erfindung der Nation. Zur Karriere eines folgenreichen Konzepts*, Frankfurt: Campus.

AN-DGIDL (Asamblea Nacional Dirección General de Investigación y Desarrollo Legislativo) 2007, *Ejes fundamentales del proyecto de reforma constitucional. Consolidación del Nuevo Estado*, Caracas: AN-DGIDL.

Antillano, Andrés 2005, 'La lucha por el reconocimiento y la inclusión en los barrios populares: la experiencia de los comités de Tierras Urbanas', *Revista Venezolana de Economía y Ciencias Sociales*, 11, 3: 205–18.

―――― 2006a, 'Comités de Tierra Urbana', in *Lo mío, lo tuyo, lo nuestro … Visiones sobre la propiedad*, edited by María Ramírez Ribes, Caracas: Informe del Capítulo Venezolano del Club de Roma, 199–212.

―――― 2006b, 'Vivimos en una tensión permanente entre el gobierno y los sectores de base', *Rebelión* (20 October 2006), Interview with Andrés Antillano, available at: http://www.rebelion.org/noticia.php?id=39653.

APPP (Asamblea de Promotores del Poder Popular) 2005, 'Síntesis del 1er Encuentro Ideológico de Promotores del Poder Popular', *Aporrea.org* (20 August 2005), available at: http://www.aporrea.org/actualidad/a16140.html.

Aporrea tvi 2014, 'Propuestas para salir de la crisis de las empresa básicas de Guayana presentó la compañera Nieves de Alcasa', *Aporrea.org* (20 December 2014), available at: http://www.aporrea.org/actualidad/n262541.html.

Aronowitz, Stanley 1991, *False Promises*, New York: McGraw Hill.

Azzellini, Dario 2007a, *Venezuela bolivariana. Revolution des 21. Jahrhunderts?*, Cologne: Neuer ISP Verlag.

―――― 2007b, 'Von den Mühen der Ebene: Solidarische Ökonomie, kollektive Eigentumsformen, Enteignungen und Arbeitermit- und Selbstverwaltung', in *Revolution als Prozess: Selbstorganisierung und Partizipation in Venezuela*, edited by Andrej Holm, Hamburg: VSA-Verlag, 38–57.

―――― 2008, 'Basisbewegung oder Staat? Der Transformationsprozess in Venezuela stößt an Grenzen', *WeltTrends. Zeitschrift für internationale Politik*, 16, 61: 55–63.

―――― 2009a, 'Venezuela, MAS and Causa Radical', in *International Encyclopedia of Revolution and Protest. 1500 to the Present*, Volume 7, edited by Immanuel Ness, Oxford: Wiley-Blackwell, 3445–8.

―――― 2009b, 'Venezuela, military uprisings, 1960–1962', in *International Encyclopedia of Revolution and Protest. 1500 to the Present*, Volume 7, edited by Immanuel Ness, Oxford: Wiley-Blackwell, 3450–1.

―――― 2009c, 'Venezuela, guerrilla movements, 1960s to 1980s', in *International Encyclopedia of Revolution and Protest. 1500 to the Present*, Volume 7, edited by Immanuel Ness, Oxford: Wiley-Blackwell, 3441–5.

―――― 2009d, 'Bolivarianism, Venezuela', in *International Encyclopedia of Revolution and Protest. 1500 to the Present*, Volume 7, edited by Immanuel Ness, Oxford: Wiley-Blackwell, 412–16.

―――― 2009e, 'Guaicaipuro (1530–1568)', in *International Encyclopedia of Revolution and Protest. 1500 to the Present*, Volume 7, edited by Immanuel Ness, Oxford: Wiley-Blackwell, 1471–2.

―――― 2009f, 'Chirinos, Jose Leonardo (?–1796)', in *International Encyclopedia of Revolution and Protest. 1500 to the Present*, Volume 7, edited by Immanuel Ness, Oxford: Wiley-Blackwell, 737.

―――― 2009g, 'Zamora, Ezequiel (1817–1860)', in *International Encyclopedia of Revolution and Protest. 1500 to the Present*, Volume 7, edited by Immanuel Ness, Oxford: Wiley-Blackwell, 3706–7.

―――― 2009h, 'Venezuela, Negro Miguel Rebellion, 1552', in *International Encyclopedia of Revolution and Protest. 1500 to the Present*, Volume 7, edited by Immanuel Ness, Oxford: Wiley-Blackwell, 3451–2.

―――― 2009i, 'Venezuela's solidarity economy: collective ownership, expropriation, and workers self-management', *WorkingUSA*, 12, 6: 171–91.

―――― 2010, *Partizipation, Arbeiterkontrolle und die Commune. Bewegungen und soziale Transformation am Beispiel Venezuela*, Hamburg: VSA.

―――― 2011, 'Workers' Control under Venezuela's Bolivarian Revolution', in *Ours to Master and to Own. Workers' Councils from the Commune to the Present*, edited by Immanuel Ness and Dario Azzellini, Chicago: Haymarket Books, 382–99.

―――― 2012, 'From Cooperatives to Enterprises of Direct Social Property in the Venezuelan Process', in *Cooperatives and Socialism. A View from Cuba*, edited by Camila Piñeiro Harnecker, Basingstoke: Palgrave Macmillan, 259–78.

―――― 2013, 'The Communal System as Venezuela's Transition to Socialism', in *Communism in the 21st Century. Vol. II: Whither Communism? The Challenges Facing Communist States, Parties and Ideals*, edited by Shannon K. Brincat, Westport: Praeger Publishers, 217–49.

―――― 2014, 'Venezuela's Social Transformation and Growing Class Struggle', in *Crisis and Contradiction: Marxist Perspectives on Latin America in the Global Economy*, edited by Susan Spronk and Jeffery R. Webber, Leiden: Brill, 138–62.

―――― 2015, *An Alternative Labour History: Workers' control and Workplace Democracy*, London: Zed Books.

Azzellini, Dario, Stephan Lanz and Kathrin Wildner (eds.) 2013, *Caracas, sozialisierende Stadt. Die 'bolivarianische' Metropole zwischen Selbstorganisation und Steuerung*, metroZones 12, Berlin: b_books.

Azzellini, Dario and Oliver Ressler 2004, *Venezuela desde abajo*, Caracas/Berlin/Vienna, film, 67mins.

―――― 2006, *5 Fábricas. Control Obrero en Venezuela*, Caracas/Berlin/Vienna, film, 81mins.

―――― 2010, *Comuna en construcción*, Caracas/Berlin/Vienna, film, 94mins.

Banko, Catalina 2008, 'De la descentralización a la "nueva geometría del poder"', *Revista Venezolana de Economía y Ciencias Sociales*, 14, 2: 167–84.

Barreto Cipriani, Juan 2007, *Poder Popular. Poder Constituyente*, Caracas: Juan Barreto Cipriani.

Baute, Juan Carlos 2009, 'Juan Carlos Baute: "Las cooperativas no desaparecerán". Se impulsa su cambio hacia un modelo socialista y comunal', Últimas Noticias (17 June 2009), available at: http://www.aporrea.org/actualidad/n136615.html

Benjamin, Walter 1965, 'Geschichtsphilosophische Thesen', *Zur Kritik der Gewalt und andere Aufsätze. Mit einem Nachwort versehen von Herbert Marcuse*, Frankfurt: Suhrkamp, 78–94.

―――― 1968, 'Thesis on the Philosophy of History', in *Illuminations*, edited by Walter Benjamin, New York: Schocken Books, 253–64.

―――― 2003, *Walter Benjamin: Selected Writings*, edited by Howard Eiland and Michael Jennings, Cambridge, MA: Harvard University Press.

Blankenburg, Stephanie 2008, 'El Estado y la revolución. Reestatización del Banco del grupo Santander', *América XXI*, 41: 18–21.

Bloch, Ernst 1986, *The Principle of Hope*, Cambridge, MA: MIT Press.

Bloch, Marc 1992, *The Historian's Craft: Reflections on the Nature and Uses of History and the Techniques and Methods of Those Who Write It*, Manchester: Manchester University Press.

Bonefeld, Werner 2008, 'La autoemancipación de las clases de trabajadoras y trabajadores como proceso abierto', *Herramienta*, Buenos Aires: Ediciones Herramienta, 39: 117–32.

Bonilla-Molina, Luis and Haiman El Troudi 2004, *Historia de la Revolución Bolivariana: Pequeña crónica, 1948–2004*, Caracas: Gobierno Bolivariano/Ministerio de Comunicación e Información.

Brecher, Jeremy 1973, 'Who Advocates Spontaneity?', *Radical America*, 7, 6: 91–112.

References

Bruce, Ian 2005, 'Venezuela promueve la cogestión', BBC (19 August 2005), available at: http://news.bbc.co.uk/hi/spanish/business/newsid_4167000/4167054.stm.

Castells, Manuel 1997, 'The Power of Identity', *The Information Age: Economy, Society and Culture*, Volume 2, Oxford: Blackwell Publishers.

Chávez Frías, Hugo 1993, *Pueblo, sufragio y democracia*, 2, Yare: Ediciones MBR-200.

―――― 2007, 'Fragmentos del Discurso de toma de posesión', in *El Poder Popular. Serie Ensayos. Propuestas para el debate*, edited by IMU (Instituto Metropolitano de Urbanismo), Caracas: IMU.

IMU (Instituto Metropolitano de Urbanismo) 2007, Caracas: IMU, 2–7.

―――― 2008, *El Poder Popular*, Caracas: Ministerio del Poder Popular para la Comunicación y la Información.

―――― 2012, 'Propuesta del Candidato de la Patria Comandante Hugo Chávez para la Gestión Bolivariana Socialista 2013–2019', available at: http://www.chavez.org.ve/Programa-Patria-2013-2019.pdf.

Colau, Ada 2008, 'Los Comités de Tierras Urbanas y el proceso de regularización de tierras en Venezuela', *Observatori DESC*, Barcelona, available at: http://www.descweb.org/?q=es/node/190.

Comisión Merco Sur Alba de Industrias Diana CA. 2014, 'Julio Borges miente sobre Industrias Diana', *Aporrea.org* (13 April 2014), available at: http://www.aporrea.org/endogeno/n248990.html.

Consejo Trabajadores Maisanta de Guanarito 2014, 'Denuncia: En la Empresa "Socialista" Pedro Camejo impera el capitalismo y el abandono', *Aporrea.org* (17 December 2014), available at: http://www.aporrea.org/contraloria/n262434.html.

CST (Consejos Socialistas de Trabajadoras y Trabajadores de Venezuela) 2009, *I Encuentro Nacional de Consejos Socialistas de Trabajadoras y Trabajadores de Venezuela* (27 June 2009), Caracas: CST.

Contreras Ramírez, Enrique 1999, *Educación para la nueva República*, Caracas: Fundación Editorial Fabricio Ojeda.

Córdova Jaimes, Edgar 2008, 'Construcción política ciudadana y desarrollo en Venezuela', *Frónesis*, 15, 2: 21–45.

Cormenzana, Pablo 2009, *La batalla de Inveval. La lucha por el control obrero en Venezuela*, Madrid: Fundación Federico Engels.

Coronil, Fernando 1997, *The Magical State: Nature, Money and Modernity in Venezuela*, Chicago: University of Chicago Press.

Della Porta, Donatella and Mario Diani 1999, *Social Movements: An Introduction*, Oxford: Blackwell Publishers.

―――― 2006, *Social Movements: An Introduction*, Oxford: Blackwell Publishers.

Denis, Roland 2001, *Los fabricantes de la rebelión*, Caracas: Primera Linea.

―――― 2003, 'La nueva ratio productiva (propuesta de un modelo alternativo de desarrollo)', *Revista Venezolana de Economía y Ciencias Sociales*, 9, 1: 233–50.

―――― 2005, *Rebelión en Proceso*, Caracas: Nuestra América Rebelde.

―――― 2007, 'La profecía de Alcasa', *Aporrea.org* (26 March 2007), available at: http://www.aporrea.org/actualidad/a32464.html.

Di Giminiani, Daniele 2007, '¿Que es la Nueva Geometría del Poder?', *Aporrea.org* (23 August 2007), available at: http://www.aporrea.org/actualidad/a40153.html.

Díaz, Benito 2006, 'Políticas públicas para la promoción de cooperativas en Venezuela', *Revista Venezolana de Economía Social*, 6, 11: 149–83.

Diniz, Ana Paula and Grisell López 2007, *Poder Popular y Democracia Participativa. Estado Social, Economía Social, Consejos Comunales*, Caracas: Ediciones Paredes.

Dos Santos, Theotonio 2006, *Concepto de clases sociales*, Caracas: El Perro y la Rana.

Echenique, Carlos and Fanny Torres, and Yecsi Zorrilla 2003, 'La política pública de participación ciudadana en Venezuela. Referencia al caso del municipio Baruta del Estado Miranda', in *Políticas públicas siglo XXI: caso venezolano*, edited by Carlos Mascareño, Caracas: Cendes, 87–118.

Ellner, Steve 2003, 'Introducción. En la búsqueda de explicaciones', in *La política venezolana en la época de Chávez*, edited by Steve Ellner and Daniel Hellinger, Caracas: Nueva Sociedad, 19–42.

―――― 2006, 'Las estrategias "desde arriba" y "desde abajo" del movimiento de Hugo Chávez', *Cuadernos del Cendes*, 23, 62: 73–93.

―――― 2008, 'Las tensiones entre la base y la dirigencia en las filas del chavismo', *Revista Venezolana de Economía y Ciencias Sociales*, 14, 1: 49–64.

El Troudi, Haiman and Juan Carlos Monedero 2006, *Empresas de Producción Social. Instrumento para el socialismo del siglo XXI*, Caracas: Centro Internacional Miranda.

ENCO (Encuentro Nacional por el Control Obrero) 2011, 'Sistematización del Encuentro Nacional por el Control Obrero y los Consejos de Trabajadores y Trabajadoras', available at: http://www.aporrea.org/endogeno/n182995.html.

Esteva, Gustavo 2009, 'Otra mirada, otra democracia', in *Rebelión.org* (02 February 2009), available at: http://www.rebelion.org/noticia.php?id=80143.

FCG (Fundación Centro Gumilla) 2008, *Estudio de los Consejos Comunales en Venezuela*, Caracas available at: http://gumilla.org.ve/files/documents/Estudio.pdf.

Fernandes, Sujatha 2007, 'Barrio Women and Popular Politics in Chávez's Venezuela', *Latin American Politics and Society*, 49, 3: 97–127.

Fernández Colón, Gustavo 2006, '¿Verticalismo burocrático o protagonismo popular?', *Aporrea.org*, available at: http://www.aporrea.org/ideologia/a28479.html.

FNCSB (Frente Nacional Comunal Simón Bolívar) and FNCEZ (Frente Nacional Campesino Ezequiel Zamora) 2007, *Manifiesto del I Encuentro Nacional de Consejos Comunales* (13 March 2007), available at: http://www.tiempodecuba.com/node/1345.

FONDEMI (Fondo de Desarrollo Microfinanciero) 2007, *Módulo Formativo. Ciclo del poder comunal*, Caracas: Fondo de Desarrollo Microfinanciero.

Fox, Michael 2006, 'CECOSESOLA: Four Decades of Independent Struggle for a Venezuelan Cooperative', in *Venezuelanalysis.com*, available at: www.venezuelanalysis .com/articles.php?artno=1755.

Freeman, Jo 1972–3, 'The Tyranny of Structurelessness', *Berkeley Journal of Sociology*, 17: 151–65.

FTSA (Frente Socialista de Trabajador@s de Alcasa) 2014, 'Frente de trabajadores pide la intervención de CVG Alcasa', *Aporrea.org* (06 March 2014), available at: http://www .aporrea.org/trabajadores/a183623.html.

Freteco 2007, 'Historic Freteco meeting – workers of occupied factories present ideas on socialist companies, workers' councils, and the building of socialism', in *Controlobrero.org*, available at: http://www.marxist.com/historic-freteco-meeting-factories060707.htm.

García-Guadilla, María Pilar 2003, 'Sociedad civil: institucionalización, fragmentación, autonomía', in *La política venezolana en la época de Chávez*, edited by Steve Ellner and Daniel Hellinger, Caracas: Nueva Sociedad, 230–51.

———— 2008, 'La praxis de los consejos comunales en Venezuela: "¿Poder popular o instancia clientelar?"', *Revista Venezolana de Economía y Ciencias Sociales*, 14, 1: 107–24.

Giachetti, Romano 1972, 'Antonio Gramsci: The Subjective Revolution', in *The Unknown Dimension*, edited by Dick Howard and Karl E. Klare, New York: Basic Books Inc., 147–68.

Giordani C. and A. Jorge 2009, *La transición venezolana al socialismo*, Valencia: Vadell Hermanos Editores.

Goldfrank, Benjamín 2001, *Deepening Democracy Through Citizen Participation? A Comparative Analysis of Three Cities*, Prepared for delivery at the 2001 meeting of the Latin American Studies Association, Washington, DC, available at: http://lasa .international.pitt.edu/Lasa2001/GoldfrankBenjamin.pdf.

Gómez, Gonzalo 2005a, 'Exposición de Ángel Nava (FETRAELEC) sobre la cogestión en el sector eléctrico (Parte I)', *Aporrea.org* (21 April 2005), available at: http://www .aporrea.org/trabajadores/n59229.html.

———— 2005b, 'Exposición de Ángel Nava (FETRAELEC) sobre la cogestión en el sector eléctrico (Parte II)', *Aporrea.org* (20 May 2005), available at: http://www.aporrea.org/ trabajadores/n60618.html.

Gramsci, Antonio 1999, 'State and Civil Society', in *Selection from the Prison Notebooks*, edited and translated Quentin Hoare and Geoffrey Nowell Smith, London: ElecBook, 445–557.

Guariguata Osorio, José Humberto 2004, 'Constituyente Municipal para la construcción del Poder Popular cogestionario', *Revista Laberinto*, 16: 10–18, available at: https:// dialnet.unirioja.es/servlet/articulo?codigo=1104777.

Gunn, Richard 1987, 'Notes on "class"', *Common Sense*, 2: 15–25.

Hardt, Michael and Antonio Negri 2000, *Empire*, Cambridge, MA: Harvard University Press.

―――― 2002, 'Globalizzazione e democrazia', *Hortus Musicus*, 10: 26–31.
―――― 2004, *Multitude: War and Democracy in the Age of Empire*, New York: Penguin.
Harnecker, Marta 2002, *Hugo Chávez Frías. Un hombre, un pueblo*, available at: http://www.nodo50.org/cubasigloXXI/politica/harnecker24_310802.pdf.
―――― 2003a, 'Democracia y Participación Popular', *Aporrea.org* (08 August 2003), available at: http://www.aporrea.org/ideologia/a4173.html.
―――― 2005a, *Los desafíos de la cogestión. Las experiencias de Cadafe y Cadela*, Caracas: La Burbuja Editorial.
―――― 2005b, *Presupuesto participativo en Caracas. La experiencia del GOL*, Caracas: Colección Testimonios.
―――― 2008, *Transfiriendo poder a la gente*. Municipio Torres, Estado Lara, Caracas.
―――― 2009, *Construyendo el Socialismo del Siglo XXI. De los Consejos Comunales a la Comuna*, available at: http://www.rebelion.org/docs/97085.pdf.
Hartling, Jay 2007, 'Building Popular Power in the Venezuelan Town of Carora', in *Venezuelanalysis* (26 April 2007), available at: http://www.venezuelanalysis.com/analysis/2359.
Harvey, David 2006, 'Space as a keyword', in *David Harvey: A Critical Reader*, edited by Noel Castree and Derek Gregory, Malden: Blackwell.
Herrera Salas, Jesús María 2004, 'Racismo y discurso político en Venezuela', in *Revista Venezolana de Economía y Ciencias Sociales*, 10, 2: 111–28.
Hobsbawm, Eric John 1995, *The Age of Extremes: The Short Twentieth Century, 1914–1991*, London: Abacus.
Holloway, John 2004a, *Clase = Lucha. Antagonismo social y marxismo crítico*, Buenos Aires: Editorial Herramienta.
―――― 2004b, 'Clase y Clasificación', in *Clase = Lucha. Antagonismo social y marxismo crítico*, edited by John Holloway, Buenos Aires: Editorial Herramienta.
―――― 2005, *Change the World without Taking Power*, London: Pluto Press.
―――― 2010, *Crack Capitalism*, London: Pluto Press.
Iturriza López, Reinaldo 2007, 'El general Kersausie y las barricadas del 27 de Febrero de 1989', *Aporrea.org* (28 February 2007), available at: http://www.aporrea.org/ideologia/a31241.html.
Kaltmeier, Olaf and Jens Kastner and Elisabeth Tuider 2004, 'Cultural Politics im Neoliberalismus. Widerstand und Autonomie Sozialer Bewegungen in Lateinamerika', in *Neoliberalismus–Autonomie–Widerstand. Soziale Bewegungen in Lateinamerika*, edited by Olaf Kaltmeier, Jens Kastner and Elisabeth Tuider, Munster: Verlag Westfälisches Dampfboot, 7–30.
Kelley, Robin 2003, *Freedom Dreams: The Black Radical Imagination*, Boston, MA: Beacon Press.
Korsch, Karl 1977, *Revolutionary Theory*, Austin, TX: University of Texas Press.

Kron, Stefanie 2004, 'Venezuela: Verfassung und staatliche Frauenpolitik', *Femina politica*, 13, 1: 56–67.
Lacabana, Miguel and Cecilia Cariola 2005, 'Los bordes de la esperanza: nuevas formas de participación popular y gobiernos locales en la periferia de Caracas', *Revista Venezolana de Economía y Ciencias Sociales*, 11, 1: 21–41.
Lander, Edgardo 2007, 'El Estado y las tensiones de la participación popular en Venezuela', osal (*Observatorio Social de América Latina*), 8, 22: 65–86.
―――― 2009, 'El proceso bolivariano y las tensiones de un proyecto alternativo. Conversación con el politólogo Edgardo Lander', in *Rebelión.org*, available at: http://www.rebelion.org/noticias/venezuela/2009/2/el-proceso-bolivariano-y-las-tensiones-de-un-proyecto-alternativo-80123.
Lanz Rodríguez, Carlos 2004, *El Desarrollo Endógeno y la Misíon Vuelvan Caras*, Caracas: Misíon Vuelvan Caras/Ministerio de Educacíon Superior.
―――― 2007, *Consejo de Fábrica y Construcción Socialista. Antecedentes teóricos e históricos de un debate inconcluso*, Ciudad Guayana: Mibam/cvg Alcasa.
Lavaca 2004, *Sin Patrón: Fábricas y empresas recuperadas por sus trabajadores. Una historia, una guía*, Buenos Aires: Cooperativa de Trabajo Lavaca Ltd.
lcc (Ley de los Consejos Comunales) 2006, Caracas: Asamblea Nacional de la República Bolivariana de Venezuela.
lcepcpp (Ley de los Consejos Estadales de Planificación y Coordinación de Políticas Públicas) 2002, in *Gaceta Oficial de la República de Venezuela* (37.509).
lclpp (Ley de los Consejos Locales de Planificación Pública) 2002, *Gaceta Oficial de la República de Venezuela* (37.463).
leac (Ley Especial de Asociaciones Cooperativas) 2001, *Gaceta Oficial de la República de Venezuela* (37.285).
Lebowitz, Michael 2006, *Construyámoslo Ahora. El Socialismo para el Siglo XXI*, Caracas: Centro Internacional Miranda.
Lenin, Vladimir Iljitsch 1932, *State and Revolution*, New York: International Publishers.
León, Osvaldo 2013, 'Una respuesta a Will Rangel y al pcv sobre los consejos obreros y el control obrero', *Aporrea.org* (12 August 2013), available at: www.aporrea.org/trabajadores/a171638.html.
Lerner, Josh 2007, 'Communal councils in Venezuela: can 200 families revolutionize democracy?', *z Magazine*, March.
loc (Ley Orgánica de las Comunas) 2010, Caracas: Asamblea Nacional de la República Bolivariana de Venezuela.
locc (Ley Orgánica de los Consejos Comunales) 2009, Caracas: Asamblea Nacional de la República Bolivariana de Venezuela.
López Maya, Margarita 2003, 'Hugo Chávez Frías, su movimiento y presidencia', in *La política venezolana en la época de Chávez*, edited by Steve Ellner and Daniel Hellinger, Caracas: Nueva Sociedad, 98–120.

────── 2008, 'Innovaciones participativas en la Caracas bolivariana: La MTA de la pedrera y la OCA de barrio Unión-Carpintero', *Revista Venezolana de Economía y Ciencias Sociales*, 14, 1: 65–93, available at: http://www.scielo.org.ve/scielo.php?script=sci_arttext&pid=S1315-64112008000100006&lng=es&nrm=iso.

LOPPM (Ley Orgánica del Poder Público Municipal) 2005, *Gaceta Oficial de la República de Venezuela* (38.204).

LOSEC (Ley Orgánica del Sistema Económico Comunal) 2010, Caracas: Asamblea Nacional de la República Bolivariana de Venezuela.

LOTTT 2012, 'Ley Orgánica del Trabajo, los Trabajadores y las Trabajadoras' (8.938), available at: http://www.lottt.gob.ve/.

Lovera, Alberto 2008, 'Los consejos comunales en Venezuela: ¿Democracia participativa o delegativa?', *Revista Venezolana de Economía y Ciencias Sociales*, 14, 1: 107–24.

Lucha de Clases 2014, 'Gran éxito del lanzamiento de la Universidad Bolivariana de Trabajadores "Jesús Rivero" en INVEVAL', *Lucha de Clases*, available at: http://www.luchadeclases.org.ve/venezuela/control-obrero/5688-gran-to-del-lanzamiento-de-la-universidad-bolivariana-de-trabajadores-jesivero-en-inveval.

Lukács, George 1971, *History and Class Consciousness: Studies in Marxist Dialectics*, Cambridge, MA: MIT Press.

Luhmann, Niklas 1991, 'Protestbewegungen', in *Protest: Systemtheorie und soziale Bewegungen*, edited by Kai-Uwe Hellmann, Frankfurt: Suhrkamp, 201–15.

Lynd, Staughton and Alice Lynd 2000, *The New Rank and File*, Ithaca, NY: Cornell University Press.

Mandel, Ernest 1974, *Control Obrero, consejos obreros, autogestión*, Mexico City: Era, S.A.

Marea Socialista 2010, in *CVG Alcasa, Trabajadores derrotan golpe de Estado orquestado por la FBT (Movimiento 21)*, available at: www.aporrea.org/endogeno/n169305.html.

Marini, Ruy Mauro 1991, *Dialéctica de la dependencia*, Ciudad de México: Ediciones Era.

Martín, Jorge 2011a, 'Venezuela & Revolutionary Vignettes. Part 1: Workers' Control vs Bureaucrats, Mafia and Multinationals in Bolívar', in *In Defence of Marxism*, available at: http://www.marxist.com/venezuela-revolutionary-vignettes-1.htm.

────── 2011b, 'Venezuela: Revolutionary vignettes. Part 2: Workers' councils sabotaged by the bureaucracy', in *In Defence of Marxism*, available at: http://www.marxist.com/venezuela-revolutionary-vignettes-2.htm.

Martin, Waldo 1986, *The Mind of Frederick Douglass*, North Carolina, NC: University of North Carolina Press.

Marx, Karl 1844, 'On the Jewish Question', available at: http://www.marxists.org/archive/marx/works/1844/.

────── 1967, *Capital*, Volume 3, New York: International Publishers.

────── 1975a, 'Marx to Ruge, Kreuznach, September 1843', in *Marx and Engels Collected Works*, Volume 3, New York: International Publishers, 141–4.

——— 1975b, 'Contribution to the Critique of Hegel's Philosophy of Law', in *Marx and Engels Collected Works*, Volume 3, New York: International Publishers, 175–87.

——— 1975c, 'Economic and Philosophic Manuscripts of 1844', in *Marx and Engels Collected Works*, Volume 3, New York: International Publishers, 229–348.

——— 1986, 'Second Draft of The Civil War in France', in *Marx and Engels Collected Works*, Volume 22, New York: International Publishers, 515–51.

——— 1990, *Capital: A Critique of Political Economy*, Volume 1, London: Penguin.

Marx, Karl and Friedrich Engels 2007, *The Communist Manifesto*, New York: International Publishers.

Massey, Doreen 2009, 'Concepts of Space and Power in Theory and in Political Practice', *Doc. Anàl. Geogr.*, 55: 15–26.

Mazzeo, Miguel 2007, *El sueño de una cosa (Introducción al Poder Popular)*, Caracas: El Perro y la Rana.

Mazzeo, Miguel and Fernando Stratta (eds.) 2007, *Reflexiones sobre Poder Popular*, Buenos Aires: Editorial El Colectivo.

MDP (Movimiento de Pobladores) 2007, *Balance del Movimiento de Pobladores*, available at: http://www.authorstream.com/Presentation/karinar129-28105-balance-de-los-comit-tierra-urbana-programa-ctu-13-08-07-education-ppt-powerpoint/.

Medina, Medófilo 2001, *El elegido presidente Chávez: un nuevo sistema político*, Bogotá: Ediciones Aurora.

Melcher, Dorotea 2008, 'Cooperativismo en Venezuela: Teoría y praxis', *Revista Venezolana de Economía y Ciencias Sociales*, 14, 1: 95–106.

Mészáros, Istvan 1995, *Beyond Capital: Towards a Theory of Transition*, New York: Monthly Review Press.

MinCI (Ministerio del Poder Popular para la Comunicación y la Información) 2007, *Líneas generales del Plan de Desarrollo Económico y Social de la Nación 2007–2013*, Caracas.

Minec (Ministerio de la Economía Comunal) 2009, *Reseña histórica*, available at: http://www.misioncheguevara.gob.ve/contenido.php?id=215 (last retrieved March 11, 2009).

Minep (Ministerio de Economía Popular) 2006, *Desarrollo, Eurocentrismo y Economía Popular. Más allá del paradigma neoliberal*, Caracas: Minep.

MinTrab (Ministerio del Poder Popular para el Trabajo y Seguridad Social) 2008, *La gestión socialista de la economía y las empresas. Propuesta de trabajadores(as) al pueblo y gobierno de la República Bolivariana de Venezuela. Conclusiones del tercer seminario nacional sobre formación y gestión socialista*. Valencia (18–19 April 2008), Caracas.

Monedero, Juan Carlos 2007, 'En donde está el peligro ... La crisis de la representación y la construcción de alternativas en América', *Cuadernos del Cendes*, 24, 64: 1–21.

Moreno, Alejandro 1999, 'Resistencia cultural del pueblo venezolano a la modernidad', *Revista Venezolana de Economía y Ciencias Sociales*, 5, 2–3: 201–15.

——— 2005, 'Reto popular a la gobernabilidad en Venezuela', in *Gobernanza. Laberinto de la democracia*, edited by María Ramírez Ribes, Caracas: Informe del Capítulo Venezolano del Club de Roma, 207–17.

MPD (Ministerio de Planificación y Desarrollo) and Dirección General de Planificación del Desarrollo Regional 2002, *Consejo Local de Planificación Pública. Guía de Organización y Funcionamiento*, Caracas.

Mppibm (Ministerio del Poder Popular para las Industrias Básicas y Minería) 2009, *Plan Guayana Socialista 2009–2019*, available at: http://www.sidor.com/images/noticias/documentos/p_guayana.pdf.

Müller-Plantenberg, Urs 2001, 'Engagement und Ausdauer. Kritische Deutsche Sozialwissenschaft und Lateinamerika', in *Jahrbuch Lateinamerika. Analysen und Berichte, Beharren auf Demokratie*, Volume 25, edited by Karin Gabbert, Wolfgang Gabbert and Bert Hoffmann et al., Munster: Verlag Westfälisches Dampfboot, 13–34.

Negri, Antonio 1994, *El poder constituyente. Ensayo sobre las alternativas de la modernidad*, Madrid: Prodhufi.

——— 1998, 'Repubblica Costituente. Umrisse einer konstituierenden Macht', in *Umherschweifende Produzenten*, edited by Maurizio Lazzarato, Antonio Negri and Paolo Virno, Berlin: ID Verlag, 67–81.

——— 2001, 'Entrevista a Toni Negri', in *Contrapoder. Una Introducción*, edited by Colectivo Situaciones, Buenos Aires: tinta limón, 107–32.

——— 2008, 'Der Ort der Biopolitik: Ereignis und Metropole. Ein Gespräch', *Wespennest*, 151, available at: http://www.eurozine.com/pdf/2008-05-28-negri-de.pdf.

Ness, Immanuel and Dario Azzellini 2011, *Ours to Master and to Own: Workers' Councils from the Commune to the Present*, Chicago: Haymarket Books.

Nicanoff, Sergio 2007, 'Prólogo', in *El sueño de una cosa*, edited by Miguel Mazzeo, Caracas: Editorial El Colectivo, 9–13.

Nolte, Detlef 2002, 'Demokratie kann man nicht essen. Zur politischen Lage', *Lateinamerika, Analysen*, 3: 149–72.

OCMPPPC (Ordenanza del Consejo Metropolitano de Planificacion de politicas públicas de Caracas) 2006, *Gaceta Oficial del Distrito Metropolitano de Caracas* (0076).

Panitch, Leo 2003, 'Theory, Democracy and the Left, una entrevista de Carlos Pessoa', available at: http://www.signsofthetimes.org.uk/panitch[textonly].html.

Pannekoek, Antón 2008, *Arbeiterräte: Texte zur sozialen Revolution*, Fernwald: Germinal Verlag.

Panzieri, Raniero 1965, 'Uso socialista de la encuesta obrera', *Instituto Europeo para Políticas Culturales Progresivas* (EIPCP), available at: http://eipcp.net/transversal/0406/panzieri/es.

Parada, Frank 2007, 'Los Consejos Comunales. La verdadera explosión del poder comunal desde las bases', *Aporrea.org* (23 February 2007), available at: http://www.aporrea.org/ideologia/a31058.html.

Parker, Dick 2006, '¿De qué democracia estamos hablando?', *Revista Venezolana de Economía y Ciencias Sociales*, 12, 1: 89–99.

Piñeiro Harnecker, Camila 2005, 'The New Cooperative Movement in Venezuela's Bolivarian Process', *Monthly Review Online Magazine*, available at: http://mrzine.monthlyreview.org/harnecker051205.html.

―――― 2007, 'Democracia Laboral y Conciencia Colectiva: un estudio de Cooperativas en Venezuela', *Temas*, 50–1.

―――― 2008, 'Principales desafíos de las cooperativas en Venezuela', *Cayapa: Revista de Economía Social Venezolana*, 8, 15: 37–60.

―――― 2010, 'Venezuelan Cooperatives: Practice and Challenges', in *Paper presented to the 28th ILPC*, New Brunswick, NJ: Rutgers University.

Poulantzas, Nicos 2000, *State, Power, Socialism*, London: Verso.

PPF (Pacto de Punto Fijo) 1958, available at: http://www.analitica.com/bitblioteca/venezuela/punto_fijo.asp.

Prensa INCE 2005, 'Hoy se firma convenio de cogestión de Inveval', *Aporrea.org* (04 August 2005), available at: http://www.aporrea.org/imprime/n64093.html.

Prensa Marea Socialista 2011, 'Entrevista al compañero trabajador Osvaldo León, militante del colectivo Control Obrero de Alcasa', *Aporrea.org* (27 January 2011), available at: http://www.aporrea.org/trabajadores/n173806.html.

Prensa MPPI (Ministerio del Poder Popular para Industrias) 2014, 'Alcasa firmó convenio con empresa italiana para instalar la segunda fase de la planta de Extrusión', *MPPI*, available at: http://www.mppi.gob.ve/?q=node/1222

PCTT (Primer Congreso de Trabajadores y Trabajadoras: Balance y Desafíos del Control Obrero y los Consejos de Trabajadores y Trabajadoras en la Construcción del Socialismo) 2013, *Ciudad Guayana*, available at: http://www.aporrea.org/trabajadores/a175710.html.

PFA (Programa Facultad Abierta) 2010, *Las Empresas Recuperadas en la Argentina: Informe del Tercer Relevamiento*. Buenos Aires: University of Buenos Aires.

Provea (Programa Venezolano de Educación-Acción en Derechos Humanos) 2008, *Informe anual*, Caracas: Provea.

Rakowski, Cathy 2003, 'Women's Coalitions as a Strategy at the Intersection of Economic and Political Change in Venezuela', *International Journal of Politics, Culture and Society*, 16, 3: 387–405.

Ramírez Rojas, Kléber 1991, *Venezuela: La IV República (o la total transformación del Estado)*, *Caracas:* Cromotip.

―――― 2006, *Historia documental del 4 de febrero*, Caracas: El Perro y la Rana.

Ramírez, Vicente 2006, '"La participación de los Goles en los Consejos Comunales", entrevista a Vicente Ramírez, promotor comunitario de la Oficina de Fortalecimiento Comunitario adscrita a la Dirección de Ejecución de Obras y Conservación Ambiental', *Proceso Urbano*, 1: 11–14.

Rancière, Jacques 2001, 'Ten Theses on Politics', *Theory & Event*, 5, 3.

Ranciére, Jacques and Steven Corcoran 2010, *Dissensus: On Politics and Aesthetics*, New York: Continuum.

Rauber, Isabel 2003, *Movimientos Sociales y Representación Política*, Buenos Aires: Pasado y Presente XXI.

———— 2006, *Poder y Socialismo en el Siglo XXI*, Caracas: Pasado y Presente XX.

RBV (República Bolivariana de Venezuela) 1999, *Constitución de la República Bolivariana de Venezuela*, Caracas: RBV.

Rebón, Julián 2004, *Desobedeciendo al desempleo: La experiencia de las empresas Recuperadas*, Buenos Aires: La Rosa Blindada.

———— 2006, *Empresas recuperadas. La autogestión de los trabajadores*, Buenos Aires: Capital Intelectual.

RNC (Red Nacional de Comuneros y Comuneras) 2011, 'Culminó con Éxito IV Encuentro Nacional de Comuneros y Comuneras', available at: http://rednacionaldecomuneros .blogspot.com/2011/08/culmino-con-exito-iv-encuentro-nacional.html.

Richard, Greti 2011, 'Sobre los Consejos de Trabajadores y Trabajadoras. Entrevista al sociólogo Alberto Bonilla', *Aporrea.org* (09 February 2011).

Romero Pirela, Rafael 2007, *Los consejos comunales más allá de la utopía. Análisis sobre su naturaleza jurídica en Venezuela*, Maracaibo: Universidad del Zulia, Ediciones del Vice Rectorado Académico.

Rucht, Dieter 1994, *Modernisierung und neue soziale Bewegungen: Deutschland, Frankreich und USA im Vergleich*, Frankfurt: Campus Verlag.

Rucht, Dieter and Friedhelm Neidhardt 2001, 'Soziale Bewegungen und kollektive Aktionen', in *Lehrbuch der Soziologie*, edited by Hans Joas, Frankfurt: Campus Verlag, 533–56.

Rucht, Dieter, Ruud Koopmans and Friedhelm Neidhardt (eds.) 1998, 'Introduction: Protest as a Subject of Social Research', in *Acts of Dissent: New Developments in the Study of Protest*, Berlin: Edition Sigma, 7–30.

Rudé, George 1995, *Ideology and Popular Protest*, Chapel Hill, NC: The University of North Carolina Press.

Ruggeri, Andrés 2005, 'Las Empresas Recuperadas en la Argentina: Informe del Segundo Relevamiento del Programa. Buenos Aires: Programa de Transferencia Científico-Técnica con Empresas Recuperadas por sus Trabajadores (UBACyT de Urgencia Social F-701)', *Facultad Abierta, Facultad de Filosofía y Letras*, Buenos Aires: Universidad de Buenos Aires.

———— 2010, 'Autogestión obrera y empresas recuperadas, límites y potenciales en el capitalismo neoliberal globalizado', *Facultad Abierta, Facultad de Filosofía y Letras*, Buenos Aires: Universidad de Buenos Aires.

Sanoja Obediente, Mario 2008, *El humanismo socialista venezolano del siglo XXI*, Caracas: Monte Ávila.

Sayago, Elio 2011, 'Entrevista con Elio Sayago, presidente de CVG Alcasa', *Lucha de Clases*, available at: http://www.luchadeclases.org.ve/lucha-obrera-leftmenu-166/7118-entrevista-elio-sayago.

Schönwälder, Gerd 1997, 'New Democratic Spaces at the Grassroots? Popular Participation in Latin American Local Governments', *Development and Change*, 28, 4: 753–70.

Scotto, Clemente D. 2003, 'La Participación Ciudadana como Política Pública. Una Experiencia en la Gestion Local', in *Políticas públicas siglo XXI: caso venezolano*, edited by Carlos Mascareño, Caracas: Cendes, 69–83.

Sierra Corrales, Francisco 2011, 'Lo que se está jugando en Guayana', available at: http://www.aporrea.org/regionales/a117561.html.

Sitrin, Marina 2006, *Horizontalism: Voices of Popular Power in Argentina*, Oakland, CA: AK Press.

―――― 2012, *Everyday Revolutions: Horizontalism and Autonomy in Argentina*, London/New York: Zed Books.

Sitrin, Marina and Dario Azzellini 2014, *They Can't Represent Us!: Reinventing Democracy from Greece to Occupy*, London/New York: Verso.

Soto, Héctor and Hugo Ávila 2006, 'Consejos Comunales Socialismo cotidiano y una agenda integradora', *Aporrea.org* (21 July 2006), available at: http://www.aporrea.org/poderpopular/a23747.html.

Soto, Scarlet 2014, 'Prometen que en 2015 Alcasa recuperará su capacidad para cubrir el mercado nacional', *Correo del Orinoco* (27/12/2014), available at: http://www.correodelorinoco.gob.ve/nacionales/prometen-que-2015-alcasa-recuperara-su-capacidad-para-cubrir-mercado-nacional/.

Sunkel, Osvaldo 1993, *Development from Within: Toward a Neostructuralist Approach for Latin America*, Boulder, CO: Lynne Rienner Publishers.

Superintendencia Nacional de Cooperativa, (Sunacoop) 2008, *Logros de gestión Sunacoop 2008*, Sunacoop: Caracas.

Thompson, E.P. 1991 [1963], *The Making of the English Working Class*, Harmondsworth: Penguin.

Tischler Visquerra, Sergio 2004, 'La crisis del canon clásico de la *forma clase* y los movimientos sociales en América Latina', in *Clase = Lucha. Antagonismo social y marxismo crítico*, edited by John Holloway, Buenos Aires: Editorial Herramienta, 103–27.

―――― 2007, 'Adorno: la cárcel conceptual del sujeto, el fetichismo político y la lucha de clases', in *Negatividad y revolución. Theodor W. Adorno y la política*, edited by John Holloway, Fernando Matamoros and Sergio Tischler, Buenos Aires: Herramienta, 111–28.

Trabajadores de CVG/Alcasa 2009, *Control Obrero*, available at: www.aporrea.org/endogeno/a86731.html.

Twickel, Christoph 2006, *Hugo Chávez. Eine Biographie*, Hamburg: Nautilus.
Valles Caraballo, Cristian 2004, *Para crecer desde dentro*, Caracas: Consejo Nacional de la Cultura.
Van Cott, Donna Lee 2002, 'Movimientos indígenas y transformación constitucional en los Andes. Venezuela en perspectica comparativa', *Revista Venezolana de Economía y Ciencias Sociales*, 3: 41–60.
Virno, Paolo 2003, 'Introducción a la edición en castellano', in *Gramática de la Multitud*, edited by Paolo Virno, Madrid: Traficantes de sueños, 15–20.
——— 2004, *A Grammar of the Multitude: For an Analysis of Contemporary Forms of Life*, Los Angeles/New York: Semiotext(e).
Wainwright, Hilary 2003, *Reclaim the State: Experiments in Popular Democracy*, London/New York: Verso.
Wallerstein, Immanuel 2000, 'A Left Politics for the 21st Century? Or, Theory and Praxis Once Again', *New Political Science*, 22, 2: 143–59.
Weber, Max 1922, 'IV. Stände und Klassen: § 1. Begriffe: Klassenlage, Klasse, Besitzklasse', in *Wirtschaft und Gesellschaft. Grundriss der verstehenden Soziologie. Erster Teil: Die Wirtschaft und die gesellschaftlichen Ordnungen und Mächte*, available at: http://www.textlog.de/7399.html.
Wilpert, Gregory 2003, *Coup Against Chávez in Venezuela*, Caracas: Fundación por un Mundo Multipolar y Venezolana para la Justicia Globa.
——— 2007, *Changing Venezuela by Taking Power*, London/New York: Verso.
Zibechi, Raúl 2006, 'Movimientos sociales: nuevos escenarios y desafíos inéditos', *OSAL (Observatorio Social de América Latina)*, 21: 221–30.
Zinn, Howard 2007, *A Power Governments Cannot Suppress*, San Francisco, CA: City Lights.

Index

Afro-Venezuelans   11, 25, 28, 55, 82
Alcasa   174, 176, 188, 191–92, 198, 200–202, 208–27, 237, 239–40, 275, 283, 290–91, 293–94, 297, 299
   bureaucracy and corruption   208, 212
   co-management   208–9, 211–14, 239, 281
   productive transformation   208
   sabotage   208, 226
   Workers' control   239
Allende, Salvador   15, 51
Althusser, Louis   7, 286
ANC (Constituent National Assembly)   44
Anderson, Benedict   286
Antillano, Andrés   28, 31–33, 66, 74–75, 113, 281, 286
Azuela, Mariano   27

Barreto, Juan   29, 85, 89, 147, 213, 224, 288
Barrio   67, 69, 132, 137, 146–47, 150, 197, 290
Barrio Adentro Mission   67
Barrio Mothers Mission   69
Benjamin, Walter   26, 59, 61, 64, 235, 242, 288
Bloch, Ernst   9, 26, 61, 288
Bloch, Marc   17, 288
Bolívar, Simón   3–4, 50, 52, 55, 60–63, 71, 73, 77, 82, 85, 91, 198–99, 224, 226, 283
Bolivarian movement   4, 26, 35, 71
Bonilla, Alberto   197, 298
Bonilla-Molina, Luís   59, 88, 288

Cacique Guaicaipuro   60, 287
Camejo   60, 210, 231, 289
Capriles, Henrique   15
Castells, Manuel   57, 289
CC (Communal Councils)   11, 81–83, 85–87, 90, 92–107, 109–10, 112–14, 116–23, 125–32, 134, 136–38, 140, 144–56, 269, 284–85
   in Caracas   81, 92, 147–48
   ni-nis   155
   and participation   138
   self-administration   83, 85, 128, 148
CECOSESOLA   164
CEFES   71, 73
CEPP   87
CFG   88

Chávez, Hugo   12–13, 15–17, 27–29, 42–43, 82–83, 91–92, 94–95, 183–85, 195–98, 201, 206–9, 226–30, 243–44, 258–60, 289–93
Ché Guevara Mission   165
Chirino, José Leonardo   60
CLPP (Local Public Planning Councils)   11, 46, 82, 86–89, 91, 97, 100, 108
CMPPP   89–90
Commune(s)   3, 11, 15–17, 46–47, 53–55, 71, 73, 76–79, 92, 99–100, 102, 110–111, 119, 121, 156, 160, 165, 171, 238, 243–62, 265, 268–71, 273, 278
Constituent Power   4, 6, 10–11, 15, 18, 33–51, 53–54, 56, 65, 81–84, 94–95, 123, 153, 156, 235, 263–64, 267, 269, 271, 276–279
Constituted Power   6, 10–11, 17–18, 29, 34–41, 46–48, 51–54, 56, 67, 71, 84, 88, 89, 91, 93, 95, 107, 117, 121, 123, 145, 147, 1153, 156, 233, 235, 241, 248, 251, 259, 261, 263–264, 267, 270, 276–80
CONAC   130
Corcoran   24, 298
CPPP   97, 100
CRBZ   52, 54, 71–72, 268
CST   174–75, 180, 192–93, 195–200, 228–29, 230, 274, 275
CTU (Urban Land Committees)   10, 45–46, 66–67, 70–75, 114, 117, 126, 128, 145–146

Darío Santillán Popular Front   30
Denis, Roland   9, 28, 31, 41–45, 63–64, 159, 281, 283, 289
Dos Santos, Theotonio   19–21, 25, 290

Ellner, Steve   3, 25, 45–46, 54, 64, 68–69, 74, 87, 158, 165–66, 171, 182, 198, 290–91, 293
Empowerment   133
Endogenous development   159
Inveval   174, 176, 178, 183, 188, 191, 202, 203–4, 205–8, 232, 235, 237–38, 239, 242, 275
Engels, Friedrich   6, 16, 289, 294–95
Esteva, Gustavo   261–62, 290

Factory Within Program (Fábrica adentro)   172, 203
Ferrer   84

FONDEMI   103–4, 134
Fourth National Encounter of Commune Members   77
Freeman, Jo   58, 291
French Revolution   23
FRETECO (Revolutionary Front of Workers of Co-Managed and Occupied Companies)   187, 191, 205, 282, 291
FSBT   196, 198, 224
Fundacaracas   130–31, 134–35, 138
Fundacomunal   47, 99–100, 102, 128, 130–31, 144–45, 147, 197, 250–51

Giordani, Jorge A.   265, 291
Gramsci, Antonio   7, 17, 63, 192, 198, 234, 291
Gunn, Richard   20–21, 291

Hardt, Michael   9, 22–24, 29, 48–49, 291
Harnecker, Martha   43, 83, 89, 91–93, 106, 110–11, 113, 117, 173, 284, 287, 292, 297
Heller, Hermann   36
Hobbes, Thomas   22–23
Hobsbawm, Eric   59, 292
Holloway, John   9, 19, 21, 292, 299

Inveval   173–74, 176, 178, 183, 188, 191, 202–8, 232, 235, 237–39, 242, 275, 282, 289, 297
    struggle for the factory   203
Iturriza, Reinaldo   15, 20, 25–26, 64, 66, 123, 244, 249, 251, 281, 292

Koopmans, Ruud   298

Lander, Edgardo   5, 10, 50, 87–88, 97, 108, 113, 115, 117, 123, 160, 259, 281, 293
Lassalle, Ferdinand   36
Law of Microfinance   165
Lenin, Vladimir   7, 286, 293
Luhmann, Niklas   57, 294

Machiavelli, Niccolò   3, 37–38
Maduro, Nicolás   15–16, 54, 185, 225, 229–30, 244, 249, 271
Mariátegui, José Carlos   11, 55, 63, 82
Marx, Karl   6, 13–14, 16, 20–21, 28, 37–38, 61, 64, 161, 198, 216, 234, 262, 265, 294–95
    on class   20
    of three classes   20

Mazzeo, Miguel   9, 30, 49, 51, 60–61, 286, 295–96
Messianic time   27
Mészáros, Istvan   54, 160–61, 252, 265, 295
MINEC   165, 295
Ministry of Popular Economy   12, 159–60
Ministry of Popular Power of the Communes   78
Miranda, Francisco   60
Misión Negra Hipólita   146
Monedero, Juan Carlos   65, 176, 290, 295
Multitude   20, 292, 300. *See* also: Negri, Hardt

Nation   286
National Assembly   71, 74, 82, 84, 86, 96, 101, 180, 184, 187, 196–97, 224, 226, 248, 251
Negri, Antonio   9, 22–24, 29, 33–43, 48–49, 63, 81, 83, 264, 291, 296
Negro Miguel   60, 287
Neidhardt, Friedhelm   57, 298
NUDES   170

Operaio, Potero   63
Opposition   15, 27–28, 45, 53, 61, 70, 88–90, 95, 107, 112, 120, 124, 127, 129, 133, 135–137, 139, 145–148, 150, 155–156, 158, 164, 183, 186, 193, 198, 202, 211, 221, 225
Organic Law of the Communal Economic System   253, 258

Pact of Punto Fijo/ *puntofijismo*   64
Pannekoek, Anton   63, 179, 192, 235, 296
Panzieri, Raniero   16–17, 63, 296
PCV (Communist Party of Venezuela)   62–63, 65, 163, 196, 266
PDVSA (Venezuelan Petroleum)   28, 103–4, 132, 134, 165, 173, 176, 202, 229, 240, 254
Pérez Jiménez, Marcos   62
Pérez Pirela, Miguel Ángel   264
Piñeiro, Camila   162, 164, 166–70, 287, 297
Plan Guayana Socialista 2019   200, 202
Popular power   5–6, 11, 15, 18, 34, 44, 49–51, 53, 55–56, 73, 76, 78, 79, 81–82, 92–93, 96, 108, 110, 113–115, 119–125, 136, 144, 196, 233, 243, 245, 251, 259–262, 264, 267–268, 277
Poulantzas, Nicos   7–8, 13, 297
PPC   43–44
Primero Justicia   129, 137

INDEX

PRV (Party of the Venezuelan Revolution)   26, 62
PRV-FALN   84, 163
PSUV (United Socialist Party of Venezuela)   64, 71, 84, 115, 145, 155, 185, 208, 224, 225–26, 250, 266
pueblo   15, 17, 23, 27–31, 47, 49–50, 72–73, 75–76, 79, 86–89, 133, 241, 259–61, 267–68, 295

Rakowski, Cathy   69, 297
Ranciére, Jacques   24–25, 298
Ribas, José Félix   60, 91, 125, 127, 132, 134, 204
Ribas Mission   125, 127, 134, 204
RNC (National Network of Communards)   52, 54, 72–73, 76, 77, 244, 251, 256, 258, 260, 268, 271
Rodríguez, Simón   4, 55, 60, 63, 71, 82, 94, 142–43, 178, 188, 229, 283–85, 293
Rucht, Dieter   57, 298
Ruge, Arnold   61, 294

Sáenz, Manuela   60
Simón Bolívar Communal Peasant City   77
Simón Bolívar National Plan   190

Simón Bolívar National Project   95
Sitrin, Marina   6, 46, 179, 191, 235, 237, 299
Spinoza Baruch   22, 37–38
Sucre Mission   125, 204

Thompson, E.P.   59, 299

Urbanization   75

Víctor Hugo   27
Virno, Paolo   22–24, 29, 296, 300
Vuelvan Caras Mission   165–66, 170

Weber, Max   20, 300
Workers' control   12–15, 17, 52, 54–55, 71–72, 80, 161, 174, 176, 178–181, 183, 185, 187–206, 208–216, 219, 221–232, 238–242, 253, 255, 260, 270–271, 273–276, 280. *See* also: Communes, Communal council

Zamora, Ezequiel   10, 46, 52, 60, 63, 71, 268, 287, 290
Zapatistas   24, 28
Zinn, Howard   52, 59, 300

www.ingramcontent.com/pod-product-compliance
Lightning Source LLC
Chambersburg PA
CBHW070910030426
42336CB00014BA/2352